P9-ASM-806

LightWave 3D® 8 Cartoon Character Creation

Volume 1: Modeling & Texturing

WITHDRAWN

No longer the property of the
Boston Public Library.
Sale of this material benefits the Library

Jonny Gorden

Wordware Publishing, Inc.

Library of Congress Cataloging-in-Publication Data

Gorden, Jonny.
  Lightwave 3D cartoon character creation / by Jonny Gorden.
    p. cm.
  ISBN 1-55622-253-X (volume 1, pbk., companion cd-rom) -- ISBN
  1-55622-254-8 (volume 2, pbk., companion cd-rom)
  1. Computer animation. 2. Three-dimensional display systems. 3. Cartoon
  characters. 4. LightWave 3D. I. Title.
  TR897.7.G67 2004
  006.6'93--dc22   2004021079
                                          CIP

© 2005, Wordware Publishing, Inc.

All Rights Reserved

2320 Los Rios Boulevard
Plano, Texas 75074

No part of this book may be reproduced in any form or by any means
without permission in writing from Wordware Publishing, Inc.

Printed in the United States of America

ISBN 1-55622-253-X

10 9 8 7 6 5 4 3 2 1
0410

LightWave and LightWave 3D are registered trademarks in the United States and other countries.
Other brand names and product names mentioned in this book are trademarks or service marks of their respective companies. Any omission or misuse (of any kind) of service marks or trademarks should not be regarded as intent to infringe on the
property of others. The publisher recognizes and respects all marks used by companies, manufacturers, and developers as a
means to distinguish their products.
This book is sold as is, without warranty of any kind, either express or implied, respecting the contents of this book and any
disks or programs that may accompany it, including but not limited to implied warranties for the book's quality, performance,
merchantability, or fitness for any particular purpose. Neither Wordware Publishing, Inc. nor its dealers or distributors shall
be liable to the purchaser or any other person or entity with respect to any liability, loss, or damage caused or alleged to have
been caused directly or indirectly by this book.

All inquiries for volume purchases of this book should be addressed to Wordware
Publishing, Inc., at the above address. Telephone inquiries may be made by calling:

(972) 423-0090

Contents

Introduction

Creating characters is one of the most rewarding aspects of 3D animation. Seeing a character that started out as a 2D concept drawing come to life through animation is a real joy.

Ever since I can remember, I've been fascinated by animation. While other kids wanted to be firemen or astronauts, my greatest dream was to make animated movies. I was constantly getting in trouble for being late for school because I was watching the morning cartoons and for drawing in my schoolbooks. Years later when I first got the chance to play with 3D animation, I was disappointed that the software wasn't capable of doing everything I imagined. I saw the potential was there, and although movies like *Jurassic Park* and *Toy Story* were still a few years away, it was enough to make me want to persevere. I'd been creating 2D animation for a while before that, but I enjoyed the unique challenges involved with 3D animation and found that it offered so many more possibilities.

Since then, consumer 3D software has evolved to become everything I had wished for in those early days, and more. Over the last few years we've reached a point where it's possible to create convincing 3D characters with all the nuances that were previously only possible in 2D animation. With recent advancements in software and computer speed, it's easier than ever to create and animate 3D characters with the quality of performance that modern audiences demand.

But even with all that potential, the computer is just a tool, a vehicle to enable the expression of your creativity. It's only with knowledge and talent that great characters are born. I have always enjoyed sharing my knowledge and teaching people what I've learned, and this series gives you the knowledge you need to unleash your talent and create world-class 3D characters.

This Series Is for You

When I started in 3D animation there was very little in the way of training, and 3D character animation was still in its infancy. Because many of the techniques that are common today just weren't available, I had to figure a lot of it out for myself. If you're just starting out in 3D character creation I envy you, because this book and its companion, *Volume 2: Rigging & Animation*, are the books that I wish I had so many times during my career.

If you have experience in creating 3D characters, this series teaches you how to take your characters to the next level and shows you the easy way to accomplish things that have always seemed difficult.

If you're an animator who doesn't enjoy character creation because all you want to do is animate, this series teaches you the fastest and easiest ways to create characters so you spend less time fighting with the character and more time animating, and have more fun doing it.

There are few resources available that deal with all of the aspects of 3D character creation. Many claim to but end up only scratching the surface, leaving out vital information or, even worse, teaching bad habits and inefficient techniques. This series shows you how to make a character capable of acting in every sense of the word, with the ability to express complex emotions that are essential to achieving high-quality animation, whether you're creating characters for use in your own animations or in a production environment. Many other resources use supplied content so they can skip important steps. This series guides you through every step along the way toward creating successful characters so you only need to use the supplied content if you choose to.

While short movies are often created by a single person, commercial animation productions usually involve a number of animators working with the characters. This series teaches those extra steps that are vital to ensure that an animator understands the animation controls, that the character is easy to animate, and that the character looks good when animated. Even if you're just creating characters for your own animation, those extra steps make posing and animating the character much quicker and easier.

There is rarely just one way to accomplish something in 3D creation or animation. While I have preferred methods that have evolved over a number of years of production experience, they're not necessarily the right way — just my way. Everyone has different preferred methods for creation and animation, and every character has different requirements. This series does what no other resource does; instead of just teaching my preferred methods, I provide many examples of alternate techniques and how and when to use them, and explain why I choose my preferred techniques.

Character creation is largely about problem solving, but as much as I'd like to, I can't give you a solution for every problem that you'll come across. My solution to this is to make sure that you have the knowledge and understand the techniques that you need to solve any problem that may arise. Most resources tell you *how* to accomplish a specific task, but the same technique is difficult to apply to your own work unless you know *why* it's used, and *when* it should and should not be used. My teaching philosophy is that why something is done a certain way and when it should be done are as important as how it's done. That way you have a solid understanding of the theory and practical knowledge behind the techniques so you can easily apply them to your own work.

This series gives you the knowledge to take what you've learned and build upon it, refining existing techniques and developing new techniques. Character creation and animation is a constantly evolving art form and thinking outside the box is how the evolution takes place. If you can take a technique further or find a more efficient way of accomplishing a task, then do it. Like everyone else, I'm always learning, and will continue to refine and develop the techniques that I've shared with you. It's what keeps this job fun and interesting, and makes ours the best job in the world.

Why LightWave 3D?

LightWave 3D is uniquely adapted to speed and ease of use while retaining the power and depth of features that are required for character creation and animation. It's easy to learn and doesn't require complex, advanced knowledge to do the basic tasks necessary for character creation. Using LightWave 3D you can create and rig characters for animation more quickly and easily than in any other package.

LightWave 3D has a very strong online community. Whenever you need help with any aspect of the program or any technique, there will always be someone there to help. This is especially important when you're first learning, but is invaluable even to experienced users. There are hundreds of plug-ins available to make your job even easier, and most of them are free. If you need something even more powerful, you can be sure that there's a commercial plug-in available to suit the task, at a reasonable price.

LightWave 3D 8 expands the character creation toolset even further, making the work involved in character creation faster and easier than ever before. This book and its companion volume take full advantage of the existing features as well as the features new to LightWave 3D 8 to ensure that you use the most efficient methods available for creating your characters.

Although it uses the toolset in LightWave 3D 8, this book is just as valuable if you're using an earlier version of LightWave or another package entirely. The essential principles and required tasks of character creation remain the same for all 3D characters, even though the steps to achieve a certain task may differ between packages. What I teach are theories that are program independent and character creation methods and techniques that are applicable to the creation of all 3D characters no matter what package is used.

How to Use the Books

I originally set out to write a single book on cartoon character creation. I knew it would be a fairly large book due to the number of topics relevant to the subject matter, but little did I realize just how big it would become. As I was nearing completion it became apparent that as one book it was far too big to publish, and I had a decision to make — either reduce the content to fit in a single book, or separate it into two books. It wasn't too difficult a decision to go with two books, as the last thing I wanted to do was to reduce the learning potential for you, the reader. So what was originally one book is now a two-volume set: *Volume 1: Modeling & Texturing* and *Volume 2: Rigging & Animation*.

Volume 1: Modeling & Texturing

Volume 1: Modeling & Texturing explains the process of creating 3D characters. Character design, modeling, and texturing are the fundamental building blocks of character animation. This book guides you through creating two characters, explaining the techniques for every step of the process including subpatch modeling, UV mapping, surfacing, and image mapping.

- **Part I — Preparation** explains what to do before you start the creation process. It shows you how to set up LightWave for character creation and what steps you need to take in the character concept, design, and planning stages.

- **Part II — Morfi** is an introduction to character creation, catering to the reader who has little or no prior experience in creating characters. It provides a quick entry to character creation so you can jump into the practical, creative work straight away, while at the same time giving you the opportunity to learn multiple techniques. Part II also includes a bonus chapter that provides a quick start to rigging.

- **Part III — Hamish** starts at a more advanced level, assuming the reader has a good understanding of the basic techniques described in Part II. It explains the process of modeling and texturing characters, including UV mapping, surfacing, and image map creation and application.

Volume 2: Rigging & Animation

Volume 2: Rigging & Animation follows on directly from Volume 1, explaining the process of preparing characters for animation. Proper rigging and animation preparation is vital for creating characters that can truly act and make an audience believe they are living, emotive beings. Volume 2 guides you through multiple rigging techniques, including bipeds and quadrupeds, advanced and alternate animation controls, and using dynamics for clothes and secondary motion, and includes a comprehensive explanation of facial animation.

- **Part I — Morph Creation** explains how to create and use morphs effectively. It describes the morphs that are necessary for facial expressions and lip sync, with examples from multiple characters, and explains the most efficient ways of creating those morphs.

- **Part II — Character Setup** explains the process of setting up characters for animation, including making the character deform well and making it easy to animate. It describes methods for automating motion to complement the animation controls, alternate rigging techniques for different control methods, and applying an existing rig to different characters. This section expands on the quick-start rigging chapter from Volume I, including all the theories behind the techniques.

- **Part III — Animation and Dynamics** explains the process of animating 3D characters. It explains how to use the controls for efficient animation practices, how to configure the character rig for different styles of animation, and how to animate facial expressions and lip sync, including the creation of custom morph controls. Additionally, it covers the use of dynamics for automated motion of clothing and secondary motion of the body.

The Appendix in each book contains descriptions of all the plug-ins included in the tutorials and on the CD, and provides information on other useful resources.

Both volumes contain the important theory behind the techniques and methods provided, so that when you complete the books you can continue to use them as a reference when creating your own characters. These books don't contain long-winded anecdotes or long, drawn-out explanations, but provide concise and complete explanations of every technique so you can learn quickly and effectively.

Each chapter starts with the most general theory, the techniques that apply to all characters and to all 3D packages. Following are the theories and techniques that are more specific to LightWave 3D. Finally, there are detailed steps in the tutorials, making use of the theories and techniques described earlier. The tutorials explain proper and efficient workflow practices and how to make the most of the LightWave 3D 8 toolset.

These books are companions to rather than replacements for the LightWave 3D manual. No matter what program you use, I highly recommend reading the manual every six months. It's only possible to learn and retain what you can comprehend. Many people only read the manual when they first learn a package, and even then rarely read it all. At that stage in the learning process you can only comprehend a certain amount of what is revealed. By reading the manual every six months you take advantage of your increased experience because you're able to comprehend more. Each time you read the manual you learn much more and retain that knowledge longer.

CD Content

Everything you need to follow the tutorials is included on the companion CD.

- There are sample objects, scenes, and images for every step along the way, enabling you to jump ahead to learn a specific topic.

- All the plug-ins used in the book are supplied, as well as many other plug-ins that can be helpful in character creation, including demo versions of some useful commercial plug-ins.

- All the images and illustrations from the book are supplied in full color.

- There are sample animations and images to inspire and delight you.

For a more complete list of the content, see the readme.txt file on the root of the CD.

Contacting the Author

You can contact me and see more of my work through my web site at www.zerogravity.com.au.

If you have any questions regarding this book, if you get stuck, or if you want some advice about a character you're creating or a technique you're developing, be sure to check out the support site at www.zerogravity.com.au/cartoon.

You can also find me loitering on a few popular forums under the name Kretin.

Chapter 1

Getting Started

Before starting on the tutorials, it's useful to set up a few preferences for working in LightWave. I've structured the following steps starting from the default installation. If you've been using LightWave for a while, you've probably already made some of these changes to suit your own way of working. If your own preferences differ from these, you may need to reinterpret some instructions along the way, as the tutorials in this book assume you have set the interface and options as specified here.

1.1 Files and Folders

LightWave works with content directories. When working on a model or a scene, LightWave looks in the Content Directory for any files it needs. Using this functionality is a great way to keep your projects separate, and also allows you to store your projects separately from the main program. Figure 1.1-1 shows the folder structure that LightWave uses.

Figure 1.1-1. LightWave's content folder structure.

When you open a new scene, the Scenes folder within the specified Content Directory is where LightWave looks first. From there you can specify a different directory, but it's always good to keep within the Content Directory if you can. Working this way makes it much easier to copy a specific project to send to someone else or to back up your work.

1. Copy the **LWProjects** folder from the CD to your hard drive, preferably somewhere other than in the LightWave folder. This is a good folder to keep all your LightWave projects in. If you open the folder you'll find the working files for the tutorials in this book, as well as a Project Template folder that you can copy and rename for each new project.

1

Note: In Windows, after you copy the folder to the hard drive, right-click on it and select Properties at the bottom of the context menu. In the Properties window, uncheck Read-only, then click Apply. In the following dialog box, choose Apply changes to this folder, subfolders and files and click OK, then OK again to close the Properties window.

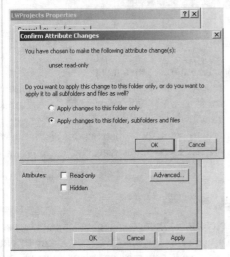

Figure 1.1-2. Changing attributes

When copying files from a CD, they're copied to the hard drive as read only. This step changes the attributes of the copied files so you can edit or modify the files.

2. To start a new project, make a copy of the **Project Template** folder and rename the copied folder appropriately for the project. This gives you all the folders LightWave needs, as well as some useful starting scenes.

You'll also see a folder in LWProjects called NewPlugins. This is where I've included the third-party plug-ins used during the course of this book. It's always a good idea to keep your third-party plug-ins separate from the plug-ins installed with LightWave. If you already have a third-party plug-ins folder, feel free to copy these plug-ins to your existing folder. If you do not, I recommend using this folder to store your third-party plug-ins from now on.

1.2 Modifying Shortcuts

Next we'll customize the shortcuts for Modeler and Layout. LightWave stores its settings in config (.cfg) files. If you don't specify where these are kept, they default to Documents and Settings in Windows or System:Preferences on Macintosh. It's better to have the configs stored in their own folder so they can more easily be modified and backed up. Additionally, you may want to have different configs for different projects or different installations of LightWave (if you have multiple versions of LightWave on the same machine).

1. Create a **Configs** folder in your LightWave directory.

2. Right-click on the shortcut for Modeler and change the **Target** to read: **C:\LightWave\programs\modeler.exe -cC:\LightWave\Configs**, changing **C:\LightWave** to the drive and directory where you have LightWave installed.

3. Repeat with the shortcut for LightWave, adding **-cC:\LightWave\Configs** to the Target.

Using these shortcuts, both Modeler and Layout will look in the C:\LightWave\ Configs folder for their config files.

If you have been using LightWave for a while and already have configs that you wish to continue using, make sure you copy your existing config files to the Configs folder.

If you want to use different configs, you can copy the shortcuts and point them to a different Configs folder, being sure to rename the new shortcuts appropriately.

> **Note:** You can also specify to disable the Hub in the shortcuts by adding -0, but since we're using the Hub we won't do that. This option can be useful to include in a copy of your main shortcuts so you can run a second copy of LightWave independently of the Hub if you want to quickly do something in a different content directory without interfering with other work you're doing.

1.3 Configuring Modeler

Options

There are two types of options in LightWave: General Options and Display Options. The shortcut keys for these are the same for both Modeler and Layout: **o** for General Options and **d** for Display Options.

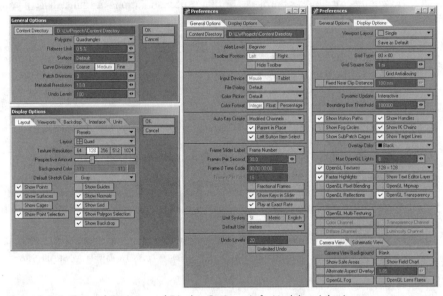

Figure 1.3-1. General Options and Display Options. Left: Modeler, right: Layout.

Launch Modeler from the shortcut so we can set up the options and window layout.

1. Press **o** to open General Options.

2. Change Patch Divisions to **3**. The reason for doing this is that Layout defaults to a subpatch level of 3. You can change this setting while working in Modeler, but if you model using a subpatch level of 3 it's easier to know if you need to adjust this setting when you import the model into Layout.

3. Change Undo Levels to a nice high number; somewhere between 50 and 100 is good.

> **Note:** General Options is also where you set the Content Directory in Modeler. Keep in mind that the Content Directory is a global setting that is the same for Modeler and Layout.

4. Click **OK** or press **Enter** to close General Options.

5. Press **d** to open Display Options. There are five tabs at the top of the window, each relating to different types of options. We'll start with the default tab, Layout.

6. The default Perspective Amount is very high, and can cause distortion in your modeling if you frequently work in Perspective view. I prefer to set it to about the middle of the 128 button (in the Texture Resolution setting). This is a more natural perspective amount to work with.

7. See Figure 1.3-2 for which Show option check boxes I have set as a default. The illustrations in the tutorials reflect my settings, but feel free to set them however you wish to best suit your preferences.

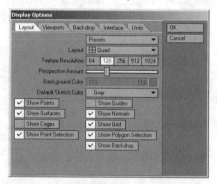

Figure 1.3-2. Display Options➢Layout.

8. Click the **Viewports** tab. Here you can adjust the default settings for each view independently. The only one we'll change is the Perspective view, or TR.

9. Click on **TR** and check **Independent Zoom** and **Independent Visibility**. You can also check **Independent BG Color** and change that to a color that best shows the models. I usually like to use a desaturated dark blue, but for the purposes of clear illustrations I've left it the default gray.

10. Notice that when you check Independent Visibility the lower options become active. Now you can adjust the way models are viewed in the Perspective view. See Figure 1.3-3 for which check boxes I have set.

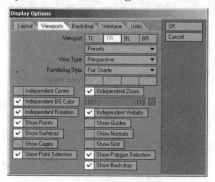

Figure 1.3-3. Display Options➢Viewports, Viewport TR.

11. We'll look at Backdrop a little later, so there's just one more setting to change now. Click the **Units** tab and change Grid Snap to **None**.

12. Click **OK** or press **Enter** to close Display Options.

Interface

The next step is to open all the panels and arrange them on the right side of the display. Having these panels open all the time makes it much easier to use the advanced tool options, select points or polygons, select and modify layers, and select and modify vertex maps, all of which is done in later chapters.

1. Select the right edge of Modeler and drag it in from the side of the display.

2. Open the Numeric panel using the button at the bottom of the interface or by pressing **n**.

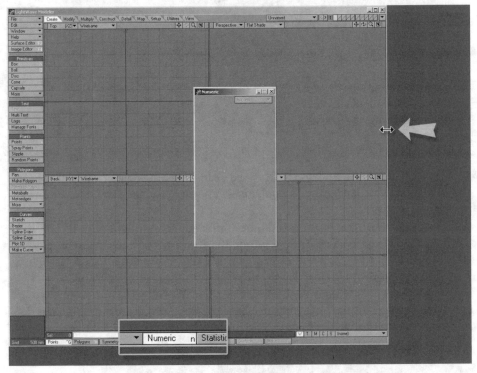

Figure 1.3-4. Drag the Modeler window to the left to make room for the panels.

3. Open the Statistics panel using the button at the bottom of the interface (or by pressing **w**).

4. Open the Vertex Maps and Layers panels from the **Window** pull-down (or press **Ctrl+F5** and **Ctrl+F6**).

5. Arrange the four windows as shown in Figure 1.3-5.

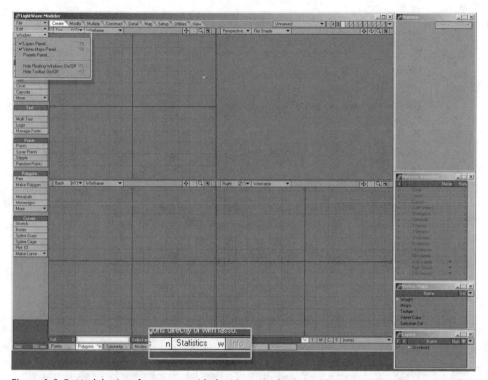

Figure 1.3-5. Modeler interface set up with the Numeric, Statistics, Vertex Maps, and Layers panels.

Now we'll install the plug-ins included on the companion CD and set up a place for them in the menu.

1. Open the Edit Plug-ins window by selecting **Utilities** ➢ **Plug-ins** ➢ **Edit Plug-ins** (or press **Alt + F11**).

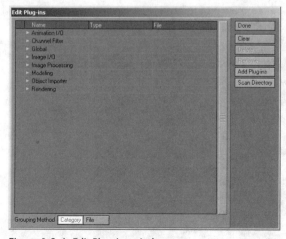

Figure 1.3-6. Edit Plug-ins window.

2. Click **Scan Directory** and browse to the **LWProjects\NewPlugins** folder on your hard drive. Select the folder and click **OK**.

3. Click **Done** to close the Edit Plug-ins window.

4. Open the Configure Menus window using **Edit**➤**Edit Menu Layout** (or press **Alt+F10**).

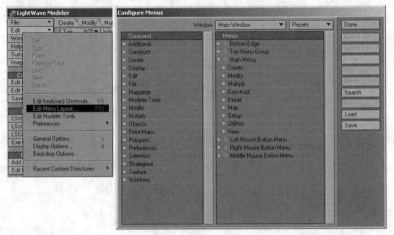

Figure 1.3-7. Configure Menus window. The left panel has a list of commands or tools, and the right panel has a list of menus. The listing under Main Menu in the Menus panel is what we are editing. This includes the tabs and tools of the main interface. When you click on a tab name, you can see the interface change in the background to display that tab, so you can see the interface update as you make changes.

5. Open the **Construct** group in the Command panel, and open **Main Menu**➤**Map**➤**General** in the Menus panel.

6. Drag **Unweld Points** from the Command panel to just below **Clear Map** in the Menus panel.

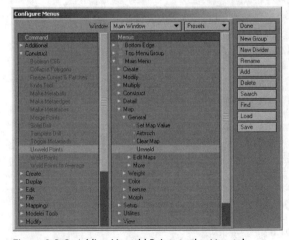

Figure 1.3-8. Adding Unweld Points to the Map tab.

7. Select **Main Menu▸View** and click **New Group**. Making a new group at this level creates a new tab.

8. Double-click on the new group and choose a name. I call it **Plugs**.

9. Expand **Main Menu▸Utilities▸Plug-ins** and drag **Additional** down to **Plugs**. If you select Plugs now, you can see all your new plug-ins under the Additional heading on the interface. Feel free to organize the plug-ins on the Plugs tab into different groups.

Figure 1.3-9. Moving Additional to the new Plugs tab.

1.4 Configuring Layout

Options

Launch Layout either from the shortcut (if it's the first time you're running it) or from Modeler via the pop-up menu button to the right of the layer buttons (see Figure 1.4-1).

Figure 1.4-1. Modeler can communicate with Layout through this menu. Once you've launched Layout from the shortcut (telling the Hub where to find it), you can also launch Layout from this menu.

First we'll set up the viewports and other options. How you configure your viewports can be a very personal preference. Almost everyone I've seen has it set differently. Because I'm doing the storytelling here, it's best to stick to my preference for now, but as always, if you're experienced enough with LightWave, feel free to use your own setup and adjust the instructions to suit. Even if you have an existing preference, I recommend trying this configuration. As we go through the tutorials I explain more about why I use this viewport layout.

1. Press **d** to open Display Options.

Figure 1.4-2. Default display options.

2. Change Viewport Layout to **2 Left, 1 Right**.
3. Change Grid Square Size to **0.25 m** (or 250 mm).
4. With Display Options still open, change the top-left viewport to **Camera View** and the right viewport to **Perspective**.
5. Change the Top (XZ) Maximum Render Level to **Front Face Wireframe**.

Figure 1.4-3. Changing Maximum Render Level.

6. Back in Display Options, check **Show Safe Areas** in the Camera View settings.
7. Click **Save as Default**.

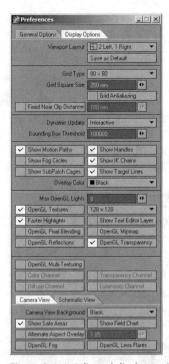

Figure 1.4-4. Adjusted display options.

We'll revisit some of these settings during the course of our work, but these are a good starting point.

Take a look at the setting for Alert Level in Modeler➤Display Options and in Layout➤General Options.

This defaults to Beginner, and controls how you're alerted to errors and warnings. Even if you're new to LightWave I'd recommend changing this to Intermediate; once you're comfortable with LightWave, change it to Expert. You still

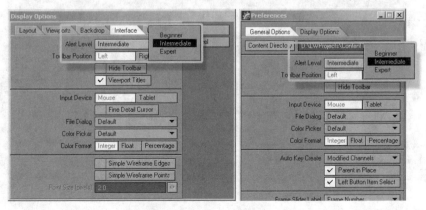

Figure 1.4-5. Alert Level. Left: Modeler, right: Layout.

get the messages, but they appear in the Information line at the bottom of the interface instead of pop-up dialog boxes. You'll be amazed at how much quicker you can work when you're not clicking OK on dialog boxes every two minutes.

Interface

It's useful to have the Scene Editor open all the time. If you have the luxury of two displays you can place the Scene Editor in the second display, leaving the viewports clear. One of the Scene Editor's most useful functions is easy item selection, but if you only have a single display you can just open Scene Editor when you need it.

> **Note:** I have become very accustomed to having two displays. I highly rec-ommend a dual display system if you're serious about doing 3D graphics or animation. This allows you to have the main program on one display and pop-up windows on the other, which can be invaluable to your work flow. Some people like to have Modeler on one display and Layout on the other, which can also be useful.

1. Select **Scene Editor➤Classic Scene Editor**.
2. Move and scale the Scene Editor window so it covers the Perspective viewport.

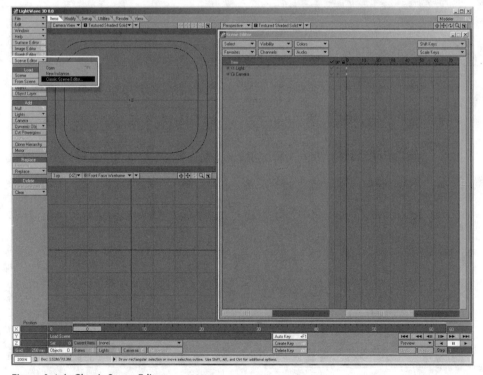

Figure 1.4-6. Classic Scene Editor.

3. If you have dual display, move the Scene Editor window to the second display; otherwise, close it.

> **Note:** There are two types of Scene Editor in LightWave 8 — the Classic Scene Editor and the new Scene Editor. The new Scene Editor is scene reliant, so there's no point in setting its position at this stage.

As we did in Modeler, we need to install the plug-ins from the CD and set up a place for them in the menu. The steps are pretty much the same for Layout as they were for Modeler.

1. Open the Edit Plug-ins window using **Utilities➢Plug-ins➢Edit Plug-ins** (or press **Alt+F11**).

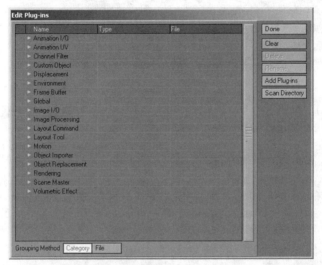

Figure 1.4-7. Edit Plug-ins window.

2. Click **Scan Directory** and browse to the **LWProjects\NewPlugins** folder on your hard drive. Select the folder and click **OK**.
3. Click **Done** to close the Edit Plug-ins window.
4. Open the Configure Menus window using **Edit➢Edit Menu Layout** (**Alt+F10**).
5. Open the **Preferences** group in the Command panel, and open the **Top Group** in the Menus panel.
6. Select **Scene Editor** in the Menus panel and click **New Group**. Double-click on the new group to rename it, deleting its name. This creates a small gap between buttons.
7. Drag **Parent in Place On/Off** from the Command panel to just below the new blank group in the right panel.

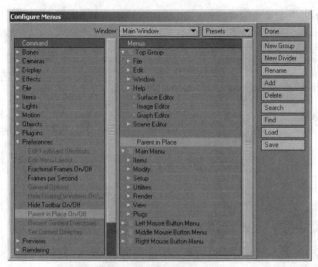

Figure 1.4-8. Configure Menus window.

8. Select **Main Menu➤View** and click **New Group**. Making a new group at this level creates a new tab.

9. Double-click on the new group and type in the same name as the tab we created in Modeler — **Plugs**.

10. Expand **Main Menu➤Utilities➤Plugins** and drag **Additional** down to **Plugs**. If you select Plugs now, you can see the Additional pull-down on the interface. Feel free to organize the plug-ins in the Plugs➤Additional tab into different groups.

Figure 1.4-9. Changing the Layout menu.

One last thing to do is to make sure that Auto Key, at the bottom of the Layout interface, is turned on.

Figure 1.4-10. Auto Key on.

I leave this on all the time, but I know some people like to turn it off when they're animating. Some motion modifiers require Auto Key to be on for interactive updates, and because I can't guarantee that everything will work as described with it turned off, you should keep Auto Key on while you're following the tutorials in this book.

Keyboard Shortcuts

You may have already noticed many interface changes in LightWave 8 from previous versions. Although we haven't covered keyboard shortcuts in this chapter, there are some significant changes to these as well. If you've used previous versions of LightWave 3D, then you're used to the LightWave shortcuts for undo, cut, copy, and paste:

- Undo   **u**
- Cut   **x**
- Copy   **c**
- Paste   **v**

These shortcuts have been changed in LightWave 8 to the Windows standards:

- Undo   **Ctrl+z**
- Cut   **Ctrl+x**
- Copy   **Ctrl+c**
- Paste   **Ctrl+v**

If you're used to the previous shortcuts and wish to continue using them in LightWave 8, you can easily revert to LightWave 7.5 keyboard shortcuts.

> **Note:** Be aware that if you revert to 7.5 shortcuts you'll lose many of the updated shortcuts in the default configuration. You may find it more beneficial just to remap the old shortcuts into the new configuration.

1. Open the Configure Keys window, **Edit>Edit Keyboard Shortcuts** (or press **Alt+F9**).

2. Click the **Presets** pull-down and select **7.0 Style** in Modeler or **7.5 Style** in Layout.

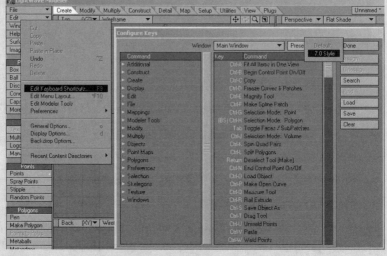

Figure 1.4-11. Edit Keyboard Shortcuts, using Presets.

Now that we've set up the basic defaults for each program, we need to save them. You can save your menu configuration separately from the Configure Menus window or, to save everything we've just done, close all three applications — Modeler, Layout, and the Hub. Closing the applications saves the settings to the config files. You can relaunch Modeler or Layout to continue working.

Part I

Preparation

Whether you're given character concepts to work from or are designing characters yourself, the following sections are important for developing characters that translate well into the 3D realm.

Chapter 2

Concept Stage

2.1 Character Design

Every 3D character should start life as a 2D character design drawing. It's very important that you establish the basis for the character before you start modeling. The shapes and forms of the 2D design determine proportions and how and where the polygons are placed, and help decide which details are modeled and which are textured.

What and Who

The first thing you need to ascertain is whether the character is human, animal, alien, fantasy creature, etc. Obviously this sets the basis for the character, but beyond this decision there are other things to consider. Characters based on animals generally fall into one of two categories — caricatured animals or anthropomorphic animals. Which of these categories your character falls into affects both its look and movement so it's an important decision to make early in the character development.

Caricatured animals, as featured in Disney's *Bambi* or *Lion King*, look, act, and move like the animals they're based on. Certain characteristics are exaggerated, especially facial features, but they retain the essential elements and body structure of the animal.

Figure 2.1-1. Caricatured animals retain the essential characteristics and motions of the animal.

Anthropomorphic animals, such as Warner Bros.' Bugs Bunny, Daffy Duck, and Wile E. Coyote, retain certain features of the animal they're based on but are more human in body shape, movement, and attitude.

Figure 2.1-2. Anthropomorphic animals maintain some of the characteristics of the animal but are generally more human in body shape and motion.

The next thing is to understand who the character is — its gender, age, background, temperament, intellect, and self-image. From there it's important to establish the unique aspect of the character — what makes the character interesting, whether it's motivation, occupation, mannerisms, or other personality quirks. Finally, it's good to know what kind of relationship this character has with other characters in the story, what conflicts there are, and how other characters perceive it (which can often be in direct opposition to the character's self-image). All of these things translate directly or indirectly to the design and visual cues of a character, how the character reacts to different situations, what kind of clothes it might wear, what accessories it might have. If you're creating a character for a specific production, there is usually a script and character descriptions that explain most of these characteristics, but there are times that you will be left to decide a lot of this yourself.

Research

Now that you've established what and who the character is, it's time to do some research. I cannot stress enough the importance of researching a character, especially if it's based on something real, which most characters are. Successful animation relies on the ability to convince an audience that your characters really exist, that their emotions are real, and that what they're doing is important. To ensure your character can do that, you need reference for every aspect of the character, including what it looks like, how it moves, what clothes it wears, what those clothes look like and how they move, and the list goes on. The more of these aspects you make up (or leave out), the less believable your character will become.

Whether your character is human, animal, or something else entirely, nine times out of ten it will be based on a real person or existing character types. If it's based on a real person, you should find either picture or video reference of that person. If that person is an actor or character in a movie, then it's easy — you just need to rent a few DVDs. If it's based on an established character type, then find pictures or video of similar characters. Using your reference, try to understand what defines that person or character. Let's say your character is a superhero. What basic characteristics define a superhero? By analyzing comic books, cartoons, and live-action movies, you will find that the stereotype (and stereotypes are often a prerequisite for cartoon characters) is a confident stance, strong jaw, large chest, spandex suit, and a cape. If your character is a cowboy, rent some John Wayne movies and look for the defining characteristics of his cowboy characters in personality and attitude, as well as clothing and accessories.

If your character is based on an animal, you need to do even more research. I spend anywhere from hours to days (even weeks) researching an animal before and during the creation of a character. The most convincing animal characters have a solid grounding in reality, and the only way to do this is to know the real animal inside out. Buy or borrow books or DVDs about the animal in question, search the web (most search engines have a section to search for images), and if possible, find the real animal in a pet shop or zoo. No matter what the animal is,

Figure 2.1-3. I recently created four frogs for a cartoon series. Each character's personality and age, and certain characteristics of the voice artist all went into deciding what kind of frog the character was based on. Instead of having four generic frogs, each character is truly unique, and because they are based on real frogs, it was much easier to adjust the shape, features, textures, and coloring for each one because I had reference right in front of me as I was creating them.

there are always dozens of variations to consider. It's not enough to know it's a monkey. What kind of monkey is it? Is it a marmoset, saki, baboon, or chimpanzee? This decision influences the character's shape, features, and how it moves. If it's a marmoset, what kind of marmoset it is will further influence its features, texture, and coloring. Making these decisions and having reference to work from goes a long way toward making your character seem alive.

If you're creating a caricatured animal, it's important to study the anatomy of the real animal and how it moves. While most animals have the same basic bone structure, each type of animal has evolved slightly differently and is capable of different poses and movements. Understanding the mechanics behind each animal's movement will influence your decisions during the modeling and rigging stages to ensure your character is capable of the same kinds of poses or movements as the real animal.

2.2 Analyzing the Concept

You have to be careful when creating character concepts for 3D characters that they translate well from two dimensions to three. Many 2D cartoon characters have features that would be difficult, if not impossible, to replicate in 3D. You need to keep this in mind when designing your character, and adjust your design if necessary. Nearly every 2D character concept needs some sort of modification when you create it in 3D, but it's a good idea to keep these modifications to a minimum.

Figure 2.2-1. The character on the left would be difficult to create in 3D. The character on the right has had a few adjustments to make it more 3D compatible.

Try drawing the character from various angles and in different poses. If you're having trouble with some angles, then it's likely you'd have the same difficulties translating that area to 3D. As you do this you also start to get a better idea of the three-dimensional form of the character, which is helpful in the modeling stage.

Figure 2.2-2. Thumbnail pose sketches for Morfi. (You can see where he got his name.)

Start thinking of the character as primitive three-dimensional forms and shapes all fitting together. In fact, this is usually taught in 2D drawing, especially when drawing animated characters, to help get the proportions correct when drawing from different angles and to make the drawings feel more three-dimensional when in motion. The reasons behind doing this for 2D and 3D are quite similar, only for 3D it's to get a better idea of the forms and shapes when you're checking your model from different angles.

Figure 2.2-3. Morfi broken down into primitive shapes.

It's sometimes useful to even draw some grid lines on your concept, following the contours of the character. This can help determine your basic polygon flow to better prepare for modeling.

Figure 2.2-4. Morfi with grid lines drawn over him to indicate polygon flow.

Eventually this becomes second nature. You won't be able to look at a 2D character (or anything else for that matter) without mentally breaking it down into primitives and polygon flow. Once you get to this stage you can rely on your mental picture of the forms, shapes, and polygon flow without needing to actually draw them over the concept.

2.3 Preparation

Read the Script

Before you start creating a character, make sure you read the script, making notes along the way. What the character does in the story will often make a big difference in the creation process. You can plan ahead for a few common scenarios, but each character always has specific things it needs to be able to do. If these things aren't taken into consideration from the beginning, you may create the character in such a way that it's very difficult to accommodate them later on, possibly even resulting in part or all of the object or rig having to be entirely recreated.

More often than not the concept sketches will give you some idea of what the character is capable of doing, but there will usually be something in the story that is quite unexpected.

> **Note:** I was an animator on a production where a robot character had ten retractable arms. The main concept image for the character had only four arms extended, and so the creator of the character had only created those four arms in the model. There was also no control method for retracting or extending those arms in the rig.
>
> A scene featuring this character called for all ten arms to retract, extend, and spin around independently of the body. None of this had been taken into account for the initial character, so I had to significantly modify the object and rig to accommodate these motions. This was work that, as an animator, I wasn't being compensated for. Since this was quite late in the production I also realized that the other animators on the project would also have had to modify the same character in order to accommodate their scenes, resulting in the same work being done multiple times by different animators.
>
> While it was partially the producer's job to make sure this work was done, and only done once, had the original creator read the script and created the character accordingly, it would not have taken much more time to create, but certainly would have saved a lot of time in the end and resulted in the animation process being more efficient and much faster.

Taking notice of the script applies to every part of the process of creating a character. The character may have features that aren't apparent in the beginning but appear later in the story that need to be included in the model. There may be unique facial expressions or model alterations that you need to include in the morphs or extra surface and texture attributes that are needed.

Keep in mind that you don't have to accommodate everything in one character. If a scene in the script calls for a character to lift off the top of his head and poke at his brain, it's likely that including that ability in the main character will result in a visible seam between the two parts of the head, and further complicate scenes where that ability isn't necessary. In cases like this you should create an alternate character that can be swapped in at that stage of the scene.

You can take this concept even further if the character is likely to be used in other scripts, by analyzing the character and thinking of things it may be required to do in later stories. You don't necessarily need to create those abilities yet, but you can allow for them in the way you create the character. Of course when it comes to future scripts you nearly always find something you could never have predicted, but with a bit of forward thinking at this stage you drastically reduce the workload when that time comes.

Size Counts

One of the most important things to consider when creating characters is the size and relative scale of the character. You may not think scale is an issue because, after all, one of the freedoms of 3D animation is that you can change the scale of objects at any stage. Let me dispel this myth right now — whether a character is interacting with just the environment or, more importantly, interacting with other characters or props, establishing the correct scale as early as possible is essential.

It's easy to ignore the scale of characters, sets, and props when creating 3D models. You can just as easily create a mouse 10 meters tall or a house 10 centimeters tall. The trouble with doing this is that once you bring all the models together in Layout you need to adjust their size. Once you've animated a scene it can be very difficult to adjust the scale of anything in the scene without redoing parts of the animation. If all the characters for your production are created with arbitrary sizes, the animators will need to rescale every character for every scene, more often than not leading to continuity problems between scenes as various animators have scaled the characters differently.

> **Note:**   I have been brought in as an animator on a few productions where the models were not created to scale. In one such production the characters had all been created to different scales, anywhere from 1 to 13 meters tall. The sets were also created to different scales and the main set, which should have been around 15 meters tall, was only 4 meters.
>
> I remember one scene in particular where a couple of characters were drawn in different sizes in the storyboards, so I had to guess what scale the characters should be. When the director had seen the first draft animation he asked that the characters be larger. Still confused by the size in the storyboards, I made them larger for the next revision, only to be told that I'd now made them too large. In the end it took three or four revisions before the director was happy with the scale of these characters.
>
> If the characters and the sets had been created to scale in the first place, there would have been none of this confusion. It would have made my job as an animator, not to mention the director's job, a whole lot easier.

Changing the scale of a character can also lead to problems with certain rigging or texturing techniques. We can make sure that the techniques we use when creating our characters stand up as well as possible to scale alterations, as it is useful to be able to adjust scale a little during animation for specific effect. Unfortunately, there are times where the only technique that can solve a particular challenge is a technique that's liable to break or need adjustment when the model or object is scaled.

With all this in mind, it's a good idea to establish the scale of a character in the concept stage, whether you create a size chart with all the characters lined up against a height marked wall or specify the height of each character on the concepts.

Figure 2.3-1. Size chart.

Once you've done this it's a quick step to set the scale of the character before you start modeling. If you're using background reference, the scale of the character is determined by the size you set for the background images. If you're not using background reference, then you can make a box that's the correct height of the character to place in a background layer and use for scale reference.

Background Images

If you're new to character modeling, it's always a good idea to have front and side references for a character to model against. As you gain more experience you can begin to rely less on background reference for some characters, but they can be an invaluable resource, even for experienced character creators.

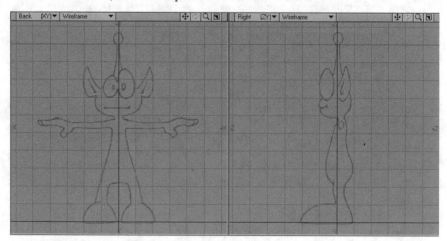

Figure 2.3-2. Front and side reference in Modeler.

If you're given a character concept, front and side views should be included, but sometimes it's left up to you to create them. If you've done all the previous steps in this chapter, you shouldn't have any problems with visualizing the character from the appropriate points of view.

1. Make sure, before you start drawing the character, that you create a center line, a base line, and a top line.

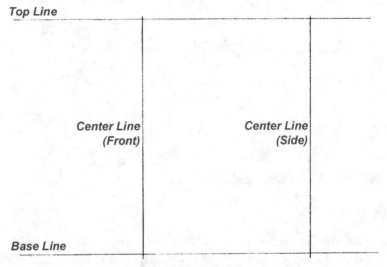

Figure 2.3-3. If you're drawing on paper, make sure these lines are parallel to the edges of the paper so when you scan the images you know the character will be symmetrical. Here I've also created a center line for the side view.

2. Draw the front view, being careful to make the left and right sides as close to each other as possible.

3. Draw the side view, placing the center line roughly in the middle of the torso.

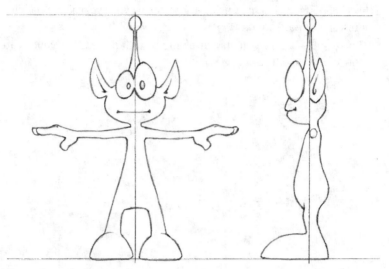

Figure 2.3-4. Front and side views.

4. Scan the image and bring it into the paint package of your choice.
5. Crop the top and bottom of the new image from the base line to the top line.
6. Adjust the Brightness and Contrast controls so the white background is a medium gray and the dark pencil lines are darker gray, just dark enough to see over the gray background. This is so you can easily see foreground and background wireframes over the images while modeling.

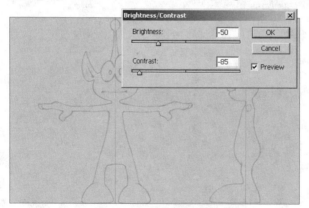

Figure 2.3-5. Adjusting brightness and contrast.

7. Select the front view from the center line to just outside the leftmost feature. Make a note of the pixel dimension of the selected area.

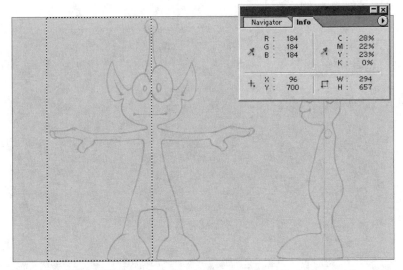

Figure 2.3-6. Selecting left side.

8. Start from the same place as the previous step and select to the right, adding to the existing selection and making sure the selected pixel dimensions are the same as the previous step. By doing this you ensure that the center of the character conforms to the center of your workspace in Modeler.

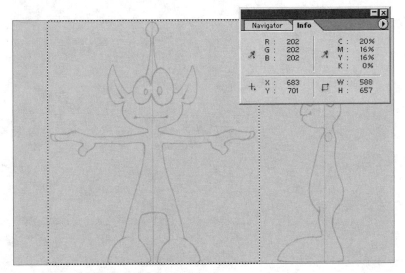

Figure 2.3-7. Adding right side to the selection.

9. **Copy** the selected area and **Paste** it into a new document.
10. **Save** the new image.
11. Repeat steps 7 to 10 for the side view.

Figure 2.3-8. Front and side views ready for saving.

Part II

Morfi

In the next two chapters we jump straight into creating a character. If you're like me, you want to get into the practical, creative work as quickly as possible, leaving the more complex techniques and explanations until later.

Chapters 4 and 5 are like a quick-start guide to character creation, guiding you through creating a very simple character in a short amount of time. You are introduced to a few techniques and concepts that are expanded upon both in later chapters and in *Volume 2: Rigging & Animation* with more complex characters. Morfi also features some unique character attributes so that different types of features found in cartoon characters can be addressed.

Chapter 3

Creating Morfi

This chapter is an introduction to subpatch modeling in LightWave 8. If you've had some modeling experience you might want to try running through this chapter quickly by just following the pictures, stopping to check the text only if you get stuck.

Figure 3-1. Meet Morfi the alien. Morfi is a fun little character who serves nicely as an introduction to character creation.

3.1 Modeler Setup

Launch Modeler and set the Content Directory (in General Options (o)) to **\LWProjects\LW8_CartoonCreation**.

> **Note:** In case you missed it earlier, in section 1.1, "Files and Folders," we copied the LWProjects folder from the CD to the hard drive.

The first step in creating a character model is to load your reference images into the background of the appropriate Modeler viewports.

1. Open Display Options (**d**) and click on the **Backdrop** tab.

2. Select **Viewport – BL** and click **Image ≻ (load image)**.

The file requester automatically takes you to the Images folder. You can find the background images used in the tutorials in the \Images\Backdrops folder.

3. Open the **Backdrops** folder and select **Template_Morfi_F.tga**.

Notice the image appears in the Back (XY) viewport on the bottom left. Now we need to set the correct size, position, and resolution of the image.

4. Change Image Resolution to **512**.

5. Set Size to **0.54** or **540 mm**.

6. Set the Y Center (the first Center setting) to roughly half the Size value, or so the base of the feet are touching the Y=0 plane. In this case, **0.265** or **265 mm** is about right.

7. Select **Viewport – BR** and load **Template_Morfi_S.tga**.

8. Fill in the same size and center settings as for the Front view.

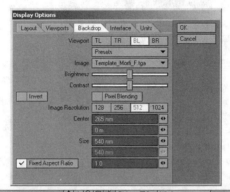

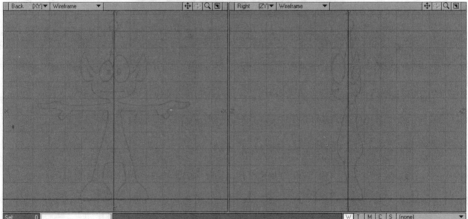

Figure 3.1-1. Backdrop settings and resulting front and side reference in Modeler.

> **Note:** You can see here that I've adjusted the brightness and contrast of the original images so the background is the same color as the viewport background, and the dark pencil lines are quite subtle. This ensures that the white wireframes of the foreground layer and the black wireframes of the background layer are easily visible over the background images.

The last step to setting up the backgrounds is to save the settings, so if you're interrupted during modeling or want to come back to it later you can load the backgrounds back in.

9. Click the **Presets** pull-down and select **Save All Backdrops**. Call the file **Backdrops_Morfi.cfg**.

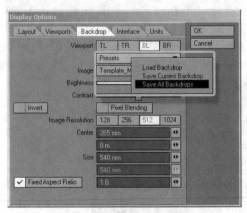

Figure 3.1-2. Display Options➤Backdrop➤ Presets➤Save All Backdrops.

10. Click **OK** to close the Display Options.

Now we're ready to move on to the next stage and start modeling.

3.2 Modeling the Body

If you haven't already, launch Modeler and load in the backdrops for Morfi that we set up in the previous stage.

1. Open Display Options (**d**) and click on the **Backdrop** tab.
2. Click the **Presets** pull-down and select **Load Backdrop**.
3. In the \Images\Backdrops folder, select **Backdrops_Morfi.cfg**.
4. Click **OK** to close the Display Options.

You can see the character is only 53 centimeters tall, which for all I know could be quite tall on his planet, but by most characters' standards is pretty small. This being the case, you need to zoom in using the magnifying glass icon or by pressing "." so the background images fill the viewports.

Torso

Since we have a background image, it doesn't really matter where we start but because it's central to all the features, we'll start by creating the torso.

1. Create an eight-sided cylinder with five segments, roughly covering the torso region of the character. You can use the settings in Figure 3.2-1 as a guide.

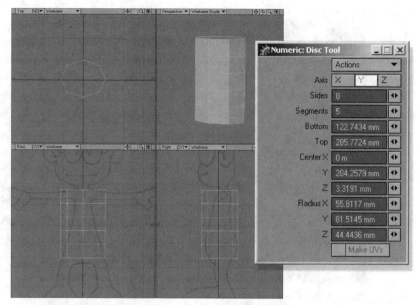

Figure 3.2-1. It's useful to start a model or section of a model with a cylinder. It helps ensure that you have a nicely rounded cross section, and gives you more polygons to play with than a box.

2. Select the top and bottom polygons of the cylinder by lassoing with the right mouse button (RMB) and delete them.

3. Press **Tab** to convert the polygons to subpatches.

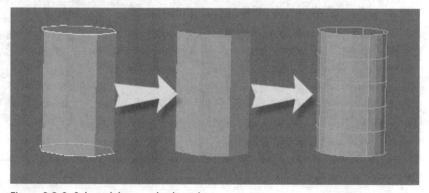

Figure 3.2-2. Select, delete, and subpatch.

4. Turn Symmetry on (**Shift+y**) and select each row of points one by one and **Stretch** (**h**) and **Move** (**t**) them until the polygons fit the torso of the background image. At this stage don't move any points vertically (up and down), only horizontally (left to right and front to back).

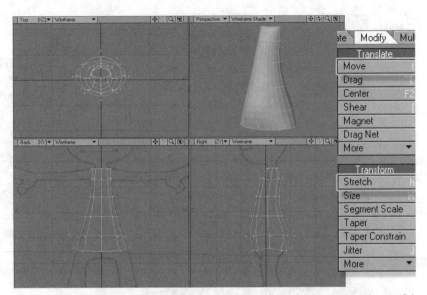

Figure 3.2-3. The points should be slightly outside the lines of the torso. Just be careful that the subpatch polygons follow the lines of the background image.

5. Select the front three and back three points of the bottom row, extend them using **Multiply➢Extend➢Extender Plus**, and move them down a little.

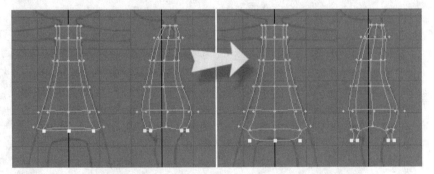

Figure 3.2-4. Extend and Move.

6. Stretch the selected points together horizontally by selecting **Stretch** (**h**), holding down **Ctrl** (constraining to a single axis), placing the mouse cursor between the points in the Right (ZY) viewport, holding down **LMB** (left mouse button), and moving the mouse left until the Numeric panel shows **0%** for the Horizontal Factor.

7. Hit **m** to merge the points together. You should have only three points at the bottom now, but if you have more (five or six) you need to weld them manually.

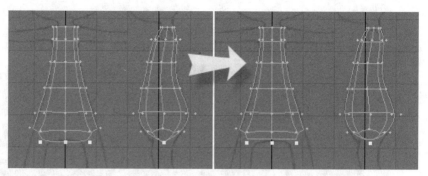

Figure 3.2-5. Stretch and Merge.

8. **Move (t)** or **Drag (Ctrl+t)** the points at the base to fit around the legs, and the top two rows of points to fit around the neck and create arm sockets.

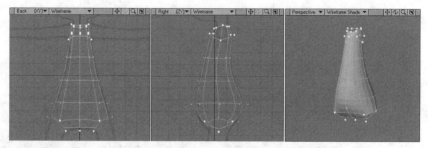

Figure 3.2-6. Move or Drag the points into position.

We want a little more definition in the legs than a four-polygon circumference allows, so we need to prepare the leg socket for an extra polygon.

9. Select the two polygons shown in Figure 3.2-7 and select the **Multiply≻Subdivide≻Knife (Shift+k)** tool. Click and drag the cursor down over the polygon in the Right (ZY) viewport.

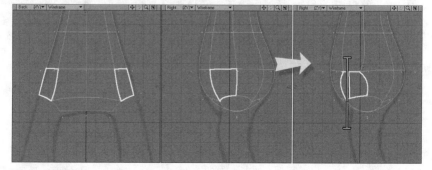

Figure 3.2-7. Create an extra edge using Knife.

10. Turn Symmetry off and select the top point of the new cut, then the top-left point of the polygon, making sure you only have one side selected, and use **Detail**≻**Points**≻**Weld** (**Ctrl+w**). Repeat for the other side.

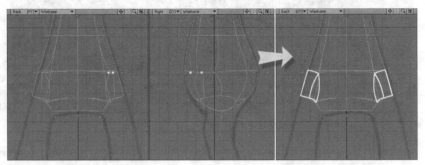

Figure 3.2-8. Weld the top of the cut.

11. Turn Symmetry back on and select the two points shown in Figure 3.2-9. **Drag** the points away from each other in the Back (XY) viewport and line them up vertically in the Right (ZY) viewport.

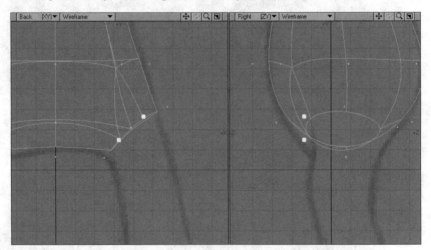

Figure 3.2-9. Adjust the points.

Legs and Feet

The legs and feet are nice and easy to make. The big feet require some careful rigging later, but since big feet are often a feature of cartoon characters it's good to cover.

1. Select the open points at the leg socket, **Extend**, and move them down. **Stretch** the points about **50%** vertically so they're roughly perpendicular to the direction of the leg.

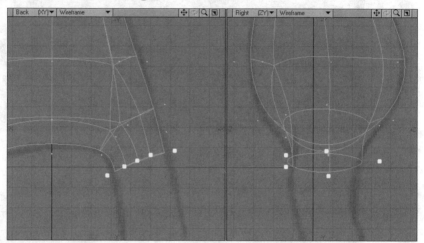

Figure 3.2-10. Extend and Stretch.

2. With the same points still selected, **Extend** and **Move** three more times, creating a row of points at the knee, ankle, and in the foot. Then **Drag** the points to fit the front and side background images.

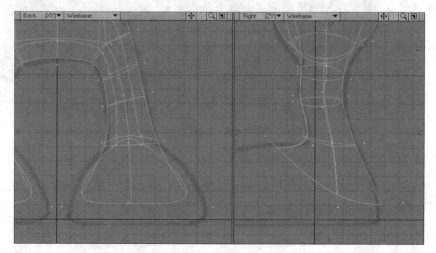

Figure 3.2-11. Extend, Move, and Drag.

3. Select the bottom three points of each foot and **Extend** and **Move** down to just below the base line of the foot.

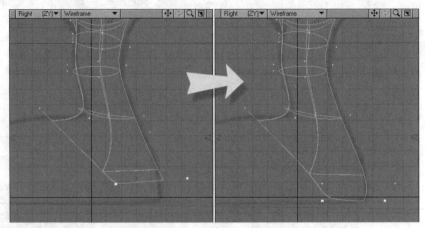

Figure 3.2-12. Extend and Move. As you do each step, adjust the points to fit the background images.

4. **Create▷Polygons▷Make Polygon**, switch to **Polygons** mode (**Spacebar**), and press **Tab** to convert the new polygons to subpatches.

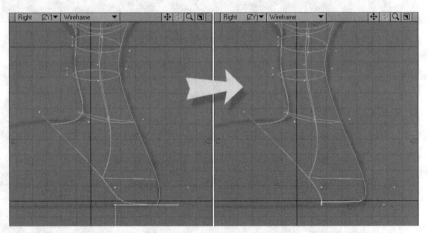

Figure 3.2-13. Make Polygon. As you do each step, adjust the points to fit the background images.

5. Select the open points at the front of the foot and **Extend** and **Move** twice, adjusting the points to shape the foot as you go.

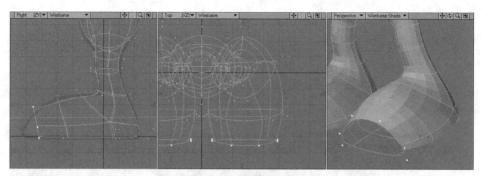

Figure 3.2-14. Extend, Move, and adjust. As you adjust the points, keep an eye on the Top and Perspective views of the foot to make sure you get a nice shape.

6. Select the open points and **Extend** once more, moving the points in for the toe.

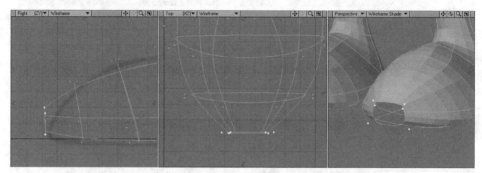

Figure 3.2-15. Extend, Move, and adjust.

7. Turn off Symmetry and **Weld** the top two points on each toe to the two points below them, welding each set of two points at a time.

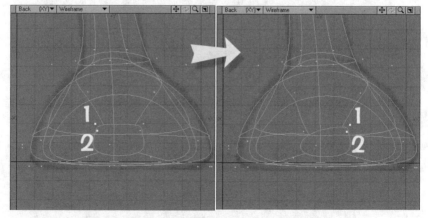

Figure 3.2-16. When welding it's easiest to select the points from the Back (XY) viewport to make sure you only select the points on one side of the model.

8. Turn Symmetry on, select the open points at the toe, and **Make Polygon**.

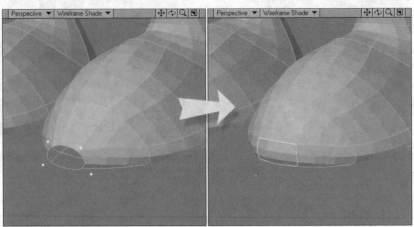

Figure 3.2-17. Make Polygon, capping off the toe.

Now let's just review where we're up to. Adjust the views so you can see the entire model (**a**) and rotate the Perspective view to get a good look at the proportions from all angles. The character is already taking shape, and he's looking pretty good so far.

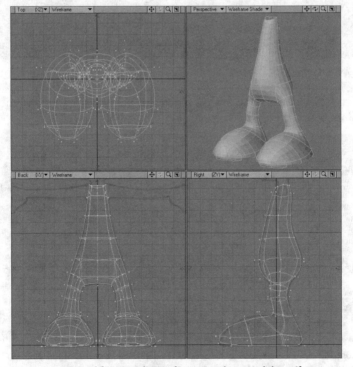

Figure 3.2-18. Feel free to adjust a few points here and there if you think they need it, and if you haven't done it already, save the object.

Note: It's a good idea to save quite often while working. The shortcut for save is "s," so it's easy to save regularly without interrupting your work flow. Once I've created a major section (or at the end of every day) I also increment the number of the working file. LightWave 8 makes this easy with FileSave Incremental, which adds a number to the filename if there isn't one, and increments the number if there is one already. When I'm working on a model I like to add "_Working_
v001," "_Working_v002," etc., at the end of the filename to keep the working versions separate from the final production models, which becomes quite important later on.

Arms

Now it's time to give Morfi some arms. Because they're skinny we can get away with a four-polygon circumference for the arms. We'll begin by creating the shoulder and the socket from which we can extend the arms.

1. Select the two side polygons of the top segment. (Check that you still have Symmetry on.) If we were to shift these polygons out for the arms we'd end up with a six-polygon circumference, so we'll do a tricky move that gives him shoulders and sets up the four-point socket.
2. **Cut (Ctrl+x)** and **Paste (Ctrl+v)** the polygons and select them again. **Drag** the lowest point up to make the peak of the shoulder.

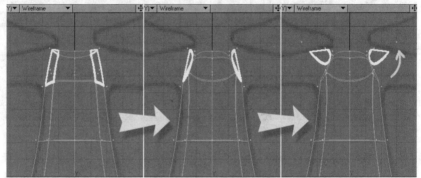

Figure 3.2-19. The Drag tool only affects selected points or polygons, so even though the point we're moving is in the same position as the points of the adjoining polygons, because we have the cut polygons selected we can separate them easily.

3. **Deselect** (/) the polygons and **Merge** (**m**).

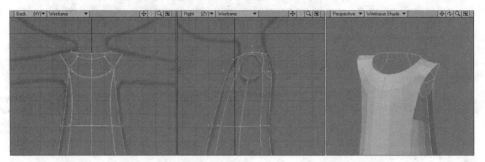

Figure 3.2-20. Now we have the shoulder and a four-point socket ready for the arms.

4. Select the four open points making up the arm socket and **Extend** and **Move** out a little. From the Back view **Stretch** the points horizontally to 0%, then select the middle points and **Stretch** them vertically together. Select the top and bottom points and from the Top view **Stretch** them together.

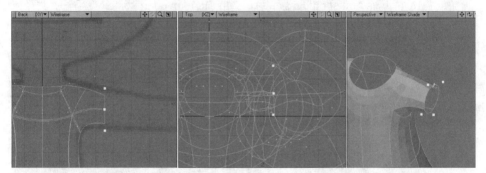

Figure 3.2-21. Stretching the points creates a neat shape as a base for the rest of the arm.

5. You may have noticed it was a bit difficult to see what we were doing from the Top view in the previous step, so to fix that, select the polygons from the chest to the feet and **Hide** (**-**) them.

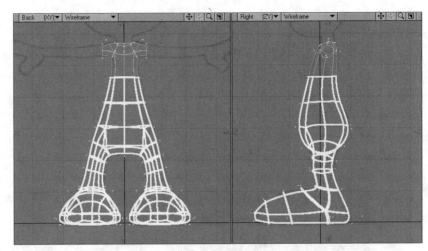

Figure 3.2-22. Hiding these polygons lets us see the arm more easily from the Top view without being obscured by the legs and feet.

6. Select the four open points again and **Extend** and **Move** four more times, adjusting the points to fit the background image.

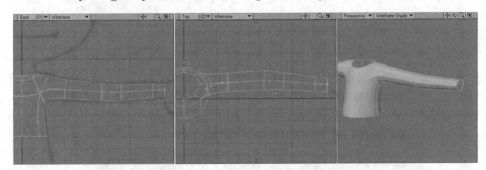

Figure 3.2-23. Use this image as a guide for positioning the points from the Top view. You can see the arm is slightly bent, which is useful for when we rig the character. Also note the narrow bands of polygons at the elbow and wrist; these will give us nice deformation at those joints.

Before we move on to the hands we need to quickly revisit the torso. I want to create some extra definition under the armpits to help keep the chest from collapsing when we rotate the arms down.

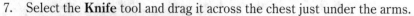

7. Select the **Knife** tool and drag it across the chest just under the arms.

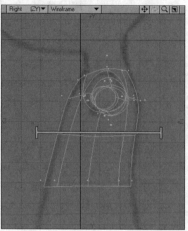

Figure 3.2-24. Creating an extra band of polygons will help create nice deformation.

Hands

Hands are often one of the most complex parts of a cartoon character. There are two main challenges we face here — keeping the polygon count low while maintaining a nice shape and arranging the polygons so the more complex polygons of the hand can join onto the simple wrist.

Since the hands require more definition than the four-polygon circumference of the wrist allows, we'll create them backward, starting with the fingers.

1. Create a box (**Shift+x**) roughly in line with the wrist from the Top view, lining it up with the backdrop in the Back view, and give it three segments in X.

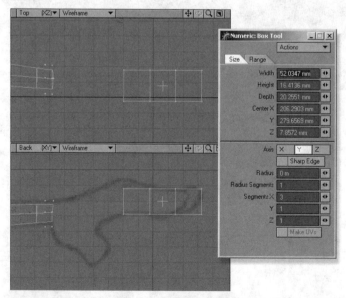

Figure 3.2-25. Use the Numeric panel to give the box three segments in X.

2. Select the end polygon on the left side of the box, closest to the wrist, and delete it. Select the remaining polygons of the box and press **Tab** to subpatch. **Deselect** (/) all the polygons.

3. Select just the top-left polygon and from the Top view use **Knife** to cut along the finger.

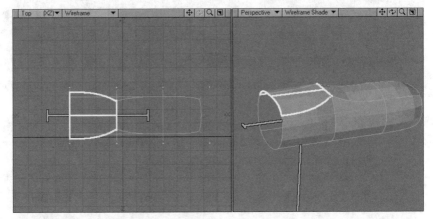

Figure 3.2-26. This cut will become the main knuckle. The knuckles are often overlooked when people make cartoon hands, but they're very important to define and shape the hand.

4. Select the right-hand point of the new cut and the point next to it and **Weld**. Then select the left-hand point of the new cut and the point on the opposite side of the finger from the last one and **Multiply➤Subdivide➤ Split (Ctrl+L)**.

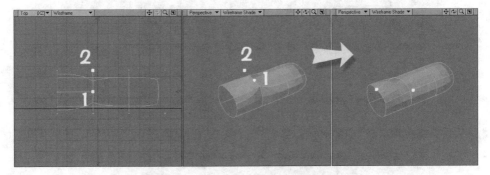

Figure 3.2-27. Use this image as a guide for which points to Weld and Split.

5. Adjust the points to fit the profile of the backdrop.

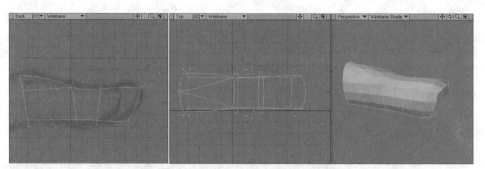

Figure 3.2-28. Adjust the points from the Top view also, using this image or your eye to gauge what looks good.

6. Select all the polygons of the finger and **Copy** and **Paste**. In the Top view, **Rotate** (**y**) the new finger **–17 °**, **Scale** (**Shift+h**) it by **90%**, and move it down next to the first finger.

7. Select the new finger. Since the fingers aren't joined, to select just one you can select one or a few polygons and press], which selects all the attached polygons to those already selected.

8. Select **Multiply**➤**Duplicate**➤**Mirror** (**Shift+v**), click in the middle of the first finger, and change the mirror axis (in the Numeric panel) to **Z**.

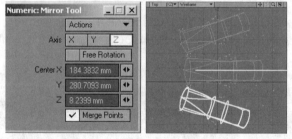

Figure 3.2-29. Mirror the new finger.

9. **Scale** the new finger by **85%** and move it next to the first finger. Then select the second and third fingers and move them down a touch.

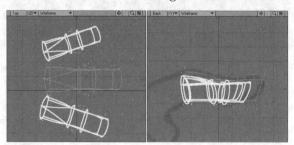

Figure 3.2-30. Use this image as a guide for positioning the fingers.

10. **Weld** the base of the fingers together by welding the points of the two outer fingers to the points at the base of the middle finger, joining the three fingers.

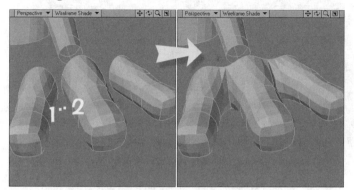

Figure 3.2-31. Weld the three fingers together.

11. Select all the points at the base of the fingers and **Extend** and **Move** back toward the wrist. Notice Extend created two extra polygons inside the hand, which we don't want, so select those and delete them. Then from the Back view, **Rotate** the extended points **15°** and **Move** down to match the backdrop.

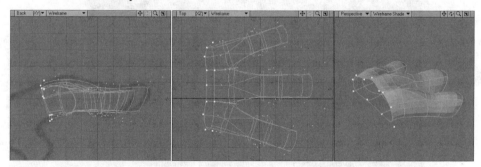

Figure 3.2-32. Feel free to adjust the point positions as you extend the hand, but it's best to do adjustments after all the hand polygons are created and you have a better overall view of the shapes and proportions.

12. With the points still selected, **Extend** and **Move** back and down again and **Weld** the top center three points.

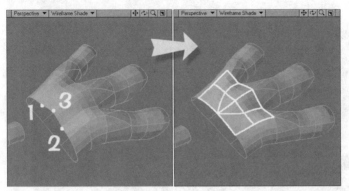

Figure 3.2-33. Remember when welding that all the points are welded to the last selected point. Follow the selection order illustrated to weld to the correct points.

13. Select all the open points of the hand and **Extend** and **Move** back and down again. **Weld** the top center three points, then **Weld** the back two points.

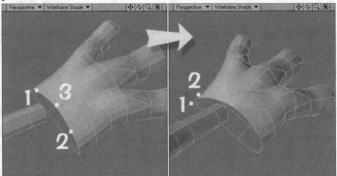

Figure 3.2-34. Working toward making the base of the hand join onto the wrist.

14. Weld the bottom two points, and finally the front two points.

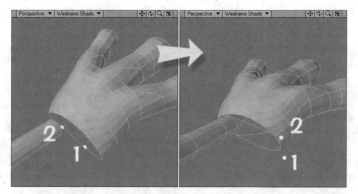

Figure 3.2-35. This has given us four points at the base of the hand that we can weld onto the wrist.

15. **Weld** the four points of the hand onto the corresponding four points on the wrist.

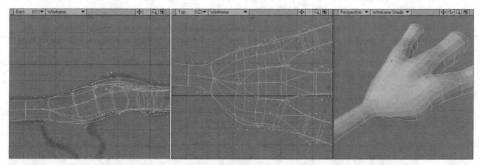

Figure 3.2-36. Once you weld the hand to the wrist you may want to tweak the points of the hand to start shaping it.

16. Now we're going to create the base of the thumb. Select the polygon shown in Figure 3.2-37. **Cut** and **Paste** the polygon, then select it again. Move the right two points away from the hand. **Deselect** the polygon and **Merge**.

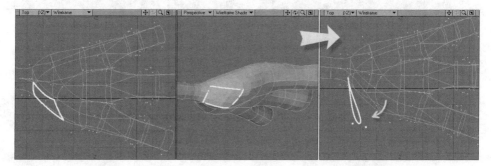

Figure 3.2-37. Here you can see the results of some shaping that I did in the previous step.

17. Select the three points in the top gap created by moving the polygon in the previous step and **Make Polygon**. Switch to **Polygons** mode and press **Tab** to subpatch the new polygon. Repeat for the three points in the lower gap. We now have four points ready to extend the thumb.

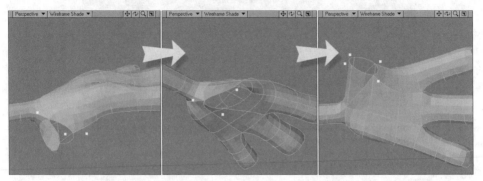

Figure 3.2-38. Make Polygon only respects subpatches if there are no open points in the selection. If there are open points, you need to subpatch the created polygons manually.

18. Select the four open points and **Extend** twice, creating the two segments of the thumb. **Move** them down and away from the hand. Then select the end points of the thumb and **Make Polygon**.

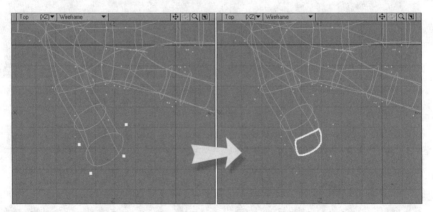

Figure 3.2-39. As you Extend, adjust the points to create a nice thumb shape.

19. Select the two three-point polygons on the top of the thumb and **Detail➤Polygons➤Merge Polys (Shift+z)**. Select the two three-point polygons on the bottom of the thumb and **Merge Polys**.

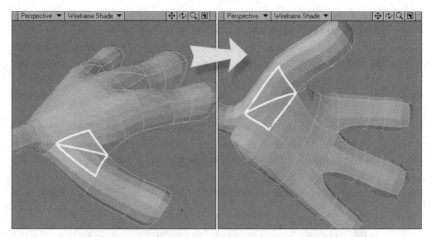

Figure 3.2-40. We'll end up with some three-point polygons in the hands, but these are obvious choices for merging into four-point polygons.

20. Select the two polygons shown in Figure 3.2-41. Switch to **Point** mode and select the two points crossing the four-point polygon. **Split (Ctrl+L)** the polygon and deselect the three-point polygon closest to the front. **Merge (Shift+z)** the remaining two selected polygons.

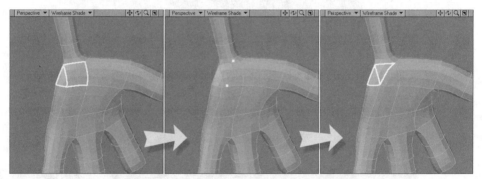

Figure 3.2-41. Switch the three- and four-point polygons to achieve better polygon flow.

> **Note:** When working with subpatches it's best to use four-point polygons where you can because they patch more nicely than three-point polygons. Don't worry too much about having three-point polygons in your model though, as they're often needed to create detail.
>
> Sometimes if you have a three-point polygon next to a four-point polygon you may want to switch them around to achieve better flow in the polygon structure. As you experiment with different options you will get a feel for what works and what doesn't so you can anticipate what structure a particular area needs.

Take a look at the hand from different angles in the Perspective view. It's looking pretty good, but there's one thing missing — the bump of the thumb muscle on the palm. We could get away with the hand as it is, but it's often those little touches that make all the difference to a character.

21. Select the two polygons of the palm at the base of the thumb. Select **Multiply▷Extend▷Super Shift**. Click and drag the cursor horizontally to adjust Inset Amount and vertically to adjust Shift Amount.

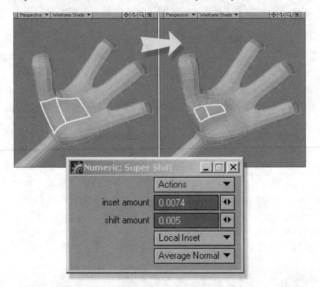

Figure 3.2-42. Super Shift allows you to bevel multiple polygons as one.

22. Select two of the points on a corner closest to the fingers, as shown in Figure 3.2-43, and **Weld**. Select the points of the other corner and **Weld**.

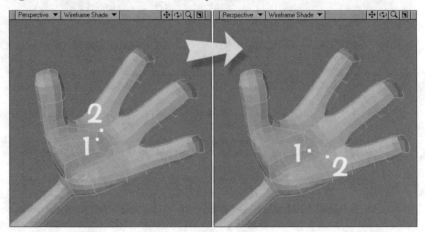

Figure 3.2-43. Welding these points creates a smooth transition into the upper part of the hand.

23. When you weld two edges together like this you end up with a two-point polygon between the two points. In the Polygon Statistics panel, click the + to the left of **2 Vertices** to select the two-point polygon and delete (**Del**).

24. Select the single remaining raised polygon and **Move** it a little toward the fingers. Tweak the remaining points to achieve a nice shape.

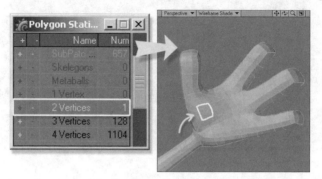

Figure 3.2-44. Moving the geometry in the Perspective view allows you to move along the axis of the view rather than golobal XYZ coordinates.

25. Select all the polygons of the hand. **Mirror** (**Shift+v**) the selected polygons on the **X** axis, centered at **0 m**. **Deselect** the polygons and **Merge** (**m**) points.

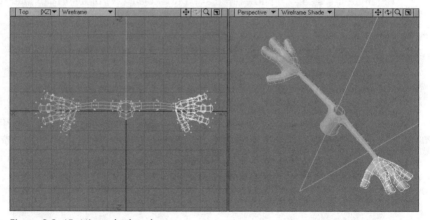

Figure 3.2-45. Mirror the hand.

26. **Unhide** (\) the legs and feet so you can see all the work you've done.

Morfi's body is now finished. As we did earlier, adjust the views so you can see the entire model (**a**) and rotate the Perspective view to get a good look at the proportions from all angles. Feel free to tweak any areas you think could be improved, but remember to turn Symmetry on first.

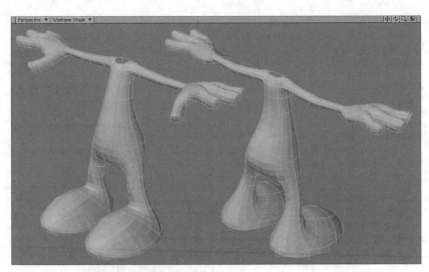

Figure 3.2-46. The finished body.

If you've modeled Morfi's body in a single session, now's probably a good time for a break. Remember to take regular breaks and do some stretching exercises while you're working so your muscles don't seize up from being in the same position for too long. Taking a little stroll around the house or office can be very beneficial, not only for your health but also to let your mind work on problems away from the computer. It's amazing how often a solution to a tricky problem can materialize out of thin air when you're on a break.

3.3 Modeling the Head

In keeping with the simple nature of the character, the features of the head are quite a bit simpler than in most cartoon characters. More detailed heads are covered later on, but Morfi's head is great for introducing the techniques involved.

1. To create the neck, select the open points at the top of the torso. **Extend** and **Move** the points up a bit and **Stretch** them, from the Back and Right views, to fit the backdrop. **Extend** the points again, moving them up and a little forward.

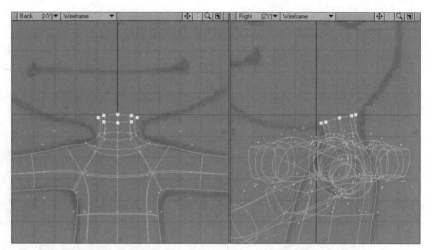

Figure 3.3-1. Creating the neck.

2. The initial stage of creating the head is just a series of Extends, making sure there are enough segments to support the features. **Extend** and **Move** six times, placing the second row at the mouth, the fourth row where the ears start, and the sixth row at the top of the smaller eye in the front backdrop. As you extend, **Stretch** each row to conform to the front and side backdrops. Use Figure 3.3-2 as a guide to position each row of points.

3. We can extend a few more times to create the antenna. **Extend**, **Move**, and **Stretch** five times up to the base of the spherical tip, creating a fairly short first segment at the base. Notice I've made each rising segment a little shorter. This is used later when we're deforming the character.

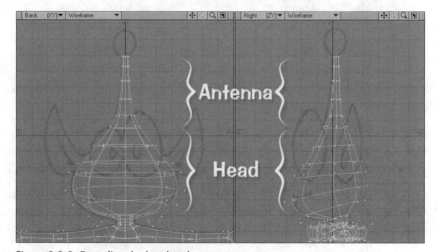

Figure 3.3-2. Extending the head and antenna.

4. To create the bulb at the top of the antenna, **Extend** once and move the points to the top of the bulb. Create two cuts in the new segment using the **Knife**. Select the middle segment of the bulb and **Stretch** it horizontally in the Back and Right views until the bulb is roughly spherical.

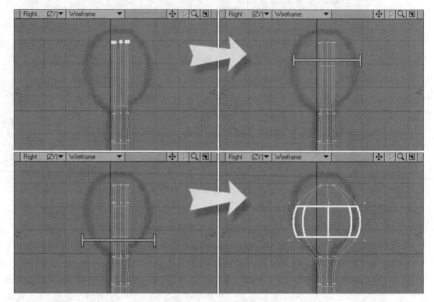

Figure 3.3-3. Notice on the side backdrop that the bulb doesn't quite match up with the front backdrop. When modeling against backdrops, usually once you get down to the smaller detail, the background sketches tend to be a little off, so at this stage use them as a rough guide for shape rather than absolute positioning.

5. Select the top row of points and **Extend**, move up a little, and **Weld**. Move the resulting top point to the middle and down to the same level as the next row of points.

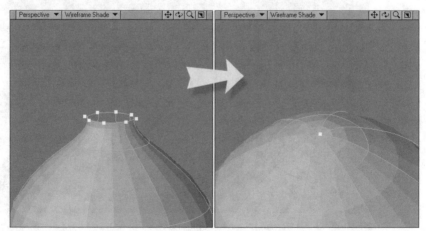

Figure 3.3-4. Capping the bulb.

6. Turn off Symmetry, select the front left three-point polygons, and **Merge Polys (Shift+z)**. Select the next two three-point polygons and **Merge Polys**. Repeat twice more until the top segment of the bulb is made up of all four-point polygons.

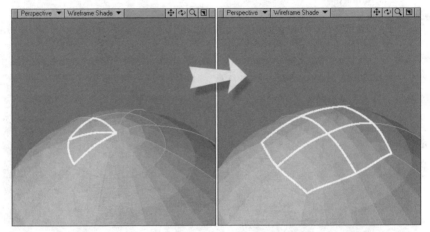

Figure 3.3-5. The benefit of having an even-numbered circumference of eight polygons or more is being able to convert the poles to a neat group of four-point polygons.

Mouth

Morfi's mouth is about the most basic you can make while retaining the ability to show the full range of expressions and phonemes. The great thing about creating a simple mouth like this one is that it makes it very easy to create morphs and to push the morphs to cartoony extremes.

1. Turn Symmetry on and select the front four polygons around the mouth. **Super Shift** with the settings shown in Figure 3.3-6. Then select the two points on each side of the mouth and **Move** them back and out to give the mouth area some extra width.

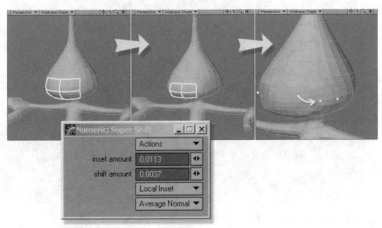

Figure 3.3-6. Use these settings for Super Shift.

> **Note:** When you use Smooth Shift or Super Shift in Symmetry mode, some-
> times the left and right sides of the shifted geometry aren't quite symmetrical. If
> this happens, delete one side of the affected area and mirror the other side.
> Select the middle points and Set Value (v) to X=0, then Merge Points to restore
> symmetry.

2. Select the four polygons shifted in the previous step and **Super Shift**
    again with the settings shown in Figure 3.3-7. Select the top three points
    of the shifted polygons and **Move** them down close to the middle points.
    Then **Move** the bottom three points up close to the middle.

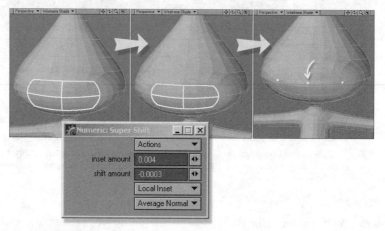

Figure 3.3-7. If you select the three points from the Right view it looks like you're only selecting two points.

3. **Move** the center point of the mouth area back to create a crease for the
    mouth. Select the two side points to the side of that point and **Move** them
    toward the center. Take this opportunity to adjust all the points around the
    mouth, fitting the geometry to the backdrops and making it look good
    from various angles in the Perspective view.

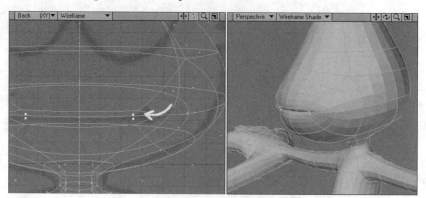

Figure 3.3-8. The mouth is starting to take shape.

4. Select the four polygons making up the crease of the mouth and **Super Shift**. (For the next few steps, select the **Super Shift** tool and immediately deselect it. This creates new geometry without shifting position or scale.) Move the selected polygons back a little, creating the lips.

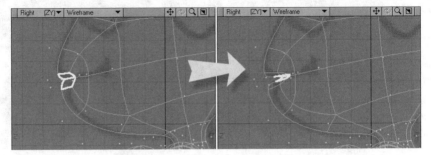

Figure 3.3-9. Creating the lips.

5. **Super Shift** and move back again. From the Right view, **Drag** the top points up and the bottom points down, and in the Back view, **Stretch** horizontally. Check against Figure 3.3-8 and tweak if necessary.

Note: Using Extender Plus on selected polygons does the same as Super Shifting in place.

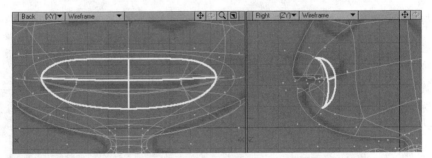

Figure 3.3-10. Creating the inside of the lips.

6. **Super Shift** three more times, and **Move**, **Rotate**, and **Stretch** each time so what you end up with matches Figure 3.3-11.

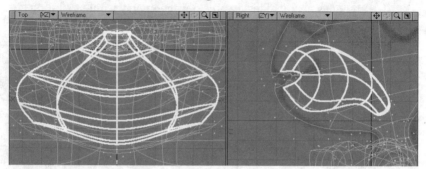

Figure 3.3-11. Creating the inside of the mouth.

Teeth and Tongue

I often see characters where the gums and tongue have been modeled separately from the mouth and just placed into position. The trouble with doing it that way is that the mouth doesn't stand up to close scrutiny, and you never know when a director is going to want a nice big close-up of an open mouth. By creating the gums and tongue emerging from the inner mouth, you can get as close as you like and it still looks great.

1. Select the top two and bottom two polygons just behind the lips. **Super Shift** and **Stretch** vertically to **90%**.

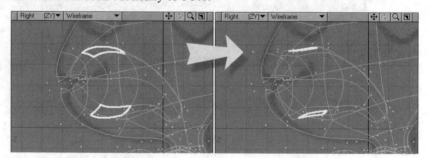

Figure 3.3-12. Creating the gums.

2. **Super Shift** again and **Stretch** vertically to **0%**. Move the teeth together by slightly overlapping the points where the teeth touch.

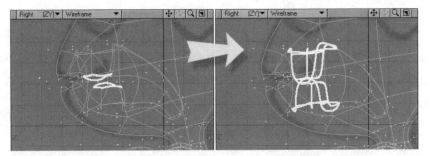

Figure 3.3-13. Feel free to tweak the teeth to the shape you want.

> **Note:** You may want to hide the outside of the head when working on details like the teeth and tongue so you can see the inside of the mouth more easily. The quickest way to do this is to select the inside of the mouth and Hide Unselected (=).

3. Select the two bottom polygons behind the teeth and **Super Shift**. Move the shifted polygons up, and from the Top view, **Drag** the points to make a nice tongue shape. From the Right view, **Rotate** the selection about **35°**.

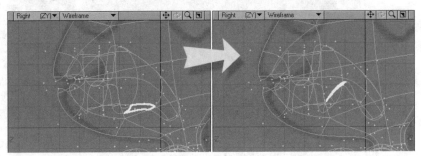

Figure 3.3-14. Creating the base of the tongue.

4. **Super Shift** again, **Rotate** about **50°** and move the selection to the back of the bottom teeth. From the Back view, **Drag** the points to shape the tip of the tongue.

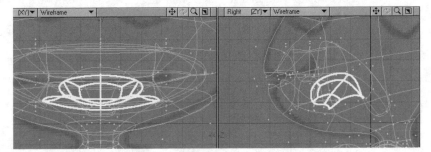

Figure 3.3-15. Use this image as a guide for how to shape the tongue.

Ears

We do some tricky moves when modeling the ears, so keep an eye on the illustrations to make sure you're on the right track. Since we do a fair amount of welding, it's probably best to only work on one side and mirror the ear when it's finished as we did with the hand.

1. Turn Symmetry off. You can also hide the right side of the head (left side when looking at the Back view) so the wireframe views don't become confusing.

2. Select the two polygons at the base of the ear. **Super Shift** and **Stretch** the shifted polygons so they're about half their original size but lying along the same plane as the original polygons.

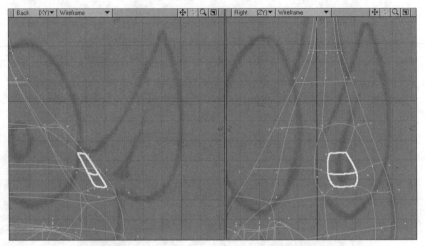

Figure 3.3-16. Shifted polygons.

3. **Super Shift** again and **Move** and **Stretch** the shifted polygons to the middle of the ear. Tweak the points a bit to start shaping the ear, and delete the end two polygons.

4. Select the middle point at the front of the ear and **Detail➤Points➤ Unweld** (**Ctrl+u**). Select the top-front polygon and **Drag** the unwelded corner up a bit, then move the remaining unwelded point down a bit.

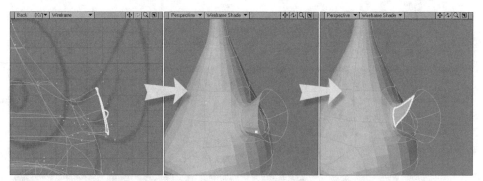

Figure 3.3-17. Unwelding the front point allows us to start creating geometry for the inside of the ear.

5. Select the three points at the front of the ear and **Extend**, moving the new points back and a little left.

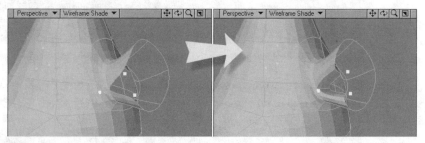

Figure 3.3-18. Creating the inner ear.

6. **Extend** again and **Stretch** the points to about half their original size. Select the two end points and **Weld**.

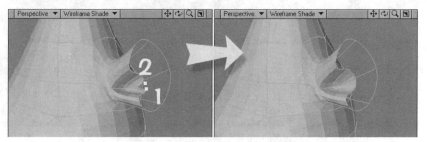

Figure 3.3-19. Finishing the shape for the inner ear.

7. **Extend** the open points. Move the extended points to the outer edge of the ear and from the Top view, **Rotate -35°. Stretch** and **Move** the points to match the backdrops.

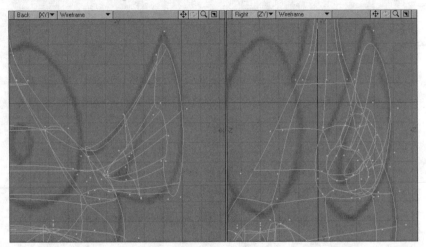

Figure 3.3-20. Feel free to tweak the points during the process to achieve a nice shape.

8. Select the top two points shown in Figure 3.3-21A and **Weld**.
9. **Weld** the two points below the top point shown in Figure 3.3-21B.

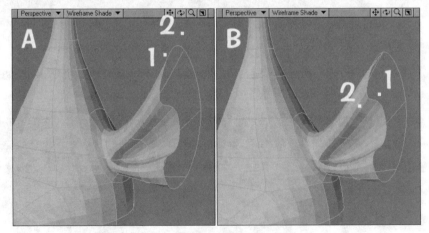

Figure 3.3-21. Welding the points simplifies the edge of the ear.

10. **Weld** the bottom two points shown in Figure 3.3-22A.

11. Finally, **Weld** the two points above the bottom point shown in Figure 3.3-22B.

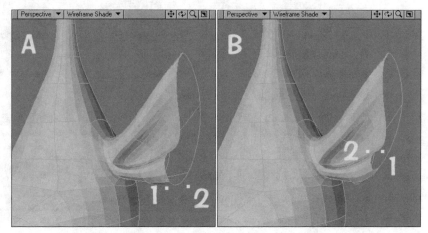

Figure 3.3-22. This results in eight points at the edge of the ear, just right for two quads.

12. Select the top four open points and **Make Polygon**. Change to **Polygons** mode and press **Tab** to subpatch the new polygon.

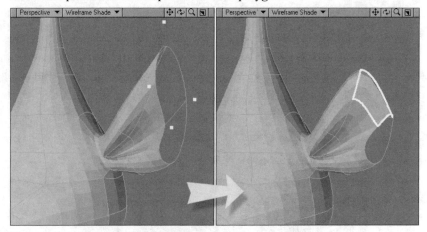

Figure 3.3-23. Capping the end of the ear.

13. Then select the remaining four open points and **Make Polygon**.

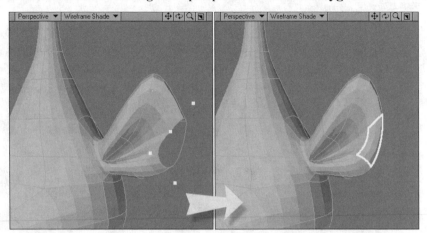

Figure 3.3-24. The last polygon is automatically subpatched as it's surrounded on all sides by subpatches.

14. Now that all the geometry is in place, you can see that the tip of the ear is quite rounded, but we need it to come to a point. You could add extra geometry to fix this, but instead we'll adjust the SubPatch Weight. Select the **Weight** button at the bottom-right of the interface. Click the pull-down menu to the right of the button and choose **SubPatch Weight**. Select the top point of the ear, where we want it pointy, and **Map**➤ **General**➤**Set Map Value** to **50%**. Notice the tip of the ear becomes more pointed immediately. Tweak all the points of the ear to match the backdrops and create a nice shape from all angles in the Perspective view.

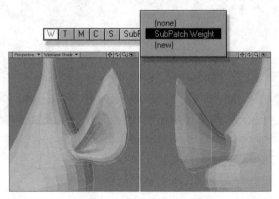

Figure 3.3-25. Adjust the SubPatch Weight, then tweak points to match the backdrops.

> **Note:** SubPatch Weight values tell the subpatches how closely to follow the points of the cage. The SubPatch Weight defaults to 0%. Higher values cause the subpatches to follow the points exactly, and lower or negative values cause the subpatches to follow loosely, or become more rounded. You can use this to tweak the look of your model without adding extra geometry.

15. The last step is to mirror the ear to the other side. **Delete** the two polygons on the right side of the head, opposite the ear. Select the ear and the head polygons at its base and **Mirror. Deselect** (/) polygons and **Merge Points**.

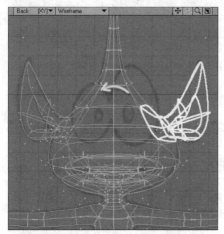

Figure 3.3-26. Once the ear is mirrored, check from all angles and tweak points to shape if necessary.

Eyes

While the eyes in the backdrops are ovals, this is a representation of the final character once the eyes are rigged and posed. We create the eyes as spheres and distort them with bones to achieve the oval shapes.

One of the unique characteristics of Morfi is that his eyes have separate eyelid geometry as opposed to the eyelids being part of the main head geometry. This also requires a slightly different rigging technique, which is explained in Chapter 4, "Rigging Morfi."

1. Select a new layer and place the body layer in the background. In the Back view, create a ball (**Shift+o**) the width of the smaller eye in the backdrop. In the Numeric panel, copy the **X** Radius to **Y** and **Z**, and set Axis to **Z**.

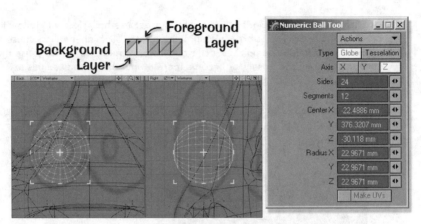

Figure 3.3-27. You can use these settings to create the eyeball.

2. Now we can create the eyelids. Select another new layer, and place the eyeball in the background layer. Create a ball using the same settings as the eyeball, only change Sides to **8** and Segments to **4**. Press **Tab** to subpatch the ball.

3. As we did with the bulb of the antenna, we need to merge the three-point polygons at the poles. From the Back view, select the top-left two polygons of the poles and **Merge Polys (Shift+z)**. Repeat around the pole until you're left with all four-point polygons.

4. **Scale** the ball to **136%**, then from the Right view, **Stretch** horizontally **97%** to make it spherical.

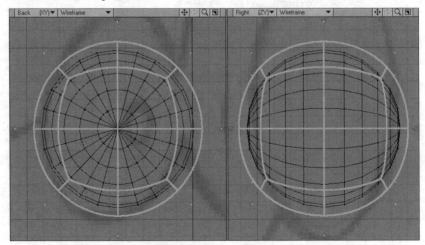

Figure 3.3-28. The eyelids should maintain an even distance from the eyeball all around.

> **Note:** When you subpatch a low-polygon ball, it tends to become ovular because of the uneven distribution of points. If you need a sphere, you need to stretch the subpatched ball to regain even scale.

5. Select the middle three points at the front of the ball and **Unweld**. Select the polygons above the unwelded points and **Merge Points** (**m**). **Drag** the points we just unwelded up a fraction. Select the polygons below the unwelded points, **Merge Points**, and **Drag** the three points down a fraction.

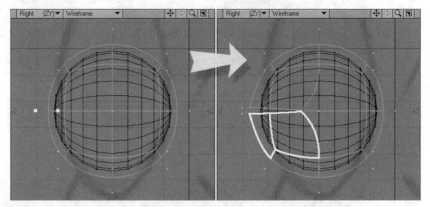

Figure 3.3-29. Creating the slit of the eyelids from the Right view.

6. **Deselect All** polygons and **Copy**, then **Smooth Shift** inward to just below the surface of the eyeball in the background layer. **Flip** (**f**) the polygons.

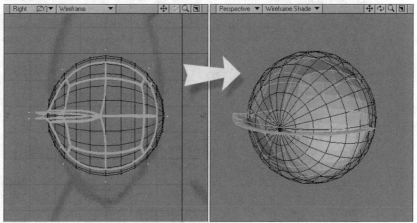

Figure 3.3-30. Creating the inside surface of the eyelids.

7. **Paste** the copied polygons and **Merge Points**. Select the polygons of the split and overlap them slightly so the subpatches meet.

71

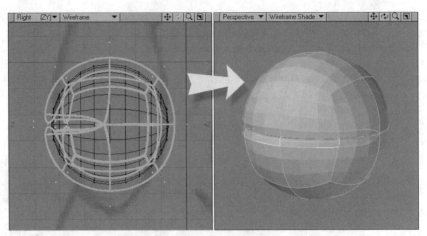

Figure 3.3-31. Giving the eyelids thickness.

8. **Cut** the eyelid and **Paste** it in the eyeball layer.
9. **Mirror** on X=0, creating the eye on the other side.
10. **Cut** both eyes and **Paste** into the body layer.

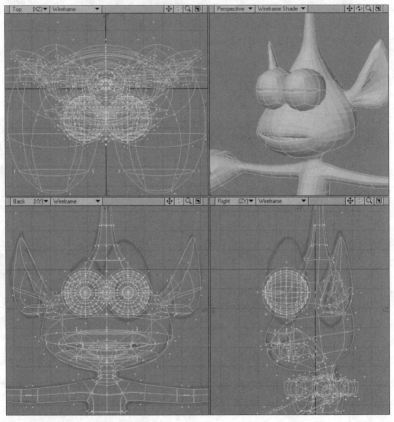

Figure 3.3-32. The finished head.

Now that the modeling is finished, take another break; then we'll move on to surfacing.

3.4 Creating Surfaces

In this tutorial I've saved all the surfacing until after the modeling is finished, but it's often a good idea to set up surface names and basic surface settings as you model.

To keep things simple, Morfi doesn't use any image maps for his surfaces. Image-mapped textures are covered in detail in Chapter 6, "Texturing." Surfacing Morfi includes applying surfaces, setting basic surface attributes, and using weight maps and gradients.

1. In the Perspective view, select a polygon on the body and one on each eyelid, then **Select Connected** (]) to select all the polygons of the body and eyelids. **Change Surface** (**q**). In the Change Surface panel, change Name to **Body**, and copy the other settings from Figure 3.4-1.

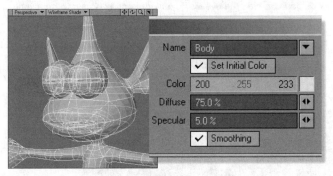

Figure 3.4-1. Use these settings for the Body surface.

2. Select the polygons of the eyeballs and **Change Surface** to **Eye_White**. Deselect all but the front two segments of the eyeballs and **Change Surface** to **Eye_Iris**. Deselect all but the front poles of the eyeballs and **Change Surface** to **Eye_Pupil**. Copy the other settings for the eye surfaces from Figure 3.4-2.

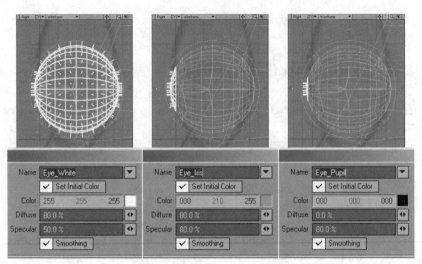

Figure 3.4-2. You can hide the eyelids if you want easier access to the eyeballs.

3. Select the four polygons at the back of the mouth and **Expand Selection**
   (**Shift +]**) five times, then **Contract Selection** (**Shift + [**) once. This
   selects all the polygons of the inner mouth. **Change Surface** to **Mouth**
   and copy the other settings from Figure 3.4-3.

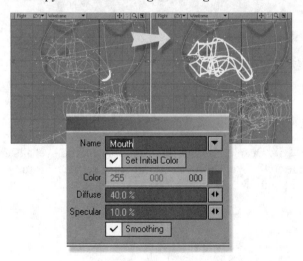

Figure 3.4-3. Use these settings for the Mouth surface.

Now that we've applied all the surfaces, it's time to finish setting up the basic surface attributes. In the previous steps we applied specularity to the surfaces, but
specularity by itself isn't enough. Specularity works hand in hand with glossiness,
specularity telling the surface how bright the highlight is and glossiness telling
the surface how large the highlight is.

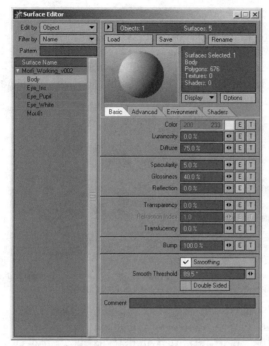

Figure 3.4-4. The Surface Editor.

4. Open the Surface Editor (**Ctrl+F3**) and you can see on the left side the object name and the surfaces applied to that object. On the right side are all the surface settings. The two settings we need to adjust now are Luminosity and Glossiness. Use the following values for each of the surfaces.

Surface	Luminosity	Glossiness
Body	--	20%
Eye_Iris	10%	60%
Eye_Pupil	--	60%
Eye_White	10%	60%
Mouth	--	40%

The luminosity for the Eye_White surface brightens the eyes a little, which tends to work well for cartoon characters.

Weights and Gradients

Gradients are a powerful texturing feature with a wide variety of uses. One valuable feature of gradients is the ability to use a weight map as the input parameter.

We'll start with the easiest one, the Dark gradient, but don't underestimate its usefulness just because it's easy to create. This weight map is used on the Diffuse channel of the surfaces to artificially darken the surface for certain areas, especially sunken areas such as the inside of nostrils or the back of the mouth.

Creating Weight Maps

1. First we need to create a weight map for the gradient. Change the Perspective view to **Weight Shade**. Select the **Weight** button at the bottom-right of the interface. Click the pull-down menu to the right of the button and choose **(new)**. In the Create Weight Map panel, change Name to **Tex_Dark** and Initial Value to **0%**.

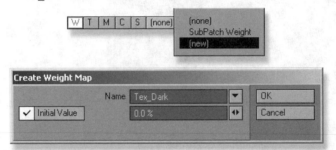

Figure 3.4-5. When creating weights for gradients, giving all the points an initial value of 0% is useful to ensure smooth transitions on subpatched polygons.

2. Now that the weight map is created we can adjust the values. Zoom close up on the base of the ear. Make sure Symmetry is on, and select the two innermost points of the inner ear. **Map➢General➢Set Map Value** to **50%**. Select the next three points of the inner ear and **Set Map Value** to **25%**.

3. Select the four polygons at the back of the mouth and **Set Map Value** to **100%**.

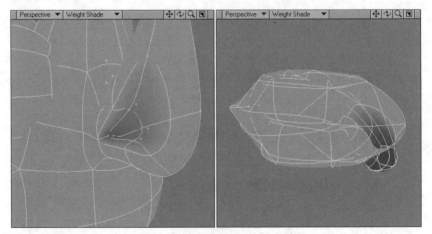

Figure 3.4-6. You can set weight values from points or polygons.

That's all we need to do with the Tex_Dark weight. Now we need to create a couple more texture weight maps for the mouth. We've given the mouth, teeth, and tongue a single surface. We can use the same technique of gradients based on weight maps to differentiate the teeth and tongue from the mouth and to create a transition from the mouth to the lips.

1. Create a new weight map called **Tex_Teeth**. Select the teeth polygons, excluding the segments joining the teeth to the mouth, and **Set Map Value** to **100%**.

2. Create a new weight map called **Tex_Tongue**. Select the tongue, excluding the segment joining the tongue to the mouth, and **Set Map Value** to **100%**.

3. Create a new weight map called **Tex_Lips**. Select the polygons at the edge of the lips and **Set Map Value** to **100%**.

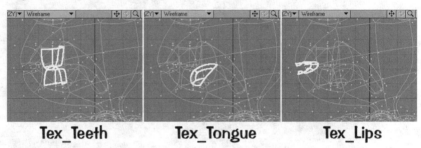

Tex_Teeth   **Tex_Tongue**   **Tex_Lips**

Figure 3.4-7. Use this image as a guide for which polygons to select to create the three mouth weight maps.

Creating Gradients

Now that all the weight maps are created, we need to apply them to gradients for our surfaces. We'll set up the gradients in the same order that we created the weights.

1. Open the Surface Editor and select the **Body** surface. Click the **T** button next to **Diffuse** to open the Texture Editor. The first texture layer is already created for us, so we just need to adjust the settings.

2. Change Layer Type to **Gradient**. Notice the settings change to reflect the Layer Type change. Change the Input Parameter to **Weight Map** and set Weight Map to **Tex_Dark**.

3. Now we need to create keys in the gradient to tell it what values to use for the different weight values. Click in the middle of the gradient bar and click again at the bottom to create two new keys. With the bottom key still selected, set its values to Value **0%**, Alpha **100%**, and Parameter **100%**. Select the middle key and set all its values to **0%**. Select the top key and set its values to Value **0%**, Alpha **0%**, and Parameter **–100%**.

4. Because we're going to use the same gradient in another surface, select **Copy** and choose **Selected Layer(s)**. Finally, click **Use Texture** to close the Texture Editor.

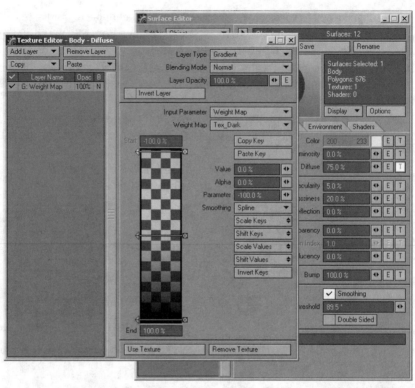

Figure 3.4-8. What we've done here is create a gradient that tells the Diffuse channel to transition from its basic value to a value of 0% as the weight map transitions from 0% to 100%.

5. Back in the Surface Editor, select the **Mouth** surface. Open the Texture Editor for **Diffuse**, and select **Paste≻Replace Selected Layer(s)**, pasting a copy of the gradient we just made. We need a few more gradients here though, so select **Paste≻Add to layers** three times. With the top layer still selected, change Weight Map to **Tex_Lips**. Change Value for all three keys to **75%**. Select the second layer, change Weight Map to **Tex_Teeth**, and change Value for all three keys to **95%**. Select the third layer, change Weight Map to **Tex_Tongue** and change Value for all three keys to **75%**. For Tex_Tongue we want the transition to be a little sharper and closer to the mouth, so for the bottom key, change Parameter to **50%**.

6. Still on the Mouth surface, open the Texture Editor for **Color**. Gradients in the Color channel work a little differently than the other surface channels; instead of Value there are RGB settings. Select **Paste≻Replace Selected Layer(s)**, then **Paste≻Add to layers**, creating two gradient layers. With the top layer still selected, change Weight Map to **Tex_Lips**. Change Color for all three keys to **200, 255, 233**. Select the second layer, change Weight Map to **Tex_Teeth**, and change Color for all three keys to white (**255, 255, 255**).

7. Open the Texture Editor for **Specularity** and **Paste▷Replace Selected Layer(s)**. Change Weight Map to **Tex_Lips** and change Value for all three keys to **5%**.

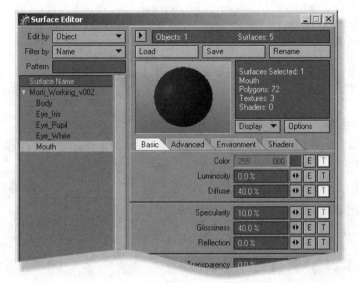

Figure 3.4-9. The finished Mouth surface with textures on three channels.

With the gradients applied, our surfaces are complete.

3.5 Creating Morphs

We're going to create some basic morphs to enable Morfi to show some emotion. We'll also create some fake morphs that are used to control the eyelid bones when we've rigged Morfi. Most production-ready characters need a few more morphs than we'll create right now. Morphs are described in greater detail in *Volume 2: Rigging & Animation*.

> **Note:** A fake morph is used to create a Morph Mixer slider that doesn't deform the geometry. The most important use of fake morphs is keeping controls consistent between characters even if they've been rigged differently. Fake morphs have many uses though, and can be used instead of LightWave's other Slider tool. Since the majority of characters have morphs, it's far easier to use morph sliders for all the slider-driven animation, keeping all your sliders in one place, rather than having two separate types of sliders for every character, each with different control methods. Apart from the controls being easier to use, another benefit of morph sliders is that they can be moved off screen instead of being limited to the viewports, so they don't obscure your view of the scene.

Before we create the morphs we need to adjust Morfi's mouth so that it's closed. While it's often easier during modeling and texturing to have the mouth open a little, using a closed mouth for the base morph is much more efficient and results in less work when animating the morphs.

1. Select the middle two polygons of the upper lip and move them down so their points line up vertically with those of the lower lip. Then select the middle two polygons of the lower lip and move them up so that it's just overlapping the top lip.

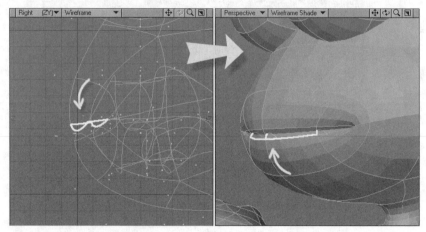

Figure 3.5-1. Closing the mouth to get ready for creating morphs.

Creating Mouth Expressions

Now we can start creating and editing the morphs, starting with a smile.

1. Select the **Morph** (**M**) button at the bottom-right of the interface. Click the pull-down menu to the right of the button and choose **(new)**. In the Create Endomorph panel, change Name to **Mouth.Smile** and click **OK**.

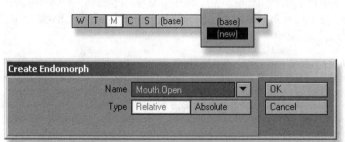

Figure 3.5-2. Morphs can be organized into groups. Morph Mixer allows regrouping but you can set initial groups in Modeler by naming the morphs Group.Name. This also makes it easier to identify morphs in the Modeler pull-down when the list starts getting long.

2. Making sure Symmetry is on, select the five points from the corners of the lips to the cheek, including the inner corner point, and move them out, up, and back a little. Then select the six points at the middle of the lips and move them out, up, and back a little.

3. Select the polygons of the mouth, as we did earlier during surfacing, and drag the two side points out, up, and back. This is so that when Morfi's mouth is open and he's smiling, the inside of the mouth matches the outside. It's important to think of these things when creating morphs. Often there are areas you can't see in the morph itself that will become visible when other morphs are mixed with it.

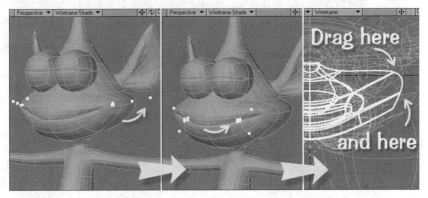

Figure 3.5-3. Creating a smile.

4. Continue tweaking points until the morph looks like Figure 3.5-4, or until you're happy with it.

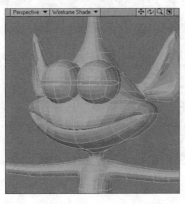

Figure 3.5-4. Finished smile morph. I've moved the cheeks and chin up a bit and enhanced the corners of the mouth by moving them up and back.

Using the same techniques we used to make the smile, create two more morphs called **Mouth.Pout** and **Mouth.Pucker**. Use the finished examples in Figure 3.5-5 as a guide.

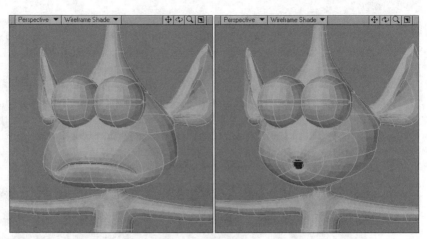

Figure 3.5-5. Left: Mouth.Pout. Right: Mouth.Pucker.

Opening the Jaw

The Mouth.Open morph is next, and it's a little trickier than the others.

1. Hide the hands so we can see what we're doing from the Right view a little better. Select the polygons of the mouth as we've done before, then deselect the top half and back row. Then in the Perspective view, select the lower part of the jaw, including the bottom lip. **Move** the polygons down and rotate **14°**. From the Back view, **Stretch** horizontally **75%**.

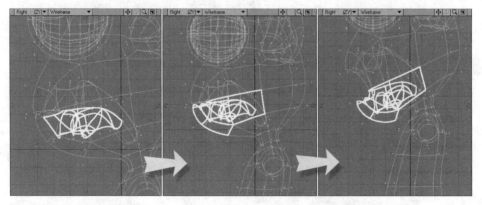

Figure 3.5-6. Opening the jaw.

2. Carefully deselect the top band of polygons, making sure not to deselect any polygons of the teeth or tongue. **Move** down again and **Rotate 40°**. Then **Stretch** vertically **120%** from the base of the tongue.

3. Tweak the points using Figure 3.5-7 as a guide. When you're finished, **Unhide** (\) the hidden geometry.

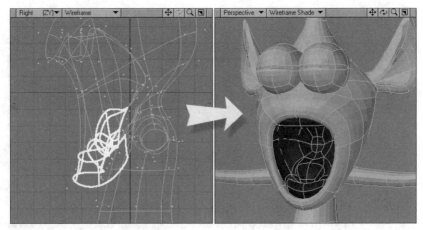

Figure 3.5-7. Finished open mouth.

Creating Eyelid Morphs

To create the fake morphs for the eyelids, we create a new point inside the model and move the point to set the morphs.

1. Select **Create➤Points➤Points** (+). In the Right view, right-click in the middle of the head to create a point.
2. Create a new morph called **Eye.Blink** and move the point up a little.

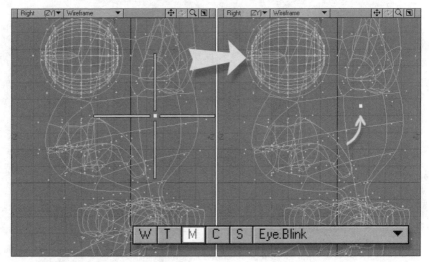

Figure 3.5-8. Creating a fake morph.

3. **Map➤General➤Edit Maps➤Copy Vertex Map** and call the new map **Eye.Blink_L**.

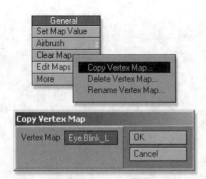

Figure 3.5-9. Copying a morph.

4. **Copy Vertex Map** three more times, calling the new maps **Eye.Blink_R**, **Eye.Lid_Up**, and **Eye.Lid_Low**.

We're done with the morphs. Congratulations, you've just finished creating Morfi. Feel free to create a few more mouth morphs if you wish, as the ones we've done here are just the very basics. You could make him sneer, grimace, stick his tongue out, or whatever your imagination can come up with.

Figure 3.5-10. Final Morfi model ready for rigging.

Now that we've modeled and surfaced the character and created the morphs, we're ready to move on to the next stage — rigging. In the next chapter we rig Morfi so he can be posed and animated, so take a break, have a stretch, and continue when you're ready.

Chapter 4

Rigging Morfi

There are two methods of creating bones in LightWave — creating skelegons in Modeler and creating bones in Layout. Of course this means there are really three ways to create bones for a character, as you can also use a combination of the two methods.

Since each method has its advantages and disadvantages you can decide which method you feel most comfortable using when rigging your own characters. Skelegons are used here to create the bones for Morfi. The bones are created in Layout for Hamish and Jack in *Volume 2: Rigging & Animation*.

4.1 Creating Skelegons

Even if you've worked with skelegons before I recommend following this section closely, as the techniques I teach for creating the skelegons of a character differ a little from most.

The trick to creating skelegons properly is to create them in a viewport perpendicular to the pitch rotation you want for the bone. The pitch of a bone is very important in character rigging. You can apply automatic compensation for joints, but it only works on the pitch rotation of the bones. Since we use joint compensation for quite a few joints, we need to make sure that the pitch is the major axis of rotation for all our bones. Creating the skelegons with this in mind minimizes the work you need to do in Layout to adjust the alignment of the converted bones.

Spine

1. Load your Morfi model into Modeler (you can find a preprepared object in \Objects\Chapters\Morfi_Working_v001.lwo).
2. Choose a new layer and place the Morfi layer in the background. **Fit All** (**a**), then **Zoom In** (**.**) twice so the head and torso are in view.
3. Select **Setup**➢**Skelegons**➢**Create Skelegons**. In the Back view, click and drag, starting from the hips and dragging up a little way, to create the first skelegon.

> **Note:** Always click and drag the first skelegon in a chain. A skelegon is created when the mouse button is released, so if you click without dragging you'll create a one-point skelegon at the beginning of the chain.

4. Click or click and drag above the first skelegon to create another one, and repeat until you have seven skelegons. Press **Enter** or select **Create Skelegons** again to finish. Select the first skelegon that you created and delete it (in case the first skelegon in a chain has its bank handle flipped 90°, which can sometimes happen), leaving six skelegons.

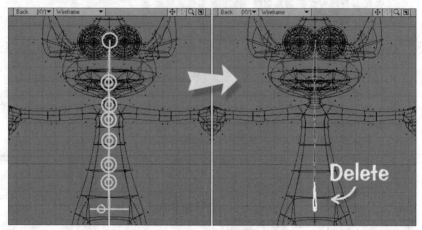

Figure 4.1-1. Creating the skelegon chain for the spine.

5. Select **Detail≻Points≻Set Value** (v). Set Axis to **X** and Value to **0** and click **OK** to align all the skelegons along the Y axis.

6. From the Right view, move the chain of skelegons so the base is where the top of the pelvis would be. Deselect the first one and move the others so the base of the second is in place, then deselect the second one and move the others until the base of the third is in place, repeating up the chain until all the skelegons are positioned correctly (see Figure 4.1-2).

7. Still in the Right view, select the fifth skelegon in the spine (the one between the shoulders) and **Stretch** it horizontally to **0%**, to make sure it's perfectly vertical. Do the same with the top (head) skelegon.

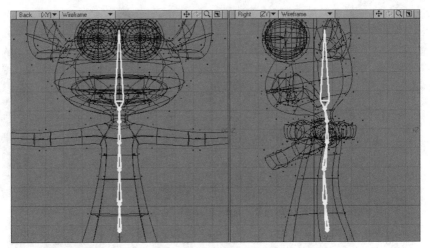

Figure 4.1-2. Instead of moving the skelegons, you could drag the points until all the skelegons are positioned correctly.

8. Select the bottom bone in the spine. Select **Setup**⮞**Skelegons**⮞**Rename Skelegon** and name the skelegon **Back01**. Rename the remaining skelegons in order: **Back02**, **Back03**, **Back04**, **Neck**, and **Head**.

Figure 4.1-3. Rename the skelegons.

Leg

1. Create a new skelegon chain in the Top view, starting from the top and pointing down (toward –Z). Create six skelegons, then delete the first to leave five skelegons.

2. **Set Value** (v), **Axis = X**, and **Value = 0** to align all the skelegons along the Z axis.

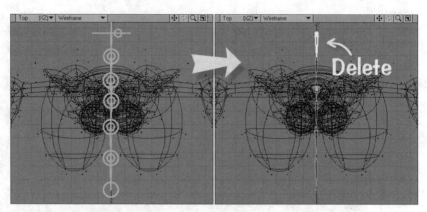

Figure 4.1-4. Creating the skelegon chain for the leg.

3. From the Right view, move the chain of skelegons up and forward so the base is at the top of the leg. Deselect the first skelegon and **Cut** and **Paste**. Reselect the pasted chain and move the skelegons into place (see Figure 4.1-5).

4. **Weld** the top of the upper leg to the base of the hip, then drag or move the end point of the hip bone back toward the base, making it fit within the leg.

5. From the Back view, select all the leg skelegons and move them right to match Figure 4.1-5.

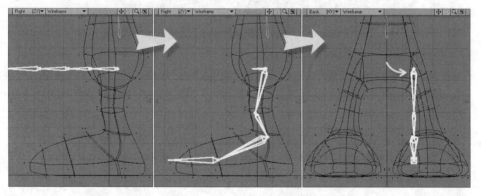

Figure 4.1-5. Notice in the Back view the bones are vertical instead of conforming to the leg. We do further rotation in Layout because if the skelegons are aligned to each other, their rotations will be aligned when they are converted into bones. This minimizes the work in Layout to adjust the bone rotations.

6. Select the top bone in the leg and **Rename Skelegon** to **Hip_LT**. Rename the remaining skelegons down the leg chain **Leg_Upper_LT**, **Leg_Lower_LT**, **Foot_LT**, and **Toe_LT**.

Pelvis

1. From the Top view, create a new skelegon pointing toward –Z. **Set Value** (v), **Axis = X**, and **Value = 0**.

2. From the Right view, move it up so the base point is close to the base point of the first spine bone (Back01).

3. With the skelegon still selected, **Copy** and **Paste**, then **Rotate 90°** from the base so it's vertical.

4. **Weld** the base points of the two new skelegons to the base point of Back01.

5. Select the horizontal skelegon or its points and **Stretch** vertically to 0%, then select the vertical skelegon and **Stretch** horizontally to 0%.

6. Select the horizontal skelegon and **Rename Skelegon** to Pelvis_Base. Rename the vertical skelegon **Pelvis**.

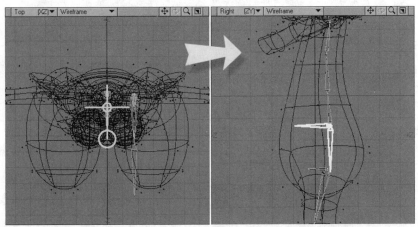

Figure 4.1-6. Creating the pelvis skelegons.

Arm

1. Create a new skelegon chain in the Back view, starting from left of the spine and pointing toward the hand (toward +X). Create four skelegons, then delete the first one, leaving three.

2. From the Top view, drag or move the skelegons into position (see Figure 4.1-7).

3. Rename the skelegons in order — **Shoulder_LT**, **Arm_Upper01_LT**, and **Arm_Lower_LT**.

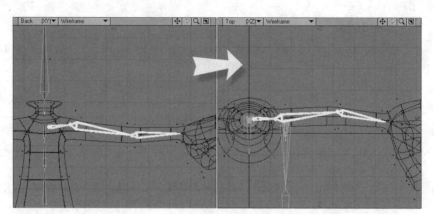

Figure 4.1-7. I've hidden some of the geometry so you can see the arms a little better. Notice the elbows and knees are a little bent. Doing this helps the IK (inverse kinematics) solution for the bones in Layout.

Hand and Fingers

Many characters have three finger bones, but we can keep the setup simple by adding just two bones for each finger.

1. Create a new skelegon chain in the Top view, starting from the middle and pointing toward the hand (toward +X). Create four skelegons, then delete the first one, leaving three.

2. Move the skelegons into position from the Top and Back views, making the first the hand, then the next two the middle finger (see Figure 4.1-8).

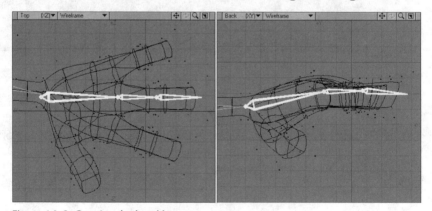

Figure 4.1-8. Creating the hand base.

3. **Copy** and **Paste** the three skelegons and drag or move the selected skelegons into the thumb position.

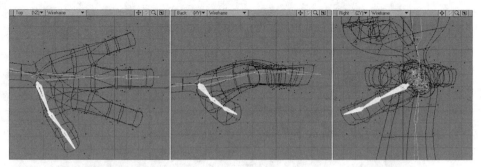

Figure 4.1-9. The thumb bones in position.

Since the thumb is on an angle, we need to adjust the skelegons so the pitch of the bones runs along the top of the thumb instead of being vertical.

4. Select the thumb skelegons and **Fit Selected (Shift+a)**. Rotate the Perspective view so you're looking down the thumb.

5. Select **Setup≻Skelegons≻Edit Skelegons**. Notice the bank handles of the bones appear, just like when you first create skelegons. The little dotted circles coming off the base of each skelegon are the handles. You can drag these to adjust the orientation of the bones when they're converted.

6. Drag the handles of all three thumb bones so they're pointing toward the top of the thumb. Press **Enter** or select **Edit Skelegons** again to confirm your editing.

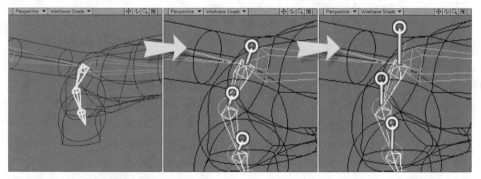

Figure 4.1-10. Adjusting the bank handles.

7. Select the hand skelegon and **Cut** and **Paste**. **Weld** the tip of the lower arm to the base of the hand, then move the hand from the Top view so it's in line with the middle of the wrist.

8. Select the two finger skelegons and **Copy** and **Paste**. From the Top view, move the selected skelegons down to the lower finger. **Scale** the skelegons to fit the finger. With those skelegons still selected, **Copy** and **Paste** again and move the selected skelegons up to the topmost finger. **Rotate** and **Scale** the skelegons to fit the finger.

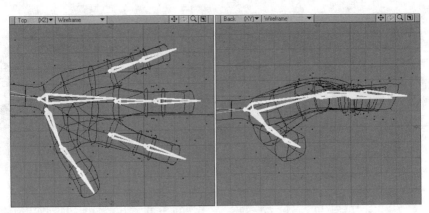

Figure 4.1-11. The fingers.

9. Rename the hand skelegon **Hand_LT**.
10. Rename the first bone of the lower finger **Finger101_LT** and the second bone of the lower finger **Finger102_LT**. Rename the middle finger **Finger201_LT** and **Finger202_LT**, the top finger **Finger301_LT** and **Finger302_LT**, and the thumb **Thumb01_LT**, **Thumb02_LT**, and **Thumb03_LT**.

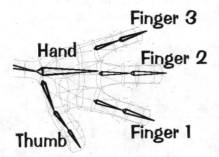

Figure 4.1-12. Naming the fingers.

Eye

With the bones for the body complete, we can create the skelegons for the eyes.

1. Create a skelegon in the Top view, from the center of the left eye (our right) down, making it long enough to just stick out from the eyeball.
2. From the Right view, move it up so it's centered vertically on the eyeball. From the Back view, **Stretch** it horizontally and vertically to **0%**. Zoom in and check that the base of the skelegon is exactly in the center of the eyeball. This will become our eye rotation bone.

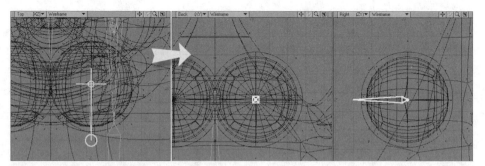

Figure 4.1-13. First eye bone.

3. With the same skelegon selected, **Copy** and **Paste**, and from the Right view drag the end point to make the copied skelegon about one-third of the size. This will become our eye base bone.

4. Select the first skelegon again and **Copy** and **Paste**. Still in the Right view, **Rotate** the selected skelegon **–90°**. If you need to, move the skelegon so its base is at the same point as the base of the other two bones. With the skelegon still selected, **Copy** and **Paste**, then **Drag** the base point of the selected bone down a little way. This will become our eye stretch bone.

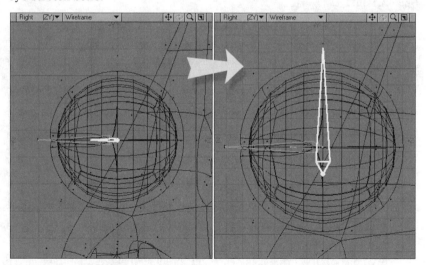

Figure 4.1-14. Main eye bones.

Note: The position of the eye stretch bone is very important, as the eyes stretch using the base position of this bone as a center. For most characters you only want the eyes to stretch up, so you'd position the bone at the base of the eyes. Positioning the bone in the center of the eye causes the eye to stretch up and down equally. In this case we want the eyes to stretch mostly up but a little down, so we've positioned the base between the middle and bottom of the eye.

5. Now we'll create the additional bones for the eyelids. Select the vertical skelegon pasted in the previous step and drag its tip down to the top of the eyelids. **Copy** and **Paste** and drag the tip of the selected skelegon down to the bottom of the eyelids.

6. Select the first eye bone, **Copy** and **Paste**, then drag the tip of the selected skelegon to the edge of the eyelids. **Copy** and **Paste** twice more, then drag the tip of the selected skelegon to the back of the eyelids.

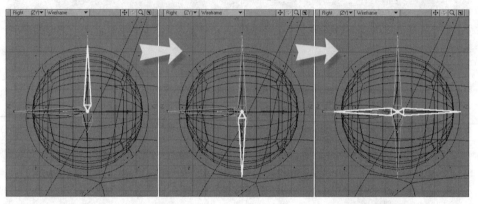

Figure 4.1-15. Eyelid bones.

7. Select **Setup**➤**Skelegons**➤**Skelegon Tree**. In the Skelegon Tree you can see all your skelegons listed with their hierarchies. You should have eight skelegons called Bone01 at the bottom of the list. Double-click on each skelegon to rename it, from the first Bone01 down, so the list reads:

    Eye_Base_LT, Eyelid_Base_LT, Eye_Stretch_LT, Eyelid_Low02_LT, Eyelid_Up02_LT, Eye_LT, Eyelid_Up01_LT, Eyelid_Low01_LT

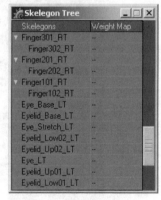

Figure 4.1-16. Skelegon Tree.

Ear and Antenna

Often a character's head only needs the head and eye bones, but Morfi has big ears and antennae that we want to be able to pose, so we need to create some extra bones for them.

1. Create a chain of four skelegons in the Back view, from just inside the head to the tip of the ear, then delete the first skelegon.

2. Move the skelegons into position.

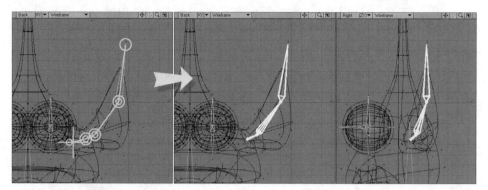

Figure 4.1-17. Ear bones.

3. Create a chain of seven bones in the Back view, from the top of the eyes to the tip of the antenna, creating a skelegon for each segment of the antenna. Delete the first skelegon.

4. **Set Value** to **Axis = X** and **Value = 0**, then from the Right view, move the chain back to the center of the antenna.

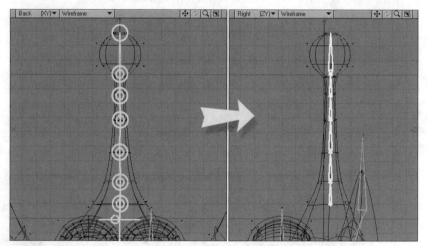

Figure 4.1-18. Antenna bones.

5. Rename the bones, from the bottom up, **Antenna01** to **Antenna06**.

Our skelegons are now complete. "But we've only done one side. What about the other side?" I hear you ask. We could mirror the skelegons and rename them all now, but it's far more efficient to mirror the bones later on in Layout, after we've converted the skelegons and adjusted some settings for the bones.

> **Note:** If you're following this using an earlier version of LightWave, mirror the skelegons on the left side now and rename the copies, changing _LT to _RT.

4.2 Weight Mapping

There's one strict rule that I have for weight maps, and that is to only create as many as you really need. Making joints deform nicely isn't difficult, but it's easy to overcomplicate it by creating too many weights. Since LightWave's bones automatically work on an object without setting weights, they also work together when sharing weights. If two or more bones in your character can share weights, you should take advantage of that, thus minimizing the work you need to do in both creating the weights and tweaking their values.

Weight maps for bones are covered in more detail in *Volume 2: Rigging & Animation*, so let's move on to creating some weight maps for Morfi.

Arms

You only need a single weight map for the arms of most cartoon characters. Sometimes you can even get away with a single weight map encompassing the arms, hands, and fingers, but separating the arms from the hands gives us more control of the wrist deformation.

1. Change the Perspective view to **Weight Shade**.
2. With the Morfi layer in the foreground and Symmetry on, select the three middle bands of polygons of the arm.

> **Tip:** When you're creating weight maps it's often useful to place the skelegon layer in the background. That way you can see where the bone joints lie in relation to the geometry you're weighting.

3. Select the **Weight** button at the bottom-right of the interface. Click the pull-down menu to the right of the button and choose **(new)**. In the Create Weight Map panel, change Name to **Arms** and Initial Value to **100%**.

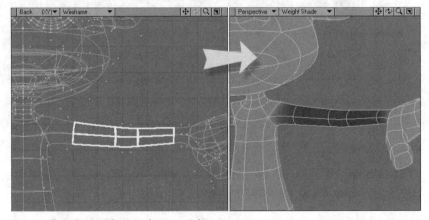

Figure 4.2-1. Setting the initial arm weight map.

> **Note:** In the following steps, unless otherwise specified, when you create a
> new weight map leave Initial Value at 100%.

4. Select the points at the wrist and **Map▸General▸Set Map Value** to
    50%, changing their value from 100% to 50%.
5. Select the top point of the shoulder and **Set Map Value** to **50%**. Select
    the front and back points of the shoulder and **Set Map Value** to **25%**.

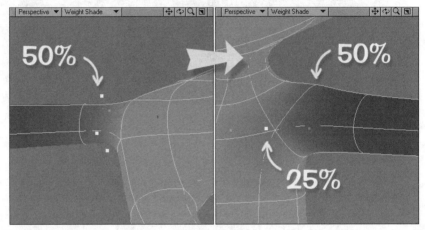

Figure 4.2-2. Adjusting the weight values for the wrist and shoulder.

Hands

A single weight map is used for the hands and fingers. The fingers are spread out
enough that the bones in each finger won't affect the other fingers.

1. Select the polygons of the hands and fingers. Create a new weight map
    called **Hands**.
2. Select the points at the wrist and **Set Map Value** to **50%**. This normal-
    izes the transition from the arm weight to the hand weight so the points
    have a combined total of 100%.

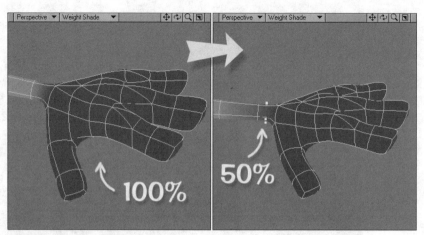

Figure 4.2-3. Hands weight map.

Head

Many characters only require a single weight map for the head, but as Morfi has bones for the ears and antennae we'll create separate weights for those.

1. Select the polygons of the head, from the top of the neck up. Create a new weight map called **Head**.

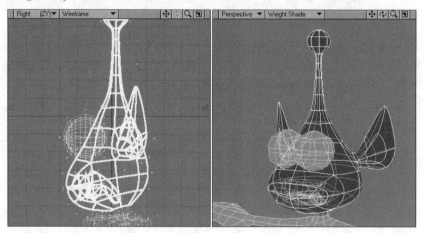

Figure 4.2-4. Initial head weight.

2. Select the points at the top of the neck and **Set Map Value** to **50%**.

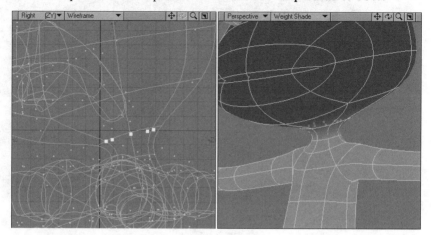

Figure 4.2-5. Initial head weight.

3. Select the end segment of the ears and **Map**≻**General**≻**Clear Map** (_).
    With the polygons still selected, create a new weight map called **Ears**.

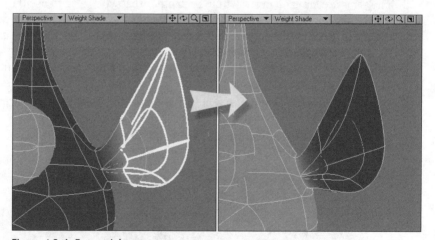

Figure 4.2-6. Ears weight map.

4. Select the **Head** weight map again, then select the antenna polygons and
    Clear Map. With those polygons still selected, create a new weight map
    called **Antenna**.

5. If you had the eyes selected when you created the Head weight map,
    select the **Head** weight map, select the eye polygons, and **Clear Map**.

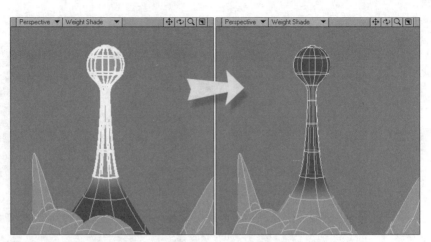

Figure 4.2-7. Antenna weight map.

Legs and Feet

The weight maps for the legs are slightly different from what we've done so far. The arms are far enough away from each other that we're able to use the same weight map for both sides of the model. Unfortunately, in most cases we can't do this for the legs, and especially in this case where Morfi's large feet are almost touching each other, so we need to create separate weight maps for the left and right sides of the legs and feet. We start by creating symmetrical weight maps and then separate them afterward.

1. With Symmetry still on, select the three segments of the legs. Create a new weight map called **Leg_LT** with an Initial Value of **50%**.

2. **View≻Selection≻Contract (Shift+[)**, so you just have the knee segment selected, and **Set Map Value** to **100%**.

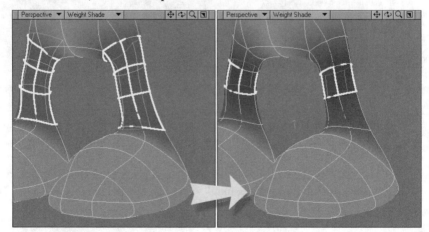

Figure 4.2-8. Leg weight map.

3. Select the points from the ankle to the middle of the foot and create a new weight map called **Foot_LT**, making the Initial Value **50%**. **Contract** the selection and **Set Map Value** to **100%**.

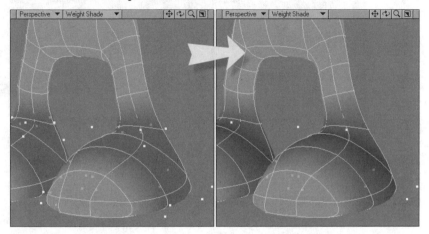

Figure 4.2-9. Foot weight map.

4. Select the points from the middle of the foot to the toe and create a new weight map called **Toe_LT** with an Initial Value of **50%**. **Contract** the selection and **Set Map Value** to **100%**.

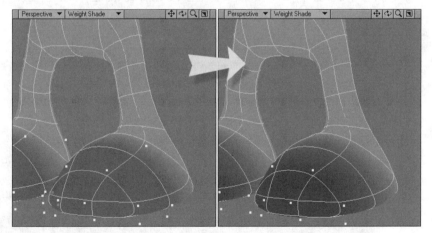

Figure 4.2-10. Toe weight map.

Now that we've created the symmetrical weight maps, we need to separate the left and right sides.

5. Turn Symmetry off and select the polygons of Morfi's right leg and foot (the left side when looking at the Back view).

6. Select the **Leg_LT** weight map, then select **Map▸General▸Edit Maps▸Copy Vertex Map**. Enter **Leg_RT** in the Copy Vertex Map panel and click **OK**.

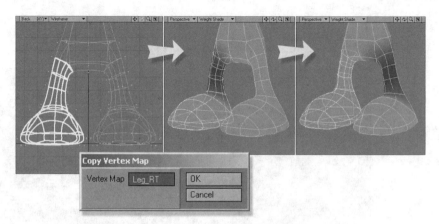

Figure 4.2-11. Separating the map into left and right sides.

7. Select the **Leg_LT** weight map again and **Clear Map**.
8. Repeat steps 6 and 7 for **Foot_LT** and **Toe_LT**, calling the new weight maps **Foot_RT** and **Toe_RT**.

Well, that wasn't too painful. Creating left and right side weight maps is fairly quick and easy when you use this method. It's really time consuming to check values of one weight, remember them, then apply the values to another weight. This method of creating weight maps means we can avoid doing that most of the time.

Body

The reason we've left the body until after the limbs and head is also so we don't have to check and remember weight map values. To do this we'll enlist the aid of a plug-in called Combine Weightmaps written by Kevin Phillips.

1. Select the polygons of the body, including the first segments of the arms, legs, and head. Create a new weight map called **Body**.

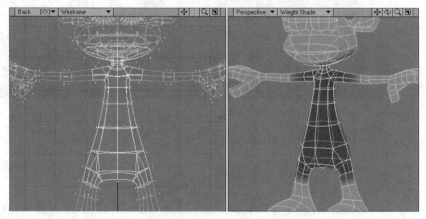

Figure 4.2-12. Initial body weight map.

2. With the polygons still selected, select **Plugs**▷**Additional**▷**Combine Weights**.

> **Note:** If you don't find the button, make sure you have followed the instructions on installing the plug-ins in section 1.3.

3. We want the destination weight map to be the one we just created, so change "to create" to **Body**. We're going to subtract the weight maps for the limbs and head from the body, so change "Take" to **Body**, change "and" to **Subtract**, and "this" to **Arms**. Turn off **Make non-mapped points equal 0%** and click **OK**.

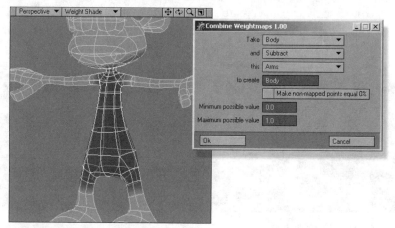

Figure 4.2-13. Subtracting the arm weight from the body weight using Combine Weightmaps.

4. Select **Combine Weights** again. Enter the same values as step 3, except change "this" to **Head**.

5. Select **Combine Weights** twice more, using the same values, except change "this" to **Leg_LT**, then **Leg_RT**.

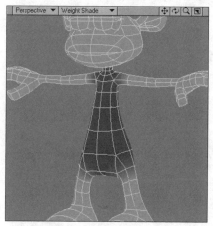

Figure 4.2-14.
Finished body
weight map.

103

Did you ever think weight mapping could be this easy? When you're not frustrated by fiddly things like normalizing a bunch of differently weighted points, weight mapping can be quite enjoyable.

Eyes

Weight mapping the eyes is often as easy as giving each eyeball a separate weight, but because Morfi has unusual eyelids it's a little more complicated.

1. Select all the polygons of the eyes and eyelids and **Hide Unselected** (=). This makes it a bit easier to see what we're doing.

2. Select the polygons of just the left eyeball (the right eye when looking at the Back view) and create a new weight map called **Eye_LT**.

3. Select the polygons of just the right eyeball and create a new weight map called **Eye_RT**.

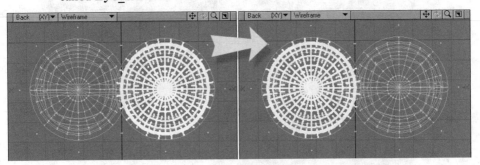

Figure 4.2-15. Eyeball selections.

4. Select both eyeballs and **Hide Selected** (-), leaving us with only the eyelids visible.

5. Select the front polygons of the upper eyelids and create a new weight map called **Eyelid_Up_LT**. Select the points at the corners of the eyelids and **Set Map Value** to **50%**. Then select the points in the upper-back quadrant of the eyelids and **Set Map Value** to **35%**.

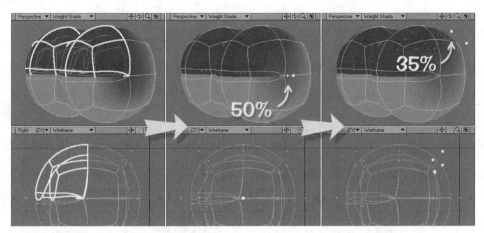

Figure 4.2-16. Creating the upper eyelid weight.

6. Select the front polygons of the lower eyelids and create a new weight map called **Eyelid_Low_LT**. Select the points at the corners of the eyelids and **Set Map Value** to **50%**. Then select the points in the lower-back quadrant of the eyelids and **Set Map Value** to **35%**.

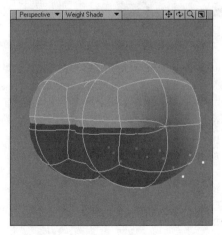

Figure 4.2-17.
Lower eyelid
weight.

7. Select the points at the back of the eyelids and create a new weight map called **Eyelid_Base_LT**. Deselect the middle points and **Set Map Value** to **65%**.

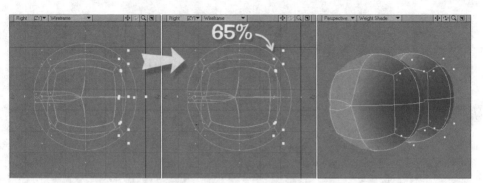

Figure 4.2-18. Creating the eyelid base weight.

8. Select the polygons of the right eyelid, select the **Eyelid_Up_LT** weight map, then **Copy Vertex Map** to **Eyelid_Up_RT**. Select the **Eyelid_Up_LT** weight map again and **Clear Map**.

9. Repeat step 8 for **Eyelid_Low_LT** and **Eyelid_Base_LT**, calling the new weight maps **Eyelid_Low_RT** and **Eyelid_Base_RT**.

10. **Unhide All** (\).

Assigning Weights to Skelegons

We're almost finished with weight maps. The last step is to assign weight maps to the skelegons.

1. Place the skelegon layer in the foreground and open the Skelegon Tree.

2. Double-click the **Weight Map** entry next to each skelegon and assign the following weight maps from the pull-down menu:

Skelegon	Weight Map
Back*	Body
Neck	Body
Head	Head
Hip_LT	Body
Leg*	Leg_LT
Pelvis*	Body
Shoulder*	Body
Arm*	Arms
Hand*	Hands
Thumb*	Hands
Finger*	Hands
Eye_Base_LT	Eye_LT
Eye_Stretch_LT	Eye_Base_LT
Eyelid_Low*	Eyelid_Low_LT
Eyelid_Up*	Eyelid_Up_LT
Ear*	Ears
Antenna*	Antenna

* indicates all the skelegons beginning with that name, so Back* means Back01 to Back04.

Notice there are some skelegons missing from the list. Those skelegons don't need weight maps assigned because they have the same name as the weight map. Those weight maps are automatically assigned to the bones in Layout, saving some mouse clicks.

Preparing for Layout

Now that we have our skelegons and weight maps completed, we need to prepare the model for the next stage where we finish the rigging in Layout.

1. Save the model under its working title.
2. Place the skelegon layer in the foreground, select all the skelegons, and **Cut**. Switch to the first layer with the model and **Paste**. This gives our model a single layer including the model and skelegons.
3. **Save As (Shift+s)**, calling it **Morfi01.lwo**. This is the model used for the final stage of rigging.

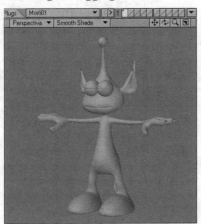

Figure 4.2-19.
The final model.

> **Note:** In most cases it's a good idea to keep your final models to a single layer. This makes referencing the model in Layout much easier as you don't have additional layer names confusing the issue.

Now that we've finished working in Modeler, it's a good time for a break before we move on to Layout. When you're ready, continue to the next section.

4.3 Layout

The rest of the rigging is done in Layout. Skelegons are converted to bones and animation controls are created so Morfi can be posed and animated. The first step is to load the character in a scene.

1. Launch Layout and check that the Content Directory (in General Options (**o**)) is set to **\LWProjects\LW8 CartoonCreation**.

2. Select **Items≻Load≻Scene** and choose **Morfi_Setup.lws**. This scene has some lights and items set up and ready for rigging Morfi.

3. Select **Items≻Load≻Object** and choose **Morfi01.lwo**. (You can find the preprepared object in \Objects\Final\Morfi01.lwo.)

4. **File≻Save≻Save Scene As (Shift+s)**, calling the new scene **Morfi_Rig01.lws**.

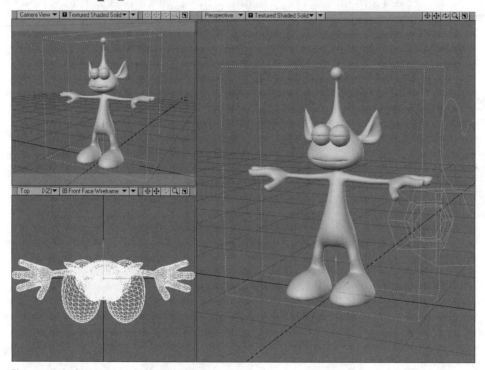

Figure 4.3-1. Scene set up and ready for rigging.

Object Properties

With the scene set up, the next thing to do is to adjust some of the properties for our Morfi object.

1. Select the **Morfi01** object and press **p** to open the Object Properties panel.

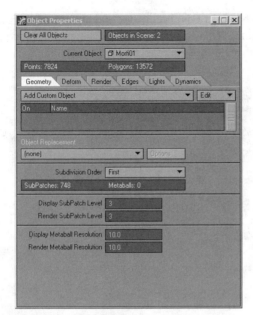

Figure 4.3-2. Object Properties panel.

2. In the Geometry tab, change Subdivision Order to **Last**. This tells the object to subdivide after the cage has been deformed by morphs, bones, and other displacements, keeping the subpatch object as smooth as possible.

3. Change Display SubPatch Level to **2** and Render SubPatch Level to **5**. This way the wireframe view isn't too dense to work with, but the rendered object is nice and smooth. The Display SubPatch Level can be set higher after we've done some work on the bones.

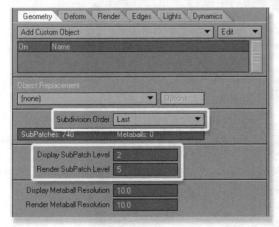

Figure 4.3-3. Object Properties geometry adjustments.

4. In the Deform tab, select **Add Displacement** and choose **Morph Mixer** from the pull-down menu. This activates the morphs in the object. Morph Mixer is covered in more detail later.

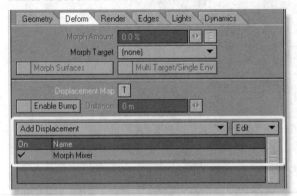

Figure 4.3-4. Object Properties deformation adjustments.

5. Press **p** again to close the Object Properties panel.

Converting Skelegons

With the object properties set we're ready to get back to rigging. We begin by converting the skelegons to bones. Remember to save often, especially when rigging; even though LightWave 8 is very stable, no software is beyond the occasional crash.

1. With the Morfi object still selected, **Setup➤Add➤Cvt Skelegons**. You should see the bones appear and a message telling you "43 bones were created."

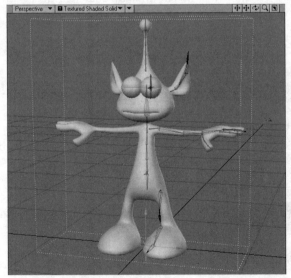

Figure 4.3-5.
43 bones created.

2. Open the Viewport Options for the Perspective view by clicking on the single arrow pull-down menu next to the Viewport Display Mode, and select **Bone X-Ray**. This enables us to see the bones within the shaded object.

Figure 4.3-6.
Turning Bone
X-Ray on.

> **Note:** You can change the default object and bone colors if you wish. Open the Scene Editor≻Classic Scene Editor and change Colors≻Default Object Color and Colors≻Default Bone Color to your preferred colors. To apply your changes, select Colors≻Apply Defaults to Scene.

Parenting the Bones

Now we need to adjust the parenting for the bones. We can do this quickly in the Classic Scene Editor.

> **Note:** If you're using an earlier version of LightWave you'll have more bones, including the left and right sides. In the following sections, repeat the steps for the bones on the right side.

1. Select **General Options** (o) and make sure **Parent in Place** is turned on. Then open the **Scene Editor≻Classic Scene Editor**. If you're working with a single monitor, position and size the Scene Editor to cover the Perspective viewport. If you have dual monitors you can move the Scene Editor to the secondary display.

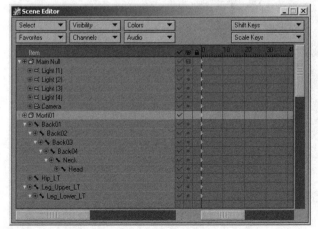

Figure 4.3-7.
Classic Scene
Editor.

> **Note:** It's a little confusing having two types of Scene Editor. In this chapter when I mention the Scene Editor, I'm referring to the Classic Scene Editor.

Notice in the Scene Editor that the bones that were connected as skelegons are already parented to each other but we have some single bones and hierarchies that need to be reorganized. Before altering parenting with Parent in Place active, make sure the Frame Indicator is on frame 0, our setup frame.

2. Make sure **Parent in Place** is on. In the Scene Editor, select **Pelvis** and drag it to just under **Pelvis_Base**, making Pelvis_Base the parent of Pelvis.

> **Note:** When you drag items in the Scene Editor, the indicator line changes size depending on where the cursor is. Release the mouse button when the indicator is shortest so it becomes a child of the item rather than being moved under the item.

3. In the same way, parent **Hip_LT** to **Pelvis_Base** and parent **Leg_Upper_LT** to **Hip_LT**. The leg hierarchy should now match Figure 4.3-8.

Figure 4.3-8.
Leg hierarchy.

4. To organize the fingers, select **Thumb01_LT**. Hold down **Ctrl**, then click to add **Finger301_LT**, **Finger201_LT**, and **Finger101_LT** to the selection. Drag the selected bones, parenting them to **Hand_LT**.

5. Parent **Shoulder_LT** to **Back04** to complete the arm hierarchy.

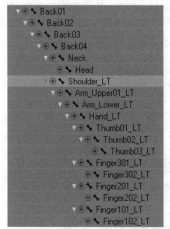

Figure 4.3-9.
Arm hierarchy.

6. Select **Ear_Base_LT** and **Antenna01** and parent them to **Head**.

7. Parent **Eye_Base_LT** to **Eye_Stretch_LT**.

8. Select all the other eye and eyelid bones and parent them to **Eye_Base_LT**.

9. Parent **Eye_Stretch_LT** to **Head**.

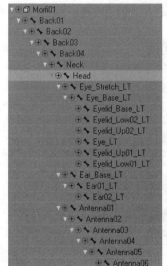

Figure 4.3-10.
Head hierarchy.

That completes the parenting. You should really check the bone rotations as you perform each step of the parenting, but as long as you create the skelegons properly the bone rotations will all be correct. Let's take a moment now to check the bone rotations anyway.

1. Move to frame 10 so you don't affect the default rotations at frame 0.

2. **Rotate** (**y**) the bones to make sure that the pitch (the green rotation handle) channels of the bones in each hierarchy are aligned, and that all the bones in each hierarchy rotate in the same direction as each other. The only exception to this is that the pitch of the fingers should be vertical, matching up with the bank orientation of the hand bone.

3. When you're done, press **Delete**, deleting the key at frame 10 for all items. Move back to frame 0 in readiness for the following steps.

All the rotations look peachy, but the leg bones still need adjusting to conform to the leg.

Adjusting the Leg Bones

To adjust the leg bones, we need to deactivate the bones, reposition them, then reactivate them in their new position.

1. Change the lower-left viewport (I call this the "working viewport") from Top to **Back**, and make sure that it's set to **Front Face Wireframe**. Zoom in and position the view so that Morfi's left leg and foot fill the viewport.

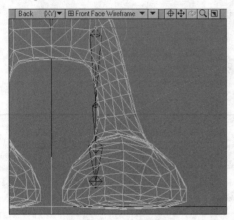

Figure 4.3-11. Back view of the leg.

2. Back in the Scene Editor, select **Hip_LT**, then hold down **Shift** and select **Toe_LT** to select all the leg bones.
3. Toggle **Bone Activation (Ctrl+r)** to deactivate the bones.

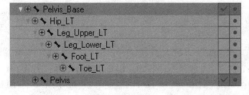

Figure 4.3-12. Notice the check mark next to each bone disappears when the bone is deactivated.

4. Select **Hip_LT** and in the working viewport, rotate the bank (the blue rotation handle) –15°, or until the tip of the upper leg bone is in the middle of the knee.
5. Press the down arrow twice to select **Leg_Lower_LT**, and rotate the heading (the red rotation handle) **5°**, or until the tip of the lower leg bone is in the middle of the ankle.

6. Zoom in so the foot bones are closer, and with **Leg_Lower_LT** still selected, drag with the right mouse button to rotate the bank to **177°**, or until the foot bone is vertical.

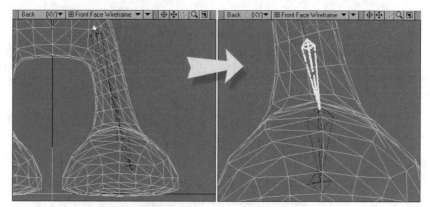

Figure 4.3-13. Rotating the leg bones.

7. Press the down arrow to select **Foot_LT** and rotate the bank **9°**, or until the bone is straight.

8. Press the down arrow to select **Toe_LT** and rotate the pitch to **–24.96°**, or until the bone is directly facing the viewport.

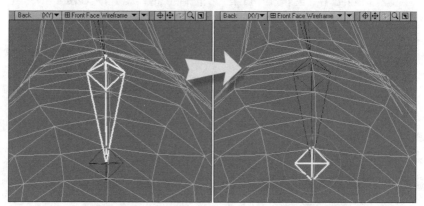

Figure 4.3-14. Rotating the foot bones.

9. Select all the leg bones in the Scene Editor and **Record Rest Position (r)** to reset the bones in their new positions.

Adjusting the Arm Bones

There are two changes to make for the arm bones. First, we'll split the upper arm into two bones, then we'll create a mechanism for the twisting of the wrist. This is our first look at the new bone tools in LightWave 8. We only use a couple of them for Morfi, since most of the work has been done using skelegons. The bone tools are used extensively when we rig Hamish in *Volume 2: Rigging & Animation*.

1. Select **Arm_Upper01_LT** and **Setup**➤**Detail**➤**Bone Split**. Leave the panel at its default values and click **OK**, splitting the bone in two.

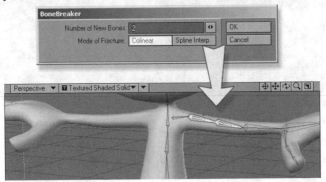

Figure 4.3-15. Splitting the upper arm bone.

2. Select the first new upper arm bone and **Items**➤**Replace**➤**Rename**, changing the name to **Arm_Upper01_LT**. Select the second new bone and **Rename**, changing the name to **Arm_Upper02_LT**.
3. Select the upper arm bones and the lower arm bone, and **Record Rest Position** (**r**).
4. To create the wrist mechanism, select **Arm_Lower_LT** and open the Bone Properties.
5. In the value for Rest Length, add **/2** to the end and press **Enter**, halving the rest length.

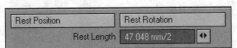

Figure 4.3-16. Changing Rest Length.

6. Select the Rest Length value and press **Ctrl+c** to copy, or write down the value so we can use it later.
7. Select the hand bone and **Setup**➤**Add**➤**Child Bone** (**=**), calling the new bone **Wrist_LT**.
8. Select **Modify**➤**Translate**➤**Move** (**t**) and change the Z position of **Wrist_LT** to **0**. You can type values directly into the XYZ or HBP numeric values in the lower-left corner of the interface.

9. Set the working viewport to Top view. Select **Modify➤Rotate➤Rotate**
    (**y**) and from the Top view, rotate the heading to **191°**, or until the heading
    of the wrist bone is aligned with the lower arm bone.

10. Set the working viewport to Back view. Rotate the pitch to **–8°**, or until
    the pitch of the wrist bone is aligned with the lower arm bone.

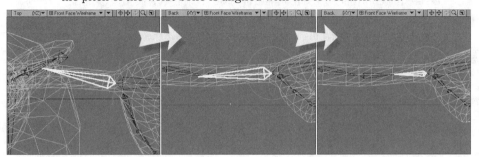

Figure 4.3-17. Positioning the wrist bone.

11. Open Bone Properties and select the Rest Length value. If you copied it
    earlier, press **Ctrl+v**, or type in the value you wrote down. You can see
    now why we did this; we've created two bones where there was only one,
    making each bone half the length of the original. While we're in the prop-
    erties, set Bone Weight Map to **Hands**.

12. Press **m** to open the Motion Options. Set Target Item to **Arm_Lower_
    LT**. Finally, press **r** to rest the bone.

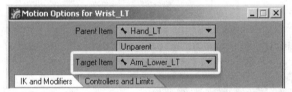

Figure 4.3-18. Setting the target item.

We've split the upper and lower arm bones, each in a different way. More about
why we've done this and how it works is explained in *Volume 2: Rigging &
Animation*.

Now that all the bones of the left side are created and positioned, it's a great
time to save if you haven't already, before moving on to create some animation
controls.

Creating Animation Controls

Animation controls allow easy access to the character for posing and animating. We create null objects for these controls, then give each one a unique appearance so that each different control is easily recognizable in the scene. We only need to create the controls for the left side, as they are mirrored across later.

1. Select **Items > Add > Null** to add a null object to the scene. Call the null **Morfi_Master**. This is the master control for the rig, allowing you to move the entire rig within the scene.

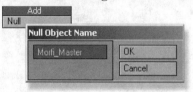

Figure 4.3-19. Add null object.

2. Add eight more nulls, calling them:

   Morfi_Mover
   Morfi_Foot_LT
   Morfi_Toe_LT
   Morfi_Ankle_LT
   Morfi_Hand_LT
   Morfi_Shoulder_LT
   Morfi_EyeStretch
   Morfi_EyeTarget

3. Set the working viewport to **Right** and select the **Center Current Item** icon. Move **Morfi_Mover** up to the pivot (base) of the Pelvis_Base bone. This is the control for moving the upper body independently of the feet.

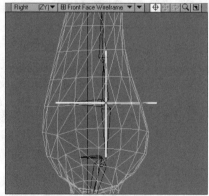

Figure 4.3-20. Positioning Morfi_Mover.

4. Parent **Morfi_Toe_LT** and **Morfi_Ankle_LT** to **Morfi_Foot_LT**. These are the controls and goals for the foot.

5. Move **Morfi_Foot_LT** in **Z** only (click and drag the Z Move handle) to the tip of the foot bone. Set the working viewport to **Back** and move **Morfi_Foot_LT** in **X** to align with the foot bones.

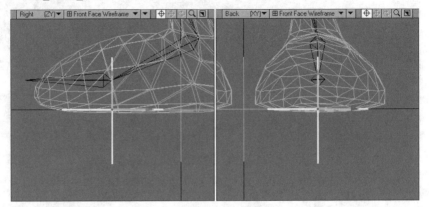

Figure 4.3-21. Positioning the foot control.

6. Set the working viewport to **Right** and move **Morfi_Toe_LT** up a bit and forward to about halfway along the toe bone.

7. Move **Morfi_Ankle_LT** to the pivot of the foot bone (zoom in as much as you need to position it fairly accurately). Rotate the heading **180°** and the pitch **24.8°**, or until the null is aligned to the angle of the foot bone.

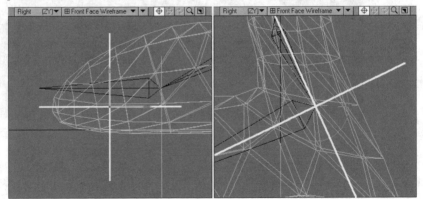

Figure 4.3-22. Positioning the toe and ankle controls.

8. Set the working viewport to **Back** and move **Morfi_Hand_LT** to the pivot of the hand bone. Set the viewport to **Top** and move the null in **Z** to finish moving it to the hand bone pivot. Rotate the heading **90°** and the pitch **–10.5°**, or until the null is aligned to the angle of the hand bone. This is the control for the arm and hand.

9. Move **Morfi_Shoulder_LT** from the Back and Top views to the pivot of **Arm_Upper01_LT**. This is the control for the shoulders.

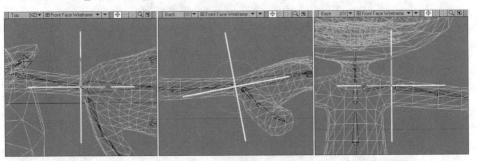

Figure 4.3-23. Positioning the hand and shoulder controls.

10. Move **Morfi_EyeStretch**, from the Right view only, to the tip of the **Eye_Stretch_LT** bone. **Items▷Add▷Clone**, adding one clone. **Items▷Replace▷Rename**, changing the name of the clone to **Morfi_EyeStretch_LT**.

11. Move **Morfi_EyeStretch_LT** in **X** from the Back view to the tip of the **Eye_Stretch_LT** bone.

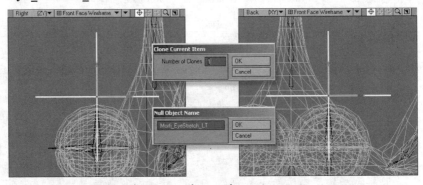

Figure 4.3-24. Positioning the eye stretch controls.

12. Move **Morfi_EyeTarget** from the Right view only to the tip of the **Eye_LT** bone. **Clone**, adding one clone, and **Rename** the clone to **Morfi_EyeTarget_LT**.

13. Move **Morfi_EyeTarget_LT** in **X** from the Top view to the tip of the **Eye_LT** bone.

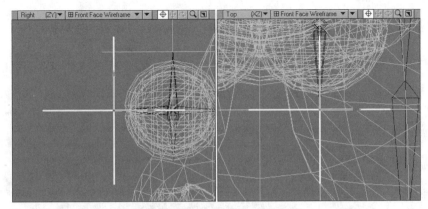

Figure 4.3-25. Left: Morfi_EyeTarget. Right: Morfi_EyeTarget_LT.

Creating Control Parents

We need to create parent items for the shoulder and eye stretch controls so their translation matches the other controls. We can use bones for these so we don't clutter up the object list too much.

1. Select the **Back04** bone and **Create Child Bone** (=), calling it **Shoulder_Base**. Move the new bone in **Z** to **0.01** or **10 mm** and rotate the pitch **90°**.

2. Open Bone Properties and adjust the Rest Length to **0.013** or **13 mm**, or until it's inside the geometry, then press **r** to rest the bone. Set Bone Weight Map to **Body** and change Strength to **0%**.

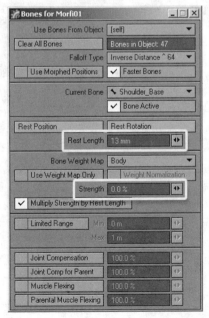

Figure 4.3-26.
Bone properties for
Shoulder_Base.

3. Select the **Head** bone and **Create Child Bone**, calling it **EyeStretch_ Base**. Rotate the new bone's pitch **90°**.

4. In Bone Properties, adjust Rest Length to **0.01** or **10 mm**, then press **r** to rest the bone. Set Bone Weight Map to **Head** and change Strength to **0%**.

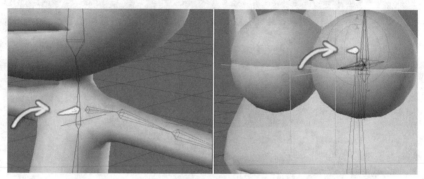

Figure 4.3-27. Left: Shoulder_Base. Right: EyeStretch_Base.

We could just parent the shoulder controls to Back04 and the eye stretch controls to Head, but that would result in their orientation being different from the other controls, which would still work but be annoying to animate. This way, all the controls move in the same direction so the animator doesn't lose momentum.

Configuring the Controls

We need to organize the hierarchies for the controls, parenting the items in the Scene Editor.

1. Parent **Morfi_EyeStretch_LT** to **Morfi_EyeStretch**.

2. Parent **Morfi_EyeTarget_LT** to **Morfi_EyeTarget**.

3. Parent **Morfi_Hand_LT** to **Morfi_Mover**.

4. Parent **Morfi_Mover, Morfi_Foot_LT**, and **Morfi_EyeTarget** to **Morfi_Master**.

5. Parent **Morfi_Shoulder_LT** to the **Shoulder_Base** bone.

6. Parent **Morfi_EyeStretch** to the **EyeStretch_Base** bone.

7. Finally, parent **Morfi01** to **Morfi_Mover**.

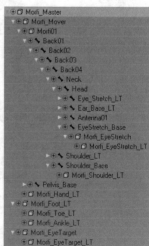

Figure 4.3-28. Control hierarchy.

Now that all the controls are in place we need to adjust their appearance so they're easily distinguishable and easy to select.

1. Still in the Scene Editor, select **Morfi_Mover**, **Morfi_Hand_LT**, **Morfi_Foot_LT**, and **Morfi_EyeTarget**. Select **Colors**≻**Color Selected Items**≻**Orange**.

Figure 4.3-29.
Changing display
color.

2. Select **Morfi_Master**, **Morfi_EyeStretch**, **Morfi_Shoulder_LT**, and **Morfi_Toe_LT**, and change their color to **Red**. (You don't have to use orange and red; these are just the colors I like to use. You can choose different colors if you wish.)

3. Select **Morfi_Mover** and open Object Properties. **Geometry**≻**Add Custom Object**≻**Item Shape**. Right-click on the **Item Shape** entry and choose **Properties** from the context menu.

4. Change Shape to **Ring** and change Scale to **0.1** or **100 mm**. Close the panel, right-click on the **Item Shape** entry again, and choose **Copy**.

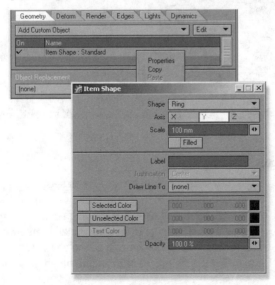

Figure 4.3-30.
Item Shape
window.

123

5. In Object Properties, click the **Current Object** pull-down and choose **Morfi_Foot_LT.**

6. Select **Edit ▷ Paste**, pasting Item Shape into the Custom Object list. Open the properties for Item Shape and change Scale to **0.075** or **75 mm**. Close the panel.

7. **Paste** the Item Shape Custom Object into **Morfi_Toe_LT** and change Axis to **X** and Scale to **50 mm**.

8. **Paste** the Item Shape Custom Object into **Morfi_Hand_LT** and change Axis to **Z** and Scale to **35 mm**.

9. **Paste** the Item Shape Custom Object into **Morfi_Shoulder_LT** and change Axis to **X** and Scale to **35 mm**.

10. **Paste** the Item Shape Custom Object into **Morfi_EyeStretch** and change Shape to **Ball** and Scale to **35 mm**.

11. **Paste** the Item Shape Custom Object into **Morfi_EyeTarget** and change Shape to **Ball** and Scale to **50 mm**.

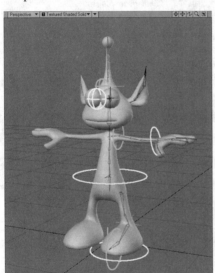

Figure 4.3-31.
Finished item
shapes.

Now that all the controls are set up, we need to adjust some of the settings for the bones.

Bone Settings

Most of the settings adjusted here relate to inverse kinematics, or IK. Applying inverse kinematics to a chain of bones or bone hierarchy allows you to position the bones using one or more control items instead of rotating each bone individually. This not only saves time when animating but has the added benefit of allowing the goal bone to be set in place while the rest of the character is moving around, which is great for planting the feet or resting a hand on something. This section is just a quick guide, as IK is explained in more detail in *Volume 2: Rigging & Animation*.

1. Select the **Hip_LT** bone and press **p** to open the Bone Properties.

2. The first setting to consider is Falloff Type. This setting affects how tightly the bones affect the mesh when sharing or not using weight maps, and affects all the bones in an object. **Inverse Distance ^ 64** is a good setting to start with for most characters.

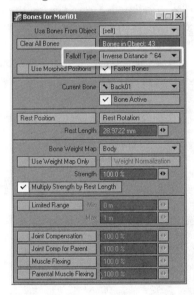

Figure 4.3-32.
Bone properties.

3. The other bone settings are dealt with later, so press **m** to open the Motion Options.

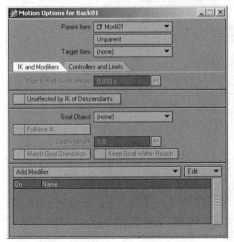

Figure 4.3-33.
Motion Options is where we apply IK and other motion modifiers.

4. We'll look at the IK and Modifiers tab a bit later, so select the **Controllers and Limits** tab. This is where you set controllers and limits for the individual rotation channels.

5. Make sure **Hip_LT** is still selected and change Bank Controller to **Inverse Kinematics**.

6. Turn off the pitch and bank (deselecting **P** and **B**) HPB Rotation channel controls at the lower-left corner of the interface. If you can only see XYZ Position channel controls, select Rotation mode (**y**) to display the HPB Rotation channel controls. Notice as you turn off the channel controls, the rotation handles for those channels change from solid to dotted lines.

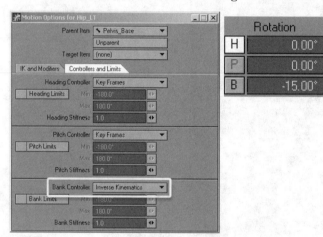

Figure 4.3-34. IK and Rotation channel controls for the hip bone.

7. For **Leg_Upper_LT** and **Leg_Lower_LT**, change Pitch Controller to **IK** and turn off all the rotation channel controls.

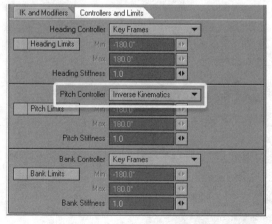

Figure 4.3-35. IK settings for the leg bones.

8. Now switch to the **IK and Modifiers** tab. This is where you set goal objects and how the item is affected by its goal.

9. Select **Foot_LT** and set Goal Object to **Morfi_Ankle_LT**. Turn on **Full-time IK** and **Match Goal Orientation** and set Goal Strength to **100**. Then turn off all the rotation channel controls.

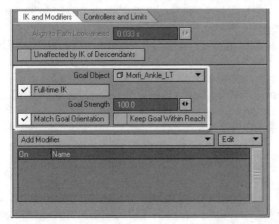

Figure 4.3-36.
IK settings for the
foot bone.

10. Select **Toe_LT** and set Goal Object to **Morfi_Toe_LT**. Turn on **Match Goal Orientation**.

When you turn on Match Goal Orientation the toe bone flips around, mangling the foot. This is because the heading of the toe control wasn't aligned correctly with the toe bone when we set it up. That can happen at this stage if you haven't evaluated the correct orientation for the control nulls. It's pretty quick to adjust it now that you can see the results.

11. Select the **Morfi_Toe_LT** control null and rotate the heading **180°**, which rotates the toe bone back to the correct place.

12. Select the **Toe_LT** bone again and turn off all the rotation channel controls.

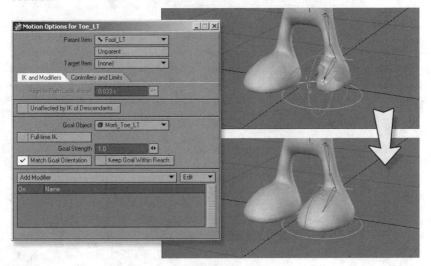

Figure 4.3-37. IK settings for the toe bone.

127

The leg settings are done. If you like, you can go to frame 10 and check the results. Check that Enable IK is turned on. Move and rotate Morfi_Foot_LT to position the foot, rotate the pitch of Morfi_Toe_LT to position the toe, and rotate the heading of Hip_LT bone to position the knee. When you're finished go back to frame 0 to continue with the arm bone settings.

1. Select the **Motion Options▸Controllers and Limits** tab again. Select the **Shoulder_LT** bone, change the heading and pitch controllers to **IK**, and turn off all the rotation channel controls.

2. Select **Arm_Upper01_LT**, change the heading and pitch controllers to **IK**, and turn off the **H** and **P** rotation channel controls, leaving only **B**.

3. Select **Arm_Upper02_LT**. Don't change the controller settings but turn off the **H** and **P** rotation channel controls, leaving only **B**.

4. Select **Arm_Lower_LT**, change Pitch Controller to **IK** and turn off all the rotation channel controls.

5. Select **Hand_LT** then select the **IK and Modifiers** tab. Set Goal Object to **Morfi_Hand_LT**, turn on **Full-time IK** and **Match Goal Orientation**, and set Goal Strength to **100**. Then turn off all the rotation channel controls.

6. Select **Arm_Upper01_LT** and set Goal Object to **Morfi_Shoulder_LT**, turn on **Full-time IK**, and set Goal Strength to **100**.

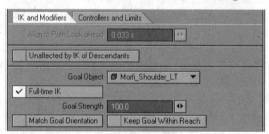

Figure 4.3-38.
Goal settings for the shoulder bone.

That's it for the arm settings. You can go to frame 10 to check the results. Move and rotate Morfi_Hand_LT to position the hand, rotate the bank of the Arm_Upper02_LT bone to position the elbow, and move Morfi_Shoulder_LT in Y to shrug the shoulders. Currently the right arm is affected by moving the left arm bones because both sides use the same weight map. This is fixed when we mirror the bones. When you're finished, go back to frame 0 to continue with the final bone settings.

1. Select the **Eye_Stretch_LT** bone and set Target Item to **Morfi_EyeStretch_LT**.

Figure 4.3-39.
Setting the target for Eye_Stretch_LT.

2. Select **Eye_LT** and set Target Item to **Morfi_EyeTarget_LT.**

Bone Strength

We need to adjust the strength of some of the bones, which is done in the Bone Properties panel.

1. Press **p** to open the Bone Properties panel, select the **Hip_LT** bone, and change Strength to **0%.**

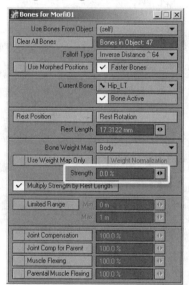

Figure 4.3-40.
Bone properties
for Hip_LT.

2. Select **Pelvis_Base** and change Strength to **0%.**
3. Select **Eye_Stretch_LT** and change Strength to **0%.**
4. Select **Eye_Base_LT** and change Strength to **0%.**

All of these bones are control bones for the working bones, so we don't want them affecting the geometry. You could deactivate the bones, but having some active and some non-active bones can become confusing. Setting the strength to 0 has the same effect as deactivating the bones, but by keeping all of the bones active you know they're all set up correctly.

Now that the IK is set up for the arms and legs, we can see what channels we need to have for the animation controls. The hand and foot controls need all their channels available, but the toe and shoulder don't. Let's set those up now.

1. Select **Morfi_Toe_LT** and press **t** to go to Move mode. Turn off all the position channel controls. Press **y** and turn off the **H** and **B** rotation channel controls, leaving only **P.**
2. Select **Morfi_Shoulder_LT** and press **t** to go to Move mode. Turn off the **X** and **Z** position channel controls, leaving only **Y.** Press **y** and turn off all the rotation channel controls.

With all the bone settings done, we're ready to mirror the rig.

Mirroring the Rig

Now that we've set up the left side of the rig, we need to mirror each hierarchy from left to right.

1. Select the **Hip_LT** bone and select **Setup⊁Edit⊁Mirror Hierarchy**.

2. In the MirrorHierarchy panel, change Mirror Goals to **YES** and Name Edit Method to **Replace String**. For Replace this string, enter **_LT**, and for with this string, enter **_RT**, then click **OK**.

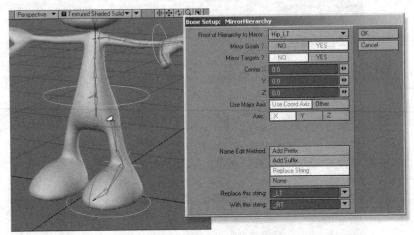

Figure 4.3-41. Mirror Hierarchy settings for the leg hierarchy.

You can see that all the leg bones and goals have been mirrored successfully, so we can continue with the other hierarchies.

3. Select the **Shoulder_LT** bone and **Mirror Hierarchy**. Change Mirror Goals to **YES** and Mirror Targets to **YES**, and replace **_LT** with **_RT**.

4. Select **Eye_Stretch_LT** and **Mirror Hierarchy**. Change Mirror Goals to **NO** and Mirror Targets to **YES**, and replace **_LT** with **_RT**.

5. Select **Ear_Base_LT** and **Mirror Hierarchy**. Change Mirror Goals to **NO** and Mirror Targets to **NO**, and replace **_LT** with **_RT**.

Well, that was easy. Mirror Hierarchy has mirrored the bones and their goals, weight maps, and IK settings. There is a little cleaning up to do though.

1. Select the **Morfi_Foot_LT** control null and **Items≻Add≻Mirror**.
    Rename the mirrored item **Morfi_Foot_RT**.

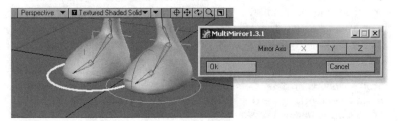

Figure 4.3-42. Mirroring the foot control.

2. In the Scene Editor, parent **Morfi_Ankle_RT** and **Morfi_Toe_RT** to
    Morfi_Foot_RT.

Figure 4.3-43.
Right foot controls.

3. Select all the default (cyan) colored control items — **Morfi_EyeStretch_
    LT, Morfi_EyeStretch_RT, Morfi_EyeTarget_LT, Morfi_
    EyeTarget_RT, Morfi_Ankle_LT**, and **Morfi_Ankle_RT** — then select
    Visibility≻Hide Selected Items. Lock the same items by clicking in the
    Lock column for each one. These are all internal control nulls that we
    don't want to see when animating.

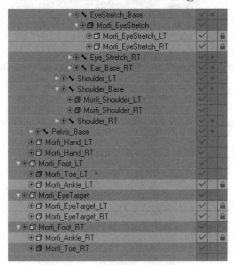

Figure 4.3-44.
Hidden controls.

Organizing the Rig

Because we haven't been very careful to create the items in a particular order, the bones and objects are all over the place in the item selection lists. Leaving it like this makes selecting items for animation very difficult. We can fix up the load order really quickly using a program called MSort, written by Scott Martindale.

> **Note:** MSort is currently only available for PC and is included on the CD. Scott is working on a new version that includes drag and drop editing, as well as much more functionality. Hopefully the new version will be available for both PC and Mac. The updated version of MSort will be available from my web site.

1. Save the scene and load **\LWProjects\Manual Sort\MSortPurple.exe**.
2. Open the Morfi rig scene, and when asked, press **Y** to sort bones as well.

Figure 4.3-45. Select Yes to sort bones.

3. The objects and bones from the scene are listed in WordPad. Cut and paste the bones and objects into your preferred selection order, leaving **Main Null** at the top of the list.

Figure 4.3-46. Initial load order listed.

> **Note:** Instead of giving my suggested order here, I've included the MSort text file, including the items from the Morfi rig after sorting, in \LWProjects\LW8_ CartoonCreation\Morfi_Rig01_MSort.txt.

4. When you've organized the selection order, save the file and quit WordPad. MSort asks if you want to keep the Edit.Me file, but I rarely see a need to do so. Press **Y** to keep it or **N** if you don't want to keep it.

5. MSort tells you the name of the updated scene file, which is always the original scene name with **_MSort** appended to the end.

Figure 4.3-47. MSort confirms the name of the reordered scene file.

MSort correctly reorders the bones and objects in the scene, but any items using targeting lose their correct target due to the order change. We'll fix that before saving over the original scene file.

6. In Layout, load **Morfi_Rig01_MSort.lws**.

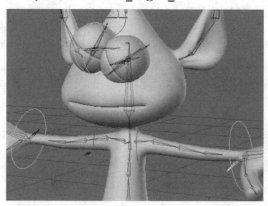

Figure 4.3-48. Targeted bones are targeting the wrong items.

7. Select the **Wrist_LT** bone and open Motion Options. Change Target Item to **Arm_Lower_LT**.

8. Change the target of **Wrist_RT** to **Arm_Lower_RT**.

9. Change the target of **Eye_Stretch_LT** to **Morfi_EyeStretch_LT**, and change the target of **Eye_Stretch_RT** to **Morfi_EyeStretch_RT**.

10. Change the target of **Eye_LT** to **Morfi_EyeTarget_LT**, and change the target of **Eye_RT** to **Morfi_EyeTarget_RT**.

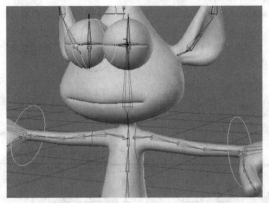

Figure 4.3-49.
Fixed targeting.

11. With all the targeting fixed, save the scene as **Morfi_Rig01.lws**, saving over the original rig scene.

4.4 Advanced Rigging

We've dealt with fairly basic rigging up to now, but the eye setup is a slightly more advanced level. We need to add some expressions to the eye stretch bones and set up some motion modifiers for the eyelid bones. Expressions and modifiers are covered in detail in *Volume 2: Rigging & Animation*.

Eyes and Eyelids

There are two main types of eyelids for cartoon characters — separate eyelids and attached eyelids.

Figure 4.4-1.
Separate eyelids are easiest to create but are best used for inorganic characters or very broad cartoon characters.

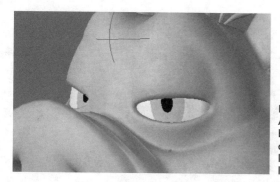

Figure 4.4-2.
Attached eyelids can
be a little more
difficult to create, but
look and behave just
like real eyelids.

Separate eyelids are usually created using separate geometry for the upper and lower lids. This works well when the eyes are embedded in the head so you can't see the back of the eyes where the seam between upper and lower lids occurs and is very easy to set up, requiring only a single bone for each eyelid.

Attached eyelids are merged with the eye socket and often don't require any bones, animating using morphs instead. If the eyes are too round, however, even attached eyelids can require bones to help them open and close without intersecting the eye geometry.

Morfi's eyes are different again, as they fall somewhere between the two types. We could make things simple by giving Morfi separate upper and lower lids, but because of his design you'd be able to see the seam between the lids at the back of the eyes, which isn't acceptable. While the eyelids are separate from the head, they are attached to each other so the controls are more like those of bulbous attached eyelids than separate eyelids.

It's also important that all the characters in a production have the same animation controls. If an animator has to figure out different control methods for each character it takes valuable time away from animating, so we need to find a way for all these types of eyelids to have a single control method.

Since the majority of cartoon characters need morphs and many have eyelid morphs, using morph sliders to drive the eyelids is a great way to maintain consistency since bones can also be driven by morph sliders. This also allows the use of a combination of morphs and bones to deform the eyelids, which provides lots of flexibility.

Eye Stretching

We'll start by adding expressions to the eye stretch bones so the eye stretch control can stretch and rotate the eyes.

1. Select the **Eye_Stretch_LT** bone and open Motion Options.
2. In the IK and Modifiers tab, select **Add Modifier▷Expression**, and open the Motion Expression panel.

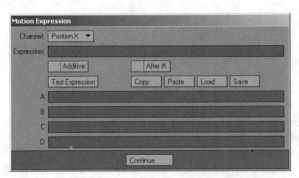

Figure 4.4-3. Motion modifier expressions allows you to place an expression on each channel of the item as well as giving you four scratch pads, A to D. I like to use these scratch pads as much as possible so the actual expressions on the channels refer only to the scratch pads. This means you can see the useful information as soon as you open the properties, without having to search through the channels.

We'll add a muscle bone expression to the eye stretch bones so they stretch to their target as it moves.

3. Type the following expression in the A scratch pad:

> **vmag(Morfi01.Eye_Stretch_LT.wpos(Time) – Morfi_EyeStretch_ LT.wpos(Time))**

The vmag expression finds the distance between two items, in this case, the pivot of the Eye_Stretch_LT bone and the Morfi_EyeStretch_LT control. You don't have to reference the object name for a bone (Object.Bone) if the bone name is unique, but it's best to do so in case you have two or more characters in a scene with the same bone names. However, the expression knows which bone you are referring to.

4. Type the following expression in the B scratch pad:

> **mapRange(A, 0, 0.0378, 0, 1)**

The mapRange expression takes an input and remaps a range from that input to a user-defined range. In this case it's taking the result of the vmag expression in A, and remapping the range 0 to 0.0378 (the bone's Rest Length and the default distance from Morfi.Eye_Stretch_LT to Morfi_EyeStretch_LT) with 0 to 1 (the bone's default Z scale).

5. Select **Channel>Scale.Z** and in the **Expression** field, type **B**.

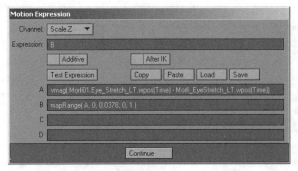

Figure 4.4-4. Scale.Z expressions.

When combined, these expressions adjust the Z scale of the bone to fit the position of its target item. Usually you would put both of these expressions in a single line, but I've separated them to make it a bit easier to understand.

6. Type the following expression in the C scratch pad:

   mapRange(A, 0, 0.0378, 0, 1) * 0.2 + 0.8

7. Select **Channel≻Scale.X** and in the Expression field, type **C**.

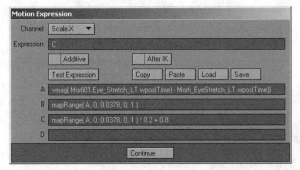

Figure 4.4-5. Add the Scale.X expression.

This adjusts the X scale of the bone with the Z scale, but a little less, so as the eyes get taller they also get a little wider, maintaining a nicer shape.

8. Type the following expression in the D scratch pad:

   (1 – Morfi_EyeStretch.scale(Time).x) * 30

9. Select **Channel≻Rotation.H** and in the Expression field, type **D**.

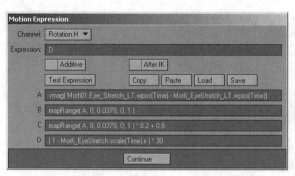

Figure 4.4-6. Add the Rotation.H expression.

This adjusts the heading rotation of the bone based on the X scale of the animation control. This means that we don't want the bone to target the control null anymore, as it will override the expression.

10. Click **Continue** in the Motion Expression panel to return to Motion Options, then change Target to **(none)**.

Now we can copy the expression to the right eye stretch bone.

11. Right-click on the expression and choose **Copy**.

12. Select the **Eye_Stretch_RT** bone and, in Motion Options, select **Edit▷Paste**.

13. Open the Motion Expression panel and in the A scratch pad change **_LT** to **_RT** for the two reference items.

14. The heading values need to be reversed for the left and right sides, so in the D scratch pad, change * **30** to * **–30**.

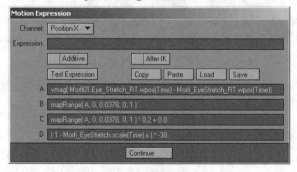

Figure 4.4-7. Expressions edited for the right eye.

15. Click **Continue**, then in Motion Options change Target to **(none)**.

Now that the expressions are done, we need to adjust the XYZ and HPB channel controls for the eye stretch control to make it easier to animate.

16. Select **Morfi_EyeStretch** and press **t** to go to **Move** mode. Turn off the **X** and **Z** Position channel controls, leaving only **Y**.

17. Press **y** and turn off the **H** and **P** Rotation channel controls, leaving only **B**.

18. Press **h** and turn off the **Y** and **Z** Scale channel controls, leaving only **X**.

Now on frame 10, play around with Morfi_EyeStretch, moving it up and down and rotating and scaling it to see how it affects the eyes.

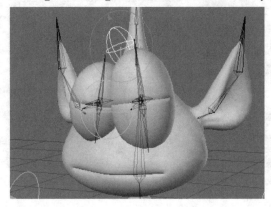

Figure 4.4-8. Eyes stretch and rotate based on the eye stretch control.

When you're finished, go back to frame 0 to continue setting up the eyelid bones.

Eyelid Automation

Now we'll link the eyelid bones to morph sliders so we don't have to manually rotate each of the bones to animate the eyelids. The first step is to place the eyelids in their default open position.

1. Set the pitch channel of **Eyelid_Up01_LT** to −90° and the pitch channel of **Eyelid_Up02_LT** to −135°. Set the pitch channel of **Eyelid_Low01_LT** to **90°** and the pitch channel of **Eyelid_Low02_LT** to **135°**.

2. Repeat for the right eyelid bones.

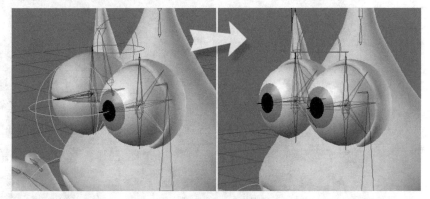

Figure 4.4-9. Rotate the eyelid bones into an open position.

With the eyelids in their default open positions we can attach the bone rotations to the morph sliders using Channel Follower.

3. Open Graph Editor and select **More▷Graph Editor Options**.

4. In the General tab, turn on **Track Item Selections**. In the Display tab, turn on **Always Show Modified**. Click **OK** to close the options panel.

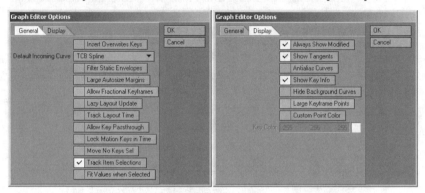

Figure 4.4-10. Graph Editor Options panel.

5. Select the **Eyelid_Up01_LT** bone and in Graph Editor, select the pitch channel on the left (the second green channel) and select the **Modifiers** tab on the right. **Add Modifier➤Channel Follower**, then open the Channel Follower panel.

6. In the Channels bin find **Morfi➤Eye➤Blink**. This is the morph channel we want to use as a control.

> **Note:** Morphs are found in the Channels list within their group name, just under an object's bones.

7. Change Scale to **9000%**.

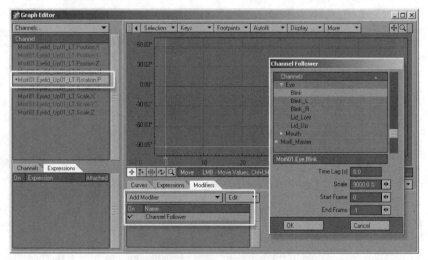

Figure 4.4-11. Scale needs to be at 9000% because morph channels, although going from 0% to 100%, are recognized in LW as only going from 0 to 1. We need the bone to rotate 90°, so we need to multiply 100% of the morph slider by 90.

8. Click **OK**, then **Edit≻Copy** the modifier.

9. Select **Eyelid_Up01_RT**, select the pitch channel on the left, and select **Edit≻Paste** on the right.

10. Select **Eyelid_Low01_LT**, select the pitch channel on the left, and select **Edit≻Paste** on the right.

11. Open the properties for the pasted Channel Follower and change Scale to **–9000%**.

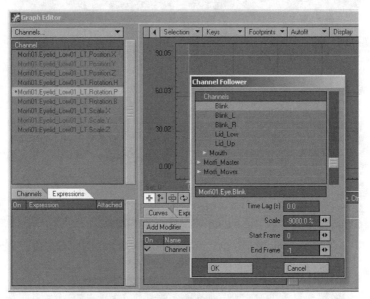

Figure 4.4-12. Settings for Eyelid_Low01_LT.

12. **Copy** the Channel Follower and **Paste** it into the Pitch channel of **Eyelid_Low01_RT**.

13. In the Pitch channels of **Eyelid_Up02_LT** and **Eyelid_Up02_RT**, **Paste** Channel Follower and change Scale to **4500%**.

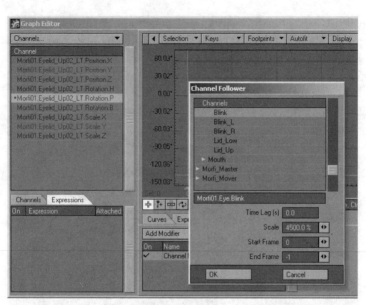

Figure 4.4-13. Settings for Eyelid_Up02_LT.

14. In the pitch channel of **Eyelid_Low02_LT** and **Eyelid_Low02_RT**, paste Channel Follower and change Scale to **–4500%**.

Now the eyelids close when you move the Blink morph slider to 100%. Feel free to test it out. We now need to add some more eyelid controls.

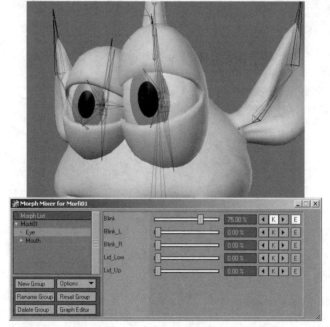

Figure 4.4-14. The eyes blink with the Blink morph slider.

Adding More Eyelid Controls

Blinking has been taken care of, but there are other eyelid controls — two to blink each eye individually and two to control the upper and lower eyelids individually. We can easily tie the eyelid bones to these morphs, as the settings have already been established. All we need to do is make copies of the Blink Channel Follower for each eyelid bone and change the morph slider control.

1.   Select the pitch channel of the **Eyelid_Up01_LT**, select the Channel Follower, and **Edit➤Copy** then **Edit➤Paste**. Paste again so there are three instances of Channel Follower.

2.   Change the second instance to follow **Morfi➤Eye➤Blink_L** and the third instance to follow **Morfi➤Eye➤Lid_Up**.

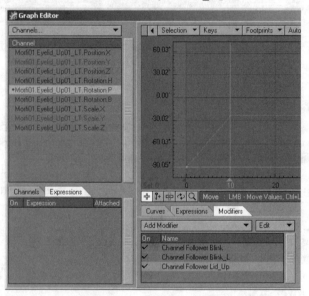

Figure 4.4-15. Three instances of Channel Follower, each following a different morph.

3.   Repeat steps 1 and 2 for **Eyelid_Up02_LT**.

4.   Do the same for **Eyelid_Low01_LT** and **Eyelid_Low02_LT**, except change the morphs to **Blink_L** and **Lid_Low**.

5.   Do the same for **Eyelid_Up01_RT** and **Eyelid_Up02_RT**, except change the morphs to **Blink_R** and **Lid_Up**.

6.   Do the same for **Eyelid_Low01_RT** and **Eyelid_Low02_RT**, except change the morphs to **Blink_R** and **Lid_Low**.

Change to frame 10 and play with the eye controls. Move Morfi_EyeStretch in Y to stretch the eyes, rotate the bank to vary the size of each eye individually, and scale in X to rotate the eyes toward each other. Move Morfi_EyeTarget to where or what you want Morfi to look at. Adjust the eye morph sliders to position the eyelids.

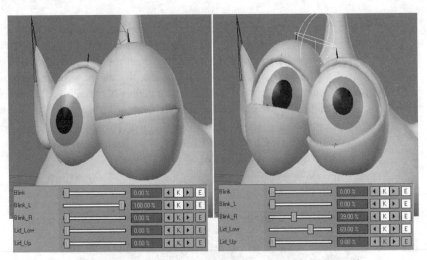

Figure 4.4-16. Adjusting the eye morphs, eye target, and eye stretch control.

Testing the Rig

The last stage is to test the rig in different poses to check the deformations. This shows us if we need to adjust the weights or Joint Compensation settings for the bones. By testing various poses with joints in bent positions I can see that some areas could benefit from joint compensation. At this stage you can test what combination of Joint Compensation and Joint Comp for Parent each joint needs by just trying them to see what looks best. Later on we'll delve further into what each of these settings mean.

1. Select **Leg_Upper_LT** and open Bone Properties. Turn on **Joint Compensation**. Do the same for **Leg_Upper_RT**.

2. Select **Leg_Lower_LT** and turn on **Joint Comp for Parent**. Do the same for **Leg_Lower_RT**.

3. Turn on **Joint Compensation** and **Joint Comp for Parent** for **Arm_Lower_LT** and **RT** and **Wrist_LT** and **RT**.

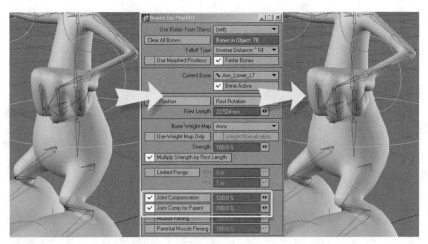

Figure 4.4-17. Enable Joint Compensation to retain the volume of a joint.

4. Turn on **Joint Compensation** and **Joint Comp for Parent** for all the thumb and finger bones.

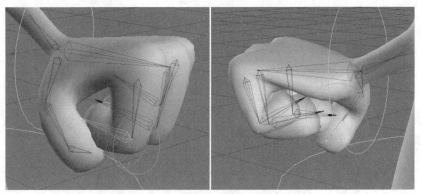

Figure 4.4-18. Finger joints often benefit from joint compensation.

Congratulations! You've just finished creating and rigging a character. Morfi is now ready for posing and animation.

Part III

Hamish

The following chapters contain a lot more reference information than those in Part II. Chapters 5 and 6 cover modeling and texturing Hamish, and the theories behind the techniques used.

These chapters build on the knowledge gained in the previous ones, so the steps are a little more advanced and assume you have a pretty good handle on the basics. If you get stuck on a particular step, do what you can to get to the same place as the illustration shows, as there's always more than one way to reach the goal, and in the end it doesn't really matter how you get there, as long as you do get there.

Chapter 5

Modeling

No doubt you have heard or read that there are two methods of modeling — box modeling and point-by-point, or detail-out, modeling. Don't think that these two methods are mutually exclusive. It's rare to find people who use only one of these methods to create a model. When you add the dozens of other ways to modify geometry, you get even further away from the idea that there are only two ways to model. What it boils down to is finding the most comfortable and efficient way for you to reach the desired result.

This chapter investigates a number of modeling methods from which you can pick and choose to apply to your own modeling.

Figure 5-1. Meet Hamish. Hamish is a perfect candidate for the more advanced character creation tutorials.

5.1 Subpatch Modeling 101

Subpatches (otherwise known as subdivision patches or subDs) are polygons that are smoothed by interactive subdivision. Subpatches are very useful for character modeling because they allow the model to have relatively few polygons and points while retaining a nice smooth surface. Polygons that aren't subpatched are known as faces. You can convert faces to subpatches and vice versa at any time when modeling (by pressing Tab), and you can select each type of polygon individually using the Polygon Statistics panel.

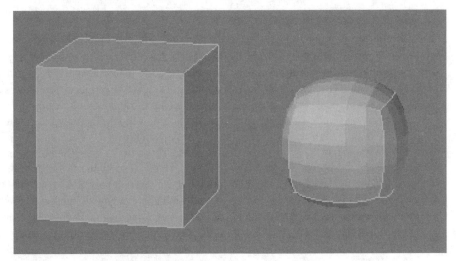

Figure 5.1-1. Left: Faces. Right: Subpatches.

Subpatch Limitations

You need to be aware when subpatch modeling that not all the modeling tools play nicely with subpatches. Most of the tools we use in the tutorials do support subpatches, but those that don't will generate faces instead of subpatches. It's usually best when working with subpatches to use the tools that support them, as it saves having to convert the new geometry to subpatches.

Only three- or four-point polygons (triangles or quads) can be subpatched, with quads generally creating a smoother subpatch surface than triangles. This means that an ideal subpatch model is made up of mostly quads, with some triangles where useful or necessary.

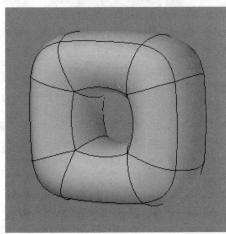

Figure 5.1-2.
Subpatch quads
and triangles.

149

Subpatch Guidelines

It's common practice, when modeling with subpatches, to keep the polygon count low. When you have a low polygon count, reducing the Display SubPatch Level and increasing the Render SubPatch Level keeps the playback speed as high as possible while keeping the subpatches nice and smooth at render time. This is a good rule to model by, but don't be afraid of adding more polygons to a model to add detail, minimize distortion, or aid deformation. Keeping the polygon count low at the expense of these things can cause problems later on.

It's important when creating subpatch models to try to keep the polygons within acceptable size relative to each other, except where you obviously need smaller detail. Having areas in your model where the polygons are vastly different in scale will either waste resources or result in visible polygons in your subpatches. Increasing the subpatch level high enough to smooth the larger polygons can create unnecessary division of the smaller polygons, and if the subpatch level is enough to smooth the smaller polygons it can underdivide the larger polygons. If all the polygons in the model are similar in scale, then the same subpatch level works equally well for the whole model.

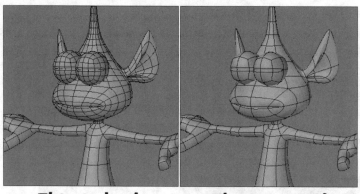

This is bad   This is good

Figure 5.1-3. Scale differences.

It can sometimes be difficult to make an area sharp or create a hard line using subpatches. One way is to create extra geometry in that area, but a more efficient way can be to adjust the SubPatch Weight as we did for the point of Morfi's ear in Chapter 3. Subpatch weight values are very useful for refining your geometry without increasing the polygon count.

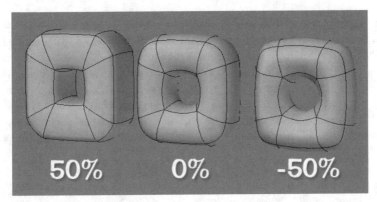

Figure 5.1-4. SubPatch weight.

One common misconception is that an entire model needs to be made up of either subpatches or faces. The truth is that a model can be made up of both subpatches and faces, so use this to your advantage. There are some things that subpatches are better used for, and some things that faces are better used for. By utilizing both in your models you have more flexibility and control over every area of your model.

Another misconception is that all the subpatch geometry in a model needs to be joined. That certainly isn't the case. You should always detach areas where you want a sharp divide between parts. Detaching subpatches does the same thing as detaching faces when Surface Smoothing is on. Because of the nature of subpatches, if you don't detach geometry, especially between areas containing different surfaces, there is often an undesirable smooth transition from one to the other.

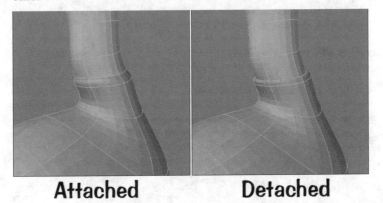

Figure 5.1-5. Detached subpatches.

Subpatch Distortion

Polygon flow is very important to character creation. Subpatch distortion due to poor polygon flow is a major cause of problems throughout every aspect of creating characters. Problems with the smoothness of the model surface, the inability to achieve nice deformations with morphs and bones, and UV mapped texture distortion are often caused by the uneven flow of polygons. The easiest way to avoid subpatch distortion is to be aware of the potential problem areas. As long as polygon flow is addressed early on, you can completely avoid many of the problems and more easily deal with the others.

Try to keep your polygon flow as uniform as possible. Neat polygon flow reduces the risk of UV distortion, makes the model easier to work with, and helps to ensure clean, predictable deformations.

The lower the polygon count, the more subpatch distortion you're likely to have. When you keep the polygon count low you usually need to twist the polygons around a fair bit to achieve the right shape. Although the model might look okay, you run the risk of deformation problems and UV texture distortion. To ensure neat polygon flow, try adding a few more polygons rather than creating all your detail with the minimum number of polygons possible.

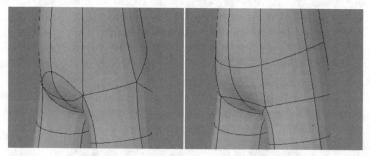

Figure 5.1-6. Increase poly count to achieve better polygon flow.

The placement of polygons is also important in avoiding subpatch distortion. Make sure you create enough polygons in the right places for an area to hold its shape when it deforms. The flow of polygons should ensure that an area can deform without falling apart.

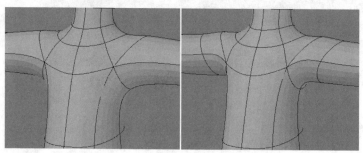

Figure 5.1-7. Add more polygons to ensure nice deformation.

You can minimize the effect of UV texture distortion by creating and positioning the polygons so that areas of strong texture detail lie inside or across the middle of polygons instead of at the corners or edges where texture distortion is most noticeable.

If you know that you want to apply small texture detail to a specific area, take some extra time when modeling to ensure optimal polygon flow in that area and that you place the polygons central to where you want the strongest detail.

Some of these things are explained in more detail as we model Hamish so you can see examples of how to apply these principles to your modeling.

5.2 Modeler Setup

Launch Modeler and make sure the Content Directory is set to \LWProjects\ LW8_CartoonCreation.

The first step is to set up the backdrops for Hamish.

1. Open Display Options (**d**) and click on the **Backdrop** tab.

2. Select **Viewport – BL** and load **\Backdrops\Template_Hamish_F.tga**.

3. Set the Image Resolution to **512**, Size to **1 m**, and Y Center to **500 mm**.

4. Select **Viewport – BR** and load **Template_Hamish_S.tga**. Fill in the same Size and Center settings as for the front view.

5. Click the **Presets** pull-down and select **Save All Backdrops**. Call the file **Backdrops_Hamish.cfg**.

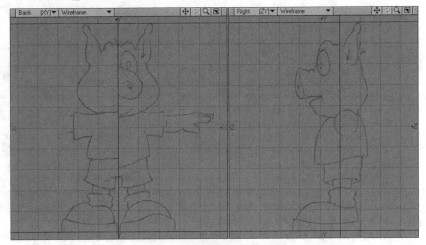

Figure 5.2-1. Front and side reference for Hamish.

Setting the backdrops to 1 m means Hamish will end up being one meter tall. Hamish is seven years old, so this is a good height for him. Now we're ready to start modeling.

5.3 Modeling the Head

Where to start modeling can be a fairly arbitrary decision; often it's just what you feel most comfortable with at the time. It can be good to start with the head, as this is the emotional center of the character. It also gets the most complex parts done early, when you usually have the most motivation. Having said that, if you're not feeling particularly motivated when you start modeling, it can be better to start with a more simple, less important part of the character.

Basic Shapes

We'll start by creating the basic shapes of the head and then work into the details. At this stage we want to create a cage for us to work more detail into later as we get to the features. We want the geometry to be simple, only complex enough to define the shape of the head and give us enough geometry to start the features of the face. Creating the basic shape with too high a polygon count makes adding the features and tweaking the shapes more difficult. If you're in doubt, keep it simple; it's much easier to add detail later than to remove it.

1. Zoom in and adjust the viewport positions so the head of the backdrops fills the viewports.

2. Create a 12-sided cylinder with 5 segments, roughly in place of the head. See Figure 5.3-1 for settings and placement. Make sure the cylinder is centered on the X axis.

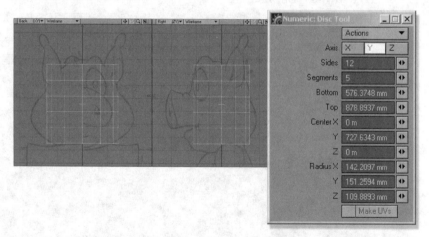

Figure 5.3-1. Start with a cylinder. You may have noticed that I start most characters with a cylinder. It's an ideal starting shape for most parts of a character, as it gives you a nice round cross section no matter how many segments you need for the detail. The number of starting segments is usually dependent on the shape of the body part and what features need to be included.

3. Delete the top and bottom polygons and press **Tab** to convert to subpatches.

4. Turn on **Symmetry**, then **Stretch** and **Move** the points to follow the major contours of the head.

5. **Extend** the top and bottom rows of points, and **Stretch** them vertically a little, creating polygons for the neck and the top of the head.

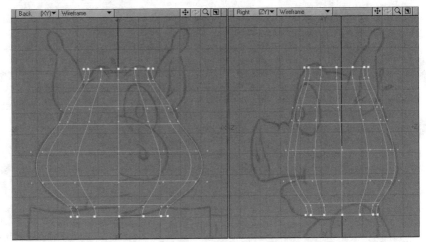

Figure 5.3-2. As you're deciding where to position your cross sections, try to think of where you need polygons to shift the features from as well as the overall shape of the head.

6. Now we need to close the top of the head. Select the top row of points. From the Right view, **Stretch** those points horizontally to **0%** and from the Back view **Stretch** the points in a little to around **60%**. **Merge Points (m)**.

7. Select the two polygons at the side of the top row of polygons (four polygons counting left and right sides), and **Merge Polygons (Shift+z)**.

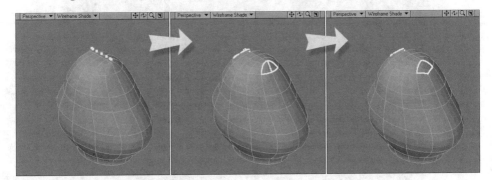

Figure 5.3-3. Closing the top of the head.

8. Although the polygons we just merged looked like triangles, they were actually quads, as the end point on either side was in the middle of the polygons. By merging the polygons, these points have become detached. We don't want any stray points floating around, so select **Point** mode and

in the Point Statistics panel, click on the **+** next to **0 Polygons** to select the two stray points. Delete the selected points.

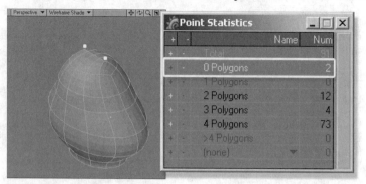

Figure 5.3-4. Check the Point Statistics and Polygon Statistics panels now and then for stray points or two-point polygons.

9. Drag the remaining points at the top of the head and arrange them so they're a little curved, rounding off the top of the head. If necessary, move them horizontally so they're in line with the middle points of the lower rows.

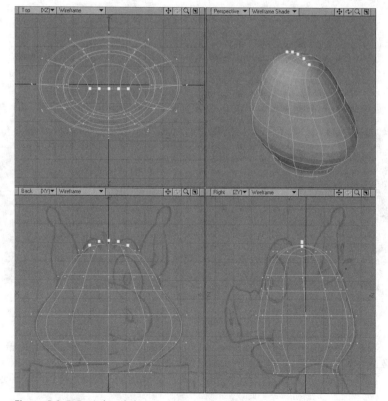

Figure 5.3-5. Basic head shape.

Eye Sockets

With the shape of the head defined we can start working on the features. As the features are created you can reposition points, tweaking the shapes, but at this early stage we're mostly concerned with creating the geometry we need. The shapes can be tweaked more effectively once all the features are built in and we can see each one relative to the others. If you do too much tweaking as you create the geometry, you double the workload, as invariably those areas will need to be adjusted to fit with the other features.

> **Tip:** It's a good idea to copy the working geometry to a new layer as you reach each stage of the model (a layer for each of Basic Shape, Eye Sockets, Nose, etc.), creating a history of sorts. While we have plenty of undos, sometimes if you've made a mistake and moved on without realizing it, it's easier to start again from the previous stage rather than reworking the geometry to fix the mistake. As you reach major milestones, such as completing the head, you can delete the previous layers and move the working geometry back to Layer 1 so the model layers don't become too unwieldy. Make it a habit to unhide (\) any hidden geometry before copying to a new layer though, as only visible geometry is copied and it's easy to forget you've got hidden geometry when you're in the groove.

1. Since we're working on the front of the head, hide the back half of the head to make it easier to see what we're doing.

2. To position the four polygons around each eye more closely around the eyes, **Move** the outside points of these polygons from the Back and Right views so they fit around the eye of the backdrops. We want them a little distance out from the eye to give us room to create the outer edge of the

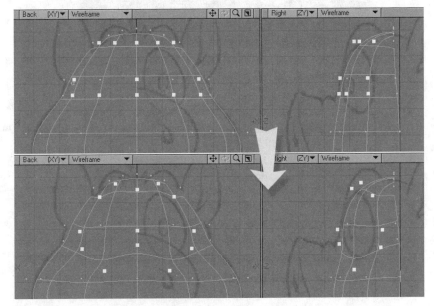

Figure 5.3-6. Shaping the polygons around the eyes.

eye socket. The middle row of points will establish where the corners of the eyes lie. We want the upper eyelids to be larger than the lower eyelids, so **Move** the middle points down to roughly level with the pupil. We can tweak the positions later, so don't worry about being too precise.

3. Now we can shift in the eye sockets. Because the polygons we want to shift lie on X=0, we can't use symmetry or else both the left and right sides will shift as one, so turn off Symmetry and select the four polygons around the left eye. **Super Shift**, inset the polygons in a little, and shift back just a touch, as shown in Figure 5.3-7. Tweak the points of the new polygons so they lie just outside the line of the eye.

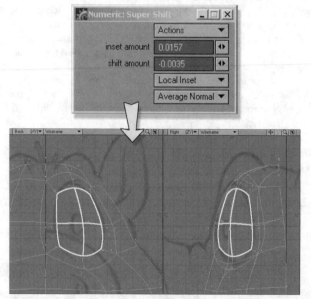

Figure 5.3-7. It's important to position the points correctly, even if the subpatch doesn't look right. Because we'll shift a few more times, the points will determine the shape to come.

4. **Super Shift** again, inset, and shift around **0.005**. The new polygons will become the base of the eyelids.

5. **Super Shift** again a decent amount to create the major part of the socket. When that's done, drag the center point back to create a nice concave shape.

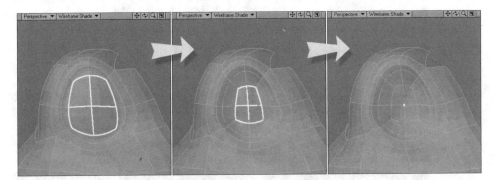

Figure 5.3-8. The eye socket doesn't have to be very deep as it will be hidden by the eyeball.

6. With the left eye socket created we just need to mirror it to the other side. Select the four polygons around the right eye and delete them. Then select the four center polygons of the left eye socket and **Expand Selection (Shift+])** three times. **Mirror (Shift+v)** on the X axis, deselect the polygons, and **Merge Points (m)**. A message will tell you that five points have been eliminated.

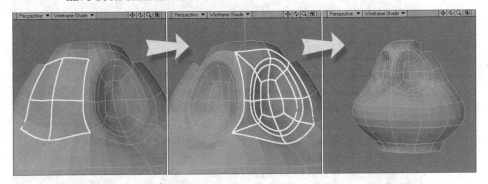

Figure 5.3-9. Mirror the eye socket.

We'll come back to the eyes and create the eyelids, eyeballs, and other details a bit later. For now it's best to continue roughing out the major features.

Nose

As I'm sure you've noticed already, Hamish has a pretty big nose. In fact, it's one of his primary distinguishing features, being a pig and all. Every character has one or more distinguishing features, something that makes it special. When you come to these features you often need to depart from the normal techniques you use. In this case, we're lucky it's not too different so we don't have to change our methods too much.

1. As we did with the eye sockets, we need to adjust the points around the area we're about to shift. Turn on **Symmetry** and select the three center points just under the nose. **Move** them up and back a little to the base of

the nose in the Right backdrop and, in the Back view, drag the outside point until it's just inside the line of the nose. See Figure 5.3-10.

2. **Move** the three center points at the middle of the nose back and down a little.

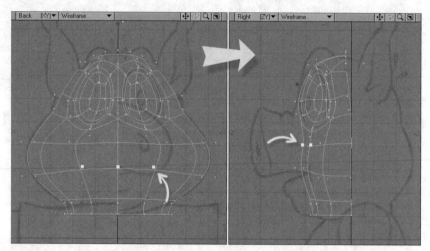

Figure 5.3-10. Making sure the nose emerges from the right place.

3. Now with the base ready we can start shifting out the nose. Select the four center polygons under the eyes and select **Extender Plus**. **Move** the polygons forward a little and, from the Right view, **Stretch** them horizontally to around **70%**, making the polygons a bit flatter.

> **Note:** Using Extender Plus on polygon selections is like Super Shifting in place.

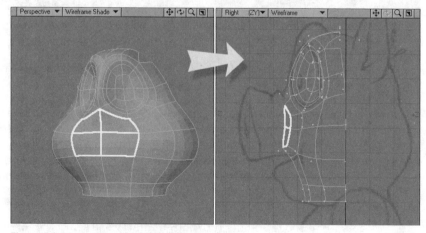

Figure 5.3-11. Creating the base of the nose.

4. **Extender Plus** again, then **Move** the polygons forward to just behind the front edge of the nose in the backdrop. From the Back view **Stretch** up a little both vertically and horizontally. Tweak the points from the Right view so they conform to the edge of the nose, matching Figure 5.3-12.

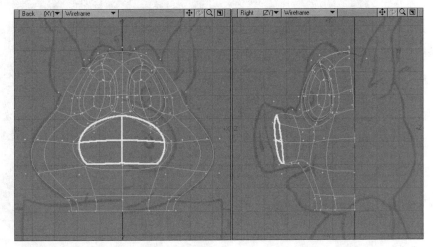

Figure 5.3-12. Creating the base of the nose.

5. **Extender Plus** again and **Move** the polygons forward to the end of the nose in the backdrop. **Stretch** and tweak to match the backdrops and Figure 5.3-13.

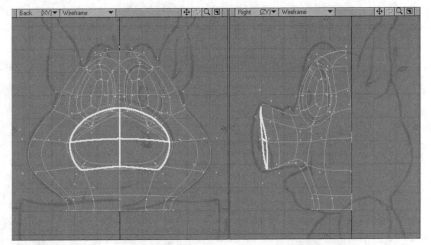

Figure 5.3-13. Creating the end of the nose.

6. **Super Shift** in place again, **Move** the polygons forward a little and, from the Back view, **Stretch** down both vertically and horizontally to match Figure 5.3-14.

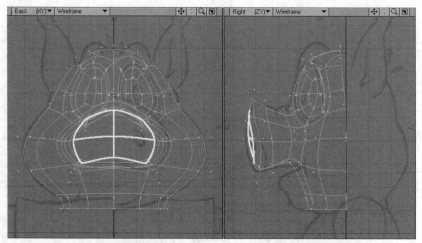

Figure 5.3-14. Creating the end of the nose.

7. Now that the basic nose geometry is done, we can make some adjustments and add some more geometry for better definition. Take a look at the top of the nose at the base, the transition from the eyes to the nose. It's not very smooth because the polygon flow isn't right. We want the geometry of the eyes to flow smoothly to the nose, so select the two polygons on either side of the eye and nose. **Spin Quads (Ctrl+k)** twice to rotate the polygons, creating a much nicer transition.

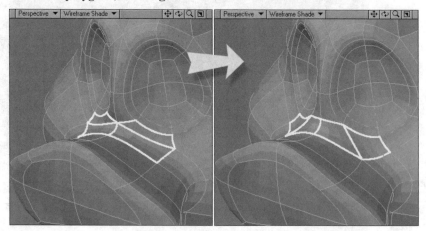

Figure 5.3-15. Spin Quads is a very useful tool for adjusting polygon flow.

8. The top of the nose isn't quite the right shape, so select the three points on either side of the top of the nose and move them up.

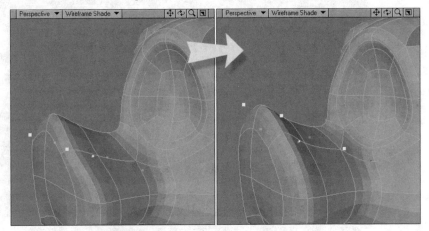

Figure 5.3-16. Refining the shape.

9. To create some extra definition, select the first row of points of the nose and **Multiply ➤ Extend ➤ Edge Bevel** about **7.5 mm**.

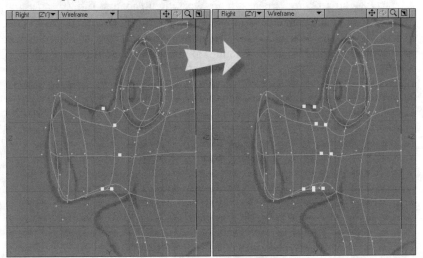

Figure 5.3-17. Edge Bevel is handy for creating a band of polygons around a row of points.

10. We need to create some extra geometry around the head, so **Unhide All** (\), then select two adjoining polygons in the horizontal band just above the middle of the nose and **Multiply ➤ Subdivide ➤ BandSaw Pro**. In the Numeric Options for BandSaw Pro, select **Enable Divide** and set the value to **65%**. Press **Enter** to confirm.

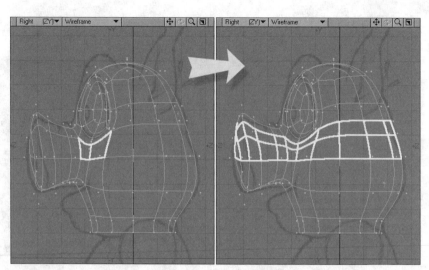

Figure 5.3-18. BandSaw is handy for creating one or more rows of points within a band of polygons.

11. Some additional bands under the nose will help the definition. Turn off Symmetry for this as we are working up against the X=0 symmetry boundary. Select the polygons shown in Figure 5.3-19 and select **Multiply▹Subdivide▹Cut**. Make sure all the options are checked and leave the rest at the default values. Click **Continue** to confirm.

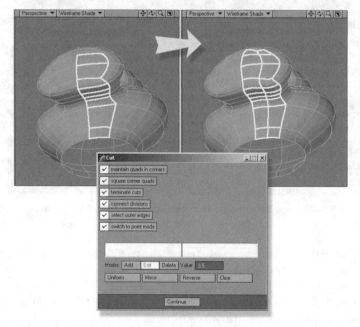

Figure 5.3-19. Cut works like BandSaw but can cut an arbitrary selection, even around corners.

> **Note:** The Cut tool can have problems with symmetry if the polygon selection crosses the X axis. If your selection crosses the X axis, it's safest to turn off Symmetry before using Cut.

12. Select the lower point of the triangle at the top of the cut and **Weld** it to the point next to it. This will have created a two-point polygon, so select that and **Delete** it.

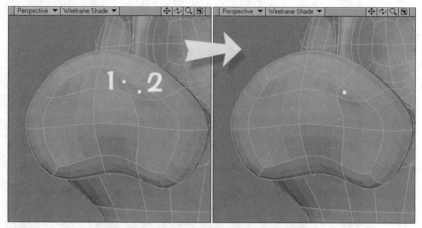

Figure 5.3-20. Welding points to maintain the flow.

13. Now select the polygons shown in Figure 5.3-21 and **Cut**. Uncheck **square corner quads** and click **Continue**. These last two cuts have the

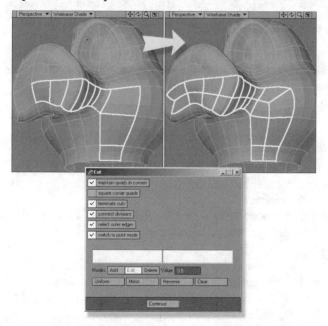

Figure 5.3-21. Turning off square corner quads relaxes the corner of the cut.

added benefit of creating a few more bands for the mouth area, which will come in handy during the next stage.

14. Because we turned off Symmetry we need to mirror what we've just done. Because it covers a fair sized area it's easiest to select the entire right side and delete it. Select the points along the mirror axis and **Set Value (v)** to **X=0**, then **Mirror (Shift+v)** on the X axis.

15. Tweak all the points of the nose to get them close to the backdrops and so the rows of points follow the contours of the nose. Check the Perspective view regularly to make sure it looks good from all angles.

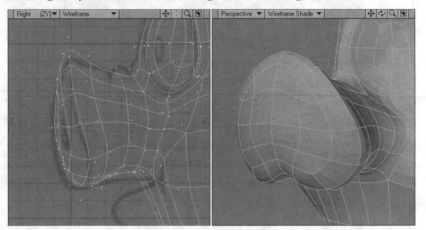

Figure 5.3-22. Cut and BandSaw work on the polygon cage rather than the subpatches, so the divisions occur between the points of the cage instead of maintaining the subpatch curvature. When working with subpatches you usually need to adjust the geometry after a Cut or BandSaw.

We'll come back to the nose to add some more detail later. For now let's move on to the mouth.

Mouth

The mouth area always needs to be created with care. You need to make sure it's detailed enough to enable the expressions and other morph shapes, and that the surrounding area has enough detail and flows well enough to enable a good deal of stretching for the morphs. You can easily paint yourself into a corner later on by not allowing for the morph deformation in your geometry.

The first thing we need to do is create some extra geometry for the mouth area. As you create the geometry, keep an eye on the polygon flow and adjust the polygons where necessary.

1. Select the bottom row of five points at the base of the nose and move them down and forward. **Rotate** them a little in line with the angle of the polygon lines leading to the points. These points will be part of the lower lip and the polygons above will become the mouth.

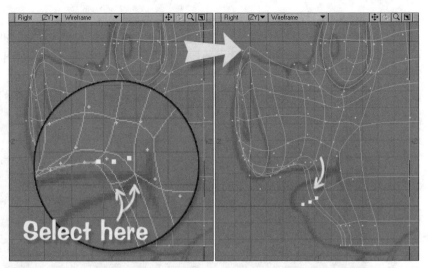

Figure 5.3-23. The decision as to where to create the mouth can be important. You need enough bands above and below the mouth to support the detail as well as the stretching from morphs.

2. Select the polygons shown in Figure 5.3-24 and **Cut**. We want two new bands, so we need to add another division. In the Cut options panel, change Modes to **Add** and click in an open area of the white display. Change Modes back to **Edit** and move the two divisions, creating three roughly equal segments. Click **Continue** to confirm the cut.

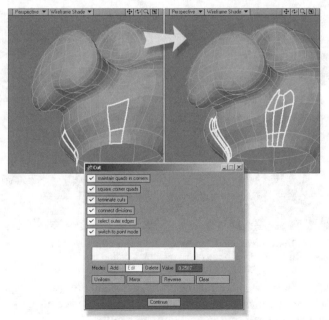

Figure 5.3-24. Cutting three segments creates a quad at the end of the cut instead of a triangle.

3. Analyzing the new geometry, I can see we need to adjust the polygons at the top-left of the cut, as we've got an edge crossing where we want the top of the mouth to be. Select the two polygons shown in Figure 5.3-25 and **Spin Quads** twice to adjust the polygon flow.

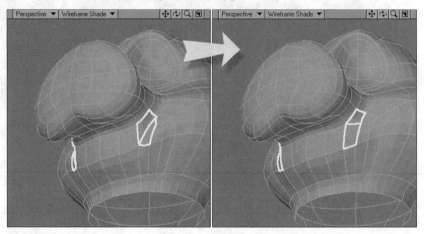

Figure 5.3-25. Spin Quads gets us out of trouble again.

4. I think we have enough vertical bands, so now we can create some horizontal bands. Select two polygons in the band below the nose and **BandSaw Pro** (leaving it at its defaults). Select two polygons in the next band down and **BandSaw Pro** again.

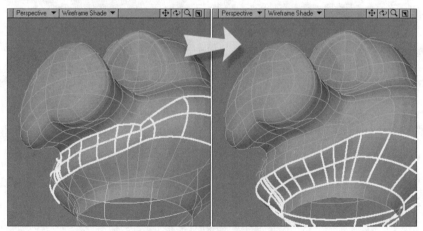

Figure 5.3-26. The vertical bands exist more to support the stretching of the mouth than for definition. The horizontal bands exist mainly to define the lips.

That's all the geometry we need for the mouth area, and there's a nice polygon flow from the nose to the mouth to the cheeks. The polygons shown in Figure 5.3-27 are the ones we will shift in to create the mouth.

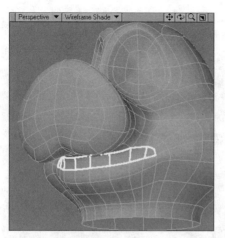

Figure 5.3-27. We'll shift these polygons in to create the lips and inner mouth.

Before we do that though, the points of the geometry we just created need some adjusting. Make sure you keep a close eye on the illustrations for the next few steps.

5. From the Back view select the points on the side of the cheek. Adjust them from the Back and Right views to fit the backdrops.

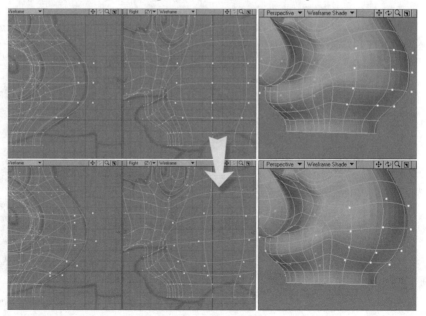

Figure 5.3-28. Adjusting the points after BandSaw.

6. Select the points of the mouth and chin and adjust them from the Right view, molding the area to create the definition of the lower lip, chin, and cheeks. See Figure 5.3-29.

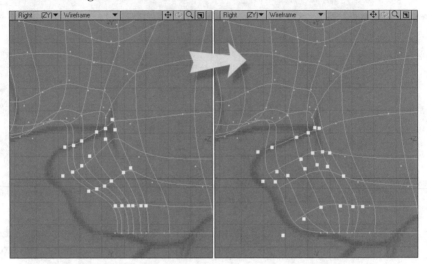

Figure 5.3-29. Starting to define the mouth area.

7. Now we want to adjust those points from the front, but it's a little difficult to see what we're doing, so change to **Polygons** mode, select the same polygons we hid before, at the back of the head, and **Hide** (-) them again.

8. Go back to **Points** mode and, with the points still selected from step 6, adjust them horizontally from the Back view to match Figure 5.3-30.

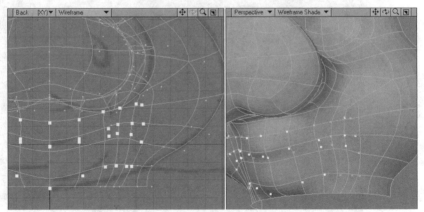

Figure 5.3-30. Creating neat polygon flow while sculpting the area.

9. Select the four points defining the cheek and move them in to match Figure 5.3-31.

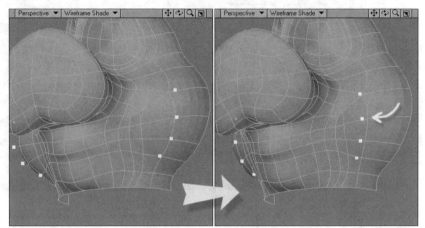

Figure 5.3-31. We want these points closer to the mouth so they have room to move out when the mouth stretches.

10. Now select the points at the top of the mouth (base of the nose) and adjust them to match Figure 5.3-32.

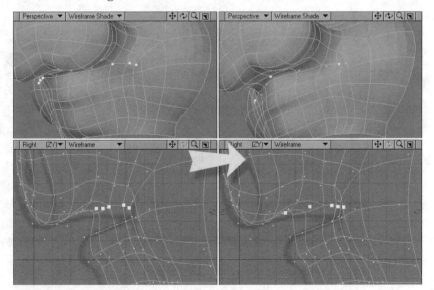

Figure 5.3-32. Shaping the top lip.

11. Select the points at the corner of the mouth. **Stretch** them down vertically and move them back. This creates the slight dimple between the corner of the mouth and the cheek.

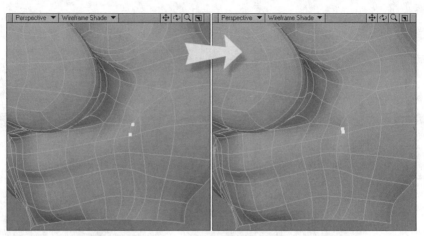

Figure 5.3-33. Creating the dimple.

Now that the whole area is taking shape we can shift the mouth polygons in to create the lips.

12. Select the polygons of the mouth shown in Figure 5.3-34. **Extender Plus** and, from the Right view, move the polygons back a little, then **Stretch** the polygons horizontally about **70%**, centered on the corner of the mouth.

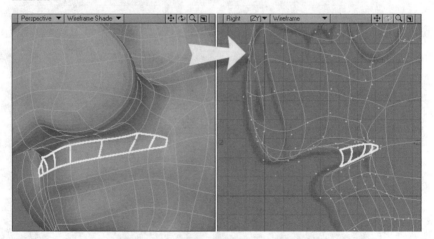

Figure 5.3-34. We typically want the lips to be thicker at the front than at the sides. Stretching the shifted polygons gives us this result.

13. While we've still got the polygons selected, it's a good time to surface these differently than the rest of the head so we can quickly and easily select them again when it comes time to detail the inner mouth. **Change Surface (q)**, type in **Mouth**, and use the other settings from Figure 5.3-35.

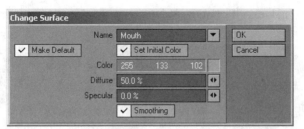

Figure 5.3-35. Mouth surface.

14. Since we're already surfacing we might as well assign a surface to the rest of the head. Remember that the back of the head is hidden, and before surfacing it needs to be visible. **Unhide All** (\), then **Invert Selection** (**Shift+'**), **Change Surface** to **Head**, and use the other settings from Figure 5.3-36.

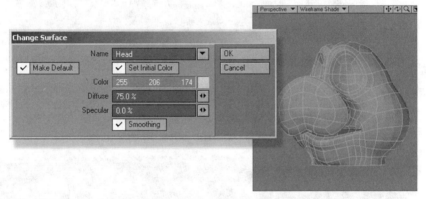

Figure 5.3-36. Head surface.

Well, that's the completed mouth area. The head is starting to take shape now.

Ears

The ears are another distinguishing feature of Hamish, although they're similar in construction to many other animal ears. Ears are often tricky to create. You usually need to do a lot of the work from the Perspective view, as when you have the folds and indents modeled it can be difficult or impossible to tell what's what from the orthographic views.

1. Start by preparing the area of the head from which the ears are shifted. There isn't enough geometry there at the moment, so a new band needs to be created. Turn off **Symmetry**, select the polygons shown in Figure 5.3-37 and **Cut**. Since we changed the Cut settings last time it was used, they need to be changed back to the default. In the Cut options panel, change Modes to **Delete** and click one of the divisions. Change Modes

back to **Edit** and enter **0.5** in the Value box. Click **Continue** to confirm the cut.

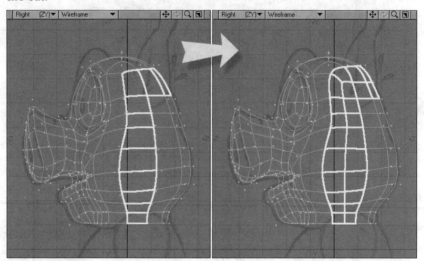

Figure 5.3-37. Cutting this band gives us enough polygons to work with for the ears.

2. Now we need to clean up the polygon flow. Select the polygons shown in Figure 5.3-38. Turn off **Symmetry** and change to **Points** mode. **Weld** the points shown in Figure 5.3-38 on each side of the model. Change back to Polygons mode and **Delete** the selected polygons.

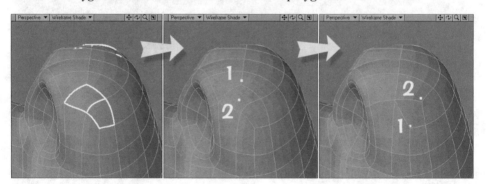

Figure 5.3-38. Adjusting polygon flow.

3. Turn on **Symmetry**, select the polygons shown in Figure 5.3-39A, and **Drag** the corners of the selected polygons from the Perspective view. Before you move each point, adjust the view so the polygons that surround the point are facing the viewport. **Drag** the corners in and adjust the sides to create a more rounded shape, matching Figure 5.3-39B.

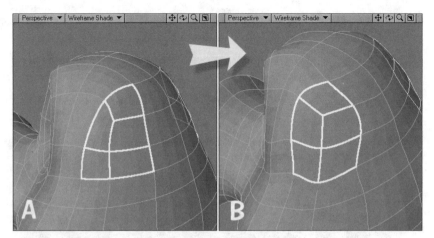

Figure 5.3-39. Creating the right shape for the base of the ears.

4. With the polygons still selected, **Super Shift** using the settings shown in Figure 5.3-40. Adjust the points of the selected polygons from the Perspective view, making sure they're even and make a nice oval.

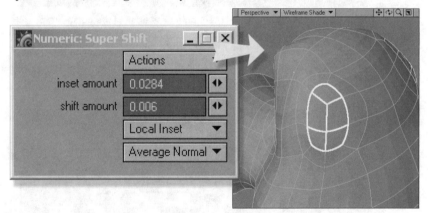

Figure 5.3-40. Shift the polygons, then tweak.

5. You may notice that as the points were adjusted in the previous step that the polygons on the other side didn't follow. This is because shifting sometimes doesn't work too well with Symmetry. Since we're doing some work on the ear that won't work with Symmetry anyway, let's delete the right side of the head. We can mirror once we've finished the ear. Turn off **Symmetry**, select the polygons of the right side, and **Delete** them.

6. Select the polygons for the ear again and **Super Shift**, using the settings shown in Figure 5.3-41. **Move** and **Rotate** the polygons to fit the backdrops.

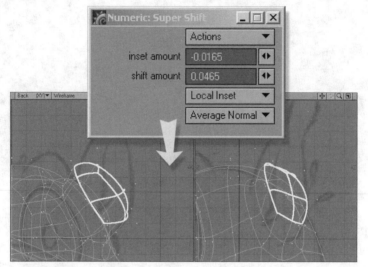

Figure 5.3-41. Creating the right shape for the base of the ears.

7. **Super Shift** again, using the settings shown in Figure 5.3-42. **Move** and **Rotate** the polygons to fit the backdrops.

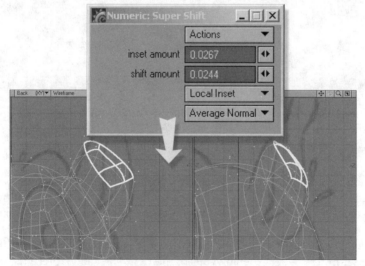

Figure 5.3-42. When adjusting the position of the shifted polygons, make sure you check that it looks okay in all the viewports.

8. Orient the Perspective view so you're looking at the bottom of the ear and **Rotate** the polygons so they're perpendicular to the direction of the ear. Finally, orient the Perspective view to face the selected polygons and adjust the points to maintain a nice, rounded oval shape.

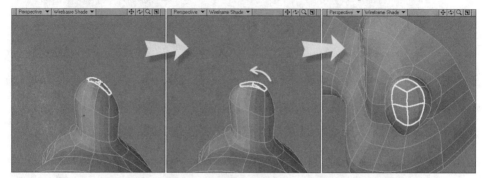

Figure 5.3-43. It's a good idea to continually check the shape as you shift, unless you shift in place, in which case the shifted polygons remain the same shape.

9. **Super Shift** again, using the settings shown in Figure 5.3-44. **Move** and **Rotate** the polygons to fit the backdrops.

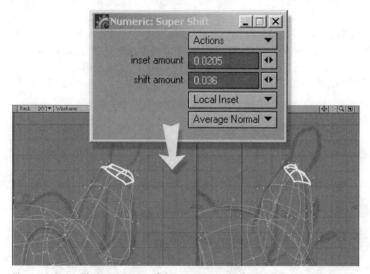

Figure 5.3-44. The main part of the ear is nearly done.

10. Sometimes working in SubPatch mode can be deceiving. The shape of the subpatches doesn't always indicate the shape of the cage. We need the points to be rounded for shifting the tip of the ear, so change to **Points** mode, then adjust the points at the top of the ear so that they (rather than the subpatches) create a nice, round circle shape. Orient the Perspective view so you're looking at the points side on and they're horizontal. From

the Perspective view, **Stretch** vertically to **0%**. Readjust their position to fit the backdrops if you need to.

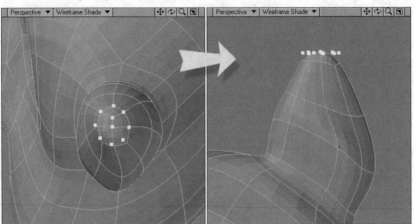

Figure 5.3-45. Adjusting the points instead of the subpatches.

11. To create the bulb at the tip of the ear, change back to **Polygons** mode and **Super Shift** in place. Move the polygons to the top of the ear in the backdrops.

12. Select two polygons of the band that make up the bulb and **BandSaw Pro**. Change Operation to **Add** and click in an open space in the segment display. Change Operation back to **Edit** and set the values for the two divisions to **45%** and **90%**.

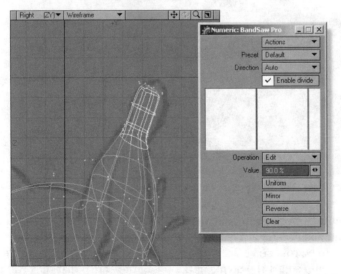

Figure 5.3-46. We've set a division very close to the lower row of points to define the bottom of the bulb.

13. Select the points in the middle row and, with the Perspective view looking down on them, **Stretch** horizontally and vertically to about **160%**.

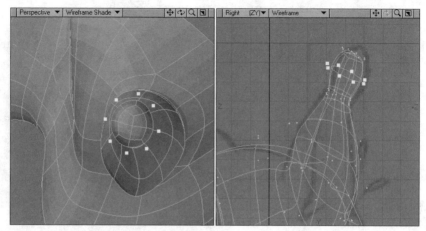

Figure 5.3-47. Creating a bulge.

14. The bulb is looking pretty good now, but let's clean up the very top. Select the two polygons shown in Figure 5.3-48 and **Spin Quads**.

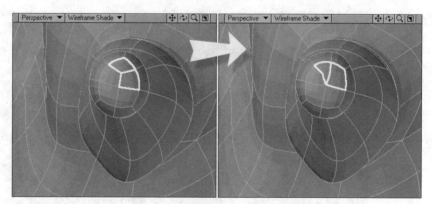

Figure 5.3-48. Cleaning up the tip of the ear.

15. Select the point in between the polygons shown in Figure 5.3-49 and **Delete**. Select the two triangles and **Merge Polygons**. Finally, move the middle point up to round off the top of the bulb.

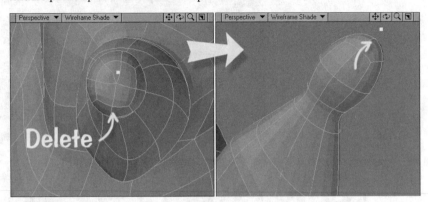

Figure 5.3-49. Cleaning up the tip of the ear.

16. Now with the geometry in place, adjust the positions of the points to neaten up the polygon flow, creating a slightly flatter front and nice rounded back for the ear.

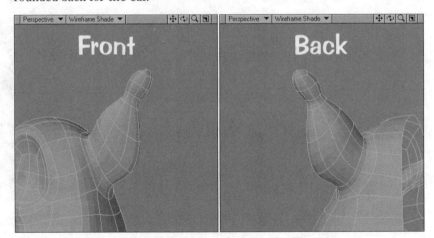

Figure 5.3-50. Use your best judgment to refine the shape of the ear. Don't worry about being too precise, as we can refine it more after we add additional detail.

17. **Deselect All** and **Mirror** so we have a full head again.

Adjusting the Shapes

Now that all the basic shapes are in place, it's time to review the overall head shape. Often the front and side views won't exactly match the original concept, or you might find that the shapes and proportions indicated by the backdrops aren't quite working in three dimensions. At this stage, while the geometry is fairly simple, we can more easily adjust the overall shapes than after we've detailed each area. Make sure Symmetry is on for these steps.

1. Check the Perspective view for areas that don't look quite smooth. Select rows of points in those areas and check all the views for points that don't follow a smooth line. Adjust the points appropriately, making sure the shapes still conform to the backdrops. Where you can while maintaining the integrity of the detail, adjust the points so they're fairly evenly spaced.

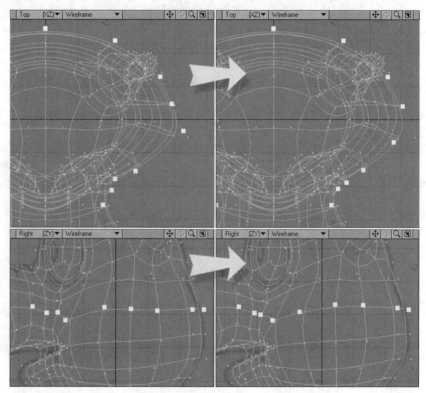

Figure 5.3-51. Aligning and smoothing points.

2. Check the model against the original concept images, adjusting for where the backdrops might not be quite accurate. Hamish's ears are a good example of this, being quite a bit larger in the backdrops than in the original concept.

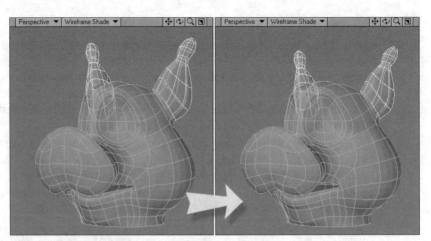

Figure 5.3-52. Adjust to the concept images.

3. Finally, adjust the model based on your own judgment, looking at it from all angles and tweaking the shapes. One adjustment I've made is to move the eye sockets slightly farther apart and rotate them to face the front a little more. Another is altering the back of the head, moving the skull back and the jowls forward a little.

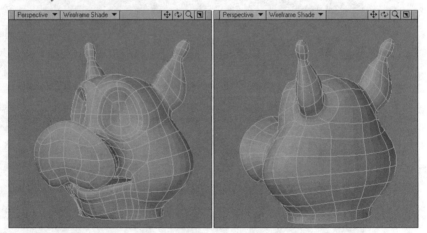

Figure 5.3-53. Adjusted model.

Creating the Details

Now that you're happy with the overall shapes and proportions, it's time to work in the details. Since the geometry can become quite complex during this stage, it's often easiest to make selections and tweak positions in the Perspective view, as it can be difficult to see what you're doing in the orthographic views.

Ears

Since we were last working on the ears we'll detail them first. Cartoon ears are usually a lot simpler than real ears, but it can still be tricky to achieve the right shapes without making a mess of the geometry. As you create detail, try to keep the polygon flow nice and neat.

1. Select the front three points of the ear shown in Figure 5.3-54, **Edge Bevel**, then **Drag** the points to create the right shape for the opening of the ear.

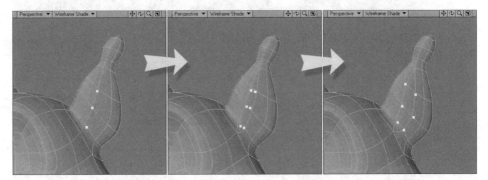

Figure 5.3-54. Creating the shape for the opening.

2. Select the beveled polygons and **Super Shift** in place.

3. Deselect the top triangle, then **Rotate** the selection, centered on the top point of the deselected triangle, from the Right and Back views to match Figure 5.3-55. **Merge Points** to join the points at the top of the opening.

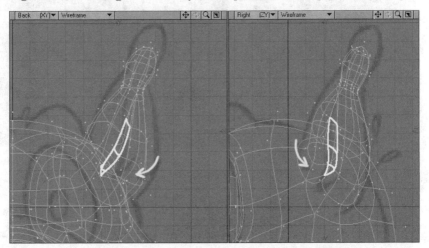

Figure 5.3-55. Deselecting the top triangle before adjusting the position leaves the top point in place so we can stay in Symmetry mode, merging instead of welding.

4. Select the two middle points of the outside edge and move them back, left, and a little down so they're in line with the points on either side.

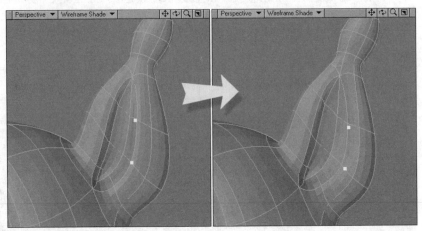

Figure 5.3-56. Shaping the outer edge.

5. Select the left three points on the inside of the opening and move them back so they're roughly in line with each other, then **Edge Bevel**.

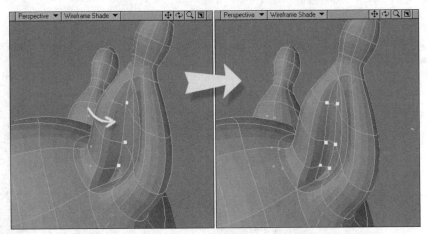

Figure 5.3-57. Defining the inner opening also makes it easy to keep it all quads.

. . . . · Modeling

Hamish

6. Select the bottom two triangles and two adjacent triangles at the top and **Merge Polygons**, then select the two remaining triangles at the top and **Merge Polygons** again.

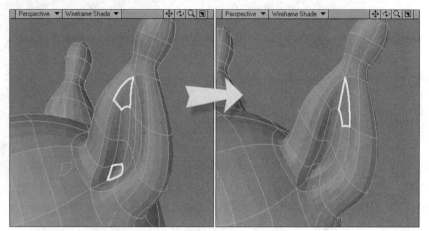

Figure 5.3-58. Converting triangles to quads.

I think that's about all the geometry we need, so now we can adjust the shapes.

7. Select the polygon shown in Figure 5.3-59 and move it forward and right. Select the points of the same polygon and, in the Back view, move the back two points in line with the front two. Deselect the bottom two points, then move the selected points back, in line with the points above and below.

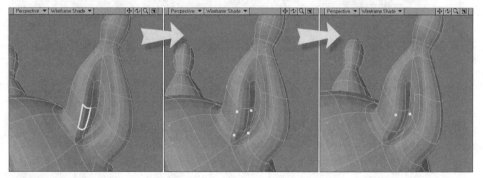

Figure 5.3-59. Although shown here in Perspective view, it's easiest to do this positioning in the orthographic views.

8. Adjust the outer opening so it's flatter and thinner.

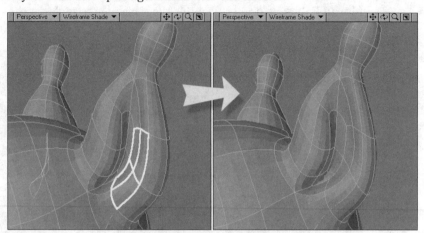

Figure 5.3-60. Adjust the points of the polygons shown here to achieve a nice shape.

9. Follow the same steps we did before when adjusting the shapes. Look at the ear from all angles, adjusting the points where necessary to create the right shapes, follow the concept images, and maintain even polygon flow.

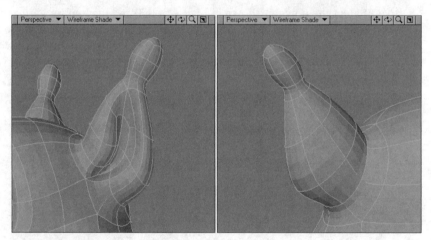

Figure 5.3-61. Final ear.

Nostrils

There are a few details we need for the nose. Obviously we need to create the nostrils, but we also need to create some wrinkles at the base and adjust the bottom points.

1. Select the polygons at the back of the head and **Hide** (-) them so we can more easily see what we're doing.

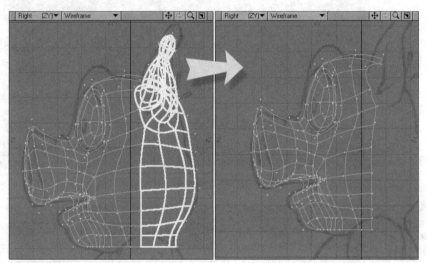

Figure 5.3-62. Hide the back of the head.

2. Starting with the nostrils, select the two polygons around the nostril in the backdrop. From the Back view, **Drag** the corners, centering them over the nostril area.

3. Add the triangle above to the selection, **Super Shift** in place, then **Drag** the corners so the points lie just outside the edges of the nostril.

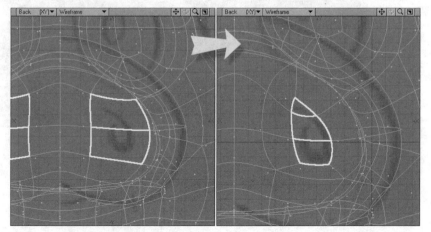

Figure 5.3-63. Adjust, shift, adjust again.

4. **Super Shift** in place again, **Drag** the corners just inside the line of the nostril, then move the polygons back a little.

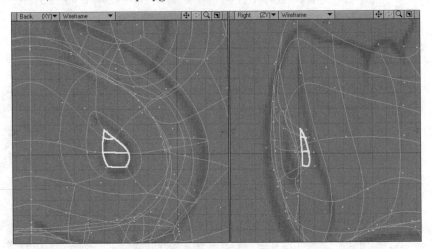

Figure 5.3-64. Creating the inner edge of the nostril.

5. Deselect the two quads and delete the selected triangle.
6. Turn off **Symmetry** and **Weld** the three open points on the left side. Do the same for the right side, then turn **Symmetry** back on.
7. Select the two triangles above the weld and **Merge Polygons**.

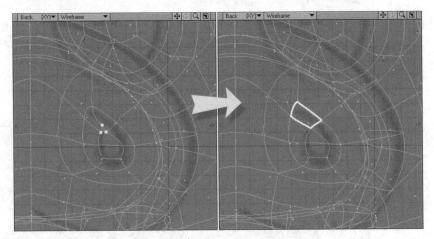

Figure 5.3-65. Cleaning up the top edge.

8. Select the inner two polygons and **Super Shift** in place, then position and scale to match Figure 5.3-66.

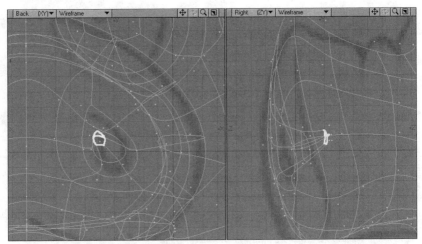

Figure 5.3-66. Creating the nostril cavity.

9. Select the two polygons of the inside edge and move them back a little, creating a nice flow around the nostril and indenting the top.

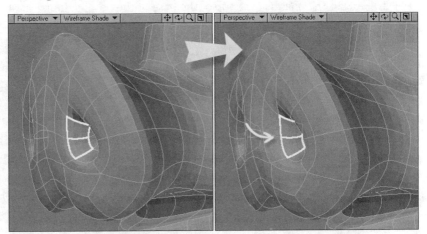

Figure 5.3-67. Shaping the nostril opening.

10. Now that all the geometry is in place for the nostrils, adjust the points at the front of the nose.

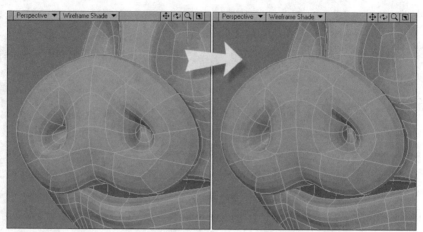

Figure 5.3-68. Adjusting the shapes.

Nose Wrinkles

The next step is to create the wrinkles or creases at the base of the nose.

1. Adjust the points at the top of the base of the nose, defining the lines we want the creases to follow.

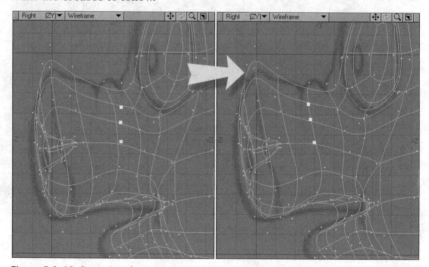

Figure 5.3-69. Preparing the geometry.

2. Select the top five points of the front row and **Edge Bevel**.

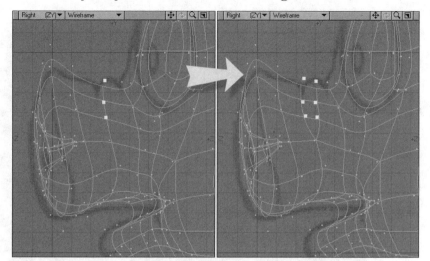

Figure 5.3-70. Creating the geometry for the outer edges of the crease.

3. Select the four quads the bevel made and **Cut** with default settings.

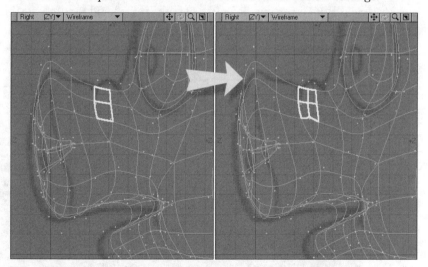

Figure 5.3-71. Creating the geometry for the inner edge of the crease.

4. Select the top five points of the back row and **Edge Bevel**. Select the four quads of the bevel and **Cut**.

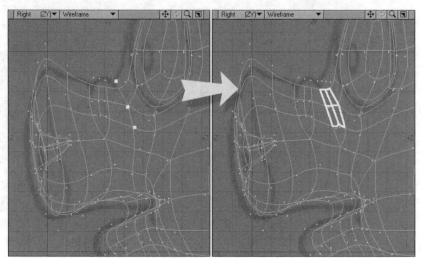

Figure 5.3-72. Creating the geometry for the back crease.

5. Select the three middle points of both creases and **Stretch** vertically to about **85%**.

6. Select the points on the outside of the creases and move up and a touch back.

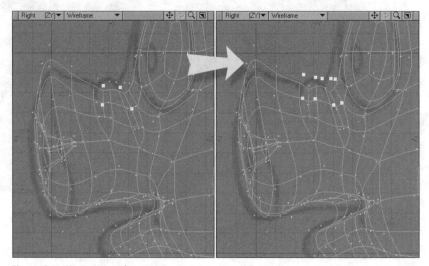

Figure 5.3-73. Forming the creases.

7. Adjust the points around the crease area.

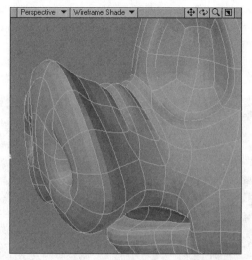

Figure 5.3-74. Creases after a bit of adjusting.

The last thing to do for the nose is to adjust the points at the bottom, making the polygons flow with the curvature of the mouth and the nose.

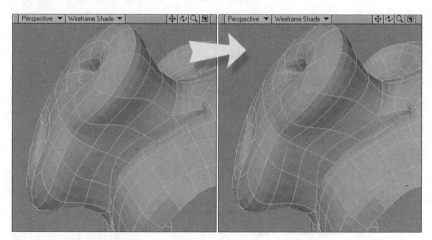

Figure 5.3-75. Adjusting the underside of the nose.

Chapter 5 ·

Part III

Eyes and Eyelids

We use a special technique for creating cartoon eyes that involves making a template for the eyeball. The template eyeball is used as reference for creating the eyelids and morphs. The final eyeballs are created a bit later.

1. Select a new layer and place the main layer in the background. Create a ball using the settings in Figure 5.3-76.

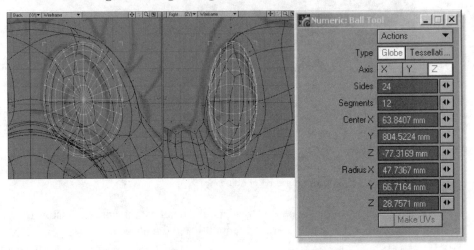

Figure 5.3-76. Creating the eyeball template.

2. **Change Surface** to **Eye_White** using the settings in Figure 5.3-77.

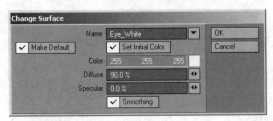

Figure 5.3-77. Eye surface.

3. Select the ball, then **Shift+click** to add the main layer to the foreground. Rotate the ball to fit just inside the eye socket. If you need to, you can scale the ball so it fits better.

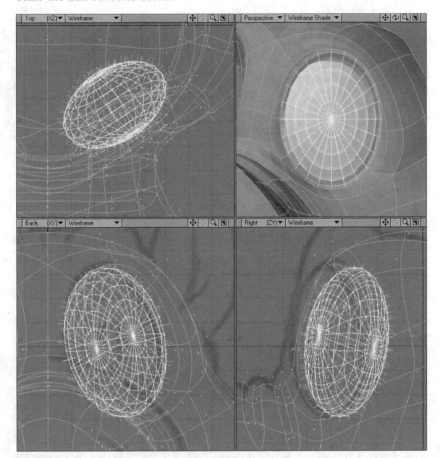

Figure 5.3-78. Rotate the eyeball from all views to fit it in the socket.

4. **Shift+click** the main layer again to turn it off and **Mirror** the eyeball.

5.   Place the main layer in the foreground and the eyeball layer in the background. Select the inside row of points of the eyelid band and, with the Perspective view facing the eye, move the points in to the edge of the eyeball.

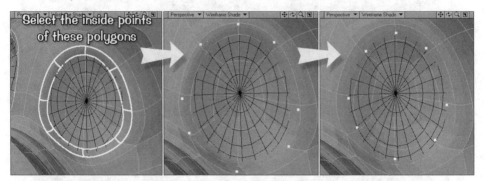

Figure 5.3-79. Moving in the Perspective view moves the geometry along the axis defined by the orientation of the viewport.

6.   Select the polygons of the eyelid band counterclockwise and **BandSaw Pro.** You should still have two divisions set, so change the values of the divisions to **25%** and **50%**.

7.   Adjust the points of the eyelids so the middle edge lies just outside the intersection of the eyeball, then select the middle band and, from the Perspective view, **Stretch** horizontally and vertically **97%**.

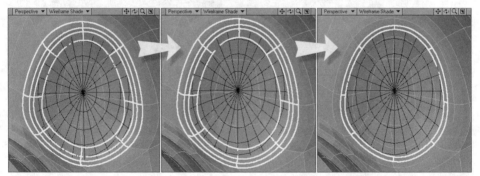

Figure 5.3-80. You can determine the final eye shape at this stage by adjusting the eyelid geometry.

8.   Because BandSaw Pro doesn't respect symmetry, **Delete** the polygons on the right side and **Mirror** the left eye area across.

That's the eyelid geometry done. We'll do more with the eyelids when we create the morphs.

Eyebrows

Hamish doesn't have hairy eyebrows, but he does have an eyebrow ridge.

1. Since we're working on the top of the head, **Unhide All** (\) to unhide the back of the head.

2. We need to do some cutting across and along the symmetry boundary in the next few steps, so turn off **Symmetry**. Select the four middle poly-gons behind the eyes and **Cut**. In the Cut options panel, add a division and set the value of the divisions to **0.3** and **0.7**. Uncheck **Select Outer Edges** and click **Continue**.

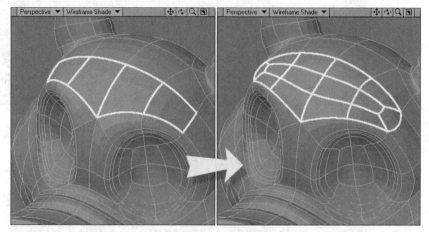

Figure 5.3-81. Creating the cross sections for the eyebrows.

3. Select the polygons shown in Figure 5.3-82 from front to back and **Cut**. In the Cut options panel, delete the division at **0.7**, check **Select Outer Edges**, and click **Continue**.

4. Select the same polygons on the other side and **Cut**. In the Cut options panel, change the division value to **0.3** and click **Continue**.

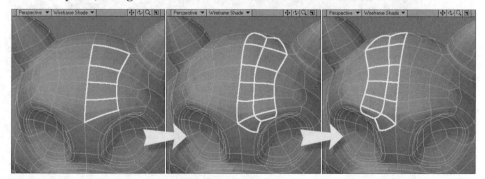

Figure 5.3-82. Creating the inside edges of the eyebrows.

5. **Weld** the two outside points of the triangle at the back of the left cut. Do the same on the right side.

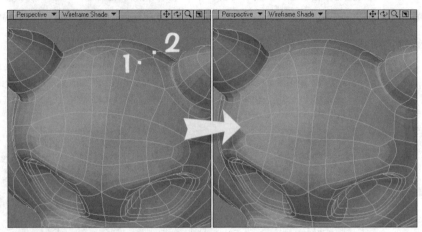

Figure 5.3-83. Cleaning up the back of the cuts.

6. **Weld** the two inside points of the triangle at the front of the left cut. Do the same on the right side.

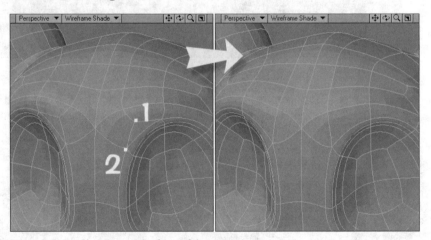

Figure 5.3-84. Cleaning up the front of the cuts.

7. Select the two polygons between the eyes shown in Figure 5.3-85 and **Cut**. In the Cut options panel, uncheck **Select Outer Edges**, change the division value to **0.5**, and click **Continue**.

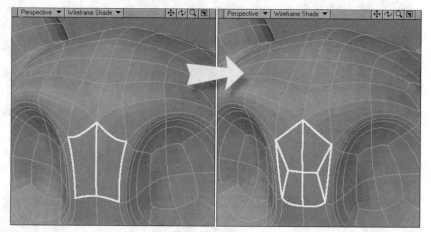

Figure 5.3-85. Cutting the geometry to create better polygon flow.

8. **Weld** the two top points of each triangle at the edge of the cut, then on each side, select the two triangles above the cut and **Merge Polygons**.

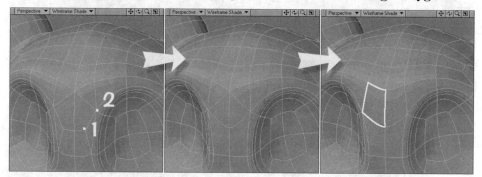

Figure 5.3-86. Cleaning up the cut.

9. Now the geometry is created. Since we've been doing lots of welding, select and delete any one- or two-point polygons.

10. With the geometry made, we can start adjusting the shapes. Turn **Symmetry** back on, select the polygon shown in Figure 5.3-87, and move it up about **14 mm**.

11. Move the two top front points of the eyebrow forward a little.

12. Select the points shown in Figure 5.3-87 and move them back.

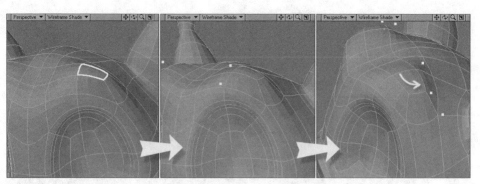

Figure 5.3-87. Forming the eyebrows.

13. Select the nine points shown in Figure 5.3-88. From the Top view, **Stretch** the points vertically to about **80%**, then move them down to match Figure 5.3-88.

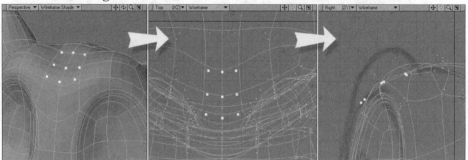

Figure 5.3-88. Adjusting the forehead.

14. Adjust the points shown in Figure 5.3-89 so they're smooth and more evenly spaced.

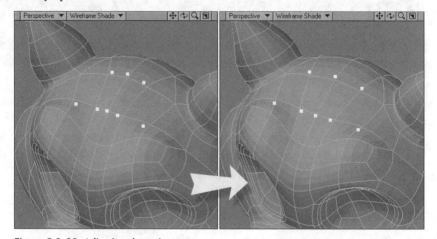

Figure 5.3-89. Adjusting the points.

Now the outside of the head is complete. Having the eyes done really makes a big difference.

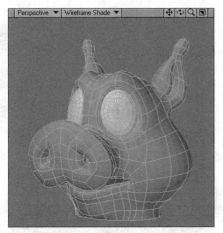

Figure 5.3-90. Hamish is starting to look like a real character now.

Adjusting the Proportions

I've noticed now that the eyes are in that the proportions are still a little different from the original concept. Before we move on to the mouth, let's adjust the proportions a little more.

1. Place the head and eyeball layers in the foreground. Select the polygons shown in Figure 5.3-91 and move down a bit. Deselect the bottom band and move down again.

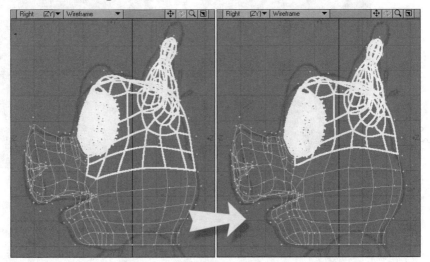

Figure 5.3-91. Make sure you include the eyeballs in the selection.

2. Select the front of the nose and from the Back view, **Stretch** horizontally to about **110%**.

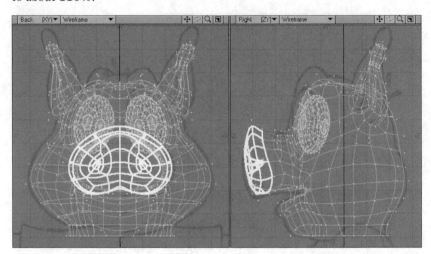

Figure 5.3-92. Resizing the nose.

3. Select the bottom band of polygons and move up a little.
4. Select the four polygons on the side of the cheeks and from the Back view, **Stretch** in a bit horizontally.

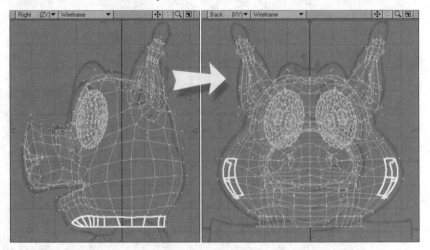

Figure 5.3-93. Adjusting the cheeks.

5. **Scale** the entire head **110%** and reposition it as close to the backdrops as possible.

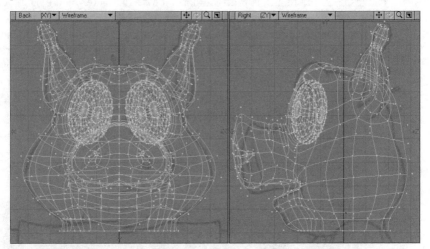

Figure 5.3-94. Scale to fit backdrops. After all those adjustments it still fits the backdrops pretty well; maybe they weren't so bad after all.

6. Finally, adjust the points, fixing any areas that might have become distorted during the last few steps and tweaking the results of the proportion adjustment. Pay particular attention to the area between the eyes and the nose.

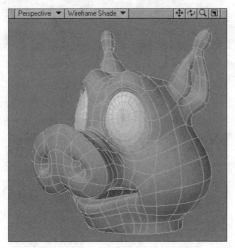

Figure 5.3-95. Shape adjustments.

Inner Mouth

The inside of the mouth is pretty important for a character model. Don't cut too many corners on the inner mouth thinking you won't see it much, because the teeth and tongue are featured extensively in expressions and lip sync, and you can see right to the back every time the character opens his mouth. There are, of course, varying degrees of complexity for the inner mouth geometry, from very simple as we created for Morfi to much more complex than we can cover here. Hamish's mouth is somewhere in between the two extremes, making it a good starting point for your average cartoon character.

1. Select the polygons with the Mouth surface from the Polygon Statistics panel.

2. **Super Shift** in place, then from the Right view **Drag** the points to match Figure 5.3-96, creating the inside of the lips.

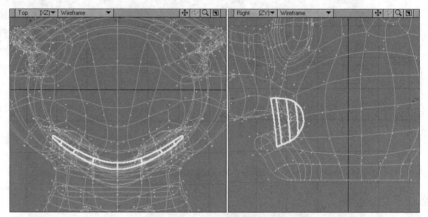

Figure 5.3-96. Make sure the top and bottom sets of points are evenly spaced, creating a nice curve from the Top view.

3. Now it's getting a bit difficult to see what we're doing with the head geometry in the way. As you gain experience you won't need to do this, but for now to make it easier to see, **Expand Selection (Shift +])** to select all the mouth polygons, then **Cut** the selected polygons and **Paste** them into a new layer. Place the main head layer in the background so you still have that as a reference.

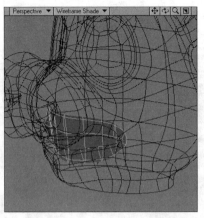

Figure 5.3-97.
Place the head in the
background instead of just
hiding it so we can still see
the head while we work
without it getting in the
way. Being able to see the
head while you make the
mouth is important to
make sure you get the
mouth geometry in the
right place.

4. Select the back eight polygons of the mouth, **Super Shift** in place, then
   move back a bit. From the Right view **Stretch** vertically from the top of
   the selection, about **85%**, and from the Top view **Stretch** vertically to
   about **70%**.

5. **Super Shift** again, move back, then from the Top view **Stretch** vertically
   to **0%**. **Drag** the points so the top and bottom points are aligned from the
   Top view. **Drag** the side points forward a little to match Figure 5.3-98.

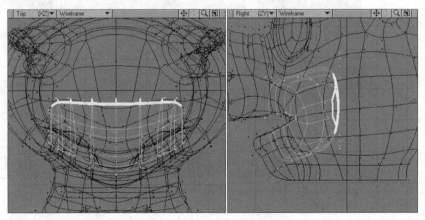

Figure 5.3-98. The first shift creates the back of the gum area, and the second starts to
define the mouth.

6. Deselect the two outer polygons on each side and **Super Shift** in place. Move the polygons back and drag the points to match Figure 5.3-99.

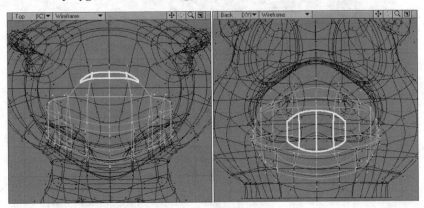

Figure 5.3-99. Creating the entrance to the throat.

7. Deselect the outside polygon on each side and **Super Shift** in place. Move and adjust to match Figure 5.3-100.

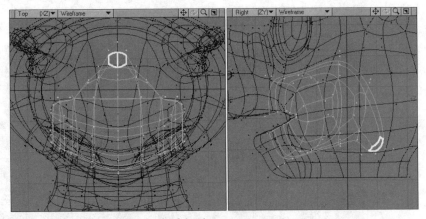

Figure 5.3-100. Creating the back of the throat.

Gums

These gums are created the same way we created the gums and teeth for Morfi, although we'll create individual teeth for Hamish.

The gum position is fairly important. You need to visualize how the lips open to determine where the gums and teeth are positioned. For Hamish they need to be placed a little higher than you might expect, as the snout is a bit deceiving. You need to imagine the top lip and nose being more human like, and position the gums and teeth about equal distance from the top lip.

1. Select the polygons shown in Figure 5.3-101A and, from the Top view, **Drag** the points to match Figure 5.3-101B, giving us more of a curve for the base of the gums.

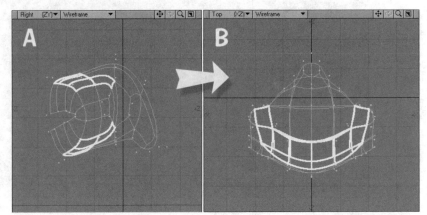

Figure 5.3-101. Preparing the base of the gums.

2. **Super Shift** in place, then from the Right view, **Stretch** the polygons vertically to **0%**. **Move** the top and bottom sets of polygons to match Figure 5.3-102.

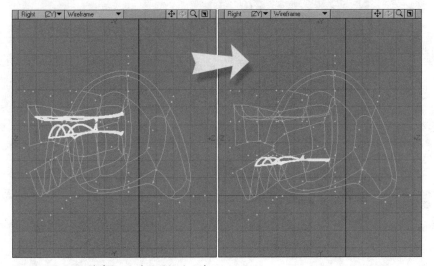

Figure 5.3-102. Shifting and positioning the gums.

3. Select the leading edge of the top and bottom gums again and adjust the points to match Figure 5.3-103.

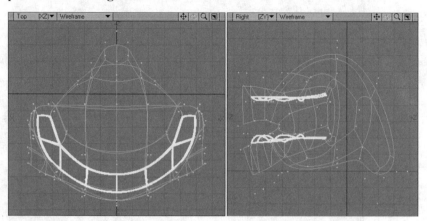

Figure 5.3-103. Adjusting the gums.

4. Select the top set of points between the lips and gums and **Move** them up, completing the gums.

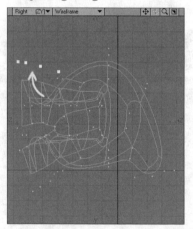

Figure 5.3-104. Giving the top gums more depth.

Tongue

The tongue geometry is pretty basic for most characters. If you're creating a snake or a frog you might want to add more bands to allow the tongue to stretch and bend more, but in general you don't need it to be too complex.

1. Select the two bottom polygons at the back of the mouth and adjust them to match Figure 5.3-105.

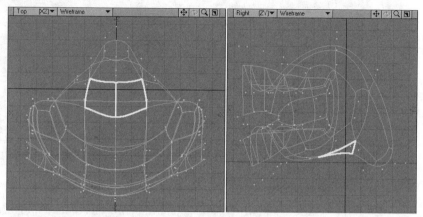

Figure 5.3-105. Preparing the base of the tongue.

2. **Super Shift** in place, then **Move** and adjust the polygons to match Figure 5.3-106.

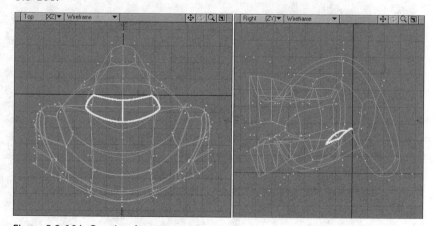

Figure 5.3-106. Creating the tongue.

3. **Super Shift** again, **Move**, and adjust the polygons to match Figure 5.3-107.

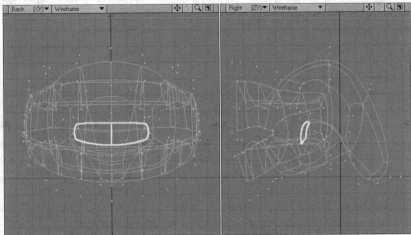

Figure 5.3-107. As you create each segment, shape the polygons to create the cross section for the tongue.

4. **Super Shift** again, **Move**, and adjust the polygons to match Figure 5.3-108, creating the tip of the tongue.

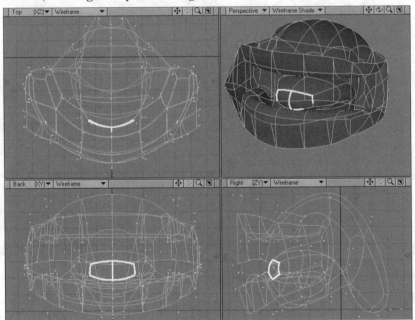

Figure 5.3-108. The tip of the tongue.

5. With the tip of the tongue selected, **Expand Selection** twice and **Move** the polygons down to the base of the mouth.

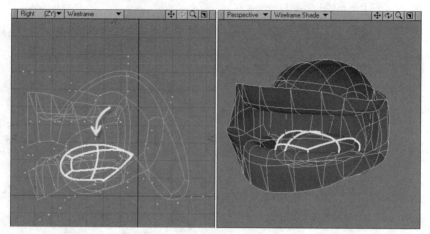

Figure 5.3-109. Adjusting the position of the tongue.

6. Now that we've created most of the inner mouth, **Cut** and **Paste** it back into the main head layer and **Merge Points.** We still want to see the mouth more easily though, so select the polygons with the Head surface and **Hide** them.

Teeth

As with the rest of the inner mouth, the teeth can range in complexity depending on your requirements. Hamish's teeth are simple but are adequate for our needs.

When creating cute or nice characters, be careful that you don't make the teeth too small, unless it's by design. Small teeth are often associated with scary or evil characters, and a character can quickly lose its appeal if it has lots of tiny teeth.

1. Select a new layer, place the main layer in the background, and turn off **Symmetry.**

2. Create a box with two Y segments. Make the box slightly thicker than the gums, starting from the top of the top gum and the bottom edge around the middle of the mouth.

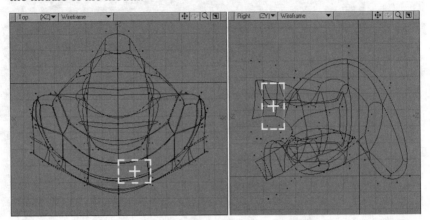

Figure 5.3-110. Our teeth are simple. If you want more detailed teeth, you can start with a more complex box or add detail in the next step.

3. Press **Tab** to convert to subpatch and adjust the points to create the shape of a front tooth.

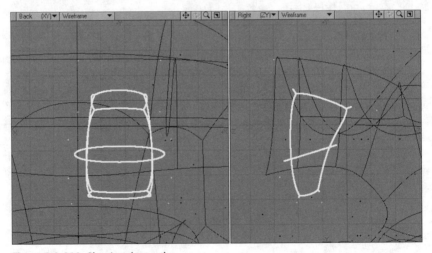

Figure 5.3-111. Shaping the tooth.

4. **Rotate** the tooth in line with the edge of the gum and **Move** it into place, checking that its position is correct by bringing the main layer into the foreground.

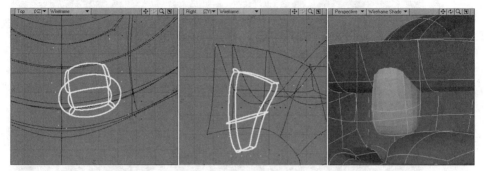

Figure 5.3-112. Adjust the tooth position with both layers in the foreground so you can see where they intersect. Instead of adding detail to the gums, the intersection between teeth and gums creates the appearance of the gums following the edge of the teeth.

5. Select the tooth, **Copy**, and **Paste**. **Move** the new tooth next to the original one and **Rotate** it in line with the gum. Adjust the points to match Figure 5.3-113.

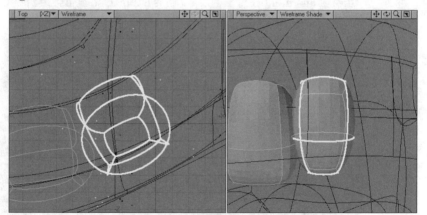

Figure 5.3-113. Adjust the shape of the second tooth to create a canine tooth. In many cartoon characters the teeth are all the same shape, but we'll create more realistically shaped teeth for Hamish so you can see how it's done.

6. **Copy** and **Paste** again, moving the new tooth next to the last one and **Rotate** it in line with the gum. Adjust the points to match Figure 5.3-114.

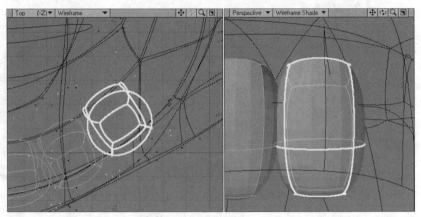

Figure 5.3-114. Position and shape the third tooth.

7. **Copy** and **Paste** again, this time moving the new tooth out a little, and **Rotate** it so it's square on the orthographic views, allowing us to do more radical adjustments on it. This tooth is a molar, so adjust the points to match Figure 5.3-115.

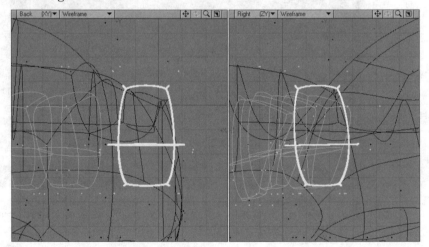

Figure 5.3-115. Shaping the molar.

8. Position the molar next to the previous tooth and **Rotate** it in line with the gums.

9. **Copy** and **Paste** the molar, then position and **Rotate** it to match Figure 5.3-116.

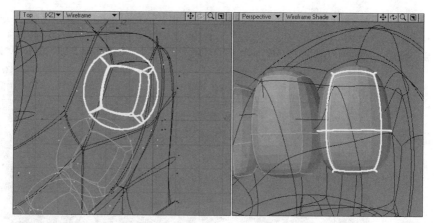

Figure 5.3-116. Positioning the molars.

10. Check the position of all the teeth with the gums in the foreground and adjust positions or points if necessary.

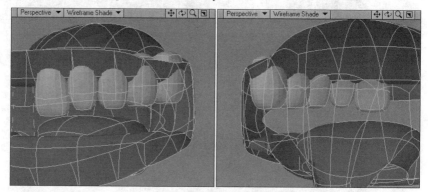

Figure 5.3-117. Make sure the intersection between teeth and gums looks right from the front and back.

11. When you're happy with the positions, place the mouth layer in the background, **Mirror**, then **Change Surface** to **Teeth**, using the other settings from Figure 5.3-118.

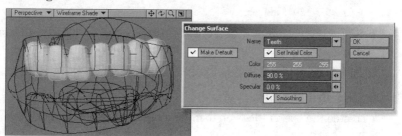

Figure 5.3-118. Surface the teeth.

12. **Mirror** the teeth again, only this time on the Y axis, placing the mirror center at the bottom of the teeth. Select the bottom row of teeth and from the Right view, **Stretch** horizontally a little from the back of the teeth.

13. Turn **Symmetry** on and select the two front teeth of the bottom row. **Move** them down a little and **Rotate** so they sit just behind the top teeth.

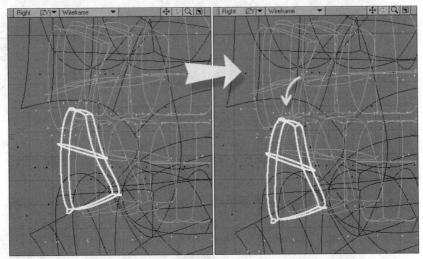

Figure 5.3-119. Mirror the teeth to create the bottom row.

14. Adjust positions and points until you're happy with all the teeth.

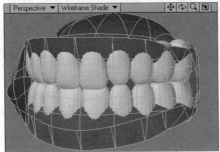

Figure 5.3-120. Final teeth.

15. Select the bottom row of teeth and **Change Surface** to **Teeth_Lower**, using the same settings as last time.

16. **Cut** and **Paste** the teeth into the main layer and **Unhide all**.

Closing the Mouth

We created the lips a little open to make it easier to create the mouth. Now that the mouth is complete, the lips need to be closed. This is an important step to prepare for creating the mouth morphs.

1. Adjust the bottom lip so it sits up against the bottom teeth.

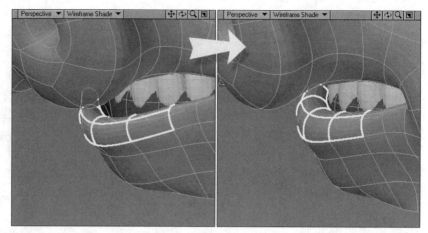

Figure 5.3-121. As I moved the lip closer I've also thickened it a little toward the middle.

2. Select the polygons around the corner of the mouth and **Move** them in, adjusting the shape of the polygons so the lips are smooth.

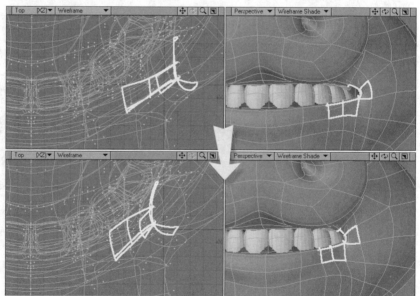

Figure 5.3-122. Move the polygons in, then adjust to create a nice shape and thickness for the lips.

3. Select the bottom lip, **Rotate** it so it's flat, then **Move** it up to the top lip, closing the mouth.

4. Adjust the points around the mouth and chin to fit the new mouth position.

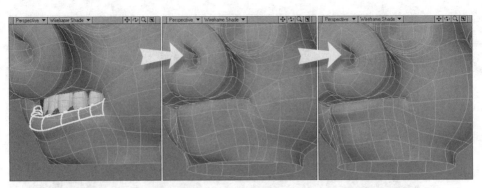

Figure 5.3-123. Closing the mouth.

Final Details

You may have noticed the bottom row of points doesn't look too good. We'll adjust those now to continue the head shape and start forming the neck.

1. Select the bottom row of points and stretch and adjust them to match Figure 5.3-124.

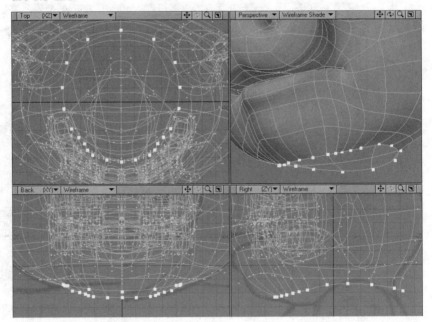

Figure 5.3-124. Adjusting the start of the neck.

2. Now we have more detail in the chin than we want for the body, so let's optimize. Turn off **Symmetry**, then **Weld** the three points shown in Figure 5.3-125. Select the resulting two triangles and **Merge Polygons**. Repeat for the other side.

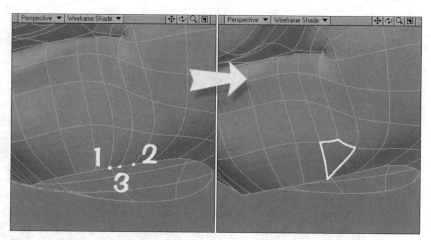

Figure 5.3-125. Refining the geometry.

We've almost finished the head now. There's just the hair and the final eyeballs to go...

Hair

As you can see from the concept, there really isn't much to the hair, just a few strands.

1. Select the point at the crown of the head and **Move** it up and back a little to create a bit more of a mound for the hair.

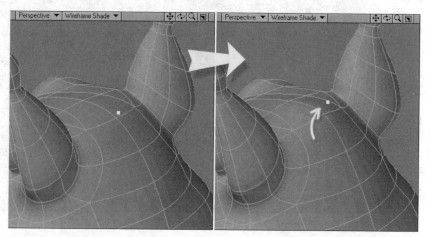

Figure 5.3-126. Preparing the head.

2. Turn off **Symmetry** and select a new layer with the head in the background layer. Create a box with three segments in Y, matching Figure 5.3-127.

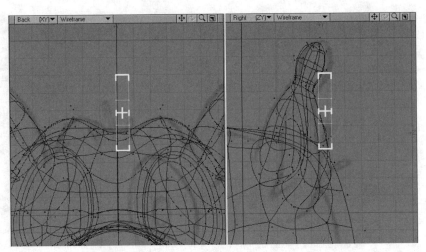

Figure 5.3-127. Create a box to start the first hair.

3. Delete the top and bottom polygons and press **Tab** to subpatch, then **Weld** the top set of points and then the bottom set of points.

4. Select the bottom point, then select **Subpatch Weight** and **Set Map Value** to **50%**.

5. Select the lower set of four points and **Stretch** horizontally and vertically about **50%** from the Top view.

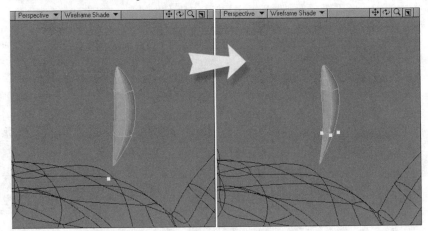

Figure 5.3-128. Shaping the hair.

6. **Copy** and **Paste** three times, each time adjusting the position and shape so you have four hairs.

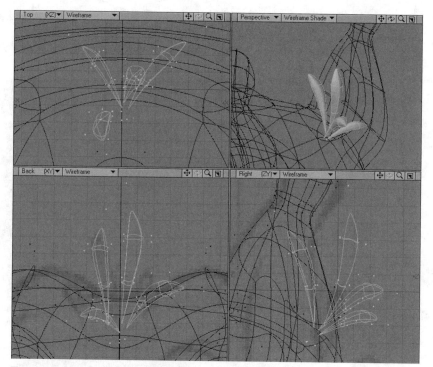

Figure 5.3-129. Creating the other hairs.

7. **Change Surface** to **Hair** using the settings in Figure 5.3-130.

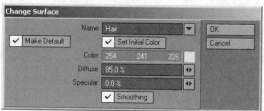

Figure 5.3-130. Hair surface.

8. **Cut** and **Paste** the hairs into the main layer.

Final Eyeballs

The eyeballs that we created earlier are templates for shaping and morphing the eye area. We'll create the final eyeballs now, although we need to keep the template eyeballs handy for the morph creation. The final eyeballs don't fit the eye area properly in the model, as they need to be perfect spheres, but don't be concerned as they're rotated and scaled with bones to fit the eye socket when the rigging is done.

1. Select the template eyeball layer, turn on **Symmetry**, then **Fit Selected** (**Shift+a**) to zoom in on just the left eyeball.

2. Select a new layer and place the template eyeball layer in the background. From the Back view, create a ball from the center of the template eyeball to the same width as the template. Copy the **Radius X** value to Y and Z and press **Enter.**

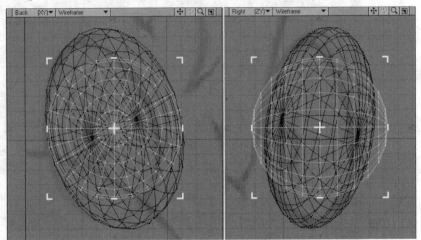

Figure 5.3-131. Create a sphere the width of the template eyeball.

3. Select another new layer and create a ball, pressing **n** to open the settings from last time. Change Segments to **24** and press **Enter.**

4. Select the first ball layer and delete the front two segments of the ball.

5. Select the second ball layer, **Copy** the front four segments, then delete the ball. **Paste** the polygons into the first ball layer and **Merge Points.**

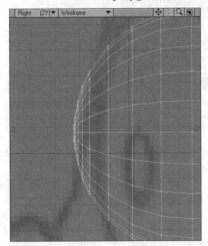

Figure 5.3-132. Creating more detail for the iris and pupil area.

6. **Change Surface** and select **Eye_White** from the drop-down menu.

7. Select the front three segments and **Change Surface** to **Eye_Iris** using the settings shown in Figure 5.3-133.

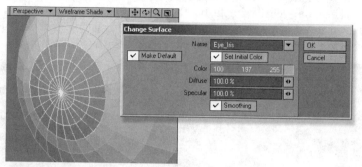

Figure 5.3-133. Iris surface.

8. **Contract Selection (Shift+[)** twice and **Change Surface** to **Eye_Pupil** using the settings shown in Figure 5.3-134.

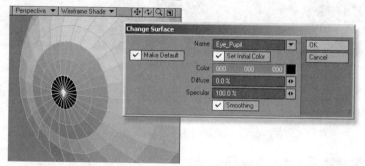

Figure 5.3-134. Pupil surface.

9. With the pupil still selected, select **Cut,** using the default settings, then **Move** the resulting points forward just a touch to maintain the curve of the eyeball.

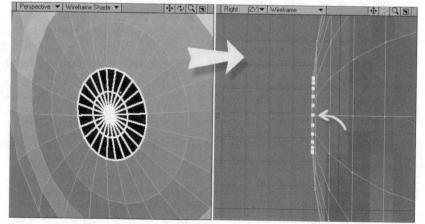

Figure 5.3-135. Pupil detail.

10. **Mirror** to create the right eyeball.

You may be asking why we didn't just create a ball and apply the surfaces to it. It's good to keep the eyeballs simple, but they need two segments in the iris and the pupil to ensure smooth specular highlights, as well as giving us enough geometry to retain the curve of the eyeballs when we dilate the pupils later on.

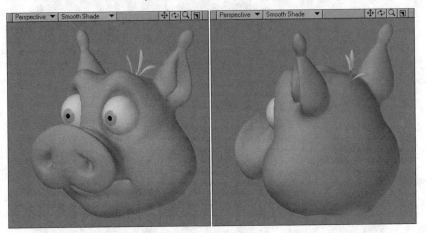

Figure 5.3-136. Finished head, showing the final pupils.

That completes Hamish's head. You should now have three layers in the model — the first layer with the head, the second with the template eyeballs, and the third with the final eyeballs.

5.4 Modeling the Body

Although the concept picture and backdrops show Hamish clothed, we'll start by creating his naked body. If your character always wears the same clothes or has tight clothing, you may choose not to create the body of your character where it is hidden by the clothing. If your character wears loose clothing, is likely to change clothes, or you want to use dynamics to animate the clothes, then it's best to create the full body under the clothing.

Because the backdrops include the clothes, we need to do some guesswork to figure out the body shape under the clothes, which isn't difficult to do in this case since the design is fairly simple. If you're in a similar situation at some point and want to be sure you get the body shapes right, it might be worth asking the concept artist (if it's not your own design) for a version of the character backdrops without clothing.

Torso

We'll start the body by creating the torso. It's a good idea to keep the torso geometry simple until you've created the arms and legs, then add any extra detail it needs. In fact, if you have a detailed torso it can be beneficial to leave detailing it until after you've rigged the character to keep weight mapping easier. Most methods of adding detail retain correct weight values, so you can weight a simple mesh and add detail, and it'll still be weighted properly. We won't be adding much detail to Hamish's torso, so we can do it before rigging.

We can create the torso by extending the points of the neck. Doing it this way means we won't have to join up the neck and body later.

1. Turn on **Symmetry**, select the bottom row of points of the head, and **Extend**. Move the points down and adjust them to match Figure 5.4-1, moving the side three points out to start the shoulders and the front points in to finish the neck.

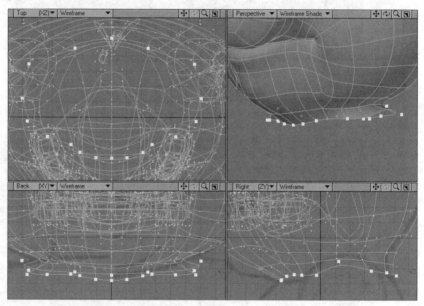

Figure 5.4-1. Continuing the neck.

2. **Extend** again, **Move** the points down to the middle of the arm and, from the Right view, **Stretch** horizontally to **112%** and adjust to match Figure 5.4-2.

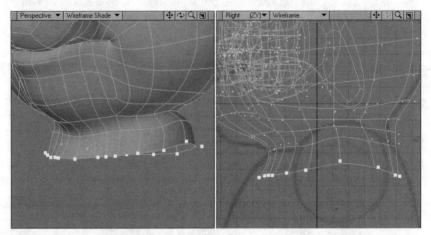

Figure 5.4-2. Starting the torso.

3. Turn off **Symmetry** and **Weld** the three points next to the front center point. **Weld** the same points on the other side. Turn **Symmetry** on, select the two triangles, and **Merge Polygons**.

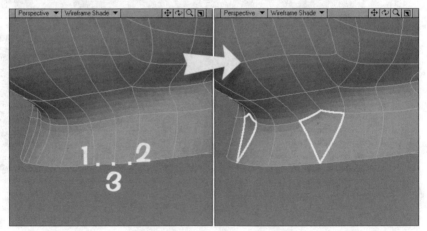

Figure 5.4-3. The cross section still has more segments than we want, so this refines the geometry for the rest of the torso.

4. Select all the points of the bottom edge and **Extend. Move** the points down to just under the shirt and adjust to match Figure 5.4-4.

5. Select the **Knife** (**Ctrl+k**) and, from the Right view, create three cuts in the torso.

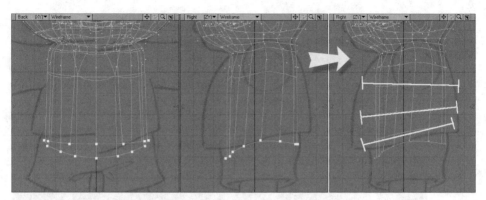

Figure 5.4-4. Creating the geometry for the torso.

6. Adjust the points of the Knife cuts to shape the stomach area.

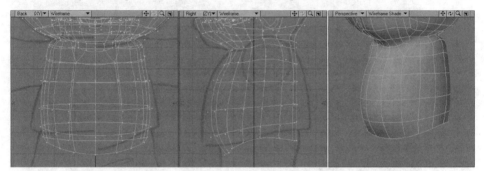

Figure 5.4-5. Adjusting the shapes. You can see we're staying just inside the clothes.

7. Adjust the points at the back to create a slight dip along the backbone.

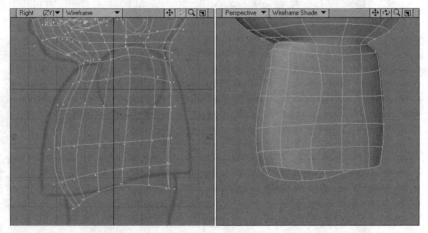

Figure 5.4-6. Adjusting the shape of the back.

Arms

We've created the torso geometry so there is an eight-polygon circumference for the arms. This gives us enough geometry to define the arms nicely. We can judge the size of the shoulder and arm by the size of the arm emerging from the shirt in the backdrop.

1. Select the four polygons around the arm of the Right backdrop and adjust the points so they lie closer to the circle of the armhole.

2. **Super Shift** in place, then from the Back view, **Rotate** the selected polygons out a little.

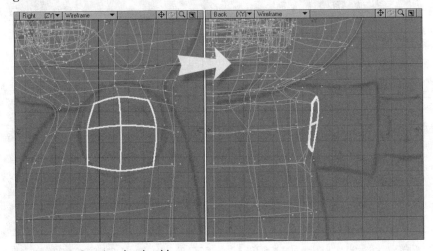

Figure 5.4-7. Creating the shoulder.

3. **Delete** the polygons, select the points, and adjust them to match Figure 5.4-8.

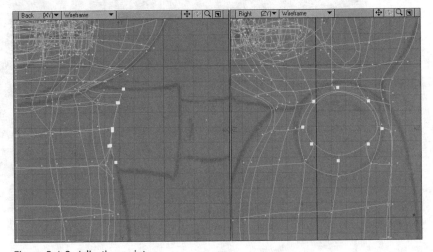

Figure 5.4-8. Adjusting points.

4. **Extend** and **Move** the points out to the elbow, adjusting them to maintain a nice circular shape.

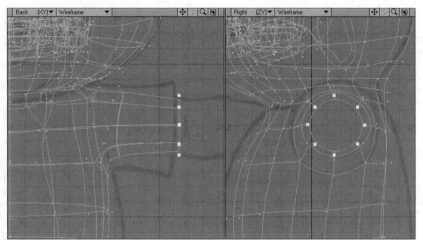

Figure 5.4-9. Adjust to keep the points aligned for easier editing.

5. **Extend** twice more, adjusting the points each time to follow the shape of the backdrop. **Rotate** the end set of points to match the rotation of the wrist.

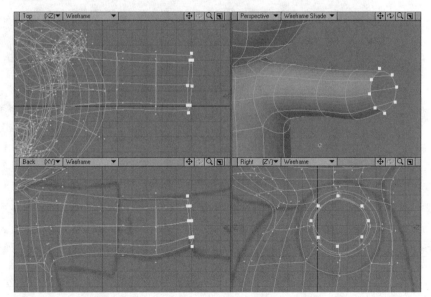

Figure 5.4-10. Creating the lower arm.

6. Select the **Knife** and, from the Front view, create a cut in the middle of the shoulder, then two more cuts on either side of the elbow joint.

7. Select two polygons at the wrist and **BandSaw Pro**, creating a segment at **20%**.

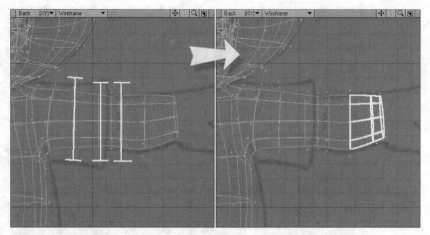

Figure 5.4-11. Creating extra cross sections allows us to shape the arm.

8. Adjust the points of the arm to create a dip on the inside of the elbow and a bump for the back of the elbow, and generally create a nice shape for the arm.

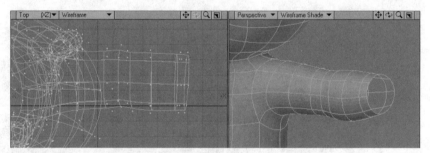

Figure 5.4-12. Notice the slight bend to the elbow.

Groin

Before we start the legs, we need to create the groin area. We'll create the groin so there's a hole for the legs.

1. Select the four front points and three back points of the bottom edge of the torso and **Extend**.

2. Adjust the points to match Figure 5.4-13, making sure not to move the two side points at the front.

3. **Deselect All** and **Merge Points**, creating two triangles at the front.

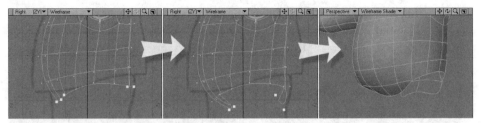

Figure 5.4-13. Creating holes for the legs.

4. Select the bottom three points of the front and **Extend**, moving them back to the middle of the legs, and adjust to match Figure 5.4-14.

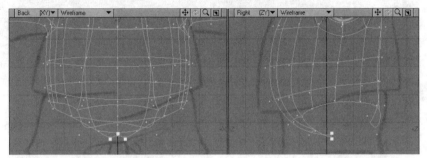

Figure 5.4-14. Extend the points.

5. Select the bottom middle point at the back and **Unweld**.

6. Turn off **Symmetry** and select the six middle polygons at the back clockwise.

7. Select **Cut**, turning off **Square Corner Quads**, then **Merge Points** and turn **Symmetry** back on.

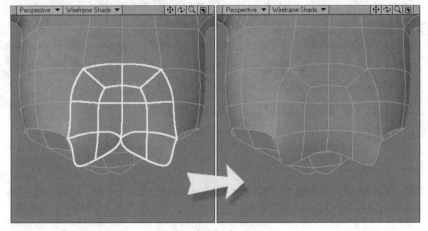

Figure 5.4-15. Creating extra geometry for the bum.

231

8. Back on the bottom row, select the three middle points at the back and **Extend**. From the Right view, move them down and in toward the middle

9. **Extend** again, and **Move** the points close to the middle. **Weld** the points just extended to the existing points in the middle, closing the groin area.

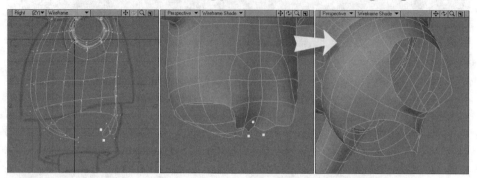

Figure 5.4-16. Closing the leg holes. Notice we've made the holes so the legs will have eight sides like the arms.

Legs

Now we're ready to extend the legs and shape the bum. As with the arms, we can judge the size of the leg under the pants by the part of the leg visible in the backdrop.

1. Select the open points at the top of the legs, then deselect the point of the large quad at the back. **Extend** and **Move** the points down. Adjust the points to form the top of the leg.

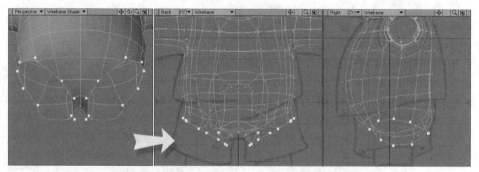

Figure 5.4-17. Extend all the points except the point of the large quad at the back.

2. Turn off **Symmetry** and **Weld** the two points on either side of the quad at the back to the point of the quad. Repeat on the other side. Turn **Symmetry** back on.

3. Now that we've got most of the geometry for the bum in place, adjust the points to form nice, rounded bum cheeks. Don't create too much of a crease in the bum at this stage; that can be done later after we've created the pants.

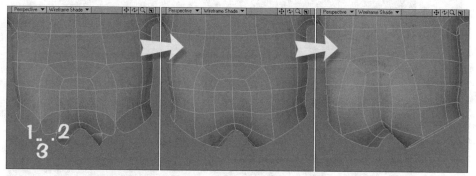

Figure 5.4-18. Shaping the bum.

4. Select the open points of the leg and **Extend**. Move the points down and adjust so the front points continue the leg and the back points create the bottom of the bum cheeks.

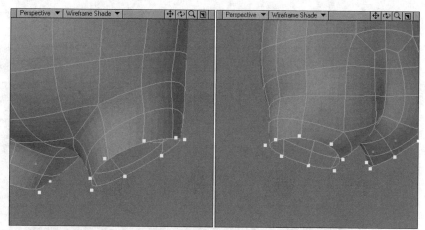

Figure 5.4-19. Continuing the bum. Make sure you have a nice, round, even cross section, as the positions of these points determine the initial shape of the legs.

5. **Extend** and **Move** the points down to the knee. Adjust the points so they're in a straight line from the Back view and follow the backdrop from the Right view.

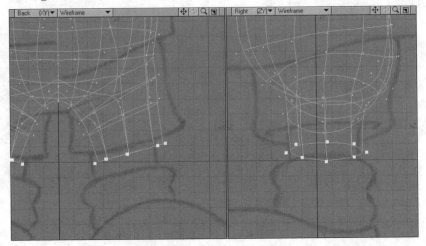

Figure 5.4-20. Creating the upper legs.

6. **Extend** again, moving the points down to the ankle. Move them back slightly.

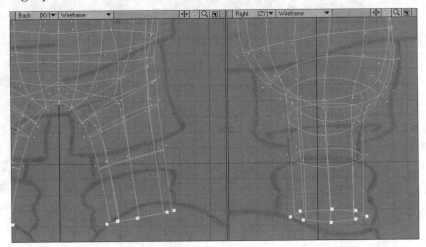

Figure 5.4-21. Creating the lower legs.

7. Select **Knife** and make two cuts, just above and below the knee.

8. Because the Knife tool doesn't work with Symmetry we're left with the right arm and leg not matching the left. Delete the right arm and leg, then **Mirror** the left arm and leg. **Deselect All** and **Merge Points**.

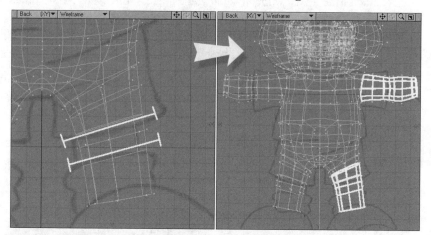

Figure 5.4-22. Create detail at the knee, then Mirror.

9. Adjust the points of the knee, creating a slight bump at the front and a crease at the back. Make any other adjustments to the legs you think are necessary.

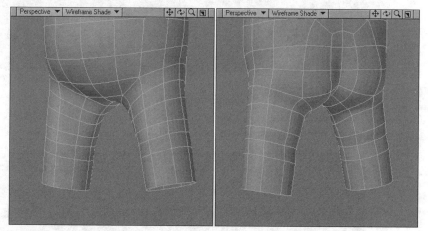

Figure 5.4-23. Finished legs.

Hands

As I mentioned earlier, the hands are often one of the more complex areas of a character model. How much detail you include in the hands really comes down to the type of character it is. Hamish's hands aren't very detailed, which is largely due to the design of the character having short, fat fingers. A character with long, thin fingers would likely need more detailed hands, with the more realistic two joints in each finger instead of just one.

Here we're dealing with three-fingered hands, which work well for many anthropomorphic and very simple human characters. I do suggest giving most human characters four fingers though, as three fingers can look strange on humans.

Since our arms have eight sides, we've got enough detail in the arms to extend the hands out from the wrists this time.

1. Turn off **Symmetry** and **Extend** the open points of the left wrist. **Move** the points to about the midpoint of the hand in the backdrop and, from the Top view, **Stretch** the points vertically a little.

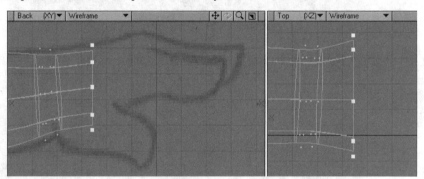

Figure 5.4-24. Extending the hand.

2. **Extend** again, moving the points to just below the knuckles. **Rotate** and **Stretch** to fit the backdrop.

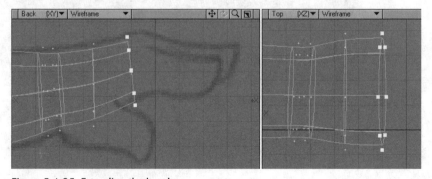

Figure 5.4-25. Extending the hand.

3. **Extend** again to the start of the fingers and, from the Top view, **Stretch** vertically a little.

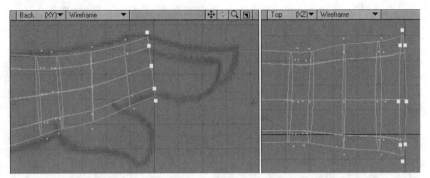

Figure 5.4-26. Extending the hand.

4. Select the two middle end points at the top of the hand and **Edge Bevel**. **Move** the resulting points so the three end polygons are roughly equal in width.

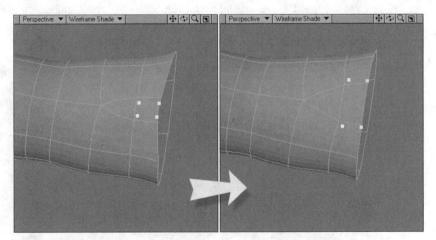

Figure 5.4-27. Creating more detail.

5. Select the middle two polygons and select **Cut**. Turn off **Select Outer Edges** and press **Continue**. Delete the end triangle made by the cut.

6. **Move** the end points on either side of the cut down a little, and the other three end points at the top up a little. This is the start of the knuckle definition, and the top of the hand is done.

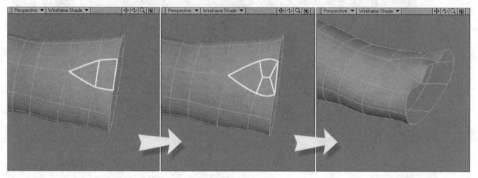

Figure 5.4-28. Defining the knuckles.

7. Now we need to define and detail the bottom of the hand, or the palm. Select the middle points of the end three rows. Move them back and move the end two points up a little.

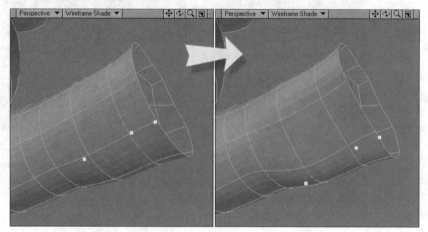

Figure 5.4-29. Preparing the palm.

8. Now select the points shown in Figure 5.4-30 and **Edge Bevel**. Drag the cursor left until the Numeric panel shows **0 m.**

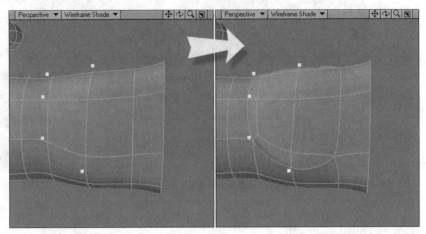

Figure 5.4-30. Adding detail.

9. Select the inner points of the beveled edge and adjust them to match Figure 5.4-31.

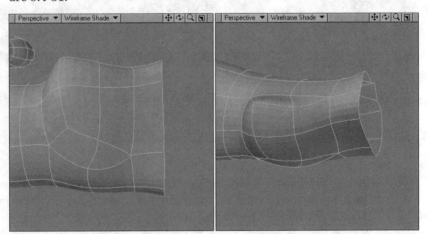

Figure 5.4-31. Adjust the points.

10. Select the two points shown in Figure 5.4-32 and **Construct≻Combine≻Bridge**, cutting the quad into two triangles.

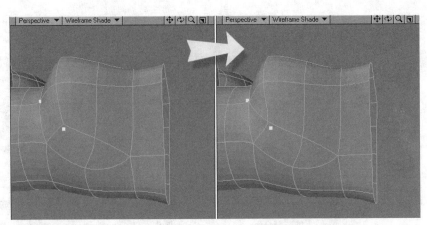

Figure 5.4-32. Bridge can be used to cut polygons.

11. Select the three polygons shown in Figure 5.4-33 and select **Cut**, using the default values.

12. Adjust the points of the cut to match Figure 5.4-33.

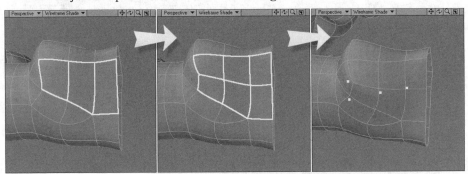

Figure 5.4-33. Defining the palm.

13. Select the three polygons shown in Figure 5.4-34 and select **Cut**, again turning off **Select Outer Edges**. Move the resulting points up a little to create the crease of the palm.

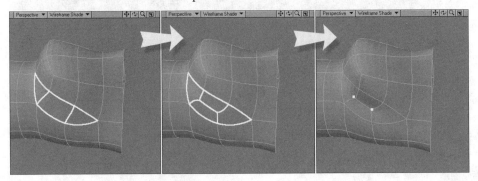

Figure 5.4-34. Creating the crease of the palm.

Fingers

Now that the hand geometry is in place we can start on the fingers.

1. Select the five end points in the middle of the hand clockwise from the Top view and **Multiply➤Extend➤More➤Extender. Move** the points out a little. Select the faces created by the Extend and **SubPatch**.

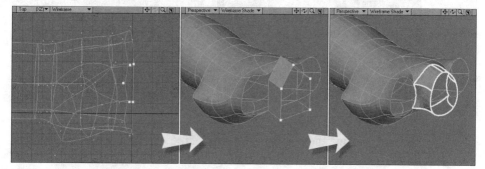

Figure 5.4-35. Extending the knuckle.

> **Note:** We used Extender for this step instead of Extender Plus because Extender creates polygons for all the selected points, rather than just extending the existing polygons, and we wanted the sides of the finger to be created at the same time as the top and bottom.

2. **Weld** the top extended point to the one next to it, then select the opposite point and the point at the knuckle and **Bridge**.

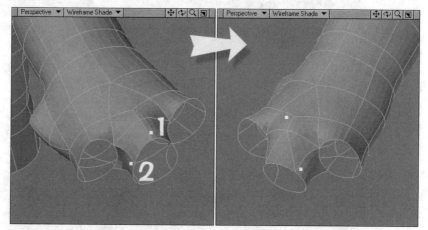

Figure 5.4-36. Refining the knuckle.

3. Select the end points of the finger and adjust them so they're even.

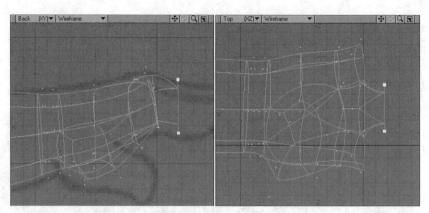

Figure 5.4-37. Preparing for extending the finger.

4. **Extend**, moving the points to the edge of the middle finger in the back-drop, then **Knife** twice across the middle of the finger.

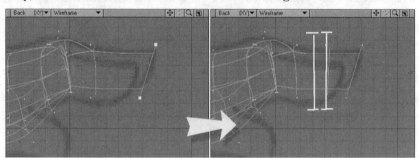

Figure 5.4-38. Extending the finger.

5. **Extend** the end points of the finger and **Scale** to about **35%**. **Move** the points out a little and center them between the previous points.

6. **Make Polygon** to cap off the end, then **Move** the points shown in Figure 5.4-39 up a little and, from the Top view, **Stretch** vertically about **135%**.

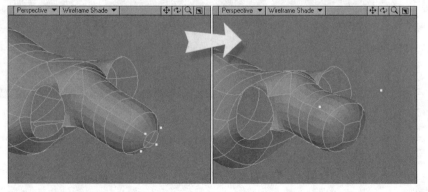

Figure 5.4-39. Capping the finger.

7. Select the polygons of the finger and **Copy**. **Paste** into a new layer, placing the main layer in the background.

8. From the Top view, move the finger down next to the existing finger and **Rotate** about **–20%**. **Scale** to about **94%**, then from the Back view, **Move** it down a touch.

9. Select the polygons of the finger and **Copy** and **Paste**. From the Top view, **Move** the selected finger up to the other side of the background finger, **Rotate** about **38%**, and **Scale** to about **83%**.

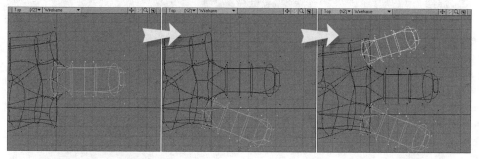

Figure 5.4-40. Creating the other two fingers.

10. Switch Background and Foreground layers (') and **Move** the three points on each side of the fingers back to just behind the fingers. This makes it easier to see what we're doing in the next few steps.

11. Switch Background and Foreground again, **Cut** the two fingers, and **Paste** them into the main layer.

12. Now we need to weld the fingers to the hand. For the joins between the fingers, **Weld** the points of the fingers to the points of the hand. For the other joins, **Weld** the points of the hand to the points of the fingers.

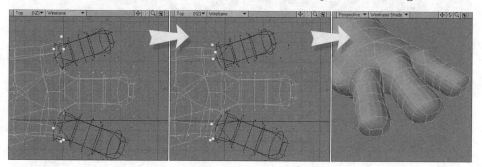

Figure 5.4-41. Joining the fingers to the hand.

13. Now with the fingers created we can create the thumb. Select the polygon shown in Figure 5.4-42 and delete it. Select the four open points and **Extend**, moving the points to match Figure 5.4-42.

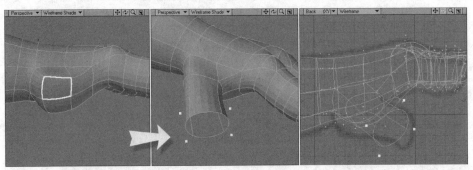

Figure 5.4-42. Extending the thumb.

14. **Extend** again and **Scale** the points to about **35%**. **Move** the points out a little and center them between the previous points. **Make Polygon** to cap the end.

15. Because the thumb is on an angle, we can't use the Knife to cut the detail in, so select two middle polygons of the thumb and **BandSaw Pro**. Add a segment if necessary, making a segment at **40%** and one at **60%**.

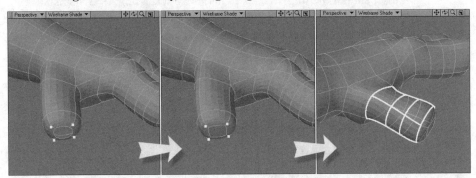

Figure 5.4-43. Capping and detailing the thumb.

16. Adjust the points of the thumb to make a nice shape, checking from all angles in the Perspective view.

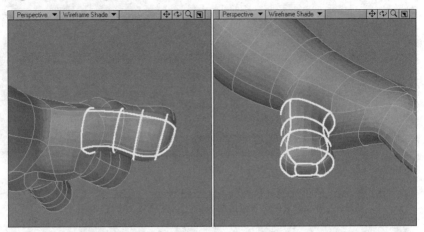

Figure 5.4-44. Adjusting the points.

17. Select the middle points at the bottom of the fingers, shown in Figure 5.4-45, and **Move** them up a touch, creating the creases in the fingers.

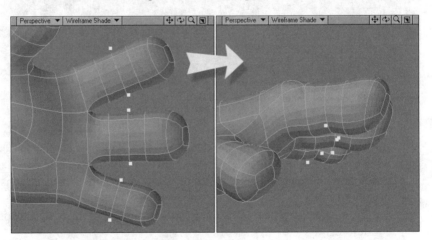

Figure 5.4-45. Creating finger creases.

18. Adjust the points of the hand, checking from all angles that it looks good.

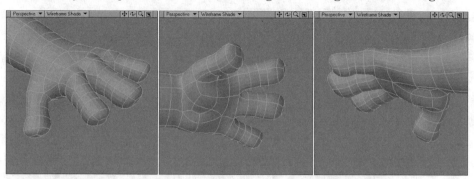

Figure 5.4-46. Adjusting the points.

19. Finally, delete the last band of polygons at the right wrist and **Mirror** the left hand and wrist. **Deselect All** and **Merge Points**.

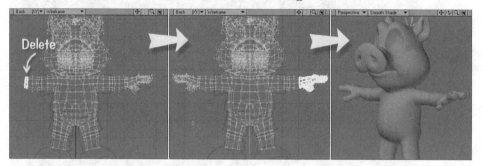

Figure 5.4-47. Mirrored hands.

Feet

Although Hamish is wearing shoes, it's useful to create the feet just in case we want him barefooted at some point. Feet are usually a lot easier to create than hands, although getting the right shapes is still important. Because Hamish will usually wear shoes, we won't make the feet too detailed.

1. So we can see what we're doing better, **Hide** all of the body except for the left leg.

2. **Extend** the bottom row of points at the ankle and adjust to match Figure 5.4-48, moving the side two points out to create the ankle bones.

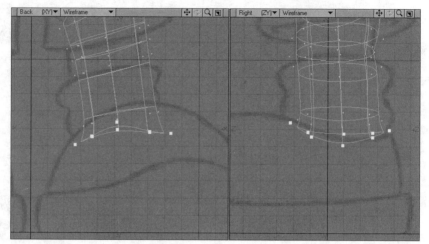

Figure 5.4-48. Creating the ankle.

3. Deselect the front point and **Extend** again. Deselect the front two points and **Move** down and adjust to match Figure 5.4-49. **Deselect All** and **Merge Points** to merge the front two points.

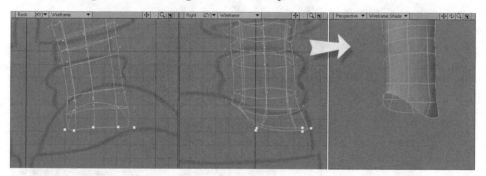

Figure 5.4-49. Extending the heel.

4. **Extend** the bottom row of points and **Move** them down and forward a little, creating the heel.

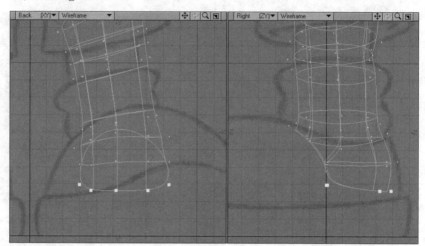

Figure 5.4-50. Finishing the heel. Notice the heel is just inside the back edge of the shoe.

5. **Extend** the front row of points, **Move** them forward and, from the Right view, **Stretch** horizontally to about **35%**. From the Top view **Stretch** horizontally to about **130%**.

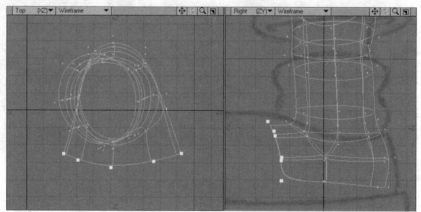

Figure 5.4-51. Extending the foot.

6. **Extend** again, moving the points forward and down a little.

7. **Extend**, moving the points forward, and, from the Right view, **Stretch** horizontally and vertically to about H=**33%**, V=**73%**. From the Top view, **Stretch** horizontally just a little, around **97%**.

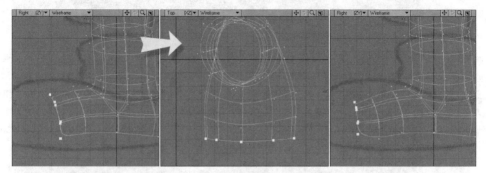

Figure 5.4-52. Top of the foot. Without a top backdrop you have to determine the shape of the foot from the top using your own judgment, although you can tweak the shapes later.

8. The foot is taking shape nicely. Let's create the bottom of the foot. Select the bottom row of points and **Extend**. **Move** down a little and, from the Top view, **Stretch** from the front of the foot to H=**60%** V=**93%**.

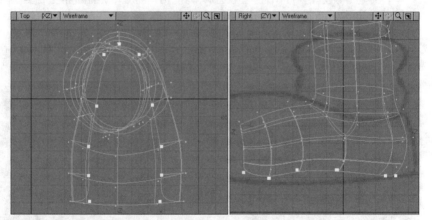

Figure 5.4-53. Extending the sole of the foot.

9. **Extend** again and, from the Top view, **Stretch** from the front of the foot again, to H=**0%** and V=**85%**.

10. From the Top view, **Weld** each set of points along the join.

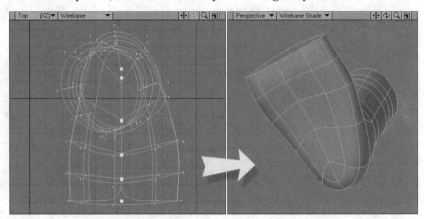

Figure 5.4-54. Finished foot geometry.

Toes

With the foot geometry in place we can create the toes. If a character had bare feet all the time you would probably want to create more detailed toes, creating geometry similar to that of the fingers. In this case we'll keep the toes simple.

1. Select each set of four points along the front of the foot and **Make Polygon**. When you have all four polygons created, change to **Polygons** mode, make sure they're all selected, and **SubPatch**.

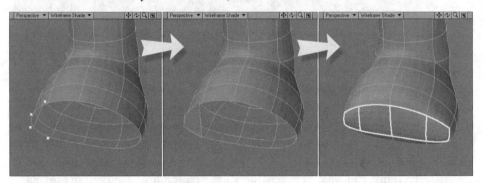

Figure 5.4-55. Capping the front of the foot.

2. Select the inside two front polygons and adjust so each polygon is similarly sized. **Extend** and **Move** forward.

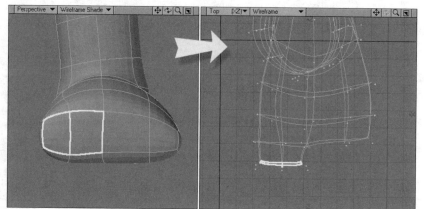

Figure 5.4-56. Extend works on a polygon selection just like Super Shift in place.

3. **Extend** again, moving the polygons forward, and adjust to match Figure 5.4-57.

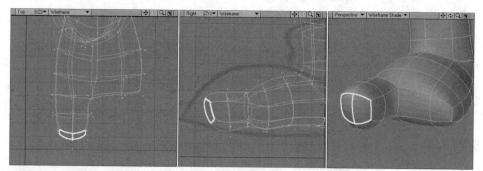

Figure 5.4-57. Finished big toe.

4. Select the middle polygon and **Extend** twice, each time moving the polygon forward a little.

5. **Extend** again, **Scale** the polygon to about **50%**, and position it just in front of the previous points, centered on the toe.

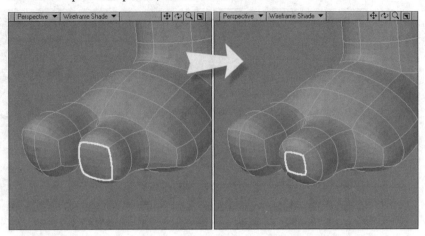

Figure 5.4-58. Middle toe.

6. Select the outside polygon, **Extend**, and **Move** forward.

7. **Extend** again, **Scale** the polygon about **50%**, and position just in front of the previous points, centered on the toe.

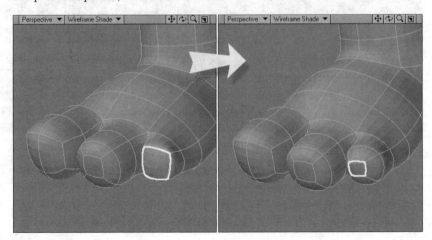

Figure 5.4-59. Little toe.

8. With all the geometry in place, adjust the points to make a nice foot shape, making sure to define the ball of the foot, the heel, the arch, and the Achilles tendon.

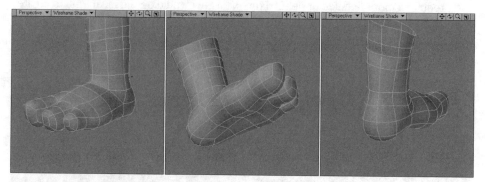

Figure 5.4-60. Adjusting the shapes.

9. **Unhide All** and delete the bottom band of polygons of the right leg. Select the left foot and bottom row of the leg, **Mirror**, and **Merge**.

Figure 5.4-61. Mirrored feet.

Detail

The only detail we need for Hamish is a belly button. Other characters may require a more detailed or defined torso, so now would be the ideal time to create any torso detail.

1. Turn on **Symmetry**, select the middle four polygons of the tummy, and **Extend**. From the Back view, **Stretch** horizontally and vertically to **116%**, then from the Right view, **Stretch** horizontally to **8%**.

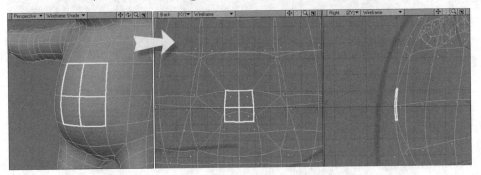

Figure 5.4-62. Creating detail for the belly button.

2. Adjust the points to create a teardrop shape.
3. Select the polygons and **Extend**, moving the polygons in a little.

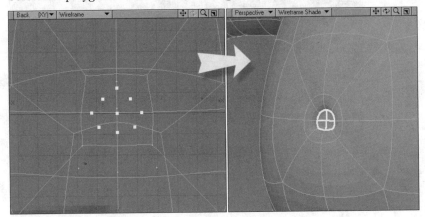

Figure 5.4-63. Shaping the belly button.

4. **Extend** again, **Stretch** in a little, and **Move** the polygons forward a touch to create an outie. If you want to create an innie, **Stretch** a little smaller and move the polygons back.

5. Adjust the points to refine the shape.

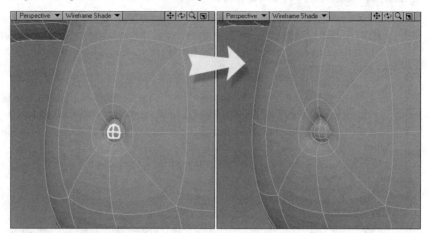

Figure 5.4-64. Finished belly button.

With the modeling of the body complete, we can start creating the clothes.

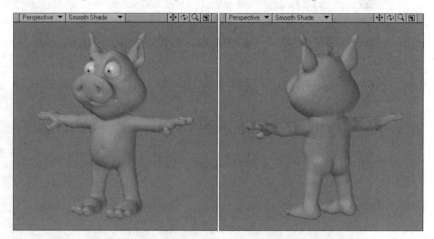

Figure 5.4-65. Completed Hamish body.

5.5 Modeling Clothes

The easiest way to create clothing is to use the body geometry as a starting point. Copy the body geometry that the article of clothing covers and adjust from there. This retains the polygon flow of the character, so the clothes deform in the same way as the body.

It can be useful to leave the creation of the clothes until after rigging. This makes it a bit easier to create the clothes, as the weight mapping is already done for the body, so you don't have to weight map the clothes again. This is especially useful when creating multiple sets of clothing, which are often required in a script where characters are wearing clothes.

In this case the clothes are simple enough that creating them before rigging doesn't create too much extra work.

Shoes

Notice that the shoes in the backdrops are turned out slightly. In this case it's because the shoes were too large to draw side by side without overlapping unless the legs were spread very wide, but it's quite common for concept artists to draw the feet this way. Because we want the feet and shoes to point forward for rigging purposes, you should use the backdrops as a rough guide only.

1. Select a new layer and place the first layer in the background. Create a disk with 16 sides centered on the foot and matching the average height of the sole of the shoe in the backdrop.

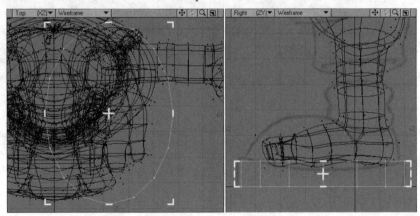

Figure 5.5-1. Match the front and back to the Right backdrop.

2. **Delete** the top and bottom polygons and **SubPatch**.

3. Adjust the top row of points to match the backdrops, allowing for the different angle.

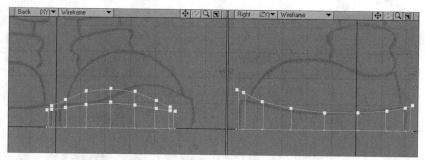

Figure 5.5-2. Shaping the sole.

4. Extend the bottom row of points and change Action Center to **Selection, Modes➤Action Center: Selection (Shift+F8)**. From the Top view **Stretch** H=80%, V=83%.

5. **Extend** the top row of points and, from the Top view, **Stretch** H=80%, V=83%.

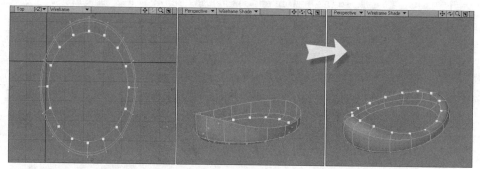

Figure 5.5-3. Giving the sole some depth.

6. Select two points in the middle band and **BandSaw Pro** with one segment at **50%**.

7. Select the points at the bottom and **Contract Selection** to select only the bottom edge. **Extend** and, from the Top view, **Stretch** to H=0%, V=90%.

8. **Merge Points**, **Delete** the two obsolete points at the front and back, and **Merge** the triangles.

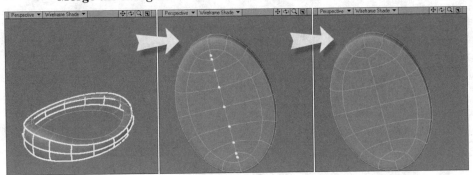

Figure 5.5-4. Capping the bottom of the sole.

9. With the soles complete we can create the main part of the shoe. Select the top edge and **Extend**, moving the points up.

10. Select the top band of polygons and **Cut** and **Paste**. Select the band again and from the Top view **Stretch** to H=**109%**, V=**114%**, then **Move** down just a touch, so the bottom edge is just inside the sole.

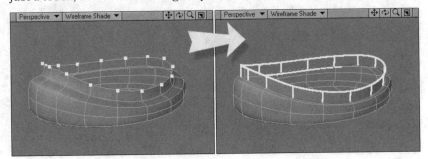

Figure 5.5-5. Creating the base of the shoe.

11. Adjust the top row of points to match the backdrop, keeping them an even distance from each other.

12. **Extend** the top points, **Move** them up, and adjust. You can do the main adjustments by stretching, but you probably want to change Action Center back to **Mouse (Shift+F5)** so you can specify the center of the stretch with the position of the cursor.

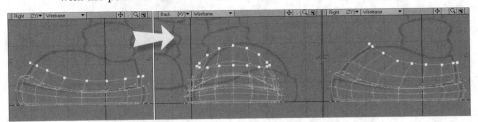

Figure 5.5-6. Extending the shoe.

13. **Extend** again, adjust the points to match the top of the shoe in the Right backdrop, and **Stretch** in from the sides.

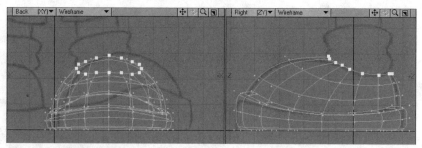

Figure 5.5-7. Final shoe shape.

14. **Extend** again, **Stretch** a little smaller, and adjust to create the top edge of the shoe.

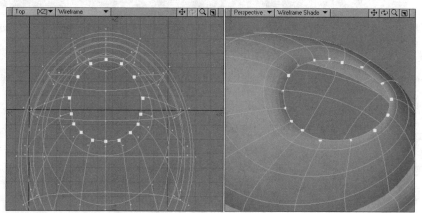

Figure 5.5-8. Creating the top.

15. **Extend** again, moving the points down to create the inside edge.

16. Check the top edge of the shoe against the ankle, making sure there's some distance between them to allow for the thickness of the sock.

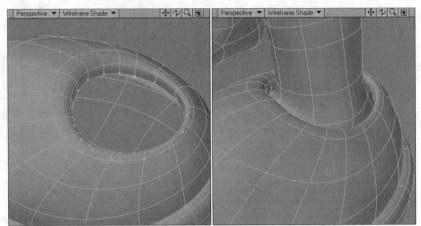

Figure 5.5-9. Adjust the points at the top of the shoe to make them roughly equal in distance all around the ankle.

17. Now select the sole and **Change Surface** to **Shoe_Sole** using the settings in Figure 5.5-10.

18. Select the main part of the shoe and **Change Surface** to **Shoe_Main** using the settings in Figure 5.5-10.

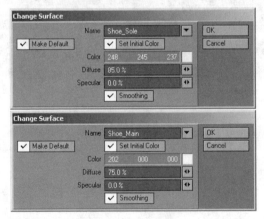

Figure 5.5-10. Shoe surface settings.

19. Now we'll create the shoelaces. Select a new layer and place the shoe layer in the background. Create a box with four segments in X that matches Figure 5.5-11.

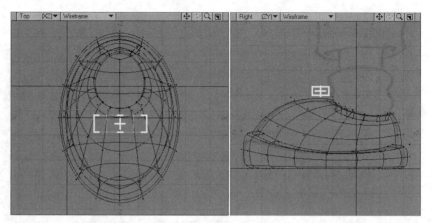

Figure 5.5-11. Initial shoelace.

20. **SubPatch,** then **Rotate** each end of the box to match Figure 5.5-12.

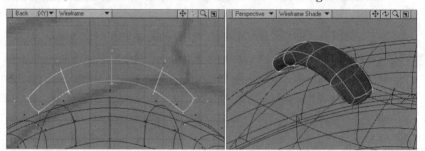

Figure 5.5-12. Shaping the shoe lace.

21. **Cut** and **Paste** into the shoe layer and position the shoelace so the ends are just inside the shoe surface.

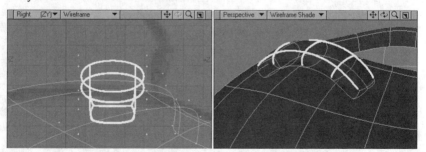

Figure 5.5-13. Positioning the shoelace.

22. **Copy** and **Paste** the lace and adjust the position and rotation to create the second shoelace.

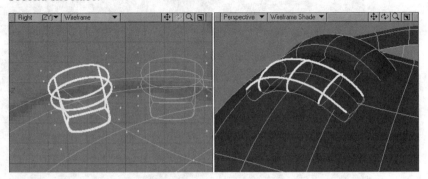

Figure 5.5-14. Creating the second shoelace.

23. Select both laces and **Change Surface** to **Shoe_Lace** using the settings in Figure 5.5-15.

Figure 5.5-15. Shoelace surface settings.

24. Now the shoe is finished, so **Mirror** to create the right shoe. Don't worry about the shoes overlapping each other; it won't affect the rigging, as each shoe will have an independent weight map.

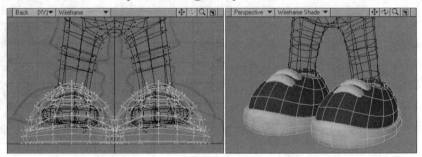

Figure 5.5-16. Mirrored shoes.

Pants

The pants, or shorts in this case, are fairly easy to create. The main thing to change from the body geometry is to decrease the indent in the center of the bum.

1. Select the polygons of the body that occupy the same space as the shorts in the backdrops and **Copy** and **Paste** into a new layer. These polygons are the start of the pants.

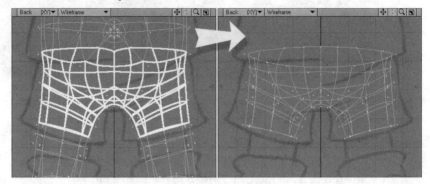

Figure 5.5-17. Copy the body geometry to a new layer.

2. Adjust the pants from the Back and Right views to match the shorts in the backdrops, leaving the top row of points as they are for now.

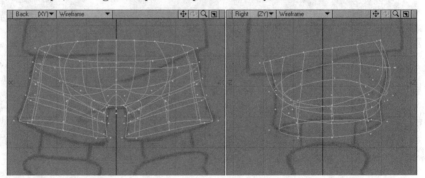

Figure 5.5-18. Shaping the pants.

3. Adjust the points along the center to decrease the crease at the bum and lower the crotch slightly.

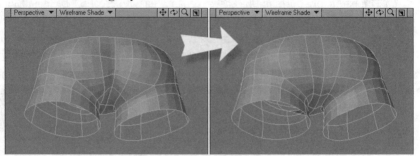

Figure 5.5-19. Shaping the bum.

4. Select the top row of points and **Stretch** from the Top view so they're just a little bigger.

5. **Extend** the points and **Stretch** them in a little. **Extend** again and **Stretch** them in more and **Move** them down a bit.

6. Place the body layer in the background and adjust the top rows of points so the top of the pants sits on the body nicely.

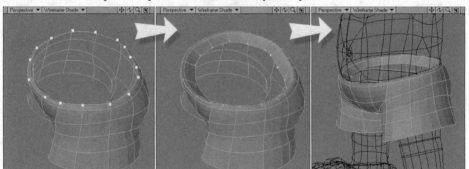

Figure 5.5-20. Creating the top edge of the pants.

7. **Extend** the bottom row of points and **Stretch** them in a bit. **Extend** twice more, each time stretching in a little and moving the points up to the next row of points on the outside of the pants.

8. Check the pants with the body layer in the foreground to make sure the open areas of the pants are hidden by the body geometry.

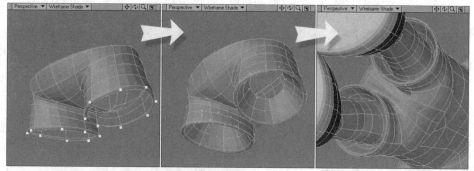

Figure 5.5-21. Creating the inside of the pant legs.

9. Create a new surface for the pants, called **Pants**, using the settings in Figure 5.5-22.

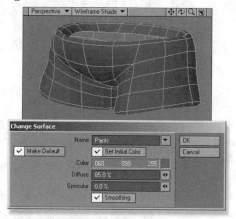

Figure 5.5-22. Pants surface.

10. Adjust the geometry to refine the shapes and create folds or wrinkles if you wish.

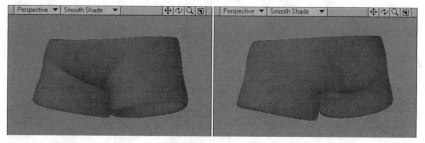

Figure 5.5-23. Finished pants with some creases under the crotch.

Shirt

The shirt starts with the body geometry, but it needs some cleaning up. We can get rid of the belly button and the extra detail at the edges, making the shirt geometry nice and even. Before we start on the shirt though, we need to clean up the polygon flow around the neck.

1. Select the two polygons shown in Figure 5.5-24a and **Spin Quads** twice, matching the flow of polygons to the line of the neck.
2. Adjust the points around the area to match the new polygon flow.

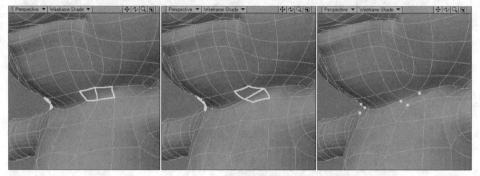

Figure 5.5-24a. Adjusting the polygon flow.

3. Select the polygons of the body that occupy the same space as the shirt in the backdrops and **Copy** and **Paste** into a new layer.

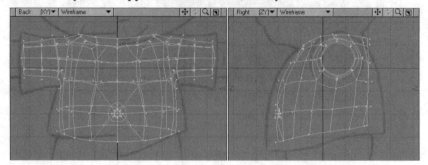

Figure 5.5-24. Copy of body geometry.

4. **Weld** all the points of the belly button. Turn off **Symmetry** and **Merge** the triangles into quads.

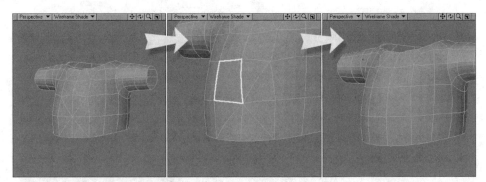

Figure 5.5-25. Removing the belly button.

5. **Weld** the three points at the back of the bottom row.

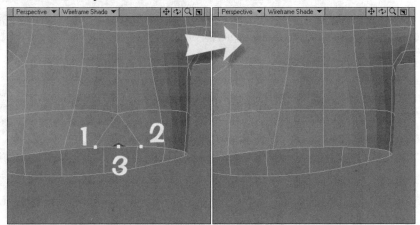

Figure 5.5-26. Cleaning up the back.

6. Select the two front center polygons of the top row and select the **Cut** tool. Make sure there's just one segment and turn on all the options. Set the segment value to around **0.7**.

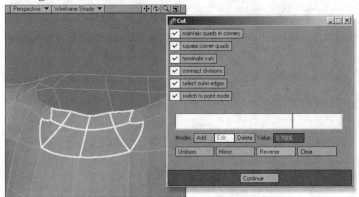

Figure 5.5-27. This makes an even band of polygons around the neck.

7. **Weld** the three points shown in Figure 5.5-28 on each side.

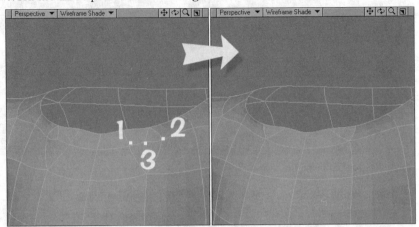

Figure 5.5-28. Cleaning up the neck area.

8. **Weld** the two points shown in Figure 5.5-29 on each side.

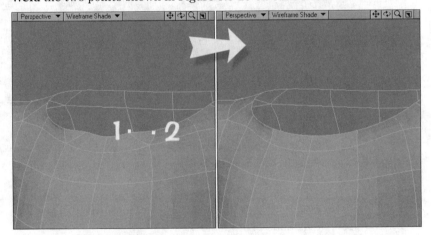

Figure 5.5-29. Now the neck is nice and neat.

9. **Smooth Shift** (**Shift+f**) to give the shirt some thickness. Offset about **11** to **12 mm** and set Max Smoothing Angle to **180**.

10. Because Smooth Shift doesn't always work well with Symmetry we'll mirror the left side of the shirt to regain symmetry. **Delete** the right side of the shirt, select the points along the middle, and **Set Value** (**v**) to **X=0**.

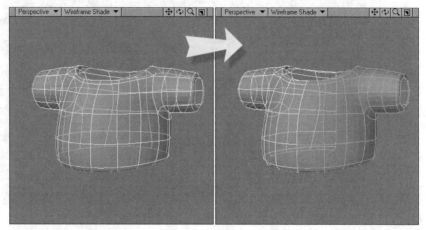

Figure 5.5-30. Smooth Shift and mirror.

11. **Deselect All** and **Mirror** (**Shift+v**).

12. Turn on **Symmetry** and adjust the shirt from all views to match the backdrops. Don't forget to widen the sleeves from the Top view to match the Back view.

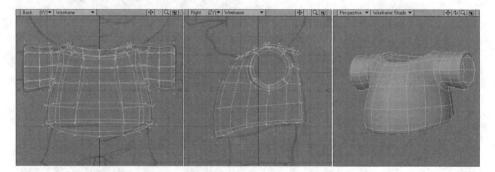

Figure 5.5-31. Shaping the shirt.

13. Delete the polygon bands at the edges of the open areas. Select the remaining polygons and **Copy**.

14. **Smooth Shift** with an offset of about **–10 mm**, **Deselect All**, and **Flip (f)** the polygons.

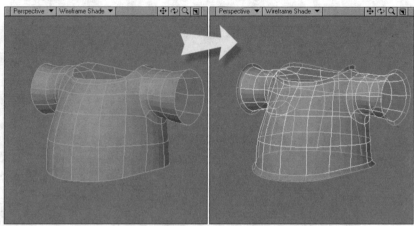

Figure 5.5-32. Smooth Shift again.

15. Create a new surface called **Shirt_Inner**, using the settings in Figure 5.5-33.

16. **Paste**, pasting the polygons we copied in step 13, and **Merge Points**.

17. Select all the polygons with the surface Head and create a new surface called **Shirt_Outer**, using the settings in Figure 5.5-34.

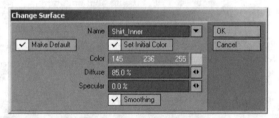

Figure 5.5-33. Shirt_Inner surface. This lets us select the inside polygons of the shirt more easily.

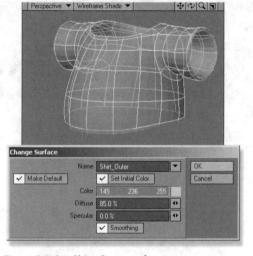

Figure 5.5-34. Shirt_Outer surface.

. . . . Modeling

Hamish

18. The shirt is looking pretty good, but it needs some cleaning up around the neck. Adjust the points until the geometry at the neck is nice and smooth.

19. Check the shirt with the body layer and adjust any areas that need it.

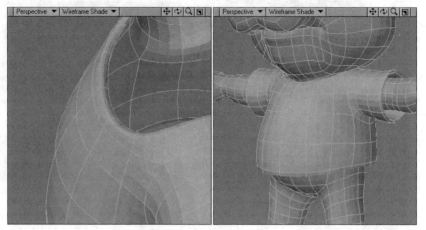

Figure 5.5-35. Adjusting the shirt.

20. Since we did some welding earlier on, use the Statistics panel to check for any one- or two-point polygons and any stray points, and delete them.

Detailing the Shirt

With the basic geometry in place, we can start creating more detail such as folds and wrinkles.

1. Select the outside polygons of the shirt shown in Figure 5.5-36.

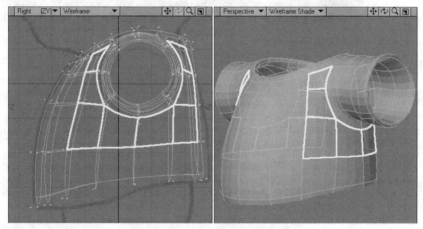

Figure 5.5-36. These polygons will have a fold through them.

2. Select the **Cut** tool. Add a new segment and use the other settings from Figure 5.5-37.

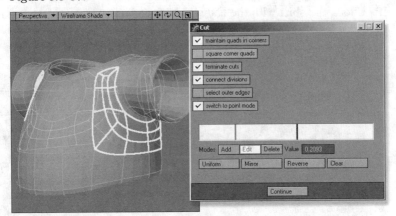

Figure 5.5-37. Cut settings.

3. Adjust the new points to create a crease under the arm.

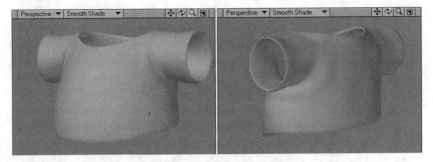

Figure 5.5-38. Finished shirt with creases under the arms.

Socks

The socks start from the ankle geometry. Be careful when creating the socks that they fit nicely between the ankle and the shoes, and make sure the detail of the folds is different on each side.

1. In the body layer, select the band of polygons on the lower leg and **Expand Selection** twice. Deselect the top two bands of polygons and **Copy** and **Paste** into a new layer.

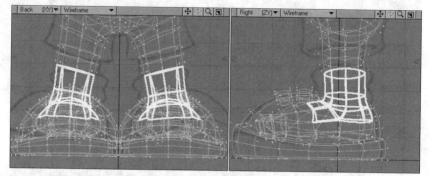

Figure 5.5-39. Selected ankle geometry.

2. Create a new surface called **Socks**, using the settings in Figure 5.5-40.

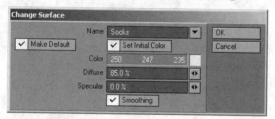

Figure 5.5-40. Socks surface.

3. Delete the points shown in Figure 5.5-41 and **Merge** the triangles.

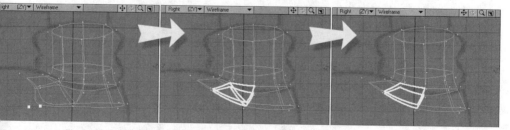

Figure 5.5-41. Cleaning up the base of the socks.

4. **Smooth Shift** by about **8 mm** and delete the bottom row created by the shift. Delete the right sock and **Mirror** the left sock, regaining symmetry.

5. Check the geometry against the body, adjusting the points to make sure the socks fit neatly between the ankles and the shoes.

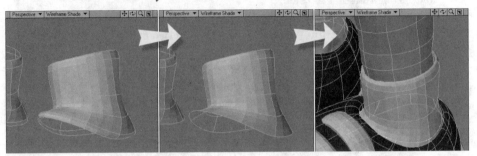

Figure 5.5-42. Smooth shift and adjust.

6. Select the second top row of points and move them down a little. **Move** the next row of points up a little, evening out the polygon sizes.

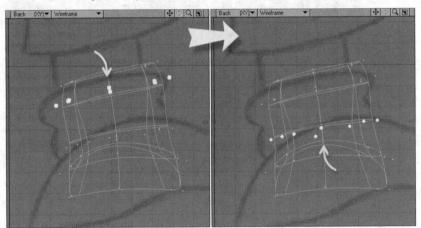

Figure 5.5-43. Point adjustments.

7. Select two polygons in the middle band and **BandSaw Pro** with one segment at **50%**. Select two polygons of the next lower band and **BandSaw Pro** again. Repeat for the right sock.

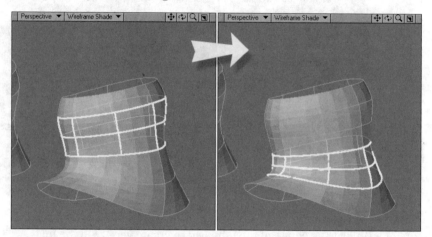

Figure 5.5-44. Creating more bands.

8. Adjust the rows, making two folds in the socks, roughly matching the backdrops.

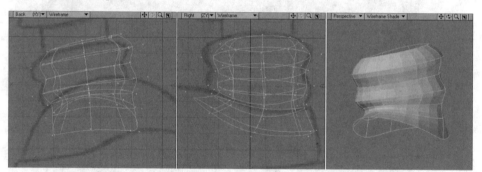

Figure 5.5-45. Initial shaping of the sock.

9. Select the top open row of points and **Extend**, scaling them in and moving them down a little.

10. Select the right sock and **Cut** and **Paste** into a new layer.

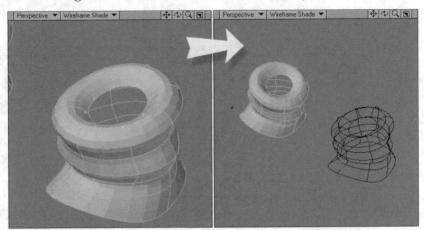

Figure 5.5-46. Creating the top band.

11. Adjust the points of the left sock to create variety in the folds.

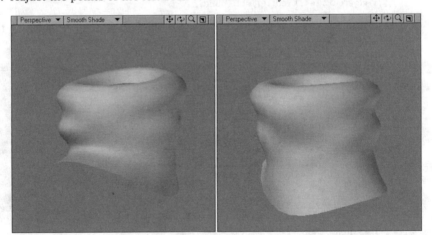

Figure 5.5-47. Adjust the folds to create variety.

12. Adjust the points of the right sock to create variety, but adjust in different places than the left sock so they're asymmetrical.

13. **Cut** and **Paste** the right sock into the layer with the left sock.

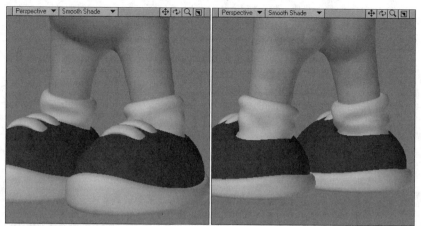

Figure 5.5-48. Finished socks.

14. Check the three clothing layers with the body and shoe layers, making any adjustments necessary.

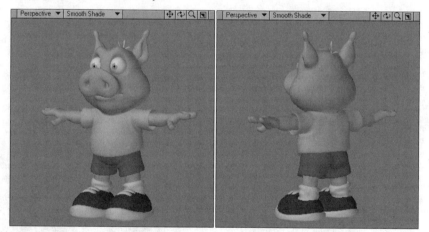

Figure 5.5-49. Hamish clothed.

You should now have seven layers including the body, template eyes, final eyes, and clothing layers.

You should now be pretty comfortable with modeling. We've covered quite a few of the modeling tools in LightWave, but there are many more. Make sure you have a good understanding of what all the tools can do so you can use the most efficient modeling methods to achieve your goal.

The most important thing when modeling characters is to start simple and work into the details. This makes it easier to create the right forms and shapes for the character, and ensures the model is only as complex as it needs to be, making every other step after modeling much easier. The more complex the model is, the harder it is to UV map, create morphs, and rig, resulting in those tasks taking a lot more time than they should.

Don't be afraid to start from scratch if the model isn't going as planned. It's often easier to start again than to fix a model that's headed in the wrong direction, whether it's due to the polygon count being too high, wrong polygon flow to support additional features, or forms and shapes that aren't working. It can sometimes take more time to adjust a bad model than to create it again, and the second time around it usually takes less time to reach the same point, with much better results.

The model is the basis for your character. Every other aspect of character creation relies on the model being as good as it can be. Spend the time and effort that it deserves and you'll be rewarded in the end.

5.6 Creating Morphs

With the modeling complete we're almost ready to move on to texturing. There are just a couple of morphs that need to be created. The eye blink and mouth open morphs we'll create now are to assist with texturing the face. Morphs and morph creation are covered in full detail in *Volume 2: Rigging & Animation*.

Eye Blink

To create the blink we just need to adjust the polygons of the eyelids. First we'll prepare the object for morphing.

1. Select the first layer and select the polygons of the body, leaving a couple of bands under the head, and **Hide** them.

2. **Fit All** and place the second layer, the template eyeballs, in the background. Make sure **Symmetry** is on and we're ready to start.

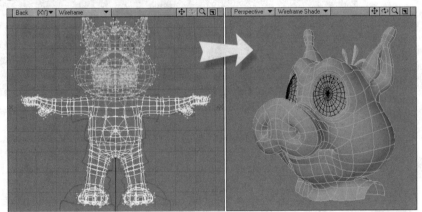

Figure 5.6-1. Ready to morph.

3. Select the **Morph** (**M**) button at the bottom-right of the interface. Create a new morph by clicking the pull-down menu to the right of the button and choosing **(new)**. Change the name to **Eye.Blink** and click **OK**.

> **Note:** If you create a new morph, then switch to another morph or back to the base without altering any geometry, the new morph will disappear. This is a housekeeping feature of vertex maps so you don't end up with redundant maps with no information in them. If this happens to you, don't panic; you just need to recreate the new morph when you're ready to adjust the geometry.

4. **Zoom** up on the left eye and select the four middle polygons of the top eyelid geometry, shown in Figure 5.6-2.

5. **Rotate** the Perspective view so you're looking side on to the eye, then **Rotate** the selected polygons about **40°** with the cursor centered on the eye.

6. Deselect the top two polygons, then **Rotate** again about **40°**.

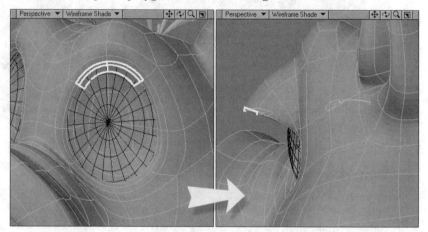

Figure 5.6-2. Rotating in the Perspective view rotates on the axis of the viewport.

7. **Shift+select** the two upper polygons again, and from the Top view **Move** the selected polygons in toward the middle of the eyeball, then **Move** them down a little.

8. Deselect the top two polygons and from the Top view, adjust the edge of the eyelid to match the curve of the eyeball while maintaining a small distance from the eyeball, then move the polygons down a little.

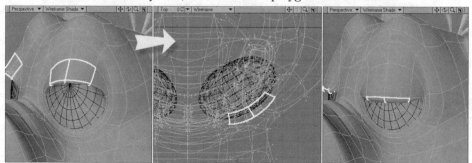

Figure 5.6-3. Try to make sure that the leading edge of the eyelid is flat.

9. Adjust the upper eyelid so it's a nice shape and maintains a roughly equal distance from the eyeball.

10. Repeat steps 2 to 7 for the lower eyelid, except only **Rotate** by **35°** each time, and adjust the lower eyelid so it sits just under and behind the upper eyelid.

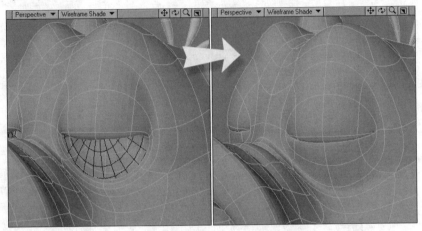

Figure 5.6-4. Create a nice rounded shape for the closed eyelids.

Mouth Open

Opening the jaw is one of the trickiest morphs to accomplish. It involves so much of the geometry and, because much of that geometry is hidden in the mouth, it can be quite fiddly. Luckily, once you've got the jaw open you won't have to worry about doing it again until the next character.

1. Create a new morph called **Mouth.Open**.

2. Select the polygons of the **Mouth** surface in the Polygon Statistics panel, then deselect the top half of the mouth and the back of the throat. Then, using the Right and Perspective views, select the polygons of the lower lip and chin. Finally, select the polygons of the **Teeth_Lower** surface.

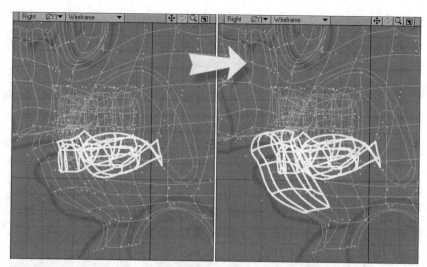

Figure 5.6-5. The most important selection is the inner mouth. The outside polygons can easily be cleared from the morph if you select and move too many.

3. From the Right view, **Rotate** the selected polygons about **30°** from just behind the teeth, then **Move** the polygons down a little.

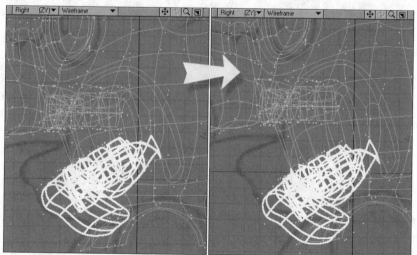

Figure 5.6-6. Rotating is the natural motion for the jaw, but it also moves down a little when it opens.

4. Now we've got the basis for the open jaw, but as you can see there's quite a bit of adjusting we need to do. The first step is to adjust the lips so they're stretched nicely around the open jaw. Adjust the lips so they create a nice oval shape around the open mouth, and move the bottom lip in against the teeth.

5. Adjust the points around the mouth, including the cheeks and chin, to smooth out the shapes. You can go back to the (base) to select points, then back to the morph to adjust if the points are hidden or difficult to select in the morph.

6. Finally, flatten the cheeks a little to promote some squash and stretch and adjust all the points to refine the shapes.

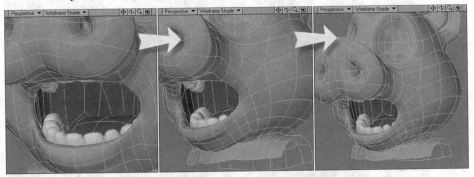

Figure 5.6-7. Adjust the points, making sure you check them from all angles.

7. **Unhide All** and **Save** the object.

Don't spend too much time on the morphs at this stage, as they're just being used to make texturing a little easier. You'll have a chance to refine them when the other morphs are created in *Volume 2: Rigging & Animation*.

Chapter 6

Texturing

Surfaces and textures enhance a model by specifying the color, how lights affect the surface, and whether it's reflective or transparent, and can provide small detail that's impractical to model. With texturing you can make a character look less like a 3D model and appear more alive and real.

6.1 UV Mapping

UV maps determine how textures are applied to the geometry. UV mapping is a daunting task for many people, but the truth is, while it can be time consuming, it's really quite easy once you understand how to apply UV maps to a character and efficient ways of creating them. Like all aspects of character creation, there is no substitute for hard work. You can't expect to press a button and have your textures perfectly arranged on the model. While some areas of a model are quick and straightforward to UV map, other areas require careful map manipulation and point adjustments to provide the best results.

Common frustrations with UV mapping in LightWave are caused by the need to unweld points to edit discontinuous UV maps, and the distortion of UV mapped textures on subpatches. Fortunately, these become far less of an issue once you learn a few simple techniques for efficient UV mapping.

Although in this case we're texturing Hamish before rigging, it's often best to leave UV mapping until after rigging as it relies so heavily on the structure of the model, which can require changes during the rigging process. As you gain experience and feel more comfortable that you won't need to make any changes to the geometry, it becomes easier to do UV mapping and texturing earlier in the process. But even then it's hard to predict when you'll need to make geometry changes during morph creation or rigging that may adversely affect existing UV maps. Unlike morphs, UV maps don't update well with geometry changes, so you can create a lot of extra work for yourself if you have to adjust them after changing the geometry.

Planning

Planning is very important to successfully UV mapping a character. There are quite a few things to account for when creating UV maps. The texture obviously needs to be applied to the model with the least amount of stretching or distortion possible. You need to decide whether a surface needs a UV map or if a standard projection will do the job. You need to determine the easiest way to UV map, or unwrap, each section of the model. You need to decide where the seams occur between UV mapped areas so they're easy to hide and in less prominent places on the model. You also need to think about the number and size of the textures so you don't blow out the memory requirements for a character with too many large textures.

UV Maps vs. Standard Projections

In most cases UV maps are preferable to standard projections for character textures. You know when you apply a UV mapped texture that it'll stay in place no matter what you do to the model. You can also position every point on a UV map to make sure there are no overlapping polygons and minimal stretching.

However, there are times when you need a texture to move around on the object or to stay in place while the object deforms. In these cases you need to use standard projections.

Standard projections also have the benefit of not distorting the texture on subpatched geometry. Although there are ways to overcome, or at least minimize, UV texture distortion, sometimes it can be easier to apply a texture using standard projections.

> **Tip:** It's also useful to create a UV map for textures using cylindrical or spherical standard projections. If you create the UV map for the polygons in the surface using the same initial values as your planned standard projection, you can use the UV map as a template for painting the texture even though you're not using the UV map for the final projection.

Analyzing the Model

Once you've determined what parts of the model to UV map, you need to work out where to create separate UV maps and the best way to create them.

It's tempting to place as much of a character as possible into a single continuous UV map. This is rarely practical, as you still end up with seams, you have less control over where the seams occur, and the texture will need to be huge to create sufficient detail.

So you need to analyze the model to determine which areas can be continuous and which cannot, then determine which discontinuous areas can share a UV map and which to separate into different UV maps. Because the face and head are such prominent and important areas of a character, it usually makes sense to give them their own UV maps. The other areas of the model should be separated where it's difficult or impractical to create a continuous map.

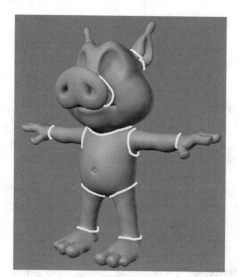

Figure 6.1-1. UV separations.

It's impossible to UV map a character without seams. You will have seams either between separate UV maps or within a UV map, and you need to work out the best positions for them. The seams should occur in areas with minimal detail so it's easier to match up the textures. Seams should also occur in less prominent areas of the model so it will be less noticeable if the textures don't match up perfectly.

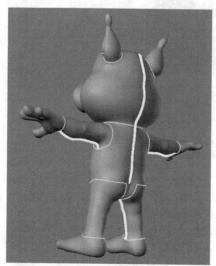

Figure 6.1-2. Seam placement.

Surfaces and UV Maps

Surfaces and UV maps can be used together in many ways. You don't have to use a single UV map for each surface. You can have multiple UV maps for a single surface, multiple surfaces for a single UV map, or a UV map for just part of a surface.

Multiple Surfaces per UV Map

Using a single UV map for multiple surfaces is useful in all sorts of ways, and can drastically reduce your workload. You can create a single UV map that covers multiple areas of the model, or apply different textures to areas of a model that use the same UV coordinates.

You can apply a texture to different surfaces using the same UV map, reducing the number of UV maps and the number of textures you need for the model. This is useful for creating detail that crosses different surfaces. It also allows you to tweak the values of each surface independently while sharing the same texture for other surface attributes.

Figure 6.1-3. The same UV map and texture is applied to the shoe soles surface and the shoelaces surface.

You can apply different textures to areas sharing the same UV mapped values. This is useful for symmetrical geometry, allowing you to create the same UV map for both sides but create asymmetrical texture detail by assigning a different surface and texture to each side. This means that you can use the same base texture image for each side so you don't have to create the same imagery twice. It's far easier to create two surfaces sharing the same UV map than it is to separate those areas within a UV map and have to paint each one individually.

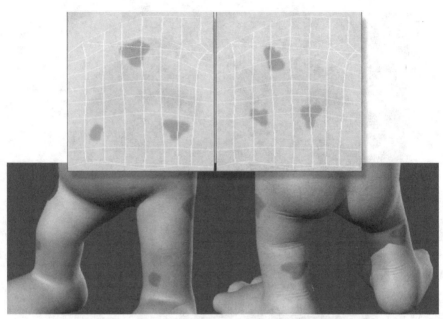

Figure 6.1-4. Each leg has a different surface and texture, but both textures use the same UV map.

Multiple UV Maps per Surface

Using multiple UV maps for a single surface is a powerful way to minimize seams by blending textures or to use different textures on the same area of a model.

You can blend two or more textures that have different mapping coordinates. This is a great way to apply different mapping coordinates to adjoining areas of a model without creating a hard seam between them. By using an alpha map for the textures you have full control over the transition between textures. You can fade one texture into another, creating a smooth blend, or change the placement or shape of the seam so it follows natural contours instead of being restricted to polygon placement.

You can apply a texture with different mapping coordinates to create localized detail. Sometimes a single UV map isn't sufficient to accurately map an area of a model, so you need to cover the less accurate areas with another texture using different mapping coordinates. Again, by using an alpha map for the local texture, you can blend the local detail into the primary texture however you like.

The important thing about using multiple UV maps on a surface is that all of the UV maps need to include all the polygons of the surface. If you don't want certain polygons of the surface to be affected by the texture, you should place them in an area of the UV map that is made transparent by the alpha map. Usually you only need alpha maps for the overlapping textures, not the base or first texture, as that'll be covered by the textures on top of it.

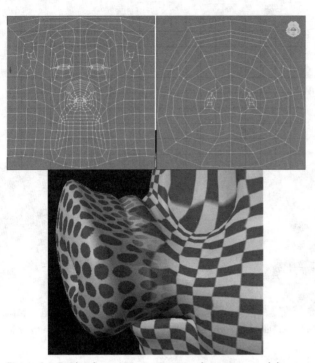

Figure 6.1-5. Blend one UV map into another using an alpha map.

UV Mapping Part of a Surface

UV mapping part of a surface is similar to creating multiple UV maps for a surface, but instead of having a UV mapped texture as a base, you have standard surface attributes or textures using standard projections. You still need to include all the polygons of the surface in the UV map, but you can keep certain polygons from being affected by the texture by including them in an area of the map that's made transparent by the alpha map.

An alternative is to create a copy of the surface for the polygons that are UV mapped. Both surfaces should have the same attributes, except for the addition of the texture on the UV mapped surface, so that they appear seamless.

Textures and UV Maps

Understanding how UV maps relate to textures or image maps is important to creating the best and most efficient textures for your character. Textures can take up a lot of system memory, and when you have multiple characters in a scene it's very important that the textures for all the characters are created efficiently so they take up as little memory as possible. It's also important to align the scale of the textures so the pixel size is roughly equal between textures applied with different UV maps or surfaces.

Aspect Ratio

UV map coordinates are different from the pixel values of a texture, although it's easy to be confused by the two. UV maps are always square, with an aspect ratio of 1:1, although that doesn't mean the textures have to be square. The UV coordinates will stretch to the aspect ratio of whatever texture you apply. So if your texture has an aspect ratio of 3:2, the UV map will stretch to fit the texture, although it will still appear to be 1:1 within the editing viewport. So don't worry when your texture is displayed square in the UV editing viewport because the full-scale texture will still be applied to the model.

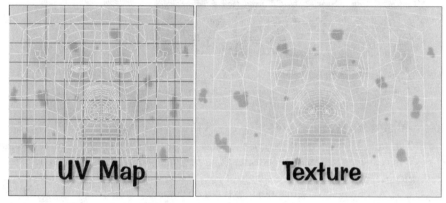

Figure 6.1-6. Left: UV Map. Right: Texture.

Understanding this enables you to create more efficient textures. By stretching the polygons within a UV map so they appear at the correct aspect ratio or scale, you can lose a lot of the potential of a texture by having large areas of unused space. This means that you need larger textures to achieve the necessary amount of detail. You should use the full UV map even though the polygons may appear stretched when you're editing the map. You can then stretch the texture to the correct aspect ratio for the polygons. By using as much of the texture as possible you can achieve the necessary amount of detail at a smaller size, saving memory.

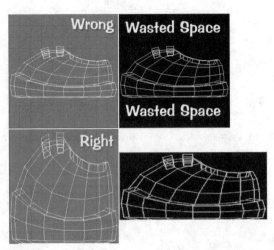

Figure 6.1-7. Top: Wasted texture space. Bottom: Using the entire texture.

Aligning Texture Size

Different UV maps will project the same texture at different sizes on the model. This can cause problems with the scale of detail and bump strength, and cause difficulties with matching up seams.

When you're UV mapping textures on adjoining areas, it's important to adjust the size of each texture to match the textures of the adjoining UV maps so the pixel sizes are roughly the same for all the textures. This makes it much easier to create the textures because you can use the same methods and brush sizes to create the details in different textures, confident that details that are common to multiple textures will appear at the same scale on the model.

Figure 6.1-8. Left: The same sized texture for all UV maps. Right: Texture sizes correctly aligned.

UV Texture Distortion

UV mapped textures can appear distorted on the object for a few reasons. The first is a result of the points being in a different position on the UV map than on the object. The second is a result of UV mapping being calculated before subdivision. The third mainly affects bump mapping and is a result of scale differences between polygons on the UV map and polygons on the object.

Mapping Faces vs. Subpatches

There is a big difference between the position of the actual points on an object and the position of points on the subpatched geometry. Texture stretching occurs as a result of creating UV coordinates from the original point positions instead of the subpatched point positions.

While this type of texture distortion can be fixed by editing the point positions, a much easier fix is to generate the UV maps from subpatches instead of faces. This creates the UV coordinates from the subpatched position of the points instead of the original position of the points. The result of this is a more accurate UV map, reflecting the position of the subpatched polygons.

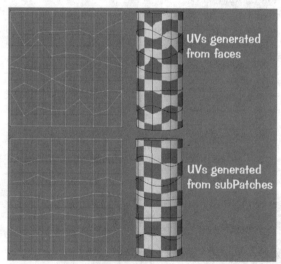

Figure 6.1-9. Always UV map subpatches from subpatched geometry to minimize stretching.

When UV mapping subpatches, you should never create UV maps from faces or unwelded geometry, as the resulting maps will require significantly more editing to eliminate texture distortion.

Subpatch Distortion

Texture distortion also occurs as a result of UV maps being interpolated linearly. The path between points is linear on a UV map, but spline interpolated on subpatches. The spline interpolation distorts the linear mapping of the UV mapped texture, which distorts the texture between the points.

291

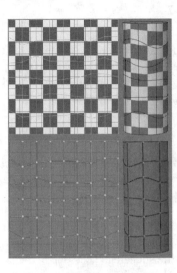

Figure 6.1-10.
Straight lines on the
texture are curved on
subpatches, creating
distortion. You can
use this to your
advantage when
creating textures.

It's not possible to overcome subpatch distortion altogether, but there are ways to minimize and control the distortion that occurs.

The best way to avoid subpatch distortion is to create neat polygon flow. Neat polygon flow creates the least amount of distortion between subpatches, so the linear interpolated texture is as accurate as possible.

You can adjust the UV map to minimize subpatch distortion. This won't remove the distortion, but it does give you some control of the amount of distortion and where it occurs so you can move the distortion to an inconspicuous area.

UV Polygon Scale

Bump mapping in LightWave is greatly affected by scale. The size of a bump mapped image affects the intensity of the bump effect; the smaller the image, the greater the bump strength.

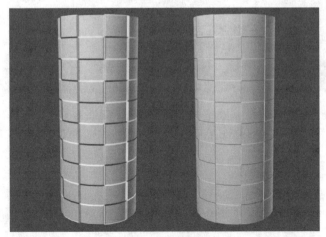

Figure 6.1-11. Left: Small texture size creates larger bumps. Right: Large texture size creates smaller bumps. Both textures and bump settings are the same except for their size.

For the same reason, for polygons that have a UV mapped bump texture applied, it's important to keep the relative scale between polygons the same on the UV map as on the object. If the relative scale between polygons differs between the UV map and the object, the bump effect will be a different strength on each polygon.

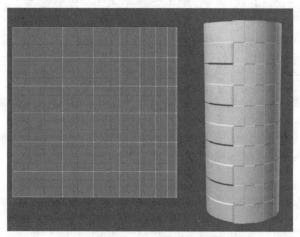

Figure 6.1-12. Bump strength increases as the texture is mapped smaller than correct scale.

The size of the textures between different UV maps also affects bump map strength, which is another reason for aligning the texture size between UV maps.

Discontinuous UVs

Discontinuous UVs are sections of a UV map that are unattached even though those sections are attached on the object. Understanding how discontinuous UVs are dealt with is an important aspect of creating UV maps.

A UV map contains UV coordinates for every point of every polygon. Even though a point may appear to be shared by multiple polygons, you can separate polygons within a UV map by specifying different UV values for that point on each polygon. This occurs when the geometry is separated within a UV map and along seams generated by cylindrical and spherical projections. When this occurs, because there is still only one physical point, the point position is only editable on one of the polygons within the UV map.

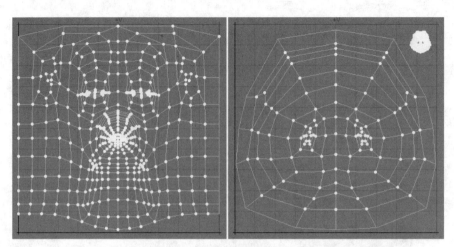

Figure 6.1-13. Notice the lack of points along one side of the discontinuous polygons.

The other aspect of point sharing is that if you separately map two sections of continuous geometry into the same UV map, the points between mapped polygons will be joined up. Sometimes this achieves the required result, but most of the time it doesn't. If you want to create separate UV coordinates for continuous geometry you have to separate the geometry first, do the UV mapping, then merge the geometry back together.

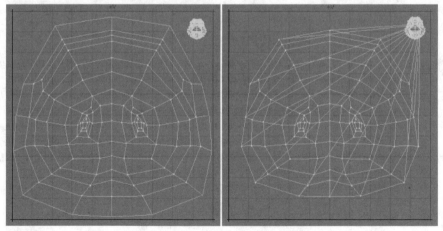

Figure 6.1-14. Left: Continuous geometry separated before mapping. Right: Continuous geometry not separated before mapping.

There are two techniques for creating discontinuous UVs, each suitable for a different type of discontinuity. You can either unweld the points or separate the different polygons by cutting and pasting.

Remember to always merge the points after separating them for UV mapping or editing.

Unwelding Points

Unwelding a point creates a separate point for each polygon that it shares. If you have multiple polygons in different places on a UV map, unwelding the shared points gives you access to the individual UV coordinates for all the polygons.

Unwelding the points causes those polygons to separate on the model as well as the UV map, so subpatches also become discontinuous. You should only unweld the points at the seam, not the entire object, so you can edit the UV map while seeing the correct subpatched result on the continuous areas of the object.

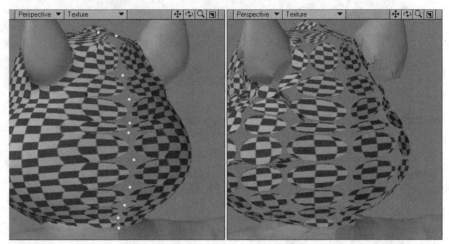

Figure 6.1-15. Left: Just the seam points unwelded. Right: All points unwelded. Notice how difficult it is to see the results of the UV map.

Unwelding creates separate points for all the attached polygons, not just the discontinuous ones, so it's often overkill to unweld. Unwelding also affects the subpatch placement of the points, so if you create UV coordinates from unwelded points you lose the benefits of mapping subpatches.

While unwelding points is sometimes the easiest way to edit existing UV mapped geometry, it's better to cut and paste to separate discontinuous sections of geometry for mapping purposes, as unwelding also positions the points in their original position instead of their subpatched position.

Cutting and Pasting

Often you don't need all the points of all the polygons separated, just a few different sections of the geometry. In these cases it's best to cut and paste the discontinuous sections instead of unwelding.

Cutting and pasting the discontinuous polygons creates separate points for just those polygons instead of all the attached polygons, so the subpatched geometry isn't as badly affected, and you can't accidentally separate continuous polygons.

Cutting and pasting retains the subpatch position of the remaining points better than unwelding. So creating discontinuous UV map coordinates is more accurate from geometry that's separated by cutting from the original instead of unwelding.

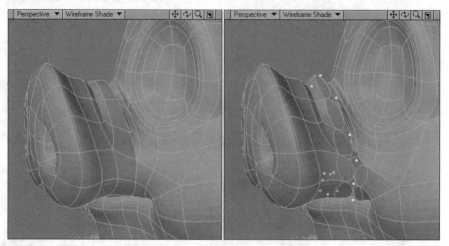

Figure 6.1-16. Left: Nose polygons separated by cut and paste. Right: Nose polygons separated by unwelding.

UV Map Creation

Creating a UV map requires deciding what geometry is to be included in the map and the initial layout of the UV map. Creating the best initial layout of a UV map is important to make the editing process as painless as possible.

There are ways to influence the initial layout of a UV map to ensure the best results from basic projections. You can manually adjust the basic projection settings to customize and improve the results. You can also create a morph with the geometry oriented differently to better align it with a projection axis and to determine where the default seams occur.

Basic Projections

The initial layout of the UV map is determined by the basic projections. Some of the basic projections are those available as standard projections. There are also a couple of extra ones that can be handy for creating UV maps. Keep in mind that these basic projections usually just provide a starting point for the UV map, not the final result.

Planar

Planar projection maps the polygons just as they appear when viewed along the chosen axis, just like the standard planar projection. This is the simplest type of projection and is also one of the most useful.

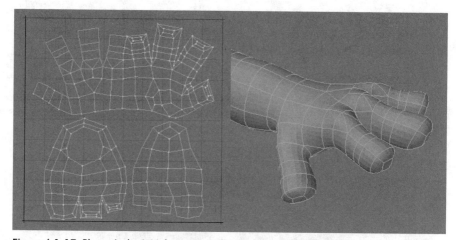

Figure 6.1-17. Planar is the initial projection for mapping the hands and feet.

Planar can be used to map one side of an object over the other, so you only need to create one texture that projects onto both sides, just like standard planar projection. Planar projection retains the relative shape of the polygons pretty well, making it useful when you want to avoid stretching the texture. This makes it a good starting point for many UV maps, as you start with a fairly accurate layout of the polygons.

Cylindrical

Cylindrical projection maps the polygons as if they were projected out from a center line, just like the standard cylindrical projection. This is the most used type of projection, as it's fairly predictable and so many things are basically cylindrical in shape.

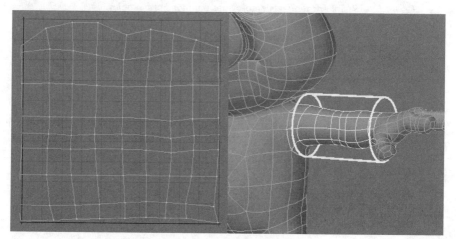

Figure 6.1-18. Cylindrical projection works well for limbs.

Cylindrical projection creates a seam along one side of the geometry, placing the points along the seam on either side of the UV map, so as long as the texture is horizontally seamless you won't have a visible seam.

Spherical

Spherical projection maps the polygons as if they were projected from a center point, just like the standard spherical projection. This is perhaps the most misunderstood type of projection.

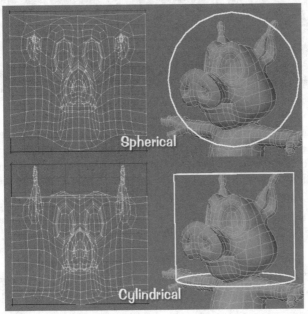

Figure 6.1-19. Spherical projection provides a better starting point for the round head than cylindrical projection.

Standard spherical projection is commonly avoided because of the difficulties of creating textures that project nicely at the poles, but it can be a powerful initial projection for UV mapping areas of a model with a round shape, as it retains the polygon shapes and relative sizes toward the poles much better than cylindrical projection.

Seams occur in spherical projections in much the same way as in cylindrical projection.

Atlas

Atlas projection maps the polygons by mapping different sections of the geometry separately to avoid overlapping areas, and to keep the aspect ratio and scale of the polygons as accurate as possible.

Figure 6.1-20. Atlas projections are difficult to edit and create textures for. Atlas projections are most useful for creating UV maps for baking textures.

Although it can be quite useful in certain circumstances, atlas projection is rarely useful for characters, as the resulting UV map is very difficult to edit and create textures for.

Quad Polygon

Quad polygon projection is the black sheep of the family. It's not included in the UV map creation options, but can be found under Map➤Texture➤Poly Map. Quad polygon projection maps each polygon to the full size of the UV map.

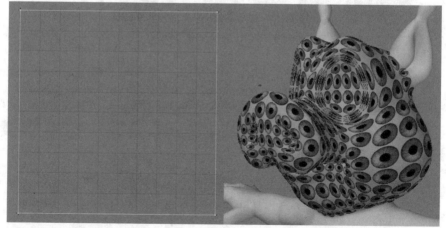

Figure 6.1-21. Quad polygon is useful for creating tiled detail.

This is really useful for creating tiled textures on a model, mapping an image to every polygon. Quad polygon projection works best when the mapped polygons are roughly equal in size and shape.

Automatic or Manual Settings

The automatic settings for the basic projections work the same way as Automatic Sizing for standard projections. The center point and scale of the selected polygons are used to generate the UV coordinates. This makes it nice and easy, but as usual, the software doesn't always do the best job and it's necessary to take control yourself. By choosing manual settings you can adjust the center point and scale of the projection, giving you more control of the outcome.

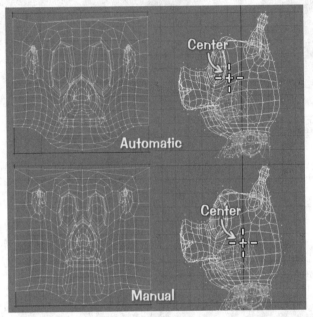

Figure 6.1-22. Manual settings often provide much better results than automatic settings.

Adjusting the settings manually isn't difficult at all. The initial automatic settings are provided, so all you need to do is adjust them. The Center settings are the most useful ones to adjust. These determine the center point of the projection so you can offset planar projections and move the center point of cylindrical and spherical projections to best suit the geometry.

Retaining Scale

Most of the time you should use the full UV map and stretch the texture to retain the scale of the UV mapped geometry, but there are times when it's useful to retain the scale of the geometry within the square aspect ratio of the UV map. It's especially useful when you're adding multiple sections to a single UV map so you can keep the scale of the geometry and use up the wasted space with more geometry.

To keep the scale of the selected geometry within the square UV map, the easiest way is to create a perfectly square box surrounding the geometry. If you include the box in the selection when you create the UV map, or make UVs on an existing map, the geometry will retain its scale. Just remember to delete the box when you're finished with UV mapping.

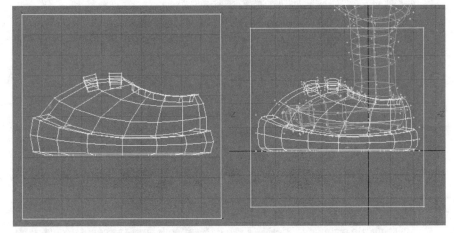

Figure 6.1-23. Adding a box keeps the correct scale within the square UV map.

Internal Seams

Seams within UV maps are determined by the orientation of the geometry being mapped. You can't change the seam axis for cylindrical and spherical projections, so to alter the position of the seam you need to adjust the orientation of the geometry.

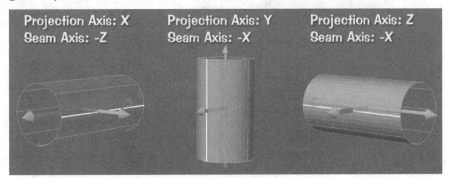

Figure 6.1-24. Projection axes and their seam axes.

If the geometry doesn't have a neat line along the seam axis, the polygons won't be aligned neatly at the sides of the UV map, but instead will be overlapping at the sides. This creates essentially the same effect, as UV coordinates wrap around, so a point that appears to be at V coordinate 1.2 will actually be mapped to 0.2.

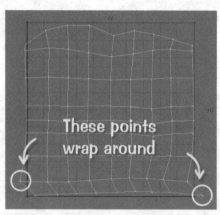

Figure 6.1-25. Overlapping points wrap around
to the opposite side of the map.

UV Morphs

Using morphs can make UV map creation much easier by allowing you to reposition the geometry in the best orientation for the initial projections without affecting the original model. You can determine where the seam occurs as well as how to align the geometry along the mapping axis so you achieve the best result.

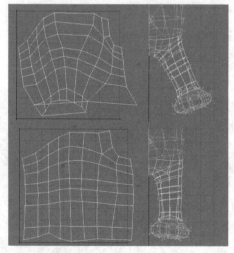

Figure 6.1-26. Top: A cylindrical projection in Y doesn't work
well for the leg on an angle. Bottom: Repositioning the leg in
a morph allows the initial projection to do a better job.

Don't try to do too much in the morph. Keep the geometry together, just moving or rotating the section you're mapping to help the initial projections. If you cut the geometry apart and start doing UV editing within the morph instead of in the UV map, you'll cause problems with subpatches later on. It's much easier to do the UV editing within the UV map than in a morph, as you can see the results as you edit, and the initial projections, which you don't have access to when editing a morph, provide a pretty good starting point.

UV Map Editing

Editing UV maps is the most time-consuming aspect of UV mapping, but it's very important to spend the time to carefully edit the UV maps to provide the best results. Even though it's time consuming, the process of editing UV maps is easy when you know a few simple techniques.

Symmetrical Editing

Symmetry is a great modeling feature that allows modifications to one side of the geometry to be reflected on the other side. When working within the UV coordinates, selecting points or polygons for UV editing works with symmetry, but modifying the position doesn't work symmetrically. This is because the symmetry axis is $X = 0$, which equates to $U = 0$ in a UV map.

To edit a UV map using symmetry, all you need to do is offset the UV map by –50% on the U axis by using Transform UV. That brings the center of the UV map to $U = 0$, and all your editing will work in full symmetry. Just remember to offset the UV map 50% on the U axis when you're finished, to bring it back into the UV boundary.

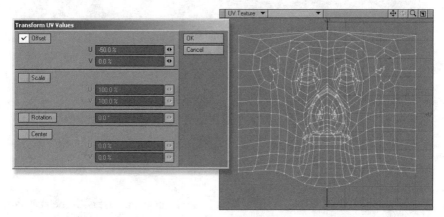

Figure 6.1-27. Symmetry boundary occurs at $U = 0$.

Transform UV

Transform UV is a very useful tool. It takes the place of the Numeric panel for modeling tools when editing UV maps.

While the standard modeling tools work when using them in the UV viewport, activating a standard tool from the Numeric panel will cause the change to occur on the object instead of the UV map. Transform UV takes the place of the numeric option of the standard tools when editing UV maps. It includes the ability to move (offset), rotate, and scale UV coordinates.

Quantize UVs

Quantize is useful when you want a neatly ordered UV map. It works a bit like editing with a grid. You can set a grid size, and the points on the UV map will snap to the closest grid point.

Checkerboard Test

The checkerboard is valuable for accurate UV map editing. The checkerboard is a checkered image that's applied to the surface using the UV map. It shows where the UV map is stretching and distorting so you can edit those areas to minimize the effect. The other benefit of the checkerboard is that you can use it to determine the correct scale and aspect ratio for the texture images.

The trick to applying a checkerboard is to use the procedural checkerboard texture instead of an image that already has a checkerboard on it. A checkered image map provides the benefit of showing the stretch and distortion, but can only give a very rough idea of the required scale and aspect ratio.

Figure 6.1-28. The same checkerboard texture is used for all UV maps.

By applying Textured Filter to a blank image, you can adjust both the scale and aspect ratio of the checkerboard for each UV map on your object so you can align the size and determine the correct aspect ratio of all the image maps before you start creating them.

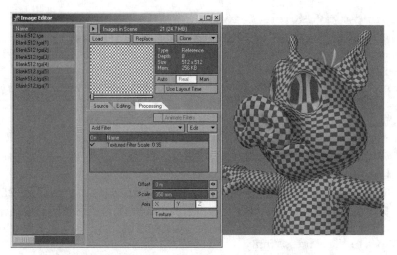

Figure 6.1-29. Textured Filter allows quick and easy scale adjustments to determine the correct scale and aspect ratio for the final textures.

6.2 Creating the UV Maps

Now we'll put all of that UV mapping information to use. We'll use a variety of methods to create the UV maps for Hamish.

UV Mapping the Head

Hamish's head is a bit more complex to UV map than many heads. The difficult part of UV mapping any geometry is mapping bits that stick out of a basic shape. For heads this is usually the ears, but for Hamish it includes the ears and the nose, as the nose is much bigger on Hamish than on many characters.

Bits that stick out often need to be mapped separately from the main shape to achieve accurate results. If you try to include them in the same UV map, the scale of the detail will be quite different between the main area and the area that sticks out.

It's useful to use the head as the primary UV map for a character. This means that the scale of all the following UV textures will be determined by the scale of the head's UV texture.

Creating a UV Morph

To set the seam down the back of the head we first need to create a morph from which to generate the UV map. The seam occurs on the –X side for a Y axis spherical or cylindrical projection, so we'll rotate Hamish so he's facing +X, making the seam run down the back of the head. We can also use the morph to place the eyelids in a better position to map.

1. Load your Hamish model into Modeler (you can find the premade object in \Objects\Chapters\Hamish_Working_v001.lwo).
2. Change the top-left viewport to **UV Texture**.
3. Create a new morph called **UV.Y-90**.
4. Select **Morph Map Mixer** and move the **Eye.Blink** slider to about **80%**.
5. Place both layers of the object in the foreground and turn off **Symmetry** if it's on. Select **Rotate** (**y**) and in the numeric values set Angle to **–90** and Axis to **Y** and press **Apply**.

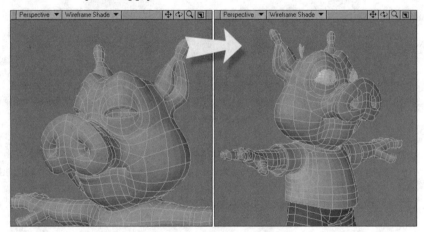

Figure 6.2-1. Adjusting the geometry in a morph helps to create a good UV map.

Creating the UV Map

The head is fairly round so we'll create the UV map using the spherical projection.

In this case there's probably about the same amount of editing needed for a cylindrical or spherical projection. Each one would require different types of adjustments. A spherical projection gives us the best initial layout for the area on the top of the head, so it's a little easier to edit.

1. Turn on **Symmetry**, select the polygons of the head down to the neck line, then deselect the polygons with the surface **Mouth**.

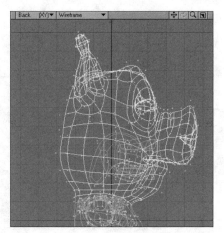

Figure 6.2-2. Selecting the polygons for the UV map.

2. Create a new UV map by using the **T** pull-down or **Map**➤**Texture**➤**New UV Map**. In the Create UV Texture Map panel, give it a name of **Head**, set Map Type to **Spherical**, and set Axis to **Y**.

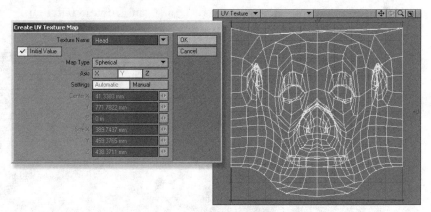

Figure 6.2-3. Automatic settings often provide substandard results.

The projection isn't very nice because the automatic settings have placed the center of the spherical projection in the center of the selected polygons. We want the center of the projection to be in the center of the main head shape, so we need to recreate the UV map with the manual settings. To determine the correct settings, place the mouse cursor in the center of the head from the side view and note the X and Y position.

3. With the polygons still selected, select **Map**➤**General**➤**Clear Map**.

4. Select **Map**➤**Texture**➤**Make UVs**. In the Assign UV Coordinates panel, change Settings to **Manual**. All the other settings will be retained from the previous step.

5. Set Center X to **0**, and Center Y to **0.72** or **720 mm**.

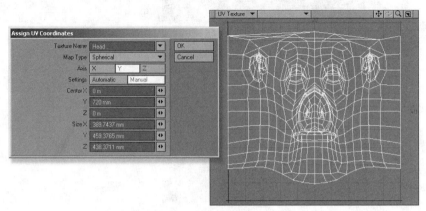

Figure 6.2-4. Manual settings allow for more control of the initial projection.

That's looking much nicer. Before we start editing the map, there are a couple of things we can clean up. The continuous polygon at the top needs to be fixed, and we'll remove the ears from the UV map and map them separately.

6. Select the top-left point on the UV map and **Unweld (Ctrl+u)**.

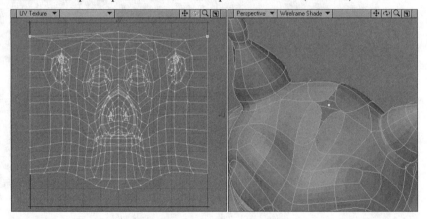

Figure 6.2-5. Unweld the attached point so the continuous polygon can be adjusted.

7. Select the overlapping polygon and **Ctrl+drag** the leftmost point over to the right side of the map, not quite all the way.

8. Select just the point that was just dragged and **Map▸More▸Set UV Value**. Leave it set to **U** and change Value to **100**.

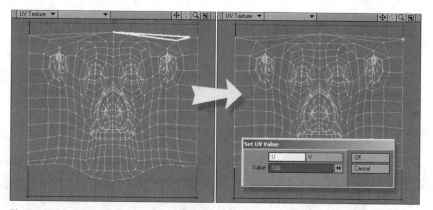

Figure 6.2-6. Fixing the continuous polygon.

9. Select the points of the bulb of the ears, expanding the selection until you have the points selected as shown in Figure 6.2-7, and **Clear Map**.

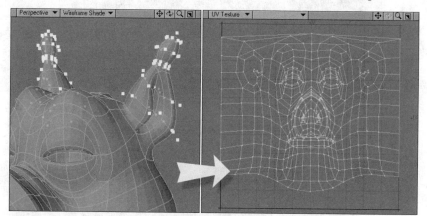

Figure 6.2-7. Remove the ears from the map, as they can't be mapped well within this layout.

Initial Editing

The first step to editing is to adjust the UV map so there are no overlapping polygons.

When editing the UV map with symmetry, the points along one side of the seam aren't selected with points on the other side of the seam, so remember to select the points on both sides of the seam when adjusting the positions of the unwelded points.

1. Select all the points at the left and right edges of the map and **Unweld**.

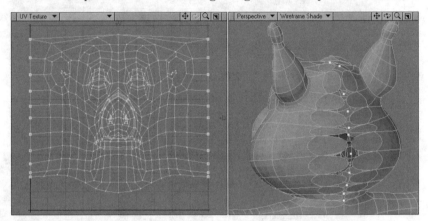

Figure 6.2-8. Unweld the seam.

2. Select **Map▸Texture▸Transform UV**, turn on **Offset**, and set U to –50% to enable symmetry editing on the UV map.

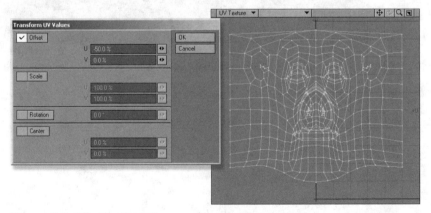

Figure 6.2-9. Offsetting the UV map enables symmetrical editing.

3. Make sure **Symmetry** is on and zoom up on the eye area on the UV map. Adjust the points so they're relatively even and there are no overlapping polygons.

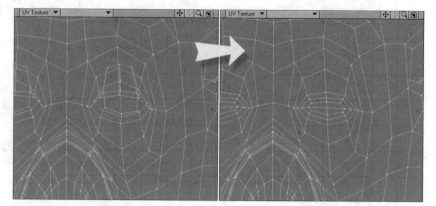

Figure 6.2-10. The polygons inside the eye socket are hidden by the eyeball so they can be squashed on the map.

4. Adjust the points at the front of the ear so there are no overlapping polygons.

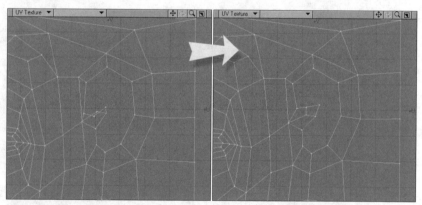

Figure 6.2-11. Cleaning up the base of the ear.

5. Select the polygons of the nose, and progressively shrink each band until there are no overlapping polygons.

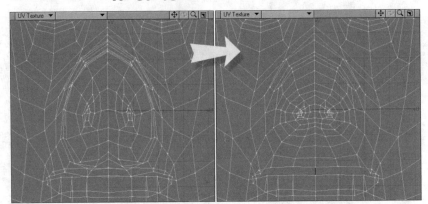

Figure 6.2-12. Bits that stick out, like the nose, need to be shrunk to fit into a continuous map. This creates different sized detail on these bits unless another UV map is used for them.

6. Adjust the points of the creases on top of the nose to neaten them up.
7. Adjust the nostrils so each band of polygons is contained within the previous one.

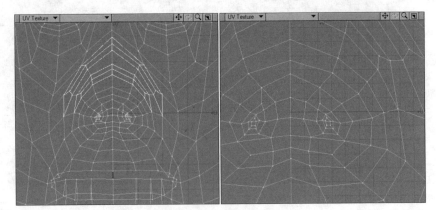

Figure 6.2-13. Making the nose coordinates neat.

8. Adjust the mouth area so there's no overlap and the points are spaced roughly according to the points on the model.

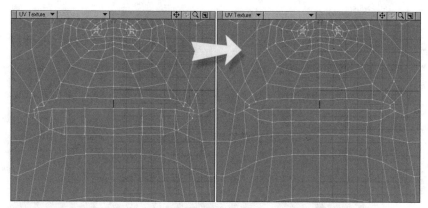

Figure 6.2-14. Try to match the scale of the lips.

9. Adjust the points at the top of the head to minimize stretching.

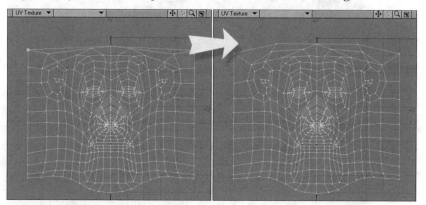

Figure 6.2-15. Adjusting the top of the head gives some control over the amount of stretching.

Checkerboard Test

Now we'll do a checkerboard test before we continue with the editing to minimize stretching and distortion. To get the full benefits of the checkerboard test, it's important to be able to adjust the scale and aspect of the checkerboard for each UV map. To do this we can create a new instance of the image for each UV map, then apply the checkerboard pattern to those instances, enabling the checkerboard for each instance to have a unique scale.

1. Open the **Image Editor** (**F6**) and load **Blank512.tga**.

2. Select **Clone➤Instance** to create a copy of the image. **Blank512.tga(1)** appears, which we'll use to test the Head UV map.

> **Note:** The first instance of the image should be left blank so the instances don't inherit the checkerboard values.

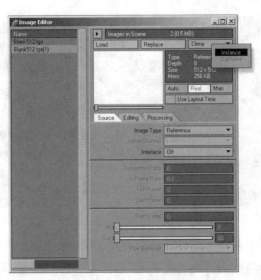

Figure 6.2-16. Cloning the blank image.

3. Select the **Processing** tab and **Add Filter**➤**Textured Filter**. Double-click the Textured Filter entry to open its properties.

4. Click the **Texture** button and change Layer Type to **Procedural Texture**, Procedural Type to **Checkerboard**, and Texture Color to **110,110,110**. Change all the Scale values to **0.1** or **100 mm**, then close the Texture Editor.

5. Set the Filter Scale to **0.25** or **250 mm** and close the Image Editor.

> **Note:** If you close Modeler and load the model later, you need to reset the Textured Filter. It retains all the same settings; it just needs waking up. Go through each instanced image in the Image Editor, open the Texture settings, and click the on/off check mark of the procedural checkerboard layer.

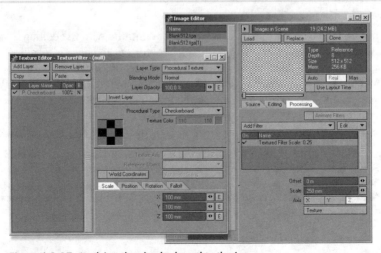

Figure 6.2-17. Applying the checkerboard to the image.

6. Open the **Surface Editor** (**F5**), select the **Head** surface, and open the Texture Editor for the Color channel.

7. Change Projection to **UV**, UVMap to **Head**, and Image to **Blank512.tga(1)**.

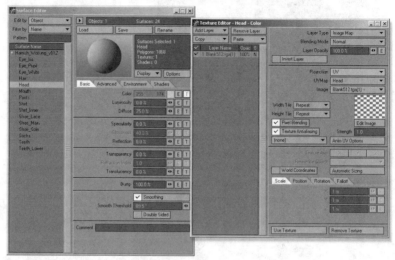

Figure 6.2-18. Applying the checkerboard to the Head surface.

8. Close the Texture Editor and Surface Editor, then change the Perspective viewport to **Textured Wire**, showing the checkerboard texture on Hamish's head.

Note: If the texture appears blurry, open the Display properties (**d**) and set Texture Resolution to 512.

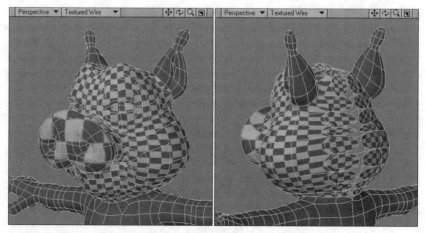

Figure 6.2-19. The checkerboard applied to the Head UV map.

9. Notice it's quite difficult to see how the texture is applied along the unwelded seam at the back of the head. **Merge Points** so you can see the effect of the checkerboard accurately at the back of the head.

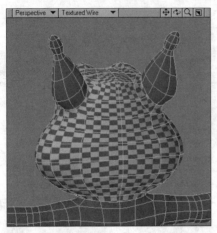

Figure 6.2-20. Merging the seam shows the texture accurately.

Editing the UV Map

Now that the checkerboard is there we can easily see where there's stretching and distortion. The points of the UV map need to be adjusted so the squares of the checkerboard are as even and close to equal size as possible. Don't worry if you can't get the checkerboard exactly square in an area. Just try to make the pattern flow evenly or flow with the polygons instead.

Notice the checkerboard is quite a different scale on the nose compared to the rest of the head. This is a result of mapping a protruding bit into the main UV map. We'll map the nose separately after editing the UV map of the head, so for now just try to get the UV map as accurate as possible around the base of the nose.

You can do most of the editing without worrying about the seam at the back of the head. When most of the points are in the right places you can unweld the seam and adjust it to match the other points in the map.

The top of the head, or the pole of the UV map, is always a tricky area. Try to get the checkerboard as smooth as possible in that area, but you won't be able to get the right scale for the checkerboard in those polygons. If you need texture detail in that area, you can add another UV map to blend a texture over the main UV map.

1. Adjust the points of the UV map, starting at the eye area and working out. Keep within the horizontal boundary set by the points of the seam.

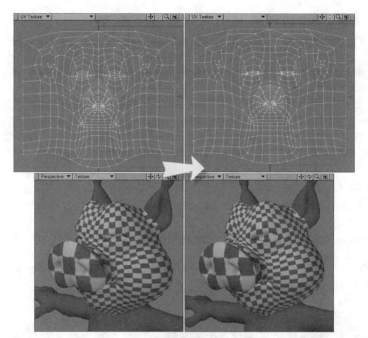

Figure 6.2-21. Edit the points to minimize stretching and distortion.

2. When you're happy that the checkerboard is as good as it can be, **Unweld** the points along the seam and adjust them vertically to match the internal points of the UV map.

3. **Scale** the UV map vertically to fit just inside the top and bottom of the UV boundary.

4. Turn off **Symmetry** and select **Transform UV,** then turn on **Offset** and set U to **50%**, moving the UV coordinates back within the UV boundary.

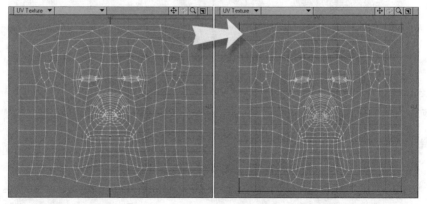

Figure 6.2-22. Adjust scale and position to fill the UV map and place the UV coordinates within the UV boundary.

5. **Merge Points** to fix the seam.

Adjusting Texture Scale

With the editing done, you can see if the squares of the checkerboard are stretched or squashed. For a cylindrical or spherical shape the squares will often be squashed, as the distance around the mapped area is more than the height of the area.

Adjusting the aspect ratio of the checkerboard texture until the checks are square gives you the opposite aspect ratio to what is needed for the image map. This means you can determine the correct scale of the image map so the pixels are square on the model, which means the detail you paint will appear at the same aspect ratio on the model as it does when you paint it.

1. Open the **Image Editor** (**F6**) and clone **Blank512.tga**.

2. Select **Blank512.tga(1)**, right-click the Textured Filter entry, and select **Copy**.

3. Select **Blank512.tga(2)** and **Paste** the Textured Filter.

> **Note:**   Making another clone maintains the original checkerboard aspect ratio and scale for use on the other UV maps.

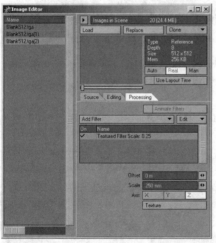

Figure 6.2-23. Create a copy of the original checkerboard settings to use for other UV maps.

4. Select **Blank512.tga(1)** and double-click the Textured Filter entry to open its properties.

5. Click the **Texture** button and change the X scale to **0.075** so the checkers appear squarer on the head.

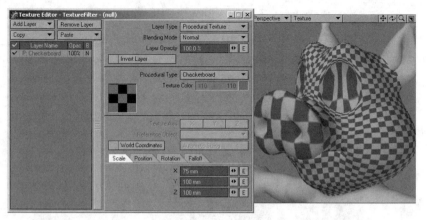

Figure 6.2-24. You should only adjust the X scale of the checkerboard texture. You can adjust the overall scale using the filter settings.

> **Note:** This means that the correct aspect ratio for the head's image map is 1.33:1 or 4:3, the same as most monitor resolutions.

We'll leave the filter scale as it is, as this is the primary UV map. The scale of all the other UV mapped textures will be adjusted to match this one.

UV Mapping the Nose

The nose needs different mapping coordinates than the head, as the nose can't fit into the head's UV map and retain the correct scale. We'll create another UV map for the nose using an initial planar projection and apply it over the head texture, blending the transition between the textures so there isn't a noticeable seam.

Although the plan is to use both UV maps on the same surface, we'll create a temporary surface for the nose so we can see both UV mapped textures as we edit the nose UV map.

1. Select the polygons of the nose, from just in front of the first crease. **Change Surface** (q), calling the new surface **Nose**.

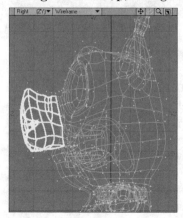

Figure 6.2-25. Select these polygons for the nose.

2. Open the Surface Editor, select the **Head** surface, right-click on it, and select **Copy**. Select the **Nose** surface, right-click on it, and select **Paste**.

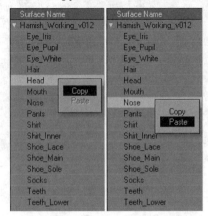

Figure 6.2-26. Copy the surface settings from the head to the nose.

3. Make sure you have the **(base)** morph selected, and with the nose polygons selected, make a new UV map called **Nose**. In the Create UV Texture Map panel, give it a name of **Nose**, set Map Type to **Planar**, and set Axis to **Z**.

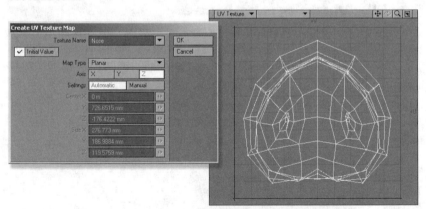

Figure 6.2-27. Initial projection for the Nose UV map.

4. Select **Transform UV**, turn on **Offset**, and set U to **–50%**.
5. Make sure Symmetry is on and adjust, progressively shrinking each band until there are no overlapping polygons.

Hamish

. . . . Texturing

6. Scale the UVs to fill the height of the map and up to the halfway point horizontally.

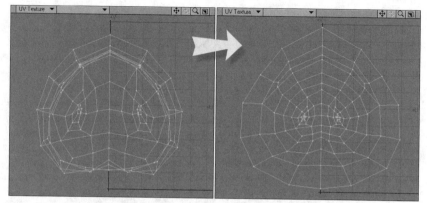

Figure 6.2-28. Edit to remove any overlapping polygons.

Editing the UV Map

We'll change the checkerboard on the nose so we can accurately edit the UV map and match the aspect and scale of the head texture.

1. Open Scene Editor, select the **Nose** surface, and open the texture for Color. Change UVMap to **Nose** and Image to **Blank512.tga(2)**.

> **Note:** When you copy filters, the settings are copied, but they sometimes don't update properly. To update the filter, open the texture and toggle the checkerboard on and off.
>
> You also need to update the checkerboards for all the textured filters if you close Modeler and reopen the model at a later stage.

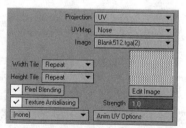

Figure 6.2-29. Now that there's a UV map it can be assigned to the nose surface.

2. Edit the UV map using the checkerboard as a reference to minimize stretching and distortions, trying to keep the size of the checks equal.

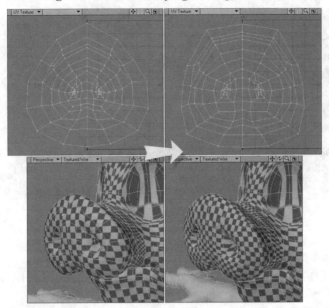

Figure 6.2-30. Adjusting the points.

3. Open Image Editor and clone **Blank512.tga**.
4. Copy the Textured Filter from **Blank512.tga(2)** to **Blank512.tga(3)**.
5. Select **Blank512.tga(2)** and double-click the Textured Filter entry to open its properties. Change the filter scale to **0.45**, making the checks on the nose about the same size as those on the head.

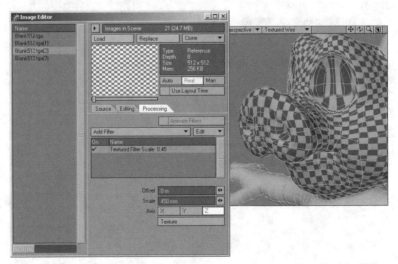

Figure 6.2-31. The checks are already square, so we just need to adjust the filter scale.

6. **Transform UV 50%** in **U** to move the UV map back within the UV boundaries.

Merging the Head

Since the UV map for the nose will be blended into the head texture, we need to include the polygons of the head in the nose UV map to avoid edge artifacts.

1. Select all the polygons in the **Nose** UV map and **Cut** and **Paste**, separating the nose polygons from the head polygons so we can create a discontinuous map.

2. Switch to the **Head** UV map and select all the polygons in the map, then switch to the **Nose** UV map and lasso all the polygons in that map, deselecting the nose but leaving the head selected.

3. **Map⟩Texture⟩Make UVs** using the previous settings (**Planar** on **Z**).

4. With the head polygons selected, stretch them so they fit into the top-right corner of the UV map.

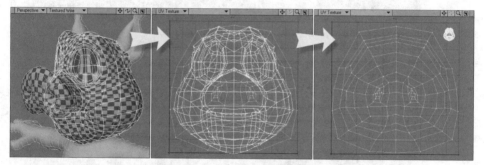

Figure 6.2-32. Placing the polygons of the head into the UV map.

5. **Deselect All** and **Merge Points**.

UV Mapping the Ears

The ears are fairly cylindrical, so that's the best initial projection. The trouble is that initial projections only work along the basic axes — X, Y, and Z. The ears are at an odd angle, so applying a cylindrical projection as they are won't provide acceptable results.

Creating the UV Morph

We need to create another morph to orient the ears for a clean cylindrical projection. There is also the issue of the ears being mirrored. If we create a UV map with the ears facing forward, or +Z, the seams will be on opposite sides of each ear. So we need to orient them so the seam occurs in the same place for both ears.

1. Create a new morph called **UV.Ears**.

2. Select the polygons of the ears by selecting the top part of the head, then deselecting all the polygons in the Head UV map.

3. With Symmetry on, **Rotate** the ears from the Back and Right views so the bulb is close to vertical.

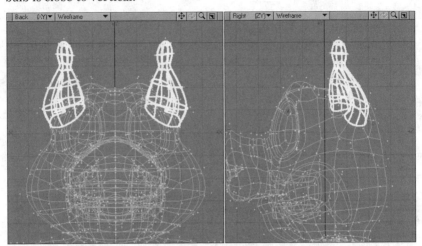

Figure 6.2-33. Orient the ears vertically.

4. **Rotate** the ears from the Top view so the back of the ears is facing –Z and the cross at the top of the bulb is straight.
5. Turn off Symmetry, select **Point** mode, and **Deselect All** points.
6. **Rotate –90** on the **Y** axis.

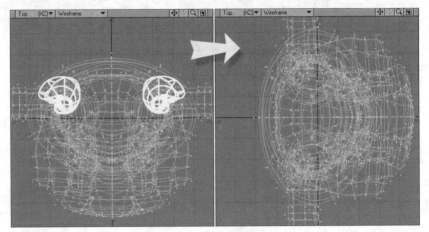

Figure 6.2-34. Rotate to align the intended seam along an axis, then rotate the model so the intended seam is facing –X.

7. Because we'll be doing some tricky editing of the UV map, select **Polygons** mode and **Cut** and **Paste** the ears, separating them from the head.

Creating the UV Map

Creating the same UV coordinates for mirrored geometry is achieved in different ways depending on the orientation of the geometry and the type of initial projection used. In this case we'll map each ear separately, then flip the coordinates of one ear to match the other.

We also want the cylindrical projection to be centered on the bulb, not on the selected polygons, so before making the UV map we'll check the X and Z coordinates for the center position.

1. Deselect the right ear, leaving the left ear selected.

2. From the Top view, place the cursor at the top point of the ear bulb and note the coordinates.

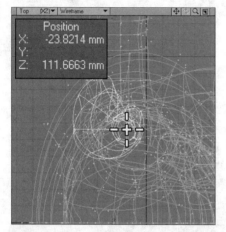

Figure 6.2-35. Check the position of the center.

3. Make a new UV map called **Ears**. Set Map Type to **Cylindrical** and Axis to **Y**. Select **Manual** settings and change the X and Z coordinates to the appropriate values. For mine they are X = **–23.82 mm** and Z = **111.67 mm**.

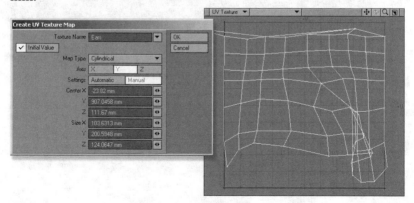

Figure 6.2-36. Initial projection for the left ear.

4. Select the polygons of the right ear only and **Make UVs**. Select **Manual** settings and change the X and Z coordinates to the same values as the previous step, except reverse the Z value. For mine they are X = **–23.82 mm** and Z = **–111.67 mm**.

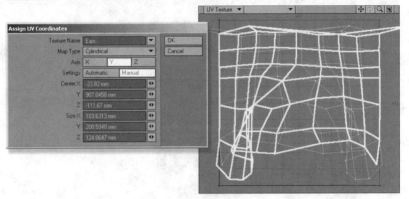

Figure 6.2-37. Initial projection for the right ear.

5. The UV coordinates for the right ear are the reverse of the left ear. To fix this, select the points at the seams and **Unweld**.

6. Select all the points of the UV map, then deselect the points of the left ear from a model viewport, leaving just the right ear selected.

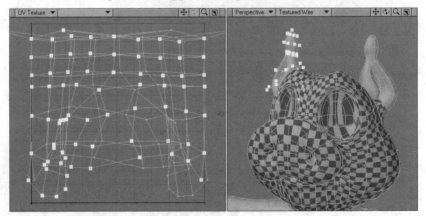

Figure 6.2-38. Selecting the points of the right ear.

7. Select **Transform UV,** then turn on **Scale** and **Center** only. Change Scale
   U to **–100%** and Center U to **50%**. This mirrors the UV coordinates
   around the center of the map so both ears have the same coordinates.

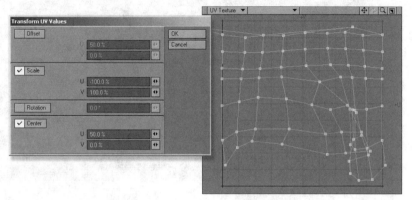

Figure 6.2-39. Mirroring the UV coordinates to match the left ear.

Adjusting the UV Map

We need to fix the overlapping polygons, then I want to change the position of the
seam so it runs down the front of the ear instead of the back of the ear. This will
hide the majority of the seam within the inner fold of the ear.

1. Switch back to the **(base)** morph so you can see the correct results of the
   editing.

2. **Unweld** the point at the top of the bulb, then drag the stray top point back
   into the UV boundary.

3. Adjust the internal points of the UV map so there are no overlapping polygons, but *don't move the points along the seam*. The points along the
   current seam should not be moved so that both sides will match up when
   we change the seam position.

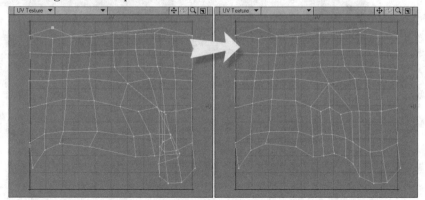

Figure 6.2-40. Fixing overlapping polygons.

4. To clean up the top row of polygons, select each polygon, one by one, and drag the top point, positioning them evenly.

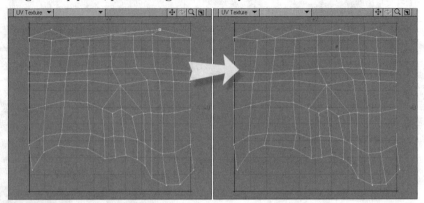

Figure 6.2-41. Adjusting the top.

5. Move the points so the points to the left of the line of the new seam are on the left side of the UV map.

6. Select the center row of points and **Set UV Value** to U = 50, then **Unweld**.

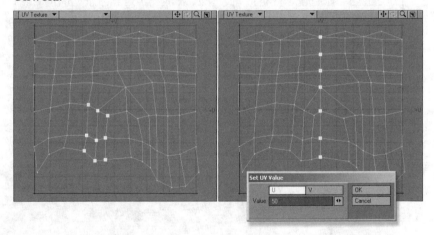

Figure 6.2-42. Preparing the geometry for the seam change.

7. Select the polygons on the left half of the UV map and **Transform UV.**
    Turn on **Offset** only and set U to **100%.** This moves the left side of the
    map to match it up with the right side.

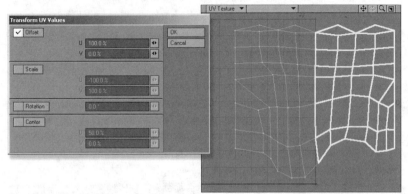

Figure 6.2-43. This is why the points at the original seam couldn't be changed. The two
sides of the map match up perfectly now.

8. Select all the polygons of the UV map and **Transform UV** again, offsetting
    U to **–50%** to bring the UV coordinates back within the UV boundary.

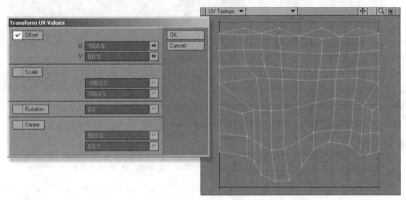

Figure 6.2-44. Bringing the map back within the UV boundary.

Editing the UV Map

We'll apply the checkerboard to the ears so we can accurately edit the UV map and match the aspect and scale of the head texture.

1. With the polygons still selected, change surface to **Ears**, then open Surface Editor and copy the **Head** surface settings to the **Ears** surface.

2. On the **Ears** surface, open the texture for Color. **Change UVMap to Ears** and Image to **Blank512.tga(3)**.

3. Open Image Editor and clone **Blank512.tga**.

4. Copy the Textured Filter from **Blank512.tga(3)** to **Blank512.tga(4)**.

5. Select **Blank512.tga(3)** and double-click the **Textured Filter** entry to open its properties. Change the scale to **0.45**, making the checks on the nose about the same size as those on the head.

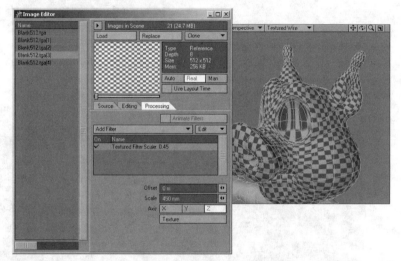

Figure 6.2-45. Since the initial UV map for the ears is relatively accurate, we can set the scale before editing. You can adjust it further after editing if it's required.

6. Edit the UV map using the checkerboard as a reference to minimize stretching and distortions, trying to keep the size of the checks equal.

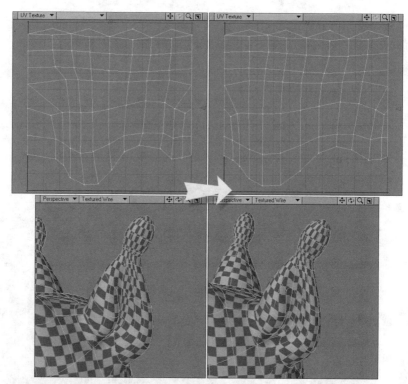

Figure 6.2-46. When editing the UV map I've only moved the points horizontally, as they're already fairly well placed vertically.

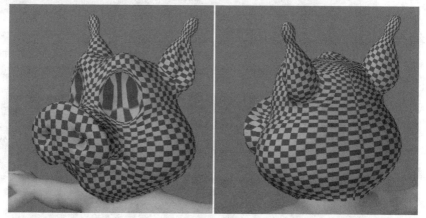

Figure 6.2-47. Final UV maps for the head. The stretching in the eye socket will be hidden by the eyeball.

Creating the Body UVs

Now we'll create the rest of the UV maps for Hamish, leaving the final editing until after they're all created.

UV Mapping the Torso

Knowing where to place the seams for the arms and legs is important when UV mapping the body. The placement of the division between torso and arms and legs is determined by stretching and distortion. Choose which UV map the polygons will be applied to by determining which one will cause the least distortion. In this case we'll place the shoulders in the UV map for the arms rather than the torso.

1. Select the **UV.Y-90** morph, and select the polygons of the torso.

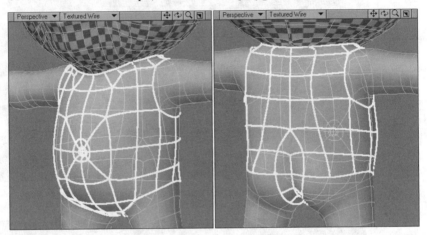

Figure 6.2-48. Selecting the torso.

2. Make a new UV map called **Body**. Set Map Type to **Cylindrical** and Axis to **Y**. Automatic settings are fine in this case.

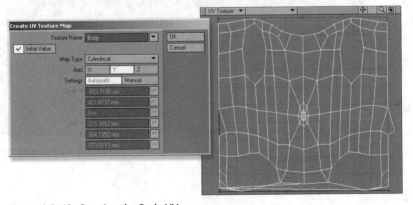

Figure 6.2-49. Creating the Body UV map.

3. **Unweld** the point at the bottom where overlapping polygons join. Select the overlapping polygons and drag the point to the middle.

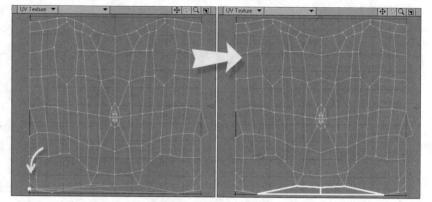

Figure 6.2-50. Cleaning up the polygons at the base.

4. Clean up the leg area, then **Unweld** the points at the edges, along the internal seam.

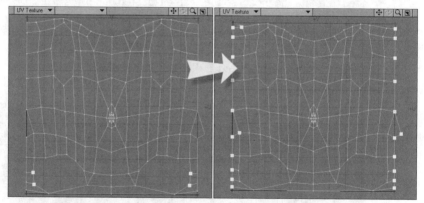

Figure 6.2-51. Unwelding the seam allows you to offset the map.

5. Offset **–50%** in U to prepare the UV map for symmetrical editing, then **Merge Points**.

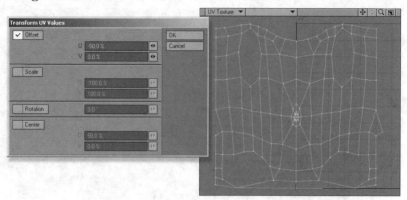

Figure 6.2-52. Offsetting the map.

UV Mapping the Arms

We need to rotate the model so the seam is created under the arms. Because the arms are parallel to each other, UV mapping is fairly straightforward.

We'll also join the arm and leg UV maps together when they're both created, so we'll only fill one half of the UV map.

1. Create a new morph called **UV.X-90**.
2. Rotate the model **–90°** on the X axis so he's lying on his back.

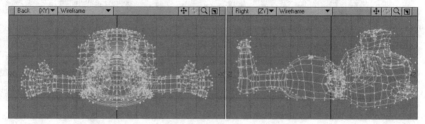

Figure 6.2-53. This orientation creates the seams under the arms.

3. Make sure Symmetry is on and select the polygons from the shoulder to the wrist. Make a note of the Z position of the center of the arms from the Right view.

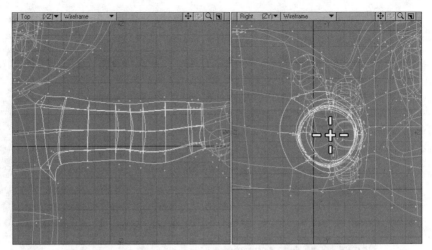

Figure 6.2-54. The ideal center is in the middle of the majority of the polygons.

4. Make a new UV map called **Arms**. Set Map Type to **Cylindrical** and Axis to **X**. Select **Manual** settings and change the Z Center to the Z position you recorded in the previous step — mine is **20 mm**.

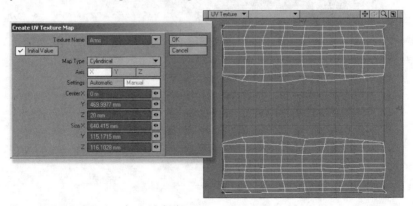

Figure 6.2-55. Creating the initial UV map.

5. **Unweld** the points along the left and right edges of the map, the internal seams, and **Deselect All**, then select all the points of the left (top) arm.

6. **Transform UV** and turn on just **Scale** and **Center**. Set V Scale to **–100%** and V Center to **50%**, placing the UV coordinates of both arms together.

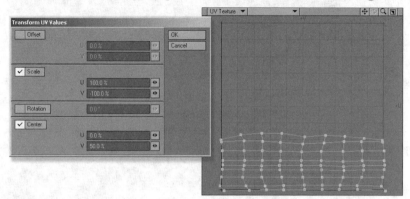

Figure 6.2-56. Mirror one side vertically.

7. Select all the points in the UV map and **Stretch** to fit the arms within the left half of the UV map and fill up more height, then **Merge Points**.

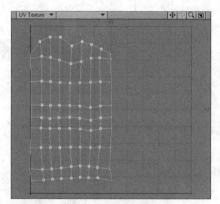

Figure 6.2-57. Position on the left side to leave room for the legs.

UV Mapping the Legs

The legs need to be rotated for the same reason as the ears — to orient them along an axis. The difference is that we want the seam for the legs to be on the inside instead of the back or front, so we'll create a different morph for each leg.

1. Create a new morph called **UV.Legs**.
2. With Symmetry on, select the polygons from the torso to the ankles.
3. **Rotate** the legs from the back view so they're oriented vertically.
4. Select **Point** mode and **Copy Vertex Map**. Call the new map **UV.Legs-180**.

5. Turn Symmetry off and **Rotate** the model **180°** on the Y axis.

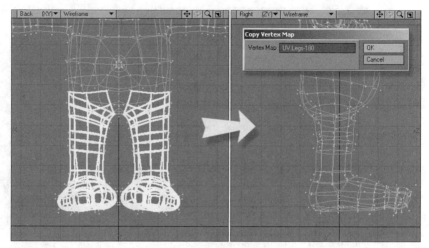

Figure 6.2-58. Create two morphs for the leg UV maps.

6. Select the **UV.Legs** morph and change to **Polygons** mode. Deselect the
    right leg, leaving the left leg selected. Make a note of the X and Z position
    of the center of the leg from the Top view.

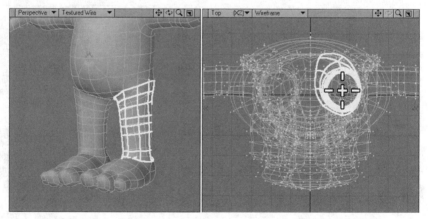

Figure 6.2-59. The leg selection.

7. Create a new UV map called **Legs**. Set Map Type to **Cylindrical** and Axis to **Y**. Select **Manual** settings and change the X and Z Center to the values recorded in the previous step. Mine are **83 mm** and **10 mm** respectively.

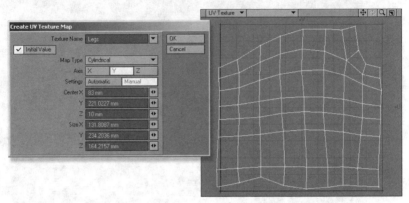

Figure 6.2-60. Mapping the left leg.

8. Switch to the **UV.Legs-180** morph and select the polygons of the right leg.

9. **Make UVs** and select **Manual** settings. Change the X to the same value as before and make Z the negative of the previous Z value.

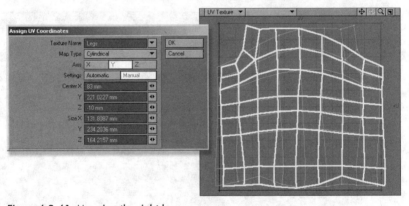

Figure 6.2-61. Mapping the right leg.

10. **Unweld** the points along the seam, then select just the points of the right leg.

11. **Transform UV** with U Scale of **–100%** and U Center of **50%** to mirror the UV coordinates.

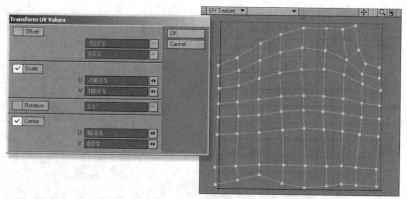

Figure 6.2-62. Mirror the right leg.

12. Select all the points in the UV map and **Transform UV** with U Scale of **50%** and U Center of **100%**.

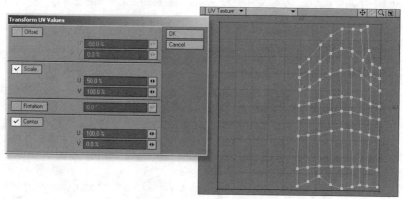

Figure 6.2-63. Position on the right side, leaving room for the arms.

Merging the Arms and Legs

To keep the number of textures down, we'll join the arms and legs UV maps. This also makes it easier to work on the seams with the torso, as they're both on the same image map.

1. With the **Legs** UV map selected, **Copy Vertex Map** to a new map called **ArmsLegs**.

2. Select the **Arms** UV map and **Copy Vertex Map** to **ArmsLegs**.

3. Select the **ArmsLegs** UV map and select all the points of the legs. **Stretch** them a little so the legs fit inside the right half of the map.

4. Select the points on the left and right edges of the arms and **Unweld**. **Stretch** them so they fit within the left half of the map, making sure there's no overlap between the arm and leg UV coordinates.

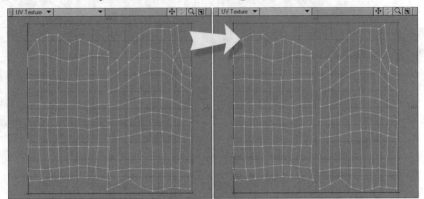

Figure 6.2-64. Merging the UV coordinates for the arms and legs.

5. **Merge Points.**

UV Mapping the Hands

The hands can be quite difficult to UV map well. We'll create simple maps for the hands that will have some stretching but minimize distortion. The stretching won't be a big issue with the planned texture detail. The important thing is to keep the right areas continuous. In this case, the bottom and sides of the fingers will be continuous so the creases under the finger joints can be textured seamlessly.

You could create a more complex UV map for the hand, mapping the hand and each finger separately for the most accurate results if you wanted highly detailed fingers.

1. With Symmetry on, select the polygons of the hands.

2. Make sure you have the **(base)** morph selected and make a new UV map called **Hands**. Set Map Type to **Planar** and Axis to **Y**, leaving it with automatic settings.

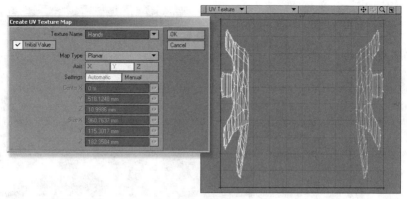

Figure 6.2-65. Initial projection for the hands.

3. Turn **Symmetry** off and deselect the left hand. **Mirror** the right-hand UV coordinates using **Transform UV** with U Scale of **–100%** and U Center of **50%**.

4. Select all the polygons in the UV map and **Stretch** so the hands fit into about a quarter of the map.

5. **Deselect All**, turn **Symmetry** on, then select just the polygons on the top side of the hands. **Cut** and **Paste**, then select the top polygons again. In the UV map, move them away from the rest of the hand.

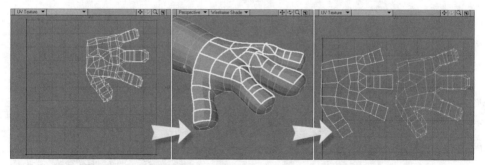

Figure 6.2-66. Separating the top of the hand.

6. **Rotate** the UV map **90°**, then select the points of the top of the hand and **Flip UVs**, choosing **Flip U**. Move the top points up to the left of the underside of the hand.

7. Adjust the underside of the hand so there are no overlapping polygons, then **Rotate** so the left edge of the underside is vertical.

8. **Rotate** the top of the hand so the right edge is vertical and move it next to the underside of the hand.

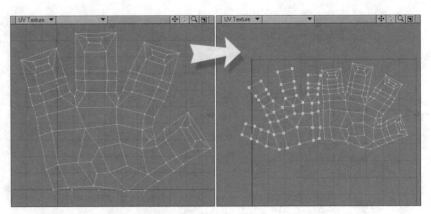

Figure 6.2-67. Fix the overlapping points, then arrange, ready to merge.

Merging Discontinuous UVs

Now we'll join the top and the underside of the hand, making one less seam to worry about.

1. Select the two lower points on each side of the seam and **Stretch** vertically and horizontally to **0%**.
2. Repeat for each pair of points along the seam until it's all joined.
3. **Move** and **Scale** the UVs so they fit into the top half of the UV map, then **Merge Points**.

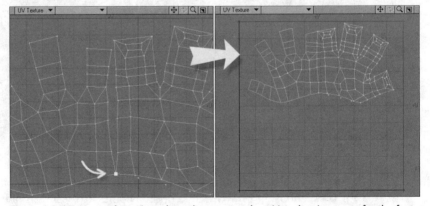

Figure 6.2-68. Merge the points along the seam and position, leaving room for the feet.

UV Mapping the Feet

The feet have the same problems as the hands. We'll create a similarly simple UV map for the feet, only this time we'll separate the base or soles of the feet, creating the seam in an area that's more inconspicuous.

1. With Symmetry on, select the polygons of the feet.

2. Make a new UV map called **Feet**. Set Map Type to **Planar** and Axis to **Y**, leaving it with automatic settings.

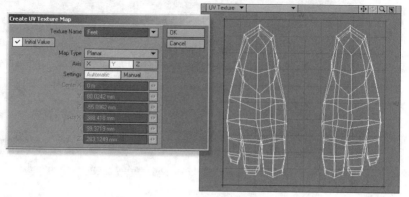

Figure 6.2-69. Initial projection for the feet.

3. Turn Symmetry off and deselect the left foot. **Mirror** the right foot's UVs using **Transform UV** with U Scale of **–100%** and U Center of **50%**.

4. Deselect the top and side polygons of the feet, leaving just the soles selected, and **Cut** and **Paste**. Move the UVs of the soles to the side of the top of the foot.

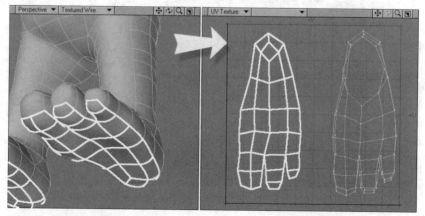

Figure 6.2-70. Separating the base of the foot.

5. **Stretch** the UVs so they're roughly the correct scale.

6. Adjust the points of the top of the foot so there are no overlapping polygons.

7. **Stretch** all the UVs to fit within the bottom half of the UV map and **Merge Points**.

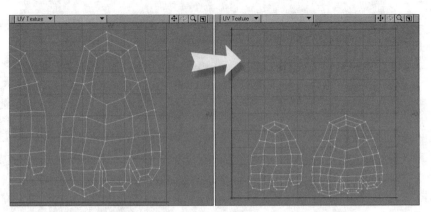

Figure 6.2-71. Adjust the points and position, leaving room for the hands.

Merging the Hands and Feet

We'll also join the UV maps of the hands and feet to keep texture numbers down.

1. With the **Feet** UV map selected, **Copy Vertex Map** to a new map called **HandsFeet**.

2. Select the **Hands** UV map and **Copy Vertex Map** to **HandsFeet**.

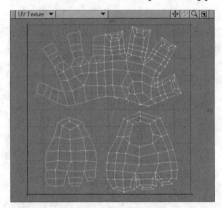

Figure 6.2-72. Merging the hands and feet.

Editing the Body UVs

With the UV maps created we can apply checkerboard textures in preparation for editing.

Creating Surfaces

The first step is to apply the appropriate surfaces to the model.

1. Select the **Body** UV map and select all the polygons in the map. **Change Surface** to **Body**.

2. Select the **ArmsLegs** UV map and select all the polygons in the map. **Change Surface** to **ArmsLegs**.

3. Select the **HandsFeet** UV map and select all the polygons in the map. **Change Surface** to **HandsFeet**.

Applying Checkerboards

We need to create a different checkerboard image for each UV map, then apply them to the surfaces.

1. Open the Image Editor and clone **Blank512.tga** three times.

2. Select **Blank512.tga(4)** and **Copy** the Textured Filter entry.

3. **Paste** the Textured Filter to the three new clones — 5 to 7.

4. Open the Surface Editor, **Copy** the **Head** surface, and **Paste** the settings to the three new surfaces — **Body**, **ArmsLegs**, and **HandsFeet**.

5. Select the **Body** surface and open the Color texture. Change UVMap to **Body** and Image to **Blank512.tga(4)**.

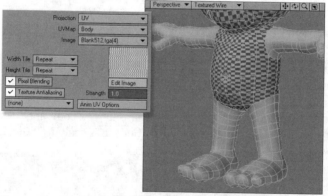

Figure 6.2-73. Applying the checkerboard to the body.

6. Select the **ArmsLegs** surface and open the Color texture. Change UVMap to **ArmsLegs** and Image to **Blank512.tga(5)**.

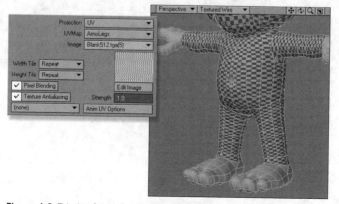

Figure 6.2-74. Applying the checkerboard to the arms and legs.

345

7. Select the **HandsFeet** surface and open the Color texture. Change UVMap to **HandsFeet** and Image to **Blank512.tga(6)**.

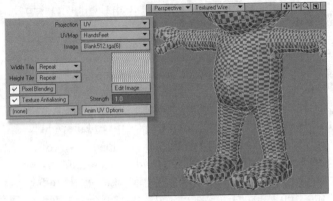

Figure 6.2-75. Applying the checkerboard to the hands and feet.

8. Close the Surface Editor, leaving the Image Editor open.

Adjusting the Checkerboards

Now we can adjust the scale settings for the checkerboards so they match the head. Always set the aspect (texture scale) first, then the overall scale (filter scale).

1. Select **Blank512.tga(4)**, the checkerboard for the body, and open the Texture settings for the Texture Filter. Set the X scale to **0.0667**.

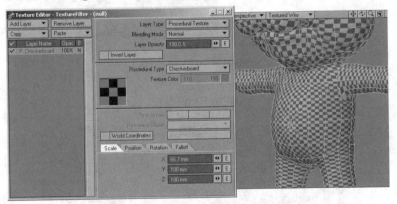

Figure 6.2-76. Adjusting the aspect ratio.

2. Close the Texture Editor and set the filter scale to **0.35**, matching the scale of the head checkerboard on the model.

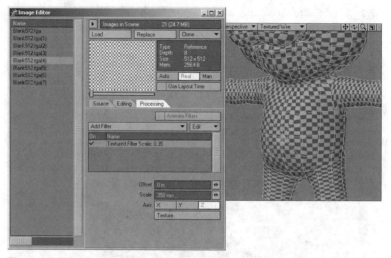

Figure 6.2-77. Adjusting the scale.

3. Select **Blank512.tga(5)**, the checkerboard for the arms and legs, and open the Texture settings for the Texture Filter. Set the X scale to **0.05**.

4. Close the Texture Editor and set the filter scale to **0.45**, matching the scale of the body checkerboard.

We'll leave the scale for Blank512.tga(6) at the default, as the checks on the hands and feet are already a good aspect ratio and scale.

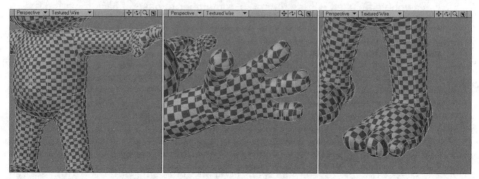

Figure 6.2-78. Checkerboards ready for editing.

347

Editing the Torso

The torso can be a tricky area to edit, especially around the groin area, which exhibits the same stretching as the top of the head. You can keep the detail low in that area so the stretching isn't apparent, and luckily it's often hidden by clothing, so it's not really an issue.

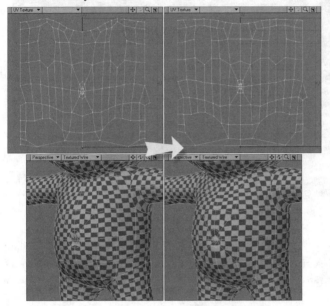

Figure 6.2-79. Body UV map before and after editing.

Once you've finished editing the torso, remember to offset it back to within the UV boundary.

Editing the Arms and Legs

The arms and legs shouldn't need much editing. The main areas to adjust are the top and bottom of the map, where the arms and legs meet the torso, hands, and feet.

First we'll adjust the seams so they're straight, which will make texturing easier.

1. Select the **ArmsLegs** UV map and **Unweld** the seams.
2. Select the left row of points on the arms and, using **Set UV Value**, set the U value to **0%**.
3. Select the right row of points on the arms and set the U value to **47%**.
4. Select the left row of points on the legs and set the U value to **53%**.
5. Select the right row of points on the legs and set the U value to **100%**.
6. Continue editing the points.

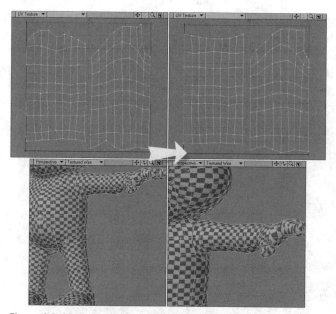

Figure 6.2-80. Arms and legs before and after editing.

Editing the Hands and Feet

The hands and feet also don't need too much editing. The main thing is to minimize distortion, as there will be some stretching on the sides of the fingers due to the way we've mapped the hands.

The first thing to fix is the floating points under the hands. These have occurred because we cut and pasted to separate the top of the hand.

1. Select the **HandsFeet** UV map and **Unweld** the floating points. Notice the equivalent points appear at the base of the top of the hand.

2. Select each pair of points and **Stretch** to **0%**, then **Merge Points**.

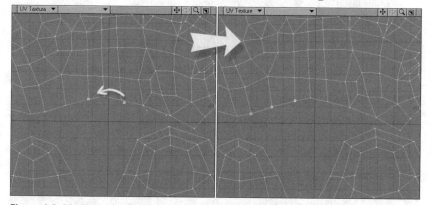

Figure 6.2-81. Fixing the floating points. Remember that we flipped the UV coordinates for the top of the hand, so the points are in reverse order. Scale the two closest points, then the middle two, then the outer two.

3. Continue editing the UVs.

4. With the UVs edited, the base of the hand is very close to the top of the feet. **Unweld** the points around the edge of the feet and swap the positions of the top and base of the foot, giving each part a bit more room.

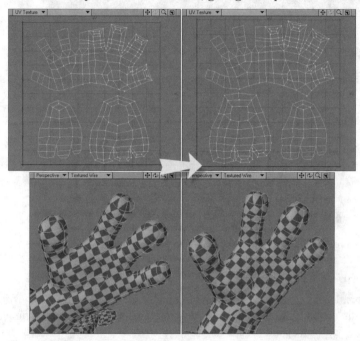

Figure 6.2-82. Hands and feet before and after editing.

UV Mapping the Clothes

We'll UV map the pants, socks, and some of the shoes, leaving the shirt and the main shoe surface to standard mapping.

Creating the Pants UVs

The pants are a difficult shape to UV map. If you needed a lot of detail in the pants it might be worth creating two UV maps for them — one for the body of the pants and one for the legs. We'll create a single UV map so you can see how to create a UV map for a complex shape with an arbitrary seam.

1. Turn off Symmetry, select the pants layer, and create a new UV map called **Pants**. Set Map Type to **Planar** and Axis to **Z**, leaving it with automatic settings.

2. Offset the map by **–50%** in U to prepare for symmetrical editing.

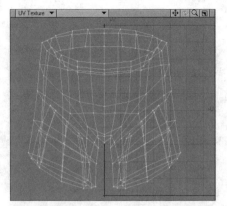

Figure 6.2-83. Initial projection for the pants.

3. Turn on Symmetry, select the center points down the back of the pants to the middle of the crotch, and **Unweld**.

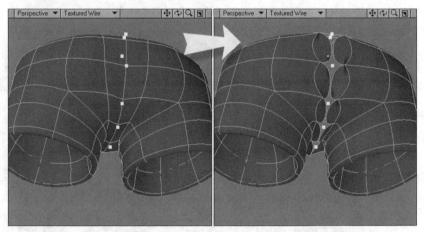

Figure 6.2-84. Manually creating the seam. The seam will run down the back of the bum and down the inside of the legs.

4. Select the points down the inside of the legs and **Unweld**.

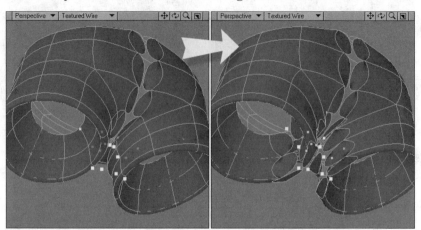

Figure 6.2-85. Continuing the seam down the inside of the legs.

5. Select the polygons of the body of the pants along the left side of the seam. Drag the center points just a little to the right.

6. Select the polygons along the right side of the seam and drag the center points a little left.

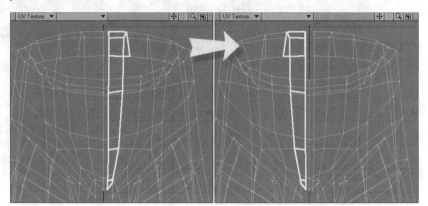

Figure 6.2-86. Offset the center points of the seam so they can be adjusted using symmetry.

7. Select the points just dragged right of the center and set the U value to 2%. Select the points dragged left of center and set the U value to –2%.

8. Select the polygons on the right side of the unwelded points and **Merge Points**. Do the same on the left side.

9. Select the polygons along the front of the seam and **Merge Points**.

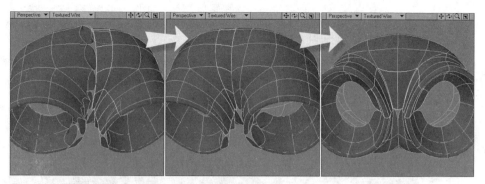

Figure 6.2-87. Merging the points except for the seam makes it easier to see that you have the correct points or polygons selected during editing.

10. Turn on Symmetry and select the polygons on the back half of the pants. On the UV map, move them out a little.

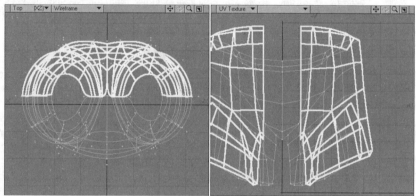

Figure 6.2-88. Starting to unwrap the UVs.

11. From the Top view, deselect the outside band of polygons, then in the UV map, move the remaining selected polygons right.

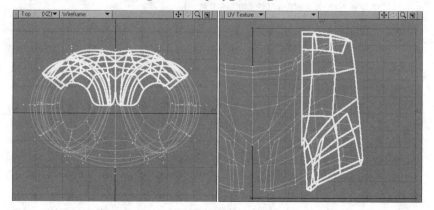

Figure 6.2-89. Unwrap the pants band by band.

12. Continue deselecting band by band, each time moving the polygons on the UV map a little more to the right.

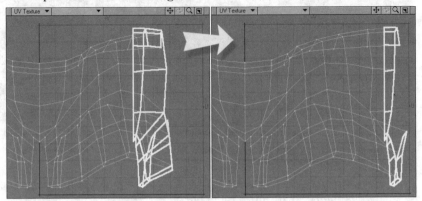

Figure 6.2-90. The last band of polygons is still overlapping; we'll fix that in a minute.

13. Clean up the top row, stretching the points vertically so they're straight.

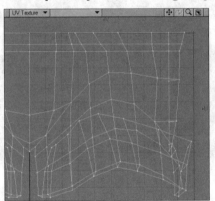

Figure 6.2-91. Adjusting the top makes it a little easier to see where the seam starts.

14. The last polygon band is still overlapping, so select the row of points making up the seam (on both sides) and move them out to the edge.

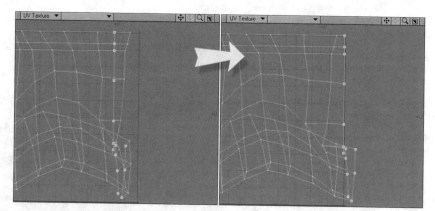

Figure 6.2-92. Unwrapping the last band of polygons.

15. Move the points inside the leg down so they're not overlapping and adjust the points on the seam so the layout is neat.

16. Finally neaten all the points, making the vertical rows straight and bringing them in to make the map the correct size.

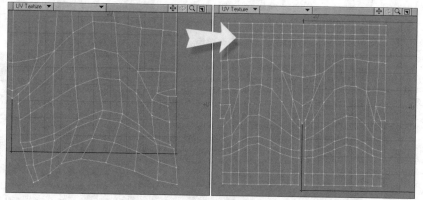

Figure 6.2-93. Clean up the map, then arrange between –50% and 50% in U.

Creating the Sock UVs

The socks are fairly simple, as they're a basic cylindrical shape.

1. Select the socks layer and create a new morph called **UV.Socks**.

2. With Symmetry on, **Rotate** the socks so the middle line of points is vertical.

3. Adjust the front points of the bottom row so they're in line with the higher points, but keeping the polygons roughly the same size.

> **Note:** This lets us use automatic settings, as the center is now correct.

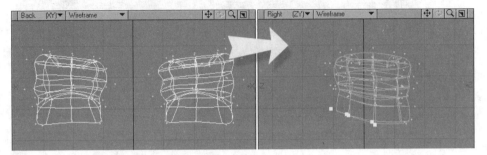

Figure 6.2-94. Adjusting the socks in a morph.

4. Rotate the right sock **180°** on the Y axis, so the seam is placed on the same side for both socks.

5. Select the left sock and create a new UV map called **Socks**. Set Map Type to **Cylindrical** and Axis to **Y**, leaving it with automatic settings.

6. Select the right sock and **Make UVs** using the same settings.

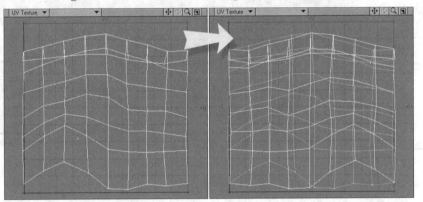

Figure 6.2-95. Initial projections for the socks.

7. **Unweld** the points at the seams, then select all the points of the right sock and mirror the UV coordinates using **Transform UV**.

8. Select each horizontal row of points and **Stretch** them so they're straight, positioning each row evenly on the map.

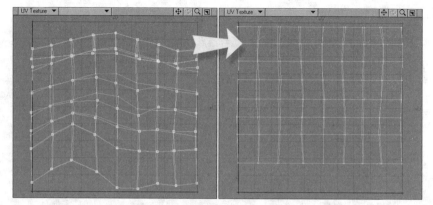

Figure 6.2-96. Adjusting the horizontal rows.

9. Select **Map**➤**Texture**➤**Point Map**➤**Quantize**. There are eight horizontal banks, so set the U Snap Grid Size to **0.125** (1 / 8 = 0.125).

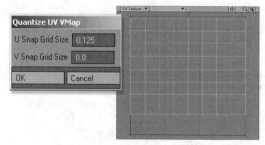

Figure 6.2-97. Because the points are fairly evenly spaced Quantize can do the rest.

10. Finally, stretch the map vertically to fit the UV space.

Creating the Shoe UVs

We'll place all the UVs for the shoes into one map, creating a single map for multiple surfaces.

1. Select the shoes layer and select the **UV.Y-90** morph.

2. Select the sole of the left shoe and create a new UV map called **Shoes**. Set Map Type to **Cylindrical** and Axis to **Y**, leaving it with automatic settings.

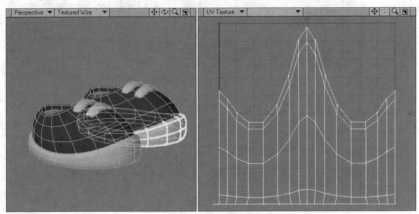

Figure 6.2-98. Initial projection for the soles.

3. Select the sole of the right shoe and **Make UVs** using the same settings.

4. **Unweld** the points of the seams and **Stretch** the UV map down.

5. Select the polygons within the bottom of the soles and **Cut** and **Paste**. Select those polygons again and **Clear Map**.

> **Note:** Because these polygons have already been mapped, you need to clear them from the map before remapping or some values will be retained when you remap them.

6. **Make UVs**, setting Map Type to **Planar** and Axis to **Y**.

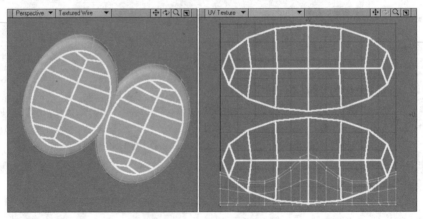

Figure 6.2-99. Initial projection for the bottom of the soles.

. . . . Texturing

Hamish

7. Deselect the polygons of the left foot and mirror vertically with **Transform UV** with a V Scale of **–100%** and V Center of **50%**.

8. Select all the polygons of the bottom soles, **Rotate** them **90°**, and **Stretch** and position them in the right side of the UV map.

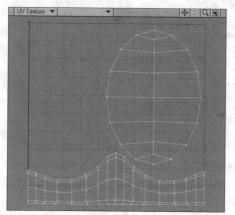

Figure 6.2-100. Repositioned UV coordinates for the soles.

9. Select the front shoelaces. Double-check that you have a morph selected, then from the Back view, **Rotate** and position them over the back shoelaces.

10. Select both shoelaces of the left shoe and position them over the shoelaces of the right shoe so that all the shoelaces occupy the same space.

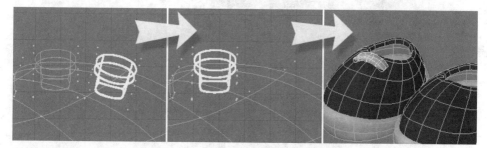

Figure 6.2-101. Repositioning the laces makes them easier to map.

11. Select all the shoelaces and **Make UVs**, using the same settings used previously.

12. **Stretch** and position the shoelace UVs in the left side of the UV map.

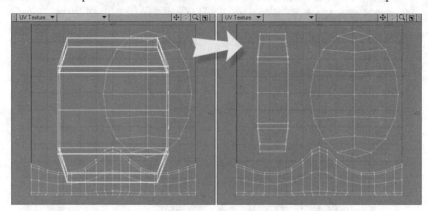

Figure 6.2-102. Mapping the laces.

Applying Checkerboards

The clothes already have correct surfaces, so we just need to apply checkerboards to them.

1. Open the Image Editor and clone **Blank512.tga** two more times.

2. Select **Blank512.tga(7)** and **Copy** the Textured Filter entry.

3. **Paste** the Textured Filter to the two new clones — 8 and 9.

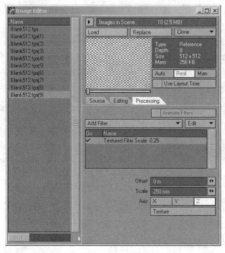

Figure 6.2-103. Clone the checkerboard.

4. Open the Surface Editor, select the **Pants** surface, and open the Texture Editor for the Color channel. Change Projection to **UV**, UVMap to **Pants**, and Image to **Blank512.tga(7)**.

5. Select the **Socks** surface and open the Texture Editor for the Color channel. Change Projection to **UV**, UVMap to **Socks**, and Image to **Blank512.tga(8)**.

6. Select the **Shoe_Sole** surface and open the Texture Editor for the Color channel. Change Projection to **UV**, UVMap to **Shoes**, and Image to **Blank512.tga(9)**. Do the same for the **Shoe_Lace** surface.

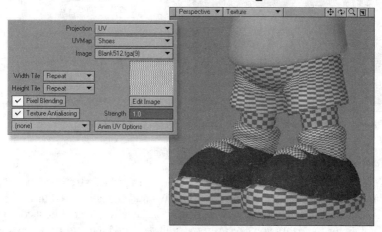

Figure 6.2-104. Clothes with default checkerboards applied.

Adjusting the Checkerboards

Now we'll adjust the scale of the checkerboards to match the body textures.

1. In the Image Editor, select **Blank512.tga(7)**, the checkerboard for the pants, and open the Texture settings for the Texture Filter. Set the X scale to **0.04**, making the checks square.

2. Close the Texture Editor and set the filter scale to **0.5**, matching the scale of the body checkerboard on the model.

3. Select **Blank512.tga(8)**, the checkerboard for the socks, and open the Texture settings for the Texture Filter. Set the X scale to **0.05**.

4. Close the Texture Editor and set the filter scale to **0.7**.

5. Select **Blank512.tga(9)**, the checkerboard for the shoes, and open the Texture settings for the Texture Filter. Set the X scale to **0.05**.

6. Close the Texture Editor and set the filter scale to **0.3**.

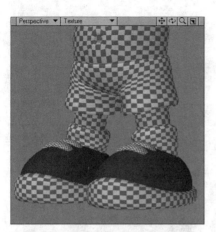

Figure 6.2-105. Adjusted checkerboards.

Editing the Clothes UVs

Now you can edit the UV maps for the clothes to reduce stretching and distortion. The socks are already good, so just the pants and shoes need editing.

Start by editing the UVs of the pants. Because we've created a continuous UV map for the pants you can't remove all the stretching, but try to position the stretching on the inside of the pants, keeping the body and outside of the legs fairly even.

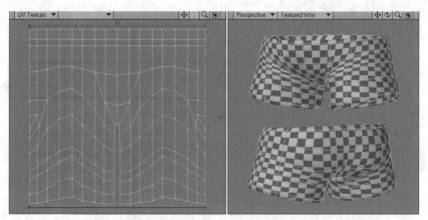

Figure 6.2-106. Pants UV map after editing.

Edit the shoe UVs so the checks are relatively square for all the different sections. Keep the laces fairly large on the map, even though the checks are much smaller than the other areas, so we can apply finer texture detail.

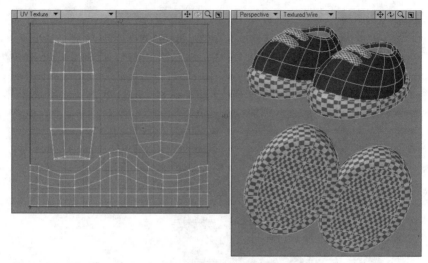

Figure 6.2-107. Shoes UV map after editing.

Preparing for Surfacing

Congratulations, you've just finished UV mapping Hamish. There are just a few more steps to prepare for surfacing.

1. Select the final eyeball layer and **Cut**. Select the first layer and **Paste**.
2. Place all the clothing layers in the foreground and **Cut**. Select the third layer and **Paste**. You should now have three layers in the object — the body in layer 1, the template eyeballs in layer 2, and the clothes in layer 3.
3. Save the checkerboard version of the object, saving as **Hamish_Working_Checkerboard.lwo**. This is very important as the checkerboard textures will be lost in the final model and we'll need to revisit the checkerboard settings.

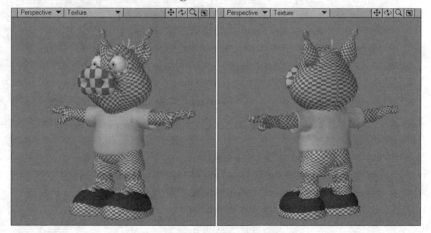

Figure 6.2-108. Hamish working object with checkerboards (layers 1 and 3 visible).

Saving the Object

Now we need to set up the model in preparation for surfacing.

1. Save the object as **Hamish_Working_v002.lwo**, or the next increment to the previous version.

2. Select the polygons of the **Nose** surface and change surface to **Head**.

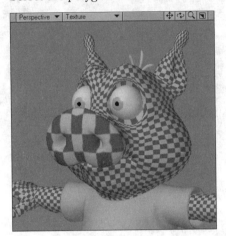

Figure 6.2-109. Changing the nose back to the head surface.

3. Open the Surface Editor and select the color texture for the **Head** surface. Set Image to **(none)**. Repeat for all the surfaces with UV maps.

Figure 6.2-110. Set all the UV mapped images to (none) in preparation for surfacing.

4. **Save** the object again.

We've covered almost every UV mapping technique, so you're now well prepared to confidently create UV maps for any part of any character.

UV mapping can be complicated and time consuming, but as you've seen it's really quite easy to do. The challenge is in deciding what areas need discontinuous

UV maps, and how best to unwrap those areas, which becomes easier with experience. From there it's just a matter of tweaking the maps using the checkerboards as a guide. To recap, the best steps for UV mapping are:

1. Create the UV map.
2. Remove overlapping polygons.
3. Assign a checkerboard.
4. Edit the UV map.
5. Adjust checkerboard aspect and scale.

The UV maps are ready for image mapping, but before the UV maps and checkerboard textures are put to use, the initial surfacing and procedural texturing should be done so you don't create more detail in the image maps than is necessary.

6.3 Surfacing

There are a number of surface attributes that don't require textures. Textures allow you to fine-tune the basic surface attributes, but you need to start with a good base. The basic attributes affect how the textures are created, so it's important to get them right before texture creation.

Surfaces and Light

The surfaces of a character are largely influenced by lighting. You can create surfaces that look wonderful under one lighting condition but terrible under another. So it's important to create the surfaces for a character using a neutral light setup and to test under different lighting conditions, such as nighttime or bright sunlight.

It's most important when surfacing multiple characters for a production that all the characters use the same lighting conditions. Since the characters share and interact in the same scenes, they all need to look correct under the same lighting. If the characters have been surfaced under different lighting conditions, it's impossible to light a scene and have all the characters look correct. You'll end up having to alter the surfaces for many characters to suit the lighting, which results in a different version of those characters for almost every scene and is terribly inefficient. As long as the characters have been surfaced under the same lighting, different lighting conditions affect all the characters equally, making the job of lighting a scene far easier and more enjoyable.

Shading Noise Reduction

Shading noise reduction is often used to reduce the noise in shadows created by area lights. While it smooths area light shadows nicely, shading noise reduction has the side effect of blurring texture detail. If you're planning to use area lights with shading noise reduction in your production, you should also perform the surfacing and texturing with shading noise reduction on so the subtle texture detail is appropriately enhanced.

Surface Preview

Before adjusting surface attributes it's useful to adjust the display options for the surface preview. The surface preview makes adjusting surface settings much quicker and easier, giving an accurate representation of the surface. If you use the surface preview, you don't need to create a test render to see the results of every surface change.

The default sample size is 1 meter, which is rarely representative of the size of the surface area in a character. If you set the sample size closer to the average size of the surfaces in your character, the feedback from the preview is much more useful.

Other preview options are useful for specific surfacing. If you're surfacing a flat object, the cube preview is more accurate. If you're surfacing transparency, it can be useful to change the preview background to checkerboard.

Basic Surface Attributes

The basic surface attributes affect the entire surface. They determine the appearance of surfaces without textures and provide a starting point for textured surfaces.

The basic surface attributes provide most of the characteristics of a surface. Most of the basic attributes are affected by other attributes, so it's important to understand how all of the attributes relate to each other.

Color, Luminosity, and Diffuse

Color and diffuse are closely related. In reality we never see these two attributes in isolation, as the apparent color of an object is filtered through its diffuseness.

The diffuse value determines how much light is absorbed before being reflected back out from the surface. This means that lower diffuse values make the surface appear less bright and darker in color. Surfaces with higher reflection often have lower diffuse values as a large amount of the light hitting the surface is reflected away before it hits the surface. A diffuse value of 75% is a good default starting point when surfacing.

Because of the diffuse value, the pure color of an object is often quite different than the apparent color of the surface. This means that it's important to establish the diffuse value of a surface before finalizing the color values. You should *never* adjust the diffuse value to change the color of a surface, as that will change the way the surface reacts to light.

Luminosity determines how much light is emitted from a surface. In most cases light isn't emitted from surfaces, so luminosity should be used very sparingly.

Luminosity should never be used to adjust the reflection of light off a surface, even though it may look good under the default lighting condition. Doing this will adversely affect the appearance of the surface under different lighting conditions.

Luminosity can be used for glowing surfaces, such as simulating the appearance of an opaque surface lit by an internal light source.

For cartoon characters, very low luminosity values can also be used on the eye surfaces to simulate the subsurface scattering of light. This exception to the luminosity rule *only* works for the eyes, as it can be effective to have a cartoon character's eyes a little brighter in low light conditions.

Specularity, Glossiness, and Reflection

Specularity is a simulation of the reflection of light sources. Specularity should be used sparingly for most characters. Hard or wet surfaces often have higher specularity values. Soft or rough surfaces usually have much lower specularity values.

The glossiness value determines the apparent smoothness of a surface. A smooth surface has a smaller specularity reflection, or higher glossiness. A rough surface has a larger specularity reflection, or lower glossiness. In most cases, lower glossiness values, or rougher surfaces, should have lower specularity values.

Color highlights introduces some of the surface's color into the specular highlights. Higher color highlight values help to simulate soft or more absorbent surfaces such as skin and cloth.

Reflection values determine the amount that a surface reflects the environment or other objects. In reality, since specularity is just a simulation of reflection, any surface with specularity has some reflection. The trouble is that apart from drastically increasing render times, reflection doesn't work the same way in 3D as in reality. In general, only hard, smooth, or wet surfaces should have reflection, and even then often specularity alone is enough to provide an adequate visual clue that a surface is reflective.

Transparency, Refraction, and Translucency

Transparency and refraction are closely connected. All transparent surfaces have some level of refraction. Refraction is the amount that light bends when it passes through the surface. The amount of refraction depends on what type of material the surface represents.

Translucency allows light to shine through from behind a surface. Many opaque and all transparent surfaces or materials allow light to shine through them. Translucency is very useful for many areas of a character. Areas where the flesh is thin are translucent, for example, ears, small noses, hair, and sometimes fingers. Translucency helps provide a little more grounding for the character by making it react more realistically to light, thus increasing its believability.

Preparing the Scene

The first step is to set up the object in the default lighting conditions.

1. Load **Hamish_Setup.lws** into Layout.
2. Select **Items➤Load➤Object** and choose **Hamish_Working_v002.lwo**, or your latest revision of the Hamish object. (You can find the preprepared object in \Objects\Chapters\Hamish_Working_v002.lwo.)

3.   Select **File**➢**Save**➢**Save Scene As (Shift+s)**, calling the new scene
     Hamish_Surfacing.lws.

Default Lighting Rig

Let's have a quick look at the lighting rig for character setup.

The main null object is the parent for the lights and camera. By rotating the
main null you can move the character around to see the surfaces in different areas
of the model. This gives you constant lighting conditions no matter the angle at
which you view the character. You can also move and rotate the camera to see a
specific area close up.

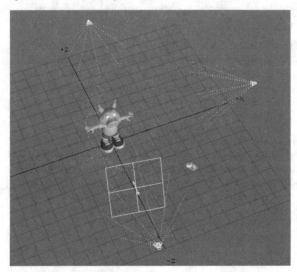

Figure 6.3-1. Setup scene.

Object Properties

With the scene set up, the next thing to do is to adjust some of the properties for
the objects.

1.   Select **Scene Editor**➢**Open (Ctrl+F1)** to open the Scene Editor.

2.   Select all the Hamish layers and open the **Object Properties** panel.

3.   In the Geometry tab, change Subdivision Order to **Last**.

4.   Select just **Layer1** and, in the Deform tab, select **Add Displacement** and
     choose **Morph Mixer** from the pull-down menu, activating the morphs in
     the object.

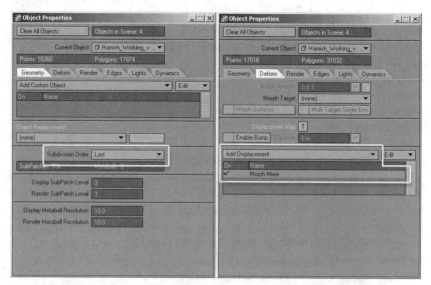

Figure 6.3-2. Setting object properties.

5. In the Scene Editor, select **Layer2**, the template eyeballs, then select the visibility icon and set it to **Hidden**. Click the active icon to uncheck it, deactivating the object.

6. Select **Layer2** and **Layer3** and parent them to **Layer1**.

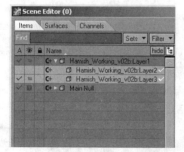

Figure 6.3-3. Setting up the layers.

7. Save the scene.

Adjusting the Surfaces

When surfaces are created you can set initial values for color, diffuse, and specularity. The first stage of surfacing is to adjust those values and set some other attributes so they look correct within the default lighting setup. Feel free to create a test render after adjusting each surface to see more accurate results. You need to render often when adjusting surfaces, as the OpenGL display doesn't show all the surface attributes accurately and doesn't have the benefit of shadows.

Surfacing the Skin

We'll start by setting the default values for the skin, the largest surface of the character.

Color and diffuse values are good, so we'll apply some specularity. Skin usually has some specularity, but only a very little. The default value should be very low, with higher specularity applied using a texture.

1. Open the Surface Editor and open the Preview Options. Change Sample Size to **0.3**.

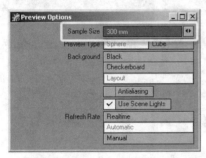

Figure 6.3-4. Change the sample size to reflect the average size of the surfaces in the character.

2. Select all five skin surfaces (holding **Ctrl** down as you select) including **ArmsLegs**, **Body**, **Ears**, **HandsFeet**, and **Head**.

3. Change Specularity to **5%** and Glossiness to **35%**.

Figure 6.3-5. You can change surface settings for multiple surfaces at the same time.

Surfacing the Mouth

The inside of the mouth has a lower diffuse value because we want it to be darker than the skin. It needs a little more specularity than the skin because it's a wet surface. To see the results of the surfacing we need to first activate the mouth open morph.

1. Select **Layer1** and open Morph Mixer. Select the Mouth group and set the **Open** morph to **100%**.
2. Select the **Mouth** surface.
3. Change Specularity to **35%** and Glossiness to **60%**.

Surfacing the Teeth

The teeth should stand out a little, so a higher diffuse value is warranted. Because they're shiny and wet they need even more specularity than the mouth.

1. Select the two teeth surfaces — **Teeth** and **Teeth_Lower**.
2. Change Diffuse to **80%** so the white surface doesn't blow out with the specularity.
3. Change both Specularity and Glossiness to **60%**.

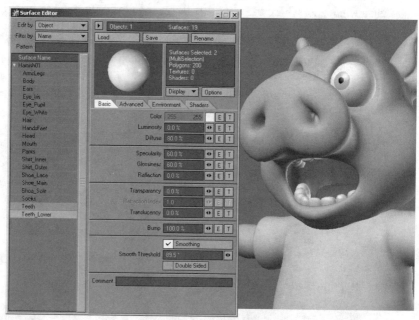

Figure 6.3-6. A small bright specular highlight gives the appearance of a hard wet surface.

Surfacing the Eyes

The eyes are a special case. Because we created the eyes as a single layer, we need to simulate the complexities of the multiple layers of a real eyeball. We can do this by giving each part of the eyeball slightly different specularity settings.

We'll also give the eyes some luminosity to simulate the subsurface scattering of light and to give them some added brightness in low-light conditions.

1. Select the **Eye_White** surface and change Luminosity to **10%**.

2. Change Specularity to **50%** and Glossiness to **70%**.

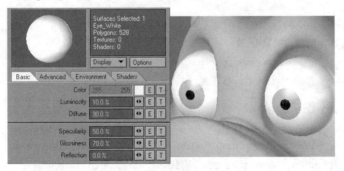

Figure 6.3-7. High diffuse settings can cause blowout.

Notice that the specularity doesn't seem to change or affect the surface. This is because of diffuse blowout. When diffuse values are high they can blow out, creating a white spot where the surface is facing the lights. We need to avoid this if possible, especially in the default lighting conditions because they're less bright than strong sunlight, so the blowout would be even worse in sunlight. We need to reduce the diffuse until there is a visible difference between the diffuse area and the specular area of the surface.

3. Change the Diffuse to **75%**, just dark enough to differentiate the specular highlight.

Figure 6.3-8. The specularity is now visible.

4. Select the **Eye_Iris** surface and change Luminosity to **10%**, Diffuse to **90%**, and Glossiness to **75%**.

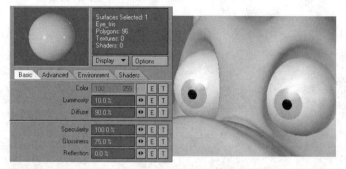

Figure 6.3-9. The diffuse values are high for the iris, but it needs to be so we achieve the correct results when the diffuse value is fine-tuned with a texture.

5. Select the **Eye_Pupil** surface and change Specularity to **150%** and Glossiness to **75%**.

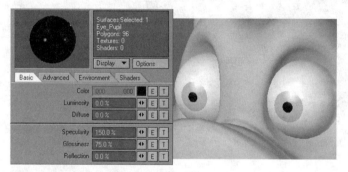

Figure 6.3-10. Pupil surface settings.

Notice Specularity is set higher than 100%. Don't be afraid of experimenting with values over 100% if you want to push an effect further. In this case, I want a nice bright but small specular highlight on the pupil.

Surfacing the Hair

We'll adjust the hair surface a little, adding some specularity and back light.

1. Select the **Hair** surface.

2. Change Diffuse to **60%**, Specularity to **20%**, and Glossiness to **30%**.

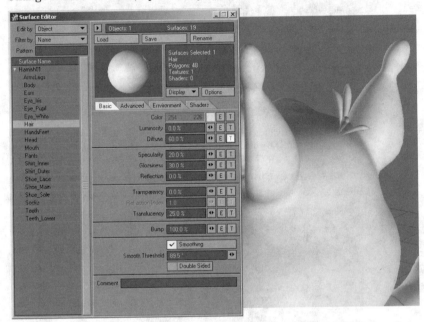

Figure 6.3-11. Surface settings for the hair. We need to do a render to test the translucency.

3. Change Translucency to **25%**.

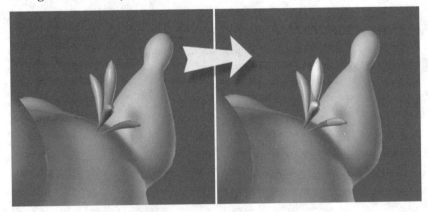

Figure 6.3-12. Before and after translucency.

Surfacing the Clothes

The initial diffuse values are fairly high for the clothes, as I want to keep them bright. We'll adjust those a little now that we can see them in the light, and give them just a tiny amount of specularity.

1. Select the two shirt surfaces and the pants surface: **Shirt_Outer**, **Shirt_Inner**, and **Pants**. Change Diffuse to **80%**, Specularity to **3%**, and Glossiness to **20%**.

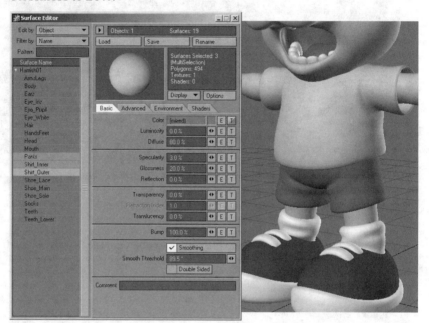

Figure 6.3-13. Clothes surface settings.

2. Select the Socks surface and change Diffuse to **80%**.

We'll leave specularity off the socks so they appear rough and matte.

Surfacing the Shoes

We'll adjust the settings for all the shoe surfaces. The soles of the shoes are rubber, so they also need some specularity.

1. Select the **Shoe_Lace** surface and change Diffuse to **80%**.
2. Select the **Shoe_Sole** surface and change Diffuse to **80%** and Specularity to **15%**.
3. Select the **Shoe_Main** surface and change Specularity to **5%** and Glossiness to **20%**.

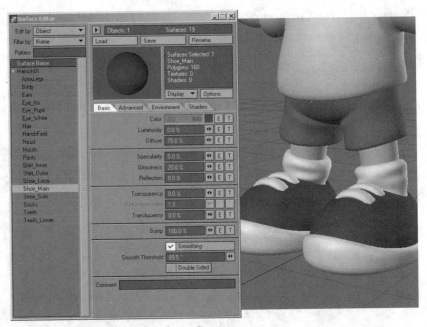

Figure 6.3-14. The shoes after surface adjustments.

With the surface settings complete, save the object, either by switching to Modeler and saving from there or in Layout by selecting File≻Save≻Save Current Object.

6.4 Gradients

Gradients have many uses for surfacing. The most useful aspect of gradients for character surfacing is their ability to use a weight map as an input parameter. We've already looked at using weight maps for bone influence. Now we'll look at using weight maps with gradients for surfacing.

Weight Maps and Gradients

Weight maps can be used with gradients to vary the surface attributes or specify certain areas where a surface attribute or texture is applied. Gradients allow you to use a weight map to apply a surface attribute by using the gradient by itself. They also allow you to use a weight map as an alpha channel for texture layers.

0% or Nothing

Creating weight maps for gradients is a bit different from creating weight maps for bones. The difference relates to when the weight map is applied. For bones, a weight map is applied before the object is subdivided. For gradients, a weight map is applied after subdivision.

Before the object is subdivided, a point with no weight map assigned is treated the same as a point with a weight map value of 0%. However, when the object is subdivided, the interpolated points inherit weight map values from the original points of the object. If two points have values of 100% and 0%, the interpolated points will inherit weight map values between those two values, as you would expect. If two points have values of 100% and nothing, the interpolated points don't inherit the weight map values, so only the point with 100% will retain a weight map value.

Figure 6.4-1. The weight maps look the same in Modeler, but the top map has a 0% value, creating a smooth transition, and the bottom map has cleared points, creating a hard transition. How hard the transition is depends on the subdivision level.

You can use this behavior to your advantage when surfacing. To create a smooth transition from a weight map value to nothing, make sure the points that you don't want affected have 0% weight map value. If you want a hard cutoff line from a weight map value to nothing, make sure the points that you don't want affected are cleared from the weight map.

Negative Values

In most cases it's easiest to create weight maps from 0% to 100%, but gradients read weight map values from –100% to over 100%.

Negative weight map values can be used in many ways. If you need two different colors applied to a surface in different places you can weight map one area with positive values and the other area with negative values, then apply the two colors to the positive and negative extremes of the gradient, reducing the number of weight maps and gradients. You can also use positive and negative weight map values to use a single weight map in multiple gradients. Since gradient values can be set differently from the weight map values, you can use negative weight map values to apply positive gradient values, and in doing so create two separate alpha gradients from a single weight map.

Other Input Parameters

Gradients have a number of other useful input parameters. Let's look at some of the most useful ones for character surfacing.

Previous Layer

Gradients are also useful for minimizing the number of image maps needed. Using gradients with the Previous Layer parameter is similar to adjusting levels in Photoshop. This means that you can use a single image map for multiple surface attributes by adjusting the output values using a gradient instead of having a separate image map for each attribute.

Bump

You can apply other surface attributes using gradients based on the overall bump amount of the surface. This is useful for applying a color to raised areas or reducing the diffuse and specularity in sunken areas. This is very useful when you have multiple bump layers so you can use a single gradient based on the overall bump amount instead of multiple textures or gradients based on each bump layer.

Incidence Angle

Incidence Angle creates a gradient based on the direction of a polygon relative to the camera. This is a useful texturing tool for characters, allowing many different effects that work well from shot to shot or scene to scene, as the gradient will automatically change for whichever camera is active.

Light Incidence

The Light Incidence parameter isn't very useful for characters. It seems like it should be useful, but the unfortunate aspect of light incidence is that it's tied to a specific light. This means that when the character is loaded into a different scene either the light has to already exist or it has to be imported with the character. So if your character has its own lights, you can confidently use light incidence based on those lights, but you shouldn't base light incidence on a scene light, as it creates complications for using the character in different scenes.

Creating Gradient Weight Maps

We'll apply some gradients to Hamish using weight maps to change the surfaces in specific areas. After we've created some other textures, we'll apply some more gradients using other input parameters.

Dark Weight Map

The first weight map to create is always the dark weight map. The dark gradient is a standard texture I use on all of my characters. This gradient darkens specific areas of the model, simulating depth where there often isn't any. Areas such as the ear canals, nostrils, and the back of the throat are where you'd start, but there are often many other areas of a model where a subtle use of this gradient can work wonders.

1. Switch to Modeler and, if it isn't already loaded, load your Hamish object.
2. Change the Perspective view to **Weight Shade**. Create a new weight map called **Tex_Dark** and set Initial Value to **0%**.

Figure 6.4-2. Giving all the points an initial value of 0% ensures a smooth transition for the gradient values.

3. **Zoom** close up on the base of the ear, and make sure **Symmetry** is on.
4. Select the innermost point of the inner ear and Set Map Value to **50%**.
5. Select the two points behind the last point and set the value to **25%**.

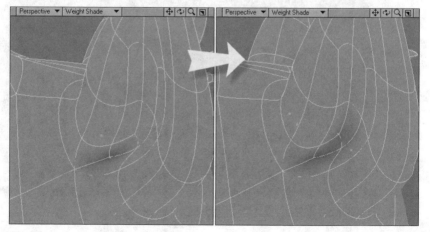

Figure 6.4-3. Weight values for the ears.

6. Select the inner bands of polygons of the nostrils and set the value to
    25%. **Contract** the selection, so just the innermost polygons are
    selected, and set the value to **100%**.

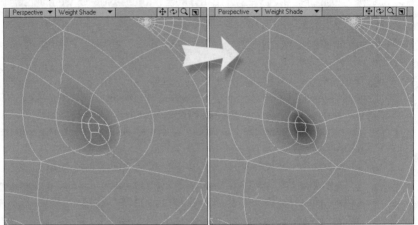

Figure 6.4-4. Weight values for the nostrils.

7. Select the **Mouth.Open** morph so you can see the inside of the mouth,
    and switch back to the **Tex_Dark** weight map.

8. Select the two polygons at the back of the throat and **Expand** the selec-
    tion. Set the value to **25%**, then **Contract** the selection and set the value
    to **100%**.

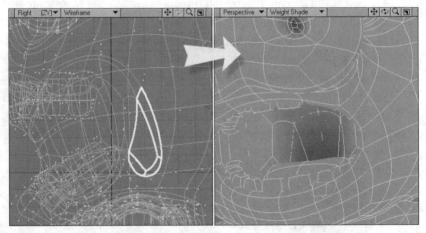

Figure 6.4-5. Weight values for the mouth.

Mouth Weight Maps

As with Morfi, Hamish has a single surface for the inner mouth, including the tongue and gums. We need to create weight maps to differentiate the gums and tongue from the mouth, and to create a transition from the mouth to the lips.

1. **Deselect All** and create a new weight map called **Tex_Lips** with an initial value of **0%**. Select the band of polygons at the leading edge of the lips and set the value to **100%**.

2. **Deselect All** and create a new weight map called **Tex_Tongue** with an initial value of **0%**. Select the tongue, excluding the segment joining the tongue to the mouth, and set the value to **100%**.

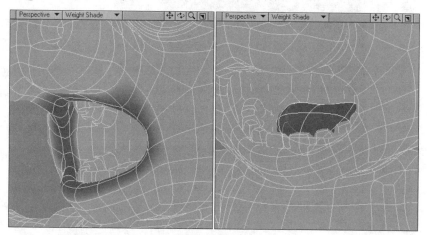

Figure 6.4-6. Lips and tongue weight values.

3. Select the polygons at the top of both gums and set the value to **50%**.

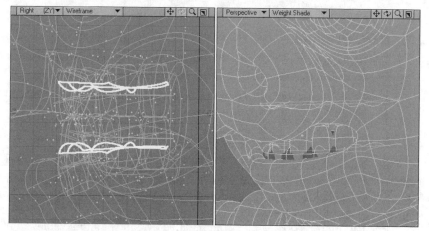

Figure 6.4-7. Polygons for the gum weight values.

Hair Weight Map

Now we'll create a weight map for surfacing the hair.

1. Select the hair polygons and create a new weight map called **Tex_Hair** with an initial value of **0%**. Deselect the bottom segment of each piece of hair and set the value to **25%**. **Contract** the selection and set the value to **100%**.

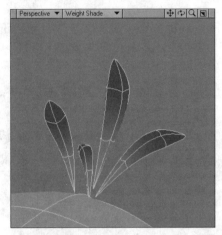

Figure 6.4-8. Hair weight map values.

Creating the Gradients

Now we'll create the gradients using the gradient weight maps. In most cases it's most useful to create a gradient that makes use of the alpha values. Use the alpha values to specify the amount of the gradient value to apply over the basic values instead of including the basic values in the gradient. This way you can use the same gradient for multiple surfaces without adjusting the gradient values.

Dark Gradient

The dark gradient can be applied to any surface. In this case we'll apply it to the Head and Mouth surfaces.

1. Switch to Layout, open the Surface Editor, and select the **Head** surface. Open the Texture Editor for the Diffuse channel.

2. Change Layer Type to **Gradient** and Input Parameter to **Weight Map**, and set the weight map to **Tex_Dark**.

3. Now we need to create keys in the gradient to tell it what values to use for the different weight values. Click in the middle of the gradient bar, then click again at the bottom, creating two new keys. With the bottom key still selected, change its settings to Value **0%**, Alpha **100%**, and Parameter **100%**. Select the middle key and set all its values to **0%**. Select the top key and set its values to **0%**, **0%**, and **–100%**.

Figure 6.4-9. Result of the dark gradient on the nostrils.

4. Select **Copy▸Selected Layer(s)**.

5. Select the **Mouth** surface and open the Texture Editor for the Diffuse channel.

6. Select **Paste▸Replace Selected Layer(s)**, pasting a copy of the gradient we just made.

Other Mouth Gradients

Now we can create the other gradients for the mouth.

1. With the diffuse texture still open, add another gradient by selecting **Paste▸Add to layers**.

2. With the new layer still selected, change Weight Map to **Tex_Tongue** and change Value for all three keys to **65%**, then **Copy Selected Layer(s)**.

3. **Paste**, adding another layer and change the Weight Map to **Tex_Lips**. Change Value for all three keys to **75%**, then **Copy Selected Layer(s)**.

4. Open the Texture Editor for the Color channel. Select **Paste▸Replace Selected Layer(s)**.

5. Now we need to get the color of the lips to use for the color gradient on the mouth. Select the **Head** surface and click the color box, opening the color picker. Select **Add to Custom Colors** and switch back to the color Texture Editor for the Mouth surface.

6. Select the color box for each key in the gradient and click the color box with the saved color to set it to the skin color.

7. Making sure the Mouth surface is selected, open the Texture Editor for Specularity and **Paste➤Replace Selected Layer(s)**. Change Value for all three keys to **5%**.

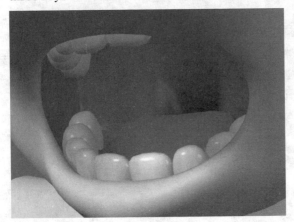

Figure 6.4-10. Result of the mouth gradients.

Hair Gradient

We'll apply the hair weight map to a gradient on the Diffuse channel.

1. Select the **Hair** surface, open the Texture Editor for the Diffuse channel, and select **Paste➤Replace Selected Layer(s)**.

2. Change Weight Map to **Tex_Hair** and change Value of all the keys to **80%**.

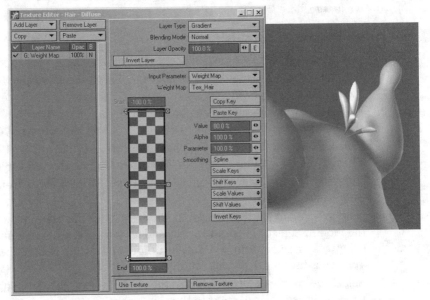

Figure 6.4-11. The hair gradient bleaches the hair toward the top, just like real hair.

We've only created gradients based on weight maps so far, but we'll look at a couple of other uses for gradients later in the texturing. Experiment with gradients using the various input parameters to get a feel for the many uses gradients have in texturing.

6.5 Procedural Textures

Procedural textures can be used for surfacing, deformation, even for motion, and they have many diverse uses for character texturing.

A major benefit to procedural textures is that they're not restricted to the same projection and resolution limitations of image maps, so they're applied evenly over the surface of any object. Another benefit to procedural textures is that they're inherently asymmetrical, whereas image mapped textures need separate UV maps or images to achieve asymmetrical texturing. Procedural textures are often quicker to create than an equivalent image map too, so before you create image maps, experiment with what detail can be achieved using procedural textures.

Viper Previews

Viper is a very useful preview tool for surfacing, especially for procedural textures. Viper updates automatically as you add or adjust surfaces and textures so you can instantly see the change in the surface without having to render. Although the surface preview does a good job for basic surface attributes, Viper shows the result of the surface on the object, which is far more useful.

You still need to render every now and then to get an absolutely accurate view of the texturing since Viper doesn't display shadows, weight mapped gradients, UV mapped textures, or reflections. You also need to render to update the Viper view when you change the camera position to view a different area; however, the time you save by using Viper is well worth it.

Applying Procedurals

We'll use procedural textures to create many of the bump details for Hamish. Bump detail such as the subtle texture of skin is notoriously difficult to texture using image maps, and very laborious to paint. You often need absurdly high resolution image maps to create the level of detail required. Using procedural textures makes it much easier to create the detail, and the size of the detail isn't limited by the resolution of the image maps.

Skin Procedurals

We'll use procedurals to create the small details in the texture of the skin. The first thing to do is to set up Viper.

1. Select **Render>Options>Enable VIPER**. Open the Viper window (**F7**) and set the preview size to **640x480**.

Chapter 6 ·

Part III

Figure 6.5-1. You need to set the preview size for Viper before rendering.

2. The face needs to be set to the default pose so there isn't any artificial stretching. Select **Layer1** and open Morph Mixer. Select the **Mouth** group and set the Open morph to **0%**.

3. Zoom up close on the face, close enough to easily see small texture detail, and render a still image (**F9**). Once the render is complete press **Render** in the Viper window to update it.

> **Note:**   You may notice that when you render close up to the surface, there are some shadow artifacts and the individual polygons are quite visible in places. These are noticeable because the subdivision level is too low for viewing that close. Don't worry about that now, as keeping the subdivision level low makes for faster rendering when testing the texturing. We'll change the final subdivision level after the texturing is complete.

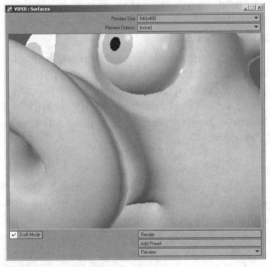

Figure 6.5-2. Viper preview of the face.

4. Open the Scene Editor, select all five skin surfaces, and open the Texture Editor for the Bump channel.

Figure 6.5-3.
Select all the skin surfaces.

5. Change Layer Type to **Procedural Texture**, Procedural Type to **Crumple**, and X, Y, and Z Scale to **5 mm**. Select **Invert Layer** and set Layer Opacity to **10%**.

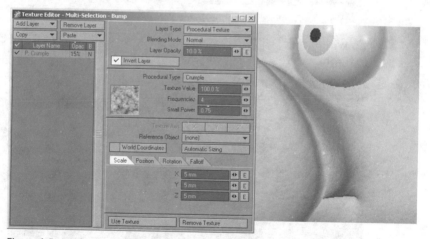

Figure 6.5-4. When adjusting procedurals, set scale first, then adjust the other values.

The Crumple texture has created the main bump detail, but I want to include some pores and raised bumps on the skin. We'll start with the pores, then use similar settings for the bumps. It can be handy to turn off the other texture layers when adjusting the settings so you can see the current layer by itself, but be sure to check it with the other layers as well so you can see if they work well together.

6. **Copy** the layer and **Paste**, adding to the layers. Deselect **Invert Layer**, change Procedural Type to **Dented**, and change X, Y, and Z Scale to **3 mm.** Change the procedural's Scale to **20,** Power to **4,** Frequency to **1,** and Octaves to **2.** Change Texture Value to **–40%** and Layer Opacity to **40%.**

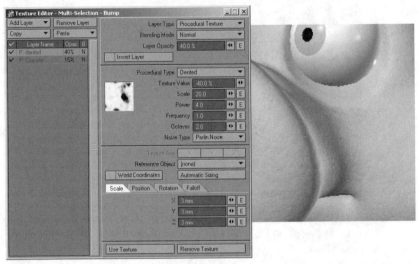

Figure 6.5-5. Creating some pores in the skin.

7. **Copy** the layer and **Paste**, adding to the layers. Change X, Y, and Z Scale to **8 mm** and Texture Value to **20%.**

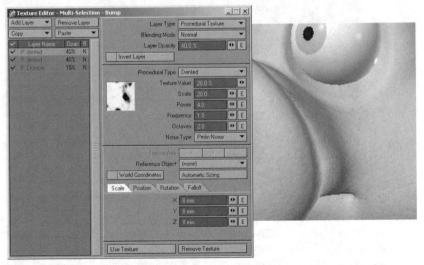

Figure 6.5-6. If you have trouble seeing the results of the texture, turn off the other texture layers so only the one you're editing is shown in the preview.

8. With the skin textures looking pretty good in Viper, do an **F9** render to check them with shadows and antialiasing, and adjust the textures if necessary.

Mouth Procedurals

We'll use procedurals to create the bump for the inside of the mouth. The first step is to open the mouth again so we can see the results of the texturing.

1. Select **Layer1** and open Morph Mixer. Select the Mouth group and set the **Open** morph to **100%**. Adjust the camera so you can see inside the mouth.

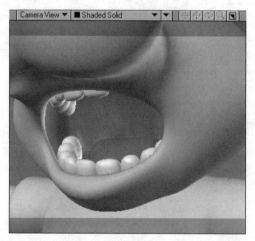

Figure 6.5-7. Getting a good view of the inside of the mouth.

2. Do a render and update the Viper window.

3. In the Surface Editor, select the **Mouth** surface and open the Texture Editor for the Bump channel.

4. Change Layer Type to **Procedural Texture**, Procedural Type to **Fractal Noise**, and X, Y and Z Scale to **5 mm**. Change Layer Opacity to **50%**.

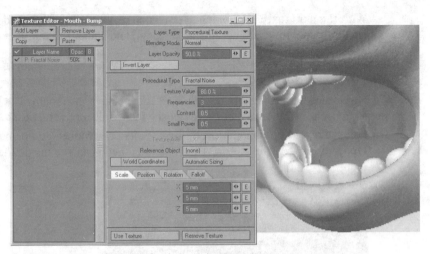

Figure 6.5-8. The main bump for the mouth.

That's given us the main bump for the mouth, but the bumps are too large for the tongue. We'll create an alpha channel for the bump texture so it isn't applied to the tongue and create a new bump texture for the tongue.

5. Select the Texture Editor for the Diffuse channel and copy the gradient for **Tex_Tongue**.

6. Select the Texture Editor for the Bump channel and paste, adding to the layers. Change Blending Mode to **Alpha** and set the values for the top and middle keys to Value **100%** and Alpha **100%**. Set the values for the bottom key to Value **0%** and Alpha **100%**. This tells the texture under the alpha layer to only apply where the Tex_Tongue weight map is 0%.

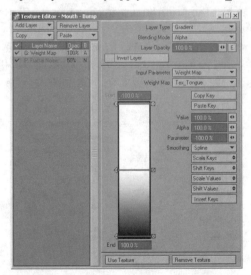

Figure 6.5-9. Creating an alpha channel from a gradient weight map lets you specify where and in what strength the texture appears on the surface.

7. **Copy** the Fractal Noise layer and **Paste,** adding to the layers. Turn off the other layers so you can see the new texture by itself and set Scale to **2 mm**.

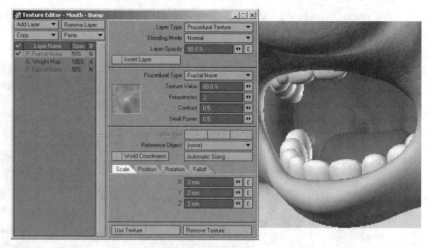

Figure 6.5-10. Smaller bump texture for the tongue.

8. **Copy** the alpha gradient layer and **Paste,** adding to the layers. Set Value for the top and middle keys to **0%**, and set Value for the bottom key to **100%**. This keeps the tongue texture from being applied to the rest of the mouth.

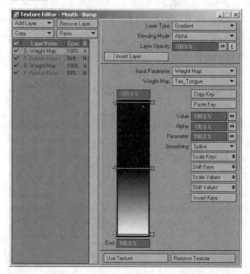

Figure 6.5-11. Notice the tongue texture disappears from Viper when you add the gradient alpha. Viper only sees the alpha value of the first key in the gradient weight map, so you need to render to make sure the alpha layers are correct.

Now we'll set some subtle bumping on the teeth. This just helps to break up the specular highlights so the teeth don't look too perfect.

9.   **Copy** the first Fractal Noise Layer of the mouth bump.

10. Select the two teeth surfaces — **Teeth** and **Teeth_Lower** — and open the Texture Editor for the Bump channel.

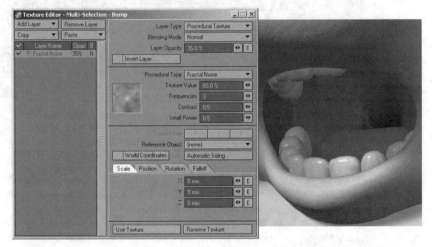

Figure 6.5-12. The bump texture for the teeth, and rendered results of the mouth textures.

11. **Paste**, replacing the layer, and change Layer Opacity to **35%**.

12. Do a render to check the bump textures, and adjust if necessary.

13. Finally, open Morph Mixer for **Layer1** and set **Mouth.Open** to **0%**.

Clothes Procedurals

We'll use procedurals to create some micro bumping of the cloth of the shirt and pants.

1.   Move the camera and main null so you have a good view of the shirt and pants, then do a render and update the Viper window.

2.   Select the **Pants, Shirt_Inner**, and **Shirt_Outer** surfaces and open the Texture Editor for the Bump channel.

3. Change Layer Type to **Procedural Texture**, Procedural Type to **Turbulence**, and Scale to **1 mm**. Change Layer Opacity to **20%**.

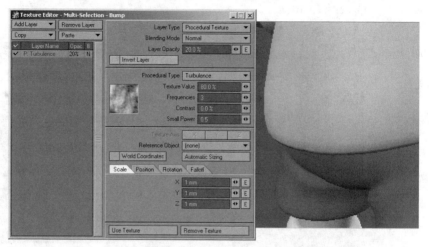

Figure 6.5-13. The small bump texture breaks up the smooth appearance of the clothes.

Shoe Procedurals

We'll use procedurals to create some bump on the soles of the shoes to simulate slightly rough rubber. We'll also create some dirt on the soles using procedural textures. Procedurals are great for creating dirt because of their random nature. Creating dirt can be a bit complex because it affects multiple channels. There's the color of the dirt, the different diffuse values, and less specularity where the dirt appears.

1. Move the camera and main null so you have a good view of the shoes, then do a render and update the Viper window.

2. Select the **Shoe_Sole** surface and open the Texture Editor for the Bump channel.

3. Change Layer Type to **Procedural Texture**, Procedural Type to **Turbulent Noise**, Texture Value to **100%**, and Scale to **5 mm**. Change Layer Opacity to **40%**.

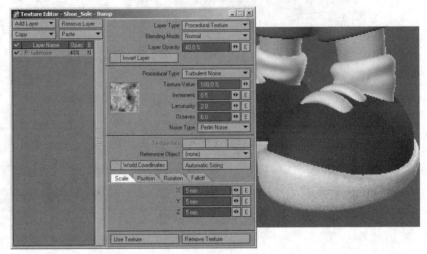

Figure 6.5-14. Creating the appearance of rough rubber.

Now we'll create the dirt textures. Once the first dirt texture is created, all its settings can be copied to use on different channels so just the strength for each needs to be adjusted.

4. **Copy** the Turbulent Noise texture layer and open the Texture Editor for the Color channel.

5. **Paste**, adding to the layers. Change Layer Opacity to **100%** and change Scale to **50 mm**.

6. With the texture size and values correct, change the color to a light brown, **175, 138, 88**.

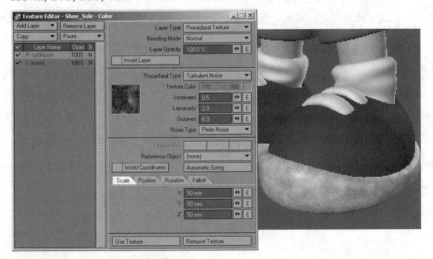

Figure 6.5-15. Making the soles dirty.

7. We don't want the dirt to be all over the surface, just on the bottom part of the soles, so change the bottom tab to **Falloff** and set Type to **LinearY** and the Y value to **1000%**.

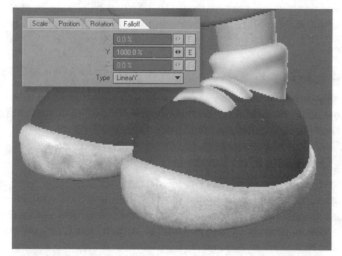

Figure 6.5-16. Falloff is another way to specify where a texture appears on a surface. The falloff is based on the position of the texture, which happens to be just in the right place for the soles of the shoes.

8. **Copy** the texture layer, open the Texture Editor for the Diffuse channel, and **Paste**, replacing the selected layer. Change Texture Value to **65%**, so the dirt is less diffuse.

9. Open the Texture Editor for the Specularity channel and **Paste**, replacing the selected layer. Change Texture Value to **2%** so the dirt is much less shiny.

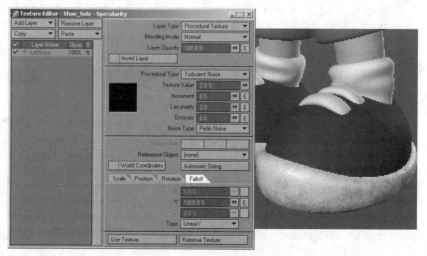

Figure 6.5-17. Final dirt after diffuse and specularity textures.

You can see there are many ways to apply procedural textures, and there are many more uses for them than we've covered here. The different settings for the procedural textures can be confusing, but the more you experiment with them, the easier it becomes to predict the outcome. Using Viper helps a lot by giving instant feedback so you can experiment with ease until you find the right combination of settings.

6.6 Image Maps

Now we can put the UV maps to use for creating the final texturing using image maps. Image maps give you more control over the texture than gradients or procedurals, allowing the creation of much more specific detail.

Image Editing Software

To complete the following tutorials you need a paint package. Photoshop is somewhat of a standard, and it's used in the tutorials, but the basic principles of layered image creation apply to most paint packages. If you use software other than Photoshop, you may need to slightly adjust the steps to suit your paint package.

Planning

Most of the planning for the image maps is done during UV mapping, but there are still some decisions that need to be made before creating the images.

Image Size

The size for the images relative to each other has been determined by the checkerboard tests during UV mapping, but that doesn't tell us the right size for the actual images. The size of the images largely depends on the type of production the character is being used for. A standard TV production doesn't need image maps as large as those of a cinema or high-definition production. A web delivered production needs even smaller images than for TV.

A general rule of thumb is to create the textures at least as large as the delivery format or render size. It's often useful to create the images at twice the size you plan to use, just in case an extreme closeup is needed where the standard image maps may show individual pixels.

Be careful not to create the images much larger than is necessary or you'll waste system memory and possibly run out of memory once a few characters are loaded into a scene.

Images vs. Other Textures

The number of images to use is also an important decision. It's a bit of a balancing act to decide whether to use a new image or an existing image adjusted using procedurals or gradients. An image uses more memory but renders faster. Procedural textures and gradients use less memory and save some creation time, but are slower to render.

Image Formats

There are benefits and disadvantages to many image file formats, but the two most commonly used formats are TGA and PNG. Both are lossless formats that support embedded alpha channels. Both take up the same amount of memory in LightWave. The added advantage of PNG is that it's compressed, so it takes up less disk space than TGA.

Color Resolution

The color resolution of images makes a big difference to the amount of memory they require. While it's important to create image maps in 24 or 32 bit, more often than not there is little or no discernable difference between an 8-bit (256 color) image and a 24-bit (16 million color) image, especially if it's used in conjunction with other textures on a surface. There is absolutely no difference between 8-bit and 24-bit grayscale images, which are used for all texture channels except color and for alpha channels.

So the final image maps should be saved as 8-bit grayscale or indexed color, if possible, only saving as 24 bit if the image suffers obvious degradation when converted to 8 bit.

Previewing Image Maps

Although Viper is invaluable when creating procedural textures, it's not as useful for image mapping since it doesn't show UV mapped textures. When you're doing image mapping it's useful to set the option to show the current texture layer in Display Options (obscurely named Show Text Editor Layer), and set the OpenGL texture resolution to the average size of your image maps. That way the current texture is shown on the object in the viewports so you can immediately see the results.

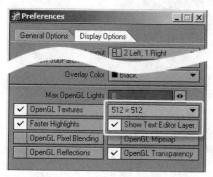

Figure 6.6-1.
Texture settings in
the Display
Options panel.

Creating the Images

We'll start by creating the initial image maps for the UV mapped textures. The checkerboards created during UV mapping determine many of the initial settings for the image maps, including relative scale and aspect ratio. The resolution of the first image map and the individual checkerboard settings determine the final resolution of the other image maps.

We need to establish a starting resolution for the image maps. From there the scale of the Textured Filter determines the initial image resolution, and the scale of the checkerboard texture determines the final image resolution. We'll set the starting resolution for Hamish's image maps to 768 pixels, a little more than standard television resolution.

While it's often useful to create the image maps at twice the final resolution, for Hamish we'll create the image maps at the final resolution to make it a bit easier. To create the initial image maps we'll use a plug-in called UV Imaginator created by Antony Scerri.

1. Load **Hamish_Working_Checkerboard.lwo** into Modeler (you can find a preprepared object in \Objects\Chapters\Hamish_Working_Checkerboard.lwo).

2. Make sure one of the viewports is set to UV Texture and open the Image Editor and the Processing tab.

3. Select the **Head** UV map, select **Plugs**➤**Additional**➤**UV Imaginator**, and choose **Entire Object**. Set Image Resolution to **768** and turn on **Wrap Drawing**. Set Image Type to **LW_PShop24** and select **Save as**, which defaults to the Images folder, and sets the name to **Hamish_Head**. Finally, press **Generate** to create the image, then press **Done** to close the panel.

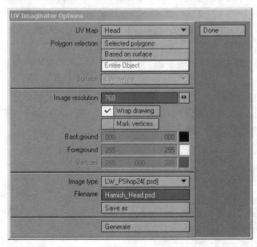

Figure 6.6-2. UV Imaginator settings.

We've just created the initial image for the head image maps. The scale of the head texture is 250 mm, or 0.25, so the size of the remaining images is based on that scale as it relates to 768 pixels. The formula for working out the size of the other images is 768 * 0.25 / Textured Filter Scale. It's handy to keep the calculator open during this process so you can work out the correct size for the images, or you can enter the formula into the Image Resolution text box. It's also useful to keep the Surface Editor open so you can double-check which checkerboard is applied to each UV map.

4. Select the **Nose** UV map and select **Blank512.tga(2)** in the Image Editor to check the Scale value.

5. Select **UV Imaginator** and set Image Resolution to **426** (768 * 0.25 / 0.45). Save as **Hamish_Nose**, generate the image, and close the panel.

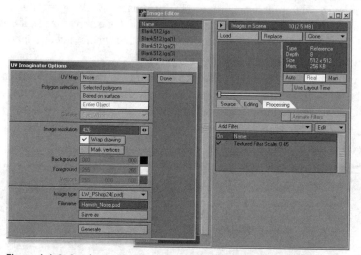

Figure 6.6-3. Set the image resolution based on the Textured Filter scale.

6. Select the **Ears** UV map and **Blank512.tga(3)** in the Image Editor.

7. Select **UV Imaginator**, leave Image Resolution at **426**, and save as **Hamish_Ears**. Generate the image and close the panel.

8. Select the **Body** UV map and **Blank512.tga(4)** in the Image Editor.

9. Select **UV Imaginator** and set Image Resolution to **548** (768 * 0.25 / 0.35). Save as **Hamish_Body**, generate the image, and close the panel.

10. Continue through all the UV maps, using the formula to calculate the Image Resolution for each one. Remember to change to the clothes layer to generate the image maps for the clothing.

Name	Image Resolution
Hamish_ArmsLegs	426
Hamish_HandsFeet	768
Hamish_Pants	384
Hamish_Socks	274
Hamish_Shoes	640

Preparing the Images

Now we need to get the working images ready for creating the final image maps.

Final Resolution

All the initial images are created, but the final resolution, or correct aspect ratio, still needs to be set. UV Imaginator creates square images, and many of the textures require a different aspect ratio. The formula for working out the final resolution is Image Width / Checkerboard X Scale (as a percentage). If the X Scale is 100, then the image will stay the same size; otherwise, it needs adjusting.

1. Load all the images into your paint package.
2. Switch to Modeler, select **Blank512.tga(1)** in the Image Editor, and open the Texture Editor for the Texture Filter. The X Scale is **75 mm**, so the size for the head image is **768** (Image Width) / **0.75**, or **1024**.
3. Switch to the paint package and resize the Hamish_Head image to **1024 x 768**.

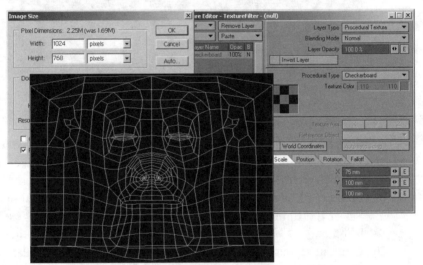

Figure 6.6-4. Resize the images based on the checkerboard X scale.

4. Repeat for all the images, using the X scale of the appropriate checkerboard to determine the final resolution.

Name	Final Size
Hamish_Nose	426 x 426 (no change)
Hamish_Ears	426 x 426 (no change)
Hamish_Body	822 x 548
Hamish_ArmsLegs	852 x 426
Hamish_HandsFeet	768 x 768 (no change)
Hamish_Pants	960 x 384

Name	Final Size
Hamish_Socks	548 x 274
Hamish_Shoes	1280 x 640

Preparing the Layers

Now we'll set up the initial layers for each image to prepare for painting. We'll create a base layer for each image and apply the UV map as an overlay.

1. Select the **Hamish_Head** image, copy the existing layer, and create a new blank layer.

2. Place the new UV map layer at the top so the blank layer is between the two UV layers.

3. Select the top UV layer and rename the layer **UVs**. Set the blending mode for the layer to **Screen** and set Opacity to **50%**. Lock the layer so you don't accidentally paint on it.

4. Check the color of the **Head** surface in Modeler and fill the blank layer with that color — **255, 206, 174**.

5. Finally, delete the original background layer.

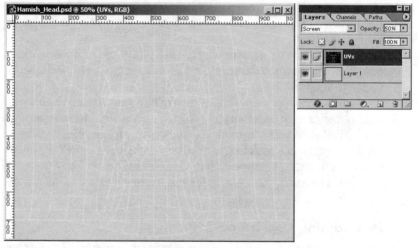

Figure 6.6-5. Layers for the head image.

6. Repeat for all the images, filling each base layer with the color of the appropriate surface.

Painting Textures

I highly recommend using a tablet for painting textures. It doesn't have to be a large or fancy one; in fact I use the smallest base model tablet because it takes up less room and does everything that I need. For a long time I didn't like a tablet. It felt strange, as I'd used a mouse to create computer graphics for many years, and was very comfortable using a mouse. After watching a friend work on textures using a tablet, and seeing how much quicker and easier it was than using a mouse, I decided to get one, and I've never looked back. Having control over the pressure makes a big difference when you're painting. You aren't restricted to the specified brush strength, and have other options available, such as the different brush shapes depending on pressure. Being able to taper a brush stroke easily makes painting things like scratches, veins, and wrinkles much easier.

Layers

Make the most of working with layers. Most textures have dark areas and light areas over a mid-range base color. If you keep the dark and light areas in separate layers it makes adjusting or changing the texture much easier.

Use different types of layer blending to your advantage. When creating dark and light variations of a base color, either for color or grayscale images, instead of painting a dark color on one layer and a light color on another layer, it's far easier to use the same color as the base and use layer blending to determine how it's applied. That way you don't have to constantly change colors when painting, and you won't accidentally paint dark in the light layer and vice versa.

Create each type of detail in its own layer. Textures are often made up of many components. There's the base color, variations of the base color, imperfections in the surface, and often a distinct pattern, especially for animal characters. If you keep each of these in its own layer, it makes creating and editing the image maps a lot easier.

If you want to try a texture but are not sure whether it will work, start by painting it on a separate layer. You can always merge it with the other layers if you decide to keep it.

Name each layer as you create it. While you're creating the image maps you usually have a good understanding of what each layer is for, no matter what each layer is called, so you may think it's unnecessary to specifically name each layer. But when you come back to it after a little while when something needs changing or you want to use the same texture detail for a different character, or if someone else needs to edit it, the layer names make it much easier to immediately find the layers that require adjusting.

Maintaining Consistency

When you're painting multiple textures for a surface, such as the six sets of image maps for Hamish's skin, it's important to maintain consistency between the images. When you create the first set of textures, create a color swatch for each color that you use. Most images only use four or five distinct colors, so the color swatch is usually quite manageable.

Once you've finished the first set of textures, copy the color swatch to all the other images for that surface so you can easily choose the same colors for all the image maps.

Dealing with Seams

There are two types of seams — internal seams and external seams. Internal seams are created by wrapping the geometry within a UV map. These are the easiest seams to deal with in the textures because the two sides of the UV map, and therefore the texture, match up perfectly. You can also see the two sides of the seam within the image, so adjusting the seam is easier.

External seams are created between UV maps. These are a little trickier to deal with, as it's more difficult to match up areas in two separate images.

The easiest way to deal with any type of seam is to keep detail away from the seam area. The simpler the seam area is, the easier it is to match up. However, it's not always possible to avoid detail near the seams.

When creating texture detail that crosses internal seams, the easiest way to deal with it is to offset the layer. Offsetting the layer allows you to paint across the seam, making sure each side matches. You can then offset the layer back to its original position.

Another way to match edges is to copy a small slice of the texture along one seam and then paste it to the other seam, giving you a starting point for matching up the detail.

The easiest way to handle external seams is to create the texture detail so it conforms to the edge of the UV map on both sides of the seam. Keep both images open so you can paint along the seam of one while using the other as reference.

If you know that a seam has varying color values, for example the base color and a lighter or darker shade of the base color, paint the exact lighter color along the seam instead of using a percentage of white or using another blending mode in order to ensure the colors match up.

Creating the Head Textures

Creating the head textures is made a bit easier by creating the smaller skin detail with procedural textures. This means that only the broad detail needs to be created. It's usually easiest to start with the color texture, as the textures for the other channels are often based on the color image.

Painting the Color Map

The color map is the starting point for the appearance of a surface. In general the color map should be quite simple, only featuring changes to the hue of a surface. Don't try to paint too much detail into the color map, as many of the surface details are better dealt with using the other surface channels.

1. In your paint package, open the **Hamish_Head** image (you can find preprepared PSD files for the following tutorials in \Images\Chapters\).

2. Create a new layer above the UVs layer. Name the layer **Swatch**. Select a small square in the top-left corner and fill it with the base color. As you paint with each new color, add that color to a new square in the Swatch layer.

3. Create a new layer above the base color and change its blending mode to **Multiply**. Name the layer **Dark**.

4. Select the base color, a large soft brush, and very low pressure or flow — about **10%** is good. Paint the darker, or redder, areas of the skin, including the eyelids, nose, lips, cheeks, and the inside edges of the ears.

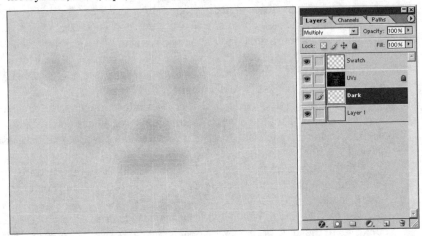

Figure 6.6-6. If you get confused as to what an area of the UV map represents, you can check it in Modeler by selecting that area of the UV map and seeing where the selected polygons are on the model.

> **Tip:** Reduce the opacity of the UVs layer to see the texture more easily. Adjust the opacity of the UVs layer up or down when creating each texture to where the UVs are just visible, so they don't obscure the underlying texture too much.

To add a bit of realism we'll give the skin a touch of color variation. Not so much a tan as lighter areas where the sun doesn't reach.

5. Select a slightly lighter pink than the base color (**255,220,197**) and add it to the color swatch. Add a new layer above the base layer called **Light**. Paint along the bottom of the UVs, fading up to the mouth and cheeks. Make sure the full strength of the color is applied to the bottom seam. Hide the other layers just to make sure, and adjust if necessary.

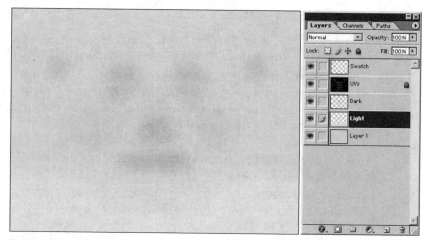

Figure 6.6-7. The Light layer has normal blending so you can be sure of the exact color of the seam.

Leaving Hamish's skin all pink is a bit dull. We'll create some spots to add some interest to the skin.

6. Select a light brown (**171,119,46**) and add it to the color swatch. Add a new layer above the Dark layer called **Spots**. Select a smaller brush and full pressure. Paint some random spots, varying the size and shape for each, but keeping the spots away from the nose.

7. Adjust the opacity of the Spots layer so the spots don't stand out quite so much. About **50%** opacity is good.

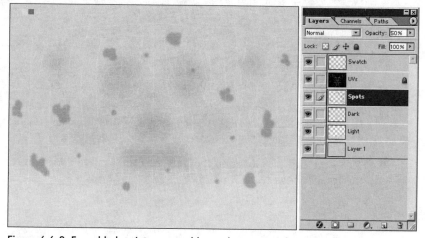

Figure 6.6-8. For added variety you could vary the opacity of each spot.

Applying the Color Map

Now that all the color elements are in place it's time to test the image on Hamish.

1. Hide the UVs and Swatch layers and save as **Hamish_Head_Col.png**.

2. Open Layout and load **Hamish_Surfacing.lws**.

3. Open the Display Options panel and change the OpenGL texture size to **512** and turn on **Show Text Editor Layer**. Make sure the Perspective view is set to **Textured Shaded Solid**.

4. Open the Texture Editor for the Color channel of the head surface, select the Image pull-down and choose **(load image)**, loading **Hamish_Head_Col.png**.

5. Rotate the Perspective view to view the texture all around the head. Check out various poses including closed eyes to make sure the texture is behaving nicely with facial deformations. If there are areas you want to change, adjust the image and resave, then in Layout open the Image Editor, select the image, and **Replace** with the same name, updating it in Layout.

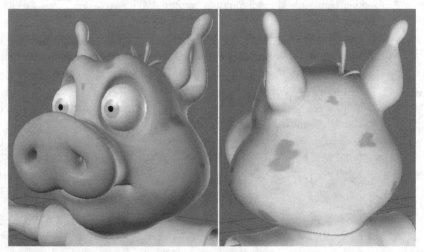

Figure 6.6-9. Check the texture in Layout, making sure all the detail is in the right place and that the spots look okay.

6. Move the camera closer so the head fills the camera view and render to the Image Viewer.

Figure 6.6-10. Rendering to the Image Viewer shows the combination of all the texturing thus far and provides a comparison for the effect of the other textures to come.

Creating the Bump Map

The basic bumps of the skin have been created using procedurals, but there are some wrinkles that need to be created using an image map. Because Hamish is young his face isn't very wrinkly, but we'll give him some wrinkles on his lips and around his ears.

I've found that wrinkles don't usually look very good on the eyelids of characters with big eyes, like Hamish. The exception is if the character is very wrinkly, in which case the wrinkles on the eyelids fit in well with the rest of the facial detail. Feel free to experiment with wrinkles on the eyelids though; it may help achieve the look you're after.

1. Create a new layer below the UVs layer and fill it with 50% gray (**128,128,128**). Name the layer **Bump**, then add the color to the color swatch.

2. Create a copy of the Bump layer, then change the opacity of the lower bump layer to **75%**. Turn off the full-strength Bump layer so some of the color layers are showing.

> **Note:** Creating a less opaque bump base layer to paint over helps by showing some of the color detail, as well as showing the painting cursors more easily.

3. Create a new layer above the Bump layers and change its blending mode to **Multiply**. Name the layer **Dark**. This layer is used to create indented areas.

4. Using a small, hard brush at about **50%** pressure, paint a series of wrinkles on the lips. Using a slightly larger softer brush, paint some wrinkles above and below the ears.

> **Tip:** Use the Smudge tool on the ends of the wrinkles to blend them.

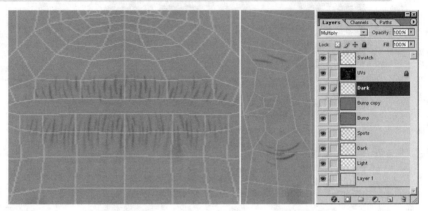

Figure 6.6-11. Painting the wrinkles.

5. Create a new layer above the Dark layer and change its blending mode to **Screen**. Name the layer **Light**. This layer is used to create raised areas.

6. Using a small soft brush at low pressure, paint between the wrinkles on the lips, accentuating the wrinkles.

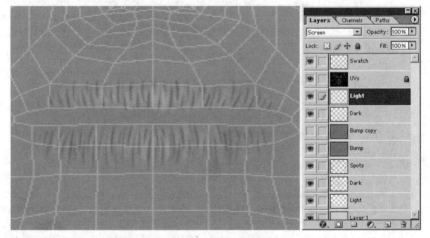

Figure 6.6-12. Painting light areas between the wrinkles accentuates them and creates a slightly different effect than dark wrinkles by themselves.

7. Create a new layer above the Light layer and change its blending mode to **Screen**. Name the layer **Spots**. Make a selection based on the color Spots layer and fill the bump Spots layer.

8. Create a new Screen blended layer, **Contract** the selection by about five pixels, and fill. Create another Screen blended layer, **Contract** the selection by five pixels, and fill. **Merge** the three Spots layers.

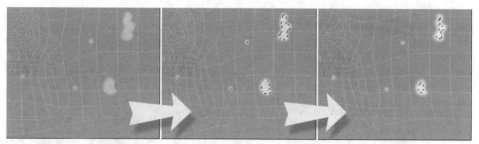

Figure 6.6-13. This technique creates a smooth mound for each spot instead of a flat raised area.

9. **Hide** the UVs and Swatch layers and turn on the full-strength Bump layer. Save as **Hamish_Head_Bmp.png**.

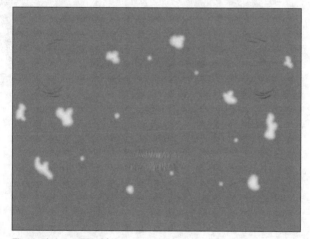

Figure 6.6-14. Final bump map.

10. Switch to Layout and open the color Texture Editor for the head surface. **Copy** the texture layer and open the Texture Editor for the Bump channel. **Paste**, adding to the layers, and move the image layer to the bottom. Change the image to **Hamish_Head_Bmp**.

11. Check the texture from the Perspective view and adjust and replace if necessary.

> **Note:** When an image is replaced in the Image Editor, the currently selected image map in the Texture Editor is changed to the replaced image. To make sure this doesn't change images assigned as textures, select the texture layer containing the image being replaced before replacing an image.

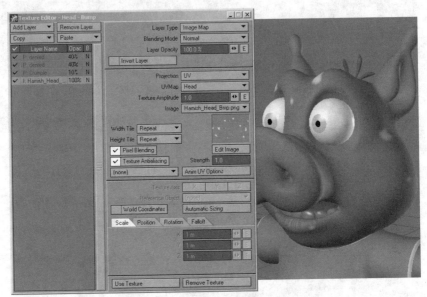

Figure 6.6-15. Apply and check the texture in Layout.

12. Do a render and compare with the previous render to see the change the bump map makes.

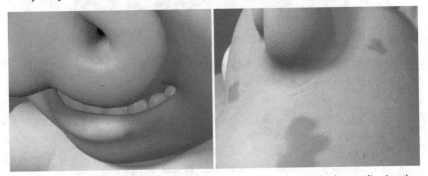

Figure 6.6-16. The result of the bump texture. Don't worry too much about adjusting the strength of the bump map at this stage — we'll do that later.

Creating the Diffuse Map

The diffuse map is based on the color and bump maps. Basically we'll slightly reduce the diffuse for the darker areas of the color map and for the wrinkles of the bump map, enhancing those areas of the surface.

1. Create a new layer below the UVs layer and fill it with 75% gray **(191,191,191)**. Name the layer **Diffuse**, then add the color to the color swatch.

> **Note:** The base color for the diffuse and specular textures should be the same as the default diffuse and specularity values of the surface.

2. Create a new layer above the Diffuse layer and change its blending mode to **Multiply**. Name the layer **Main**. Make a selection based on the color Dark layer and fill the diffuse Main layer.

3. Create a new layer above the Main layer and change its blending mode to **Multiply**. Name the layer **Spots**. Make a selection based on the color Spots layer and fill the diffuse Spots layer.

4. Create a new layer above the Spots layer and change its blending mode to **Multiply**. Name the layer **Wrinkles**. Make a selection based on the bump Dark layer and fill the diffuse Wrinkles layer.

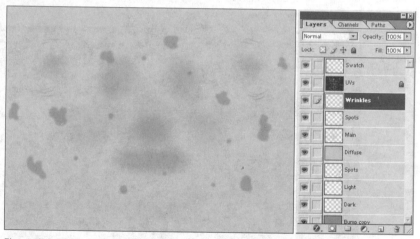

Figure 6.6-17. Don't feel restricted to only using the existing layers to create the diffuse map. Feel free to paint more diffuse variation if you want other areas to have different diffuse values.

5. Adjust the opacity of all three diffuse layers so the Main layer reaches about **65%** black value, and so the spots and wrinkles are quite faint. Change Layer Opacity of Main to **75%**, Spots to **15%**, and Wrinkles to **25%**.

6. Turn off the UVs and Swatch layers and save as **Hamish_Head_Dif.png**.

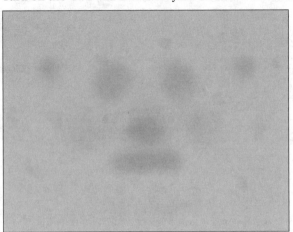

Figure 6.6-18. Adjusted opacity of the diffuse layers.

7. In Layout, apply the texture to the Diffuse channel of the head surface below the gradient texture. Set Layer Opacity to **30%**. Do a render to check the effect of the diffuse texture.

Figure 6.6-19. Adjusting the texture layer's opacity gives another level of control over the strength of the texture.

Creating the Specular Map

The skin is looking pretty good, but it looks a bit dry. To give the skin some realistic shininess we need a specular texture. Like the diffuse texture, the specular map is based on the color and bump maps. The difference is that the darker areas are lighter for the specular map, increasing the specularity for those areas.

1. Create a new layer below the UVs layer and fill it with 5% gray (**13,13,13**). Name the layer **Specular**, then add the color to the color swatch.

2. Create a new layer above the Specular layer called **Main**. Make a selection based on the color Dark layer and fill the specular Main layer with white.

3. Create a new layer above the specular Main layer called **Spots**. Make a selection based on the color Spots layer and fill the specular Spots layer with white. Adjust Layer Opacity to **50%** so the spots aren't so bright.

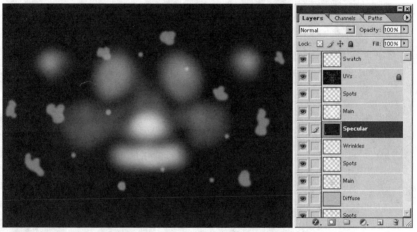

Figure 6.6-20. As with the diffuse map, feel free to paint more specular variation than exists in the previous layers.

4. Turn off the UVs and Swatch layers and save as **Hamish_Head_Spc.png**.

5. In Layout, apply the texture to the Specularity channel of the head surface. Set Layer Opacity to **30%**. Do a render to check the effect of the specularity texture.

Figure 6.6-21. Result of the specular texture.

That's looking good, but still isn't quite right. The highlights are all the same size or glossiness, making the surface look more like plastic than skin. Usually on areas of varying specularity, higher specularity values require higher glossiness values to look correct. To achieve this we'll apply the specular map to the Glossiness channel.

6. **Copy** the texture layer for the Specular channel and **Paste** it into the Glossiness channel. Change Layer Opacity to **50%**. Do a render to check the effect of the glossiness texture.

Figure 6.6-22. Result of the glossiness texture.

That looks much better. The areas with low specularity have large highlights, indicating a rougher or softer surface, and the areas with high specularity have smaller highlights, indicating a smoother, harder, or wetter surface.

With all the head textures complete you can experiment with the opacity of the textures to achieve just the right look for the skin surface. It's important to find the right look at this stage because the final settings of the textures on the head surface determine the settings of the textures on the other skin surfaces.

Creating the Nose Textures

The nose area uses a different UV map because there isn't enough room in the UV map of the head to fit the same level of detail. While the textures for the head UV map have given a good idea of what's needed for the nose textures, we didn't have to be too careful texturing the nose area because we'll be overlaying different images for the nose.

The nose textures are blended into the head textures using an alpha texture. For single textures it's easiest to embed the alpha channel in the texture itself, but because there are four textures for the nose it's more efficient to create a single alpha texture that's used for all the nose textures.

Painting the Alpha Map

The alpha map determines where the nose textures are visible. We want to fade the nose textures into the head textures, so the alpha map needs to fade from white (where the texture is fully opaque) to black at the edges of the UVs (where the texture is fully transparent).

Before we create the alpha map we'll copy the color swatch from Hamish_Head to Hamish_Nose so it's easy to use the same colors for the nose textures.

1. Open **Hamish_Nose.psd**.
2. Select **Hamish_Head.psd** and **Copy** the **Swatch** layer. Select **Hamish_Nose.psd**, select the **UVs** layer, and **Paste**, adding the swatch above the UVs layer. Rename the new layer **Swatch**.
3. Create a new layer above the base layer and fill it with black (**0,0,0**). Name the layer **Alpha**.
4. Create a new layer above the Alpha layer called **White**. Select a large soft brush and paint white inside the UVs, fading out to the edge of the UVs. Make sure there is no white (fully black) at the edges of the UVs.

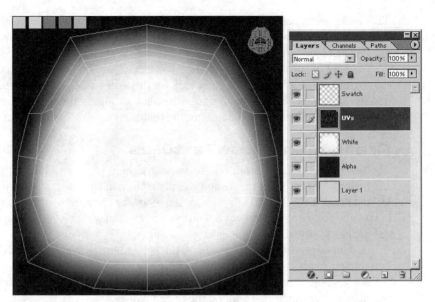

Figure 6.6-23. Notice the polygons of the head, where we don't want the nose texture to appear, are in the black area of the alpha texture.

5. Hide the UVs and Swatch layers and save as **Hamish_Nose_A.png**.

Painting the Color Map

It's useful to start by checking which polygons in the UV map represent the end of the nose. In Modeler, select the Nose UV map and in one of the other viewports, select the polygons at the tip of the nose. This shows where the tip of the nose is on the UV map.

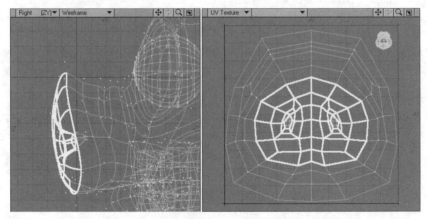

Figure 6.6-24. Check the relationship between the UVs and the model.

Follow the same process to create the nose color texture as creating the head color texture. Paint dark layer of the color texture so it just overlaps the tip of the nose, and add a few spots.

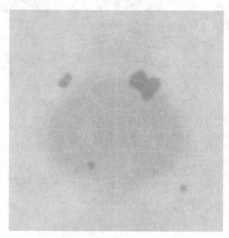

Figure 6.6-25. Color texture for the nose.

Applying the Color Map

Applying the map is a little different than the head texture, as it needs the additional alpha texture.

1.   Save the color map as **Hamish_Nose_Col.png**.
2.   In Layout, open the Texture Editor for the Color channel of the head surface. **Copy** the existing layer and **Paste**, adding to the layers. In the new layer, change UVMap to **Nose** and for Image, load the nose color texture.
3.   Check the texture in the Perspective view and adjust if necessary.

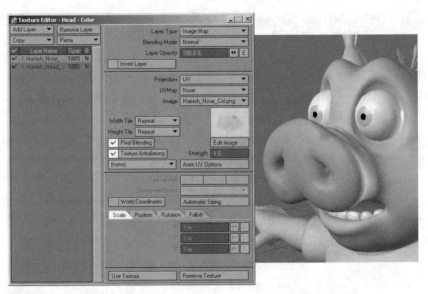

Figure 6.6-26. Check the texture in Layout.

4. **Copy** the Nose texture layer and **Paste**, adding to the layers. Change Blending Mode to **Alpha**. For Image, load the nose alpha texture.

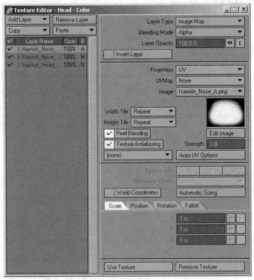

Figure 6.6-27. Add the alpha texture layer to blend the nose texture into the head texture.

5. Do a render to see the effect of the nose texture. Render from the side to check the blended area between the head and nose textures.

Creating the Bump Map

Follow the same process to create the nose bump texture as creating the head bump texture. Create some subtle wrinkles around the nostrils and add the spots in the same way as with the head texture.

In addition to the wrinkles and spots, create some large soft dark and light areas on the tip of the nose to break up the smoothness of the surface a little.

Figure 6.6-28. Bump texture.

Save the image as **Hamish_Nose_Bmp.png** and apply the bump map in the same way as the color map. Add the bump map above the head bump map layer, and add the alpha layer above the nose bump map, so all the procedural textures are above the image maps.

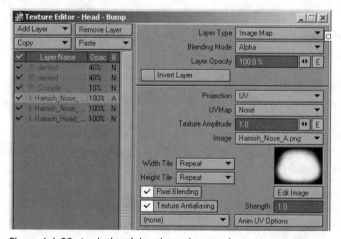

Figure 6.6-29. Apply the alpha above the nose bump texture.

Creating the Diffuse Map

Follow the same process to create the nose diffuse texture as creating the head diffuse texture.

Once the diffuse layers are created, the process changes a little. The head diffuse layer is applied with 30% opacity. If we apply the nose diffuse layer at 30% opacity, it won't overlay the head diffuse layer properly. Instead, the diffuse texture layers need to be adjusted so they're at 30% strength.

1. The Main layer is at 75%, so change it to **23%** (30% of 75).
2. The Spots layer is at 15%, so change it to **5%**.
3. The Wrinkles layer is at 25%, so change it to **8%**.
4. Save as **Hamish_Nose_Dif.png**.

Figure 6.6-30. Diffuse texture.

Apply the diffuse map the same way as the bump map with the alpha channel included, making sure the gradient is above all the image layers.

Creating the Specular Map

Follow the same process to create the nose specular texture as creating the head specular texture.

As with the diffuse texture, the head specular layer is applied at 30%, so adjust the specular texture layers to 30% of their strength — Main at **30%** and Spots at **15%**.

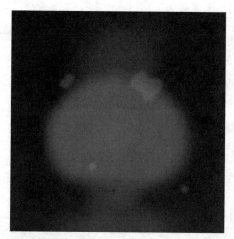

Figure 6.6-31. Specular texture.

Apply the specular map the same way as the other nose maps with the alpha layer included.

Creating the Glossiness Map

The specular map is used in the Glossiness channel for the head, but it's at a different opacity than the Specularity channel. This means that in order to overlay the nose textures correctly we need to include an additional glossiness texture.

The glossiness texture is different from the specular texture, because the base of the head specular map used on the Glossiness channel is different from the default glossiness value of the surface. We need to simulate the same blending conditions within the texture.

1. Make a copy of each specular layer and move the copies above the original specular layers.

2. Change the name of the Specular copy layer to **Gloss**.

3. Add a new layer below the Gloss layer and fill with 35% black (**89,89,89**), the same as the default glossiness value.

4. The head specular map is used at 50% opacity on the Glossiness channel, so we need to change all the gloss layers to 50% of the original head specular opacity values, including the base Gloss layer. Set Gloss to **50%**, Main copy to **50%**, and Spots copy to **25%**.

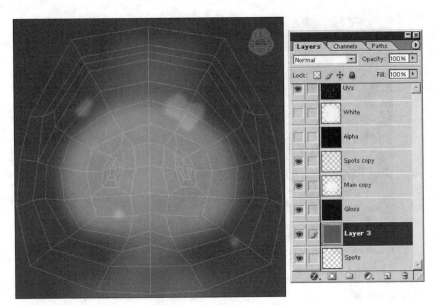

Figure 6.6-32. Glossiness texture.

5. Hide the UVs and Swatch layers and save as **Hamish_Nose_Gls.png**.
Apply the glossiness map the same way as the other nose maps.

Figure 6.6-33. Results of the combined nose textures.

. . . . Texturing

Hamish

With all the textures for the head surface complete, do some renders from various angles to check that the nose textures are blending nicely into the head textures.

Figure 6.6-34. Check the blended area between the nose and head textures.

Creating the Ear Textures

For the most part the ear textures are created in the same way as the head textures.

Creating the Color Map

The dark layer of the color texture is the most important, as it needs to match up with the same layer in the head texture as well as matching up on either side of the ear texture.

When creating the dark layer for the ears, keep the head image open with the UVs showing so you can match up the texture as closely as possible. When you've got it close, apply the ear texture to the ear surface in Layout and check the Perspective view to see how well the head and ear color textures match up.

> **Note:** Because of the alpha map for the nose texture, you need to disable the two nose textures on the head surface so you can see the head color map at the same time as the ear color map.

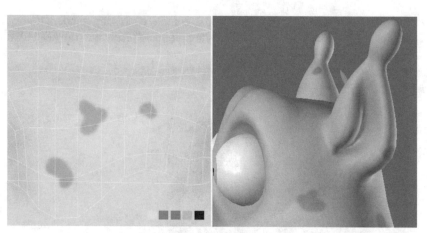

Figure 6.6-35. Check the color texture in Layout to see how it matches up with the head texture.

Adjust the texture until it matches up as closely as you feel is necessary. You may need to go back and forth between adjusting and checking the texture a couple of times to get the textures matching up so the seam is no longer visible.

Creating the Other Maps

The other maps are based on the color map, so as long as the color map matches the head texture, you know the other maps will also match up. Use the same techniques and opacity values to create and apply the ear textures as the equivalent maps for the head textures.

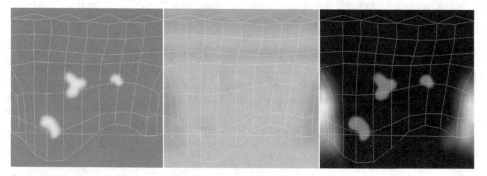

Figure 6.6-36. Bump, diffuse, and specular maps for the ears.

I've made the bulb at the top of the ears a little darker than the default skin tone. When you create the specular map, delete or erase the section on the bulb so it isn't shinier than the rest of the skin, leaving the shiny area just on the inside of the ear and on the spots.

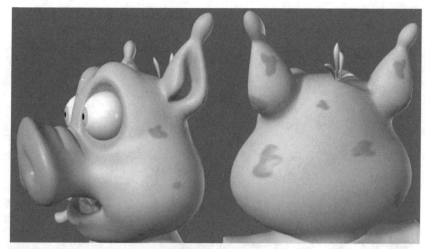

Figure 6.6-37. Results of the combined ear textures.

Creating the Body Textures

The color texture for the body is a little different because of the lighter area we created on the head for where the sun don't shine. Fill the base color for the body texture with the lighter skin color used on the head, as the sun doesn't reach the body very often.

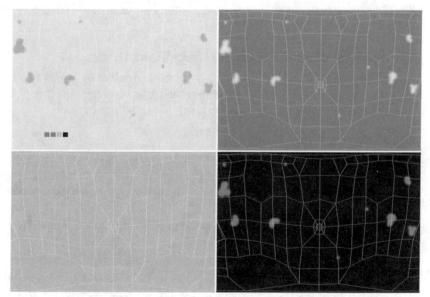

Figure 6.6-38. Clockwise from top left: color, bump, specular and diffuse textures.

I've made the textures for the body quite simple, as it's rarely seen. Feel free to add more detail to the body if you wish.

To see the results of the body, arm, and leg textures, set the visibility of the clothes layer to **Hidden** and deactivate it.

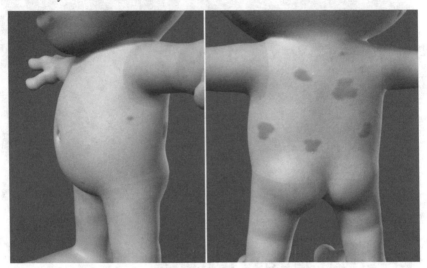

Figure 6.6-39. The results of the body textures.

Notice when you render that the seam between the body and arms and legs is very obvious, because of the lighter color of the body, but the top of the body texture matches up perfectly with the neck. Just as we did for the head, we'll adjust the arm and leg textures so they're lighter toward the seams, matching up with the body color.

Creating the Arm and Leg Textures

Creating the color ArmsLegs texture is made a little trickier by having two sets of geometry in the same UV map. Once the color texture is done, the other maps follow the same process as the head textures.

Creating the Color Map

The Light layer is the important one for the ArmsLegs color texture, as it crosses the internal seams of both the arms and the legs. The trick is to paint along the inside seam first (the seam in the middle of the texture), then copy the section outside the UVs to the other seam.

1. After copying the color swatch, create two layers above the base layer called **Light** and **LightLegs**.
2. Start with the first **Light** layer (the layer for the arms). Paint the lighter pink at full strength along the top of the UVs, fading down to about halfway between the top and the middle of the UVs. Paint along the right seam, fading to the next polygon segment to the left and overlapping the UVs by about the same amount to the right.

Figure 6.6-40. Create the detail overlapping the inside seam.

3. Make a selection running alongside the seam of the arms and covering the overlapping section. Move the selected section to the left edge of the UV map.

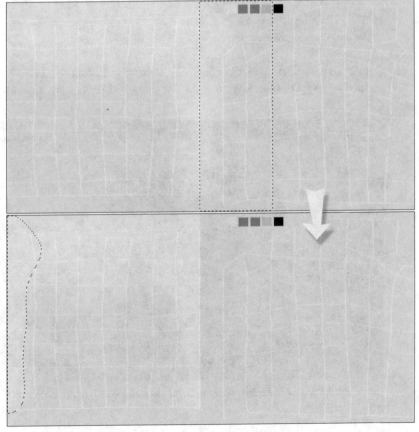

Figure 6.6-41. Move the overlapping detail to the opposite seam.

4. Repeat steps 2 and 3 for the **LightLegs** layer, but only extend the light section of the legs down to the calves.

This provides perfectly matching internal and external seams between the arms and legs and the body.

Create the other color layers the same way as the head color texture, slightly darkening the front and back of the elbow and knee, and creating some spots.

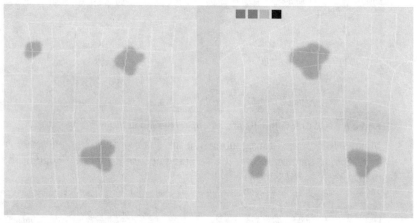

Figure 6.6-42. Final color texture.

Check the color layer with the body color texture in Layout to ensure it matches up nicely. Once the color layer matches, you know the other layers will also match up.

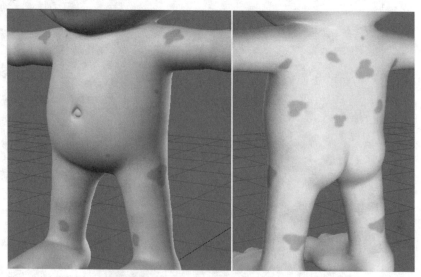

Figure 6.6-43. Check the color texture in Layout to make sure it matches up with the body texture.

Creating the Bump Map

Start the bump map in the same way as the head bump map, creating the appropriate layers.

1. Start creating the arm wrinkles by painting creases on the inside of the elbows, then create some wrinkles for the elbow. The other wrinkles for the arms require the same method of creation as the Light layer of the color texture, as the wrinkles cross the internal seam.

2. Create wrinkles under the arm and under the wrist, crossing the inside UV seam. For each of the Dark and Light layers, select and move the overlapping section to the left side of the map to create matching seams.

3. Create wrinkles under the bum, at the back of the knees, and on the Achilles tendon at the back of the ankles.

4. Finally, create the bump texture for the spots.

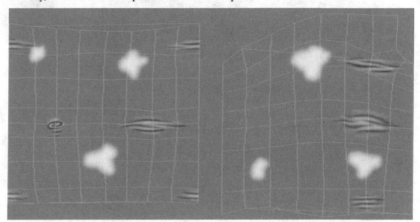

Figure 6.6-44. Bump texture.

5. Save and test the map in Layout to make sure the wrinkles are in the right places.

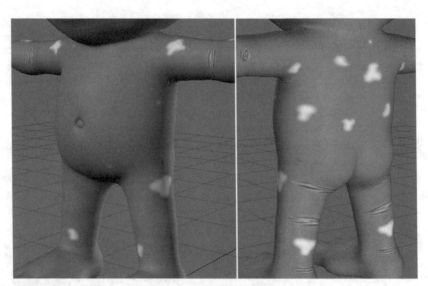

Figure 6.6-45. Checking the bump texture on the character.

Creating the Other Maps

Use the same techniques and opacity values to create and apply the ArmsLegs textures as the equivalent maps for the head textures.

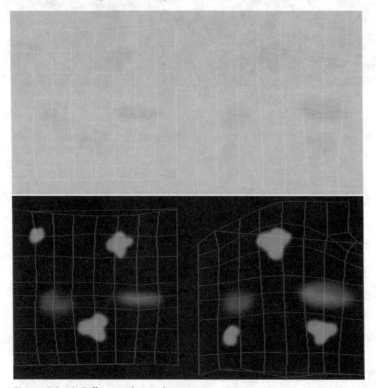

Figure 6.6-46. Diffuse and specular textures.

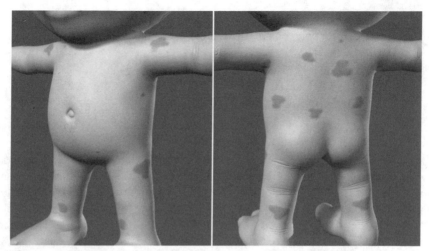

Figure 6.6-47. Result of the combined textures.

Creating Asymmetrical Maps

The spots on the arms and legs are obviously symmetrical. We can fix that by creating different textures to use on the right arm and leg. The good thing is that we can reuse most of the texture details, as it's really only the spots that are noticeably symmetrical.

The easiest way to apply the asymmetrical textures is to change the surface for the right arm and leg. We'll do that first.

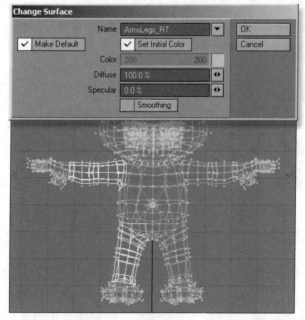

Figure 6.6-48. Create a new surface for the right arm and leg.

1. In Modeler, select the polygons of the **ArmsLegs** surface.
2. Deselect the polygons on the left side and change surface to **ArmsLegs_RT**.
3. Open the Surface Editor and copy the **ArmsLegs** surface to the **ArmsLegs_RT** surface, then save the object.

Now we'll create the asymmetrical textures for the new surface.

4. Back in the paint package, create new layers above all of the Spots layers, renaming each new layer **Spots_RT**.
5. In the **Spots_RT** layer for the color texture, paint new spots using the original spots as reference, creating the new spots a bit different in shape and position than the original ones. Set Layer Opacity to **50%** and hide the original spots.

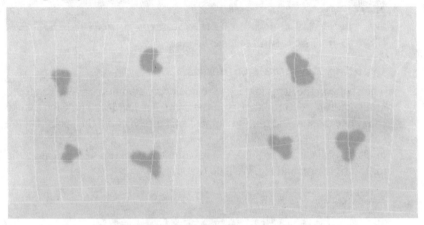

Figure 6.6-49. New spots for the right side.

6. Create the other Spots layers using the color spots in the same way as the original Spots layers for each type of texture.
7. Save right-sided versions of each of the ArmsLegs textures, for example, **Hamish_ArmsLegs_RT_Col.png**, etc.
8. In Layout, apply the new right-sided textures to the appropriate surface channels of the **ArmsLegs_RT** surface.

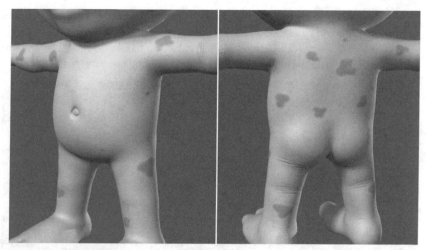

Figure 6.6-50. The spots are now asymmetrical.

Creating the Hand and Foot Textures

Creating the hand and foot textures follows the same process as the arm and leg textures. The tricky part is aligning the hand color texture with the arm texture, but you can follow the same process as aligning the ear texture with the head.

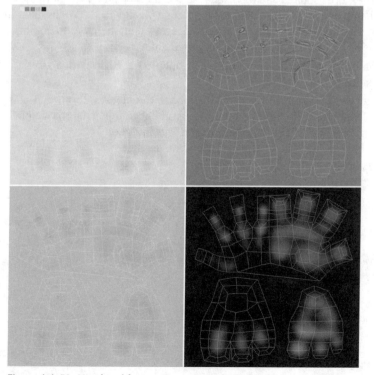

Figure 6.6-51. Hand and foot textures.

I've left the foot textures quite simple for the same reason as the body — they'll rarely be seen and can be detailed more if required later on.

The wrinkles are a little more complex for the hands, so take your time with them, checking regularly in Layout to make sure they're in the right places.

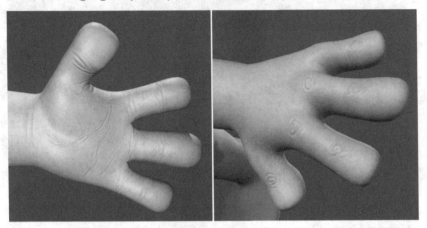

Figure 6.6-52. Result of the combined textures.

Adjusting the Procedural Bump

With the textures applied and the hands viewed up close, it's evident that the procedural bump textures on the skin are too strong for the hands. We'll adjust the procedural dented textures on the arms and legs, fading them out to nothing on the hands and feet by using a weight map gradient.

1. In Modeler, create a new weight map called **Tex_Skin** with an initial strength of **0%**.

2. Select the polygons of the arms just above the elbows. From that point set the weight values so there's an even gradient to full strength weight values on the hands. Do the same for the legs and feet.

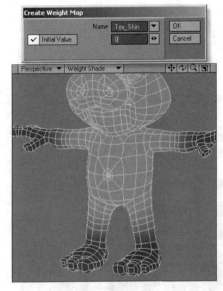

Figure 6.6-53. Create the weight map at full strength on the hands and feet, fading out along the arms and legs.

3. In Layout, open the Texture Editor for the Bump channel of the **ArmsLegs** surface.

4. Create a new Gradient layer. Set Blending Mode to **Alpha** and Input Parameter to **Weight Map**, and use **Tex_Skin**.

5. Create keys at **0%** and **100%**. Set the values of the top two keys to **100%** and the bottom key to **0%**. This tells the texture to apply where the weight map isn't, so it fades out toward the hands and feet.

6. **Copy** the Gradient layer and **Paste**, adding to the layers. Position the gradient layers so there's one above each dented layer.

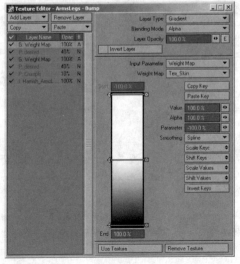

Figure 6.6-54. Alpha layer for the procedural bumps.

7. Open the Texture Editor for the Bump channel of the **ArmsLegs_RT** surface and paste twice, adding to the layers. Position the Gradient layers above each dented layer.

8. Open the Texture Editor for the Bump channel of the **HandsFeet** surface and remove the two dented layers.

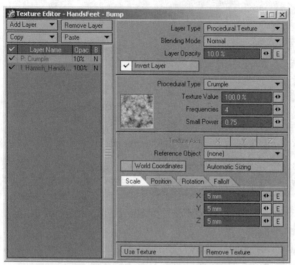

Figure 6.6-55. Simplifying the Bump channel for the HandsFeet surface.

9. Render a few views to check the results.

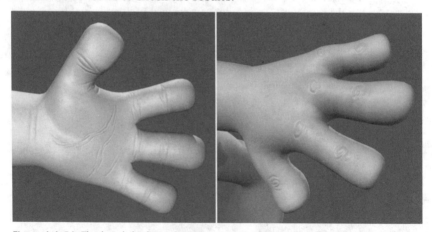

Figure 6.6-56. The hands look much nicer now without the dented bump layers.

> **Note:** You can add the weight map and alpha texture layers to any part of the skin you want to be a little smoother, such as the eyelids and tummy.

Before moving on to the clothes textures, render a few views of the naked body to check that all the textures are working nicely.

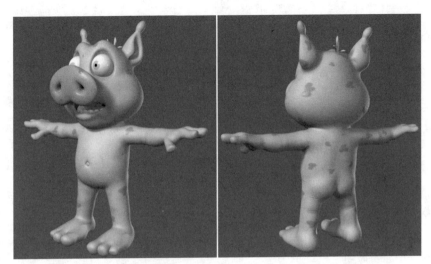

Figure 6.6-57. Finished body textures.

Clothes Textures

The clothes textures don't need to be as complex as the skin textures. For the most part we'll just create bump maps and apply the bump map to a couple of other channels as well as the Bump channel.

Sock Textures

The socks just need a bump map. I've used a burlap texture to create the bump map.

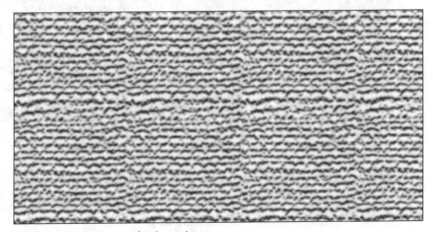

Figure 6.6-58. Bump map for the socks.

1. Set the visibility of Layer3, the clothes layer, to **Texture Shaded Solid**, and set it to **Active**.

2. Apply the sock bump map to the Bump channel of the socks surface and change Layer Opacity to **25%**.

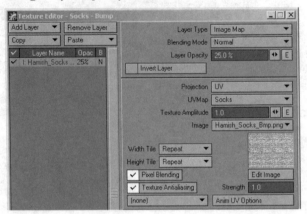

Figure 6.6-59. Bump texture layer.

3. Open the Texture Editor for the Color channel and change the image to the sock bump map.

4. Create a new Gradient layer above the texture, leaving Input Parameter on **Previous Layer.** Create a new key at the bottom of the gradient and set the color of the bottom key to the sock color, **250,247,235.** Change the color of the top key to a slightly darker color, **225,216,194.**

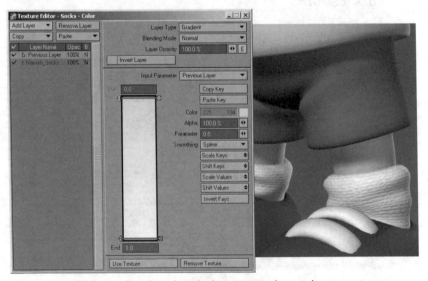

Figure 6.6-60. Color gradient based on the lower texture layer values.

Shoe Textures

The shoes also just need a bump map for the UV mapped areas. I've used a variety of filters to create the detail for the shoes UV map. The texture fades to black at the bottom of the soles UVs and around the edges of the base of the soles, so there's a distinct separation between the two sections.

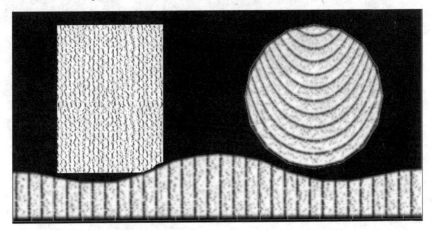

Figure 6.6-61. Bump map for the shoes.

1. In Layout, apply the bump texture to the Bump channel of the **Shoe_Soles** surface.

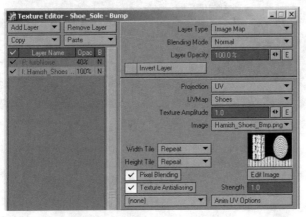

Figure 6.6-62. Bump texture layer.

2. **Copy** the layer to the Diffuse channel, under the procedural layer, and set to **10%** opacity.

3. Remove the UV Image texture layer from the Color channel.

4. Apply the texture to the **Shoe_Laces** surface in the same way as the soles surface.

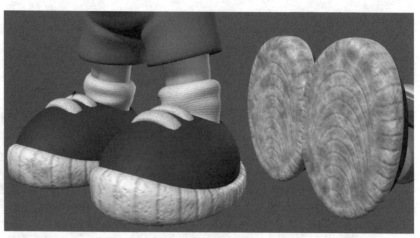

Figure 6.6-63. Result of the combined shoe textures.

Pants Textures

I've created a bump and a color texture for the pants using the burlap texture.

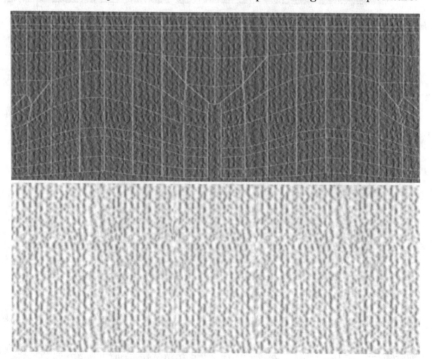

Figure 6.6-64. Color and bump textures.

1. In Layout apply the pants bump texture to the Bump channel of the **Pants** surface.

2. Apply the color texture to the Color channel. For the texture I've created I don't want the color to be too obvious, so I've set the opacity to **20%**.

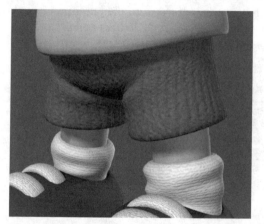

Figure 6.6-65. Result of the pants textures.

Eye Texture

I usually use a standard iris texture for all my characters, so I've included the texture to be used for Hamish's irises. Because it's a standard texture, the UV map for the irises needs to be created around the image, instead of the image being created around the UV map as we've done with the other textures.

1. In Modeler, select the polygons of the Eye_Iris surface, and deselect the right iris.

2. Create a new UV map called **Eye_Iris** using **Planar** projection on the **Z** axis.

3. Select the right iris and **Make UVs**, using the same settings.

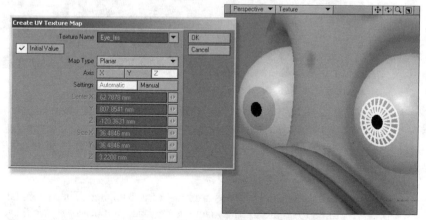

Figure 6.6-66. Create the UV map with the left iris, then add the right iris so the UV coordinates are the same for both.

441

4. In the image pull-down at the top of the UV Texture viewport, select **(load image)** and load **Images\Iris_Dif.png**.
5. Adjust the UVs so they fit the texture, with the outer points just outside the iris area and the inner points just inside the pupil area.

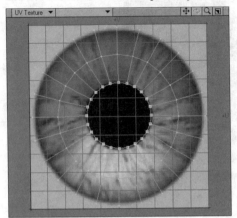

Figure 6.6-67. Adjust the UV coordinates based on the iris image.

6. Switch to Layout and open the Texture Editor for the Diffuse channel of the **Eye_Iris** surface.
7. Change Projection to **UV**, UVMap to **Eye_Iris**, and Image to **Iris_Dif.png**.
8. Render to test the texture and adjust the opacity if necessary.

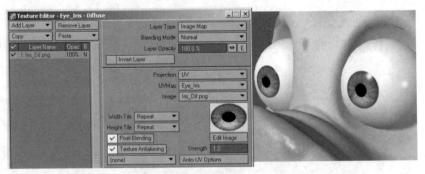

Figure 6.6-68. Result of the iris texture on the Diffuse channel.

The lighter area on the lower part of the iris simulates the effect of light on a real iris. By not including a texture on the Color channel, the same iris texture can be used on characters with different colored eyes by changing the basic surface color.

Projected Textures

All the textures for the UV maps are finished and applied. There are just a couple more textures to create for the main shoe surface and the shirt. We'll use planar projection for these textures.

Creating the Images

To create a template for the planar textures we'll take a screenshot of the polygons in the surface.

1. In Modeler, select the polygons of the **Shoes_Main** surface and **Hide Unselected** (=). Take a screenshot and paste it into a new image in your paint package.

2. Fill the base layer of the image with the shoe color, **202,0,0**. Resize the image width to **768** pixels, using Constrain Proportions to set the height. Save as **Hamish_Shoes_Main.psd**.

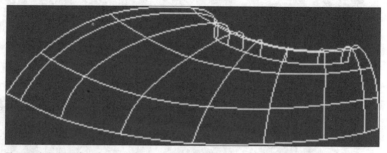

Figure 6.6-69. The shoe image ready for texturing.

Shoe Textures

Create a color and bump texture for the shoes. I've just created a white spot below the ankle for the color texture, and included the spot and toe and heel layers for the bump map. The base of the bump map is darker so the detail stands out more.

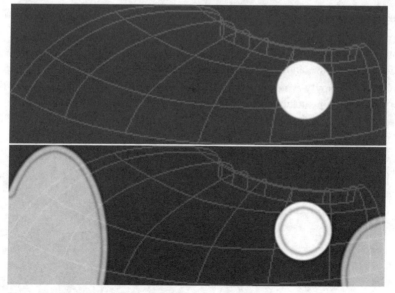

Figure 6.6-70. Color and bump textures.

443

1. In Layout, apply the shoe bump texture to the Bump channel of the
    Shoes_Main surface using **Planar** projection on the **X** axis. Choose
    Automatic Sizing to set the scale and position of the texture.

2. **Copy** the bump texture and **Paste** it into the Diffuse and Specularity
    channels, setting them to low opacity — **5 to 10%**.

3. **Paste** into the Color channel and change the image to the color shoe
    texture.

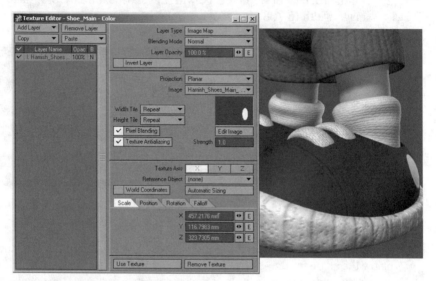

Figure 6.6-71. Results of the shoe textures.

Shirt Textures

I've prepared an image to use on the front of the shirt. *Space Pigs* is Hamish's
favorite TV show, and Captain Hogswash is his all-time, biggest ever hero. Feel
free to create or use an image of your own for the shirt though.

1. In Layout apply **Images\SpacePigs_Col.png** to the Color channel of the
    Shirt_Outer surface using **Planar** projection on the **Z** axis. Choose
    Automatic Sizing to set the initial scale and position of the texture.

2. Change the Tile settings to **Reset** so the image doesn't repeat.

3. Change the X and Y Scale to **0.175** and the Z Scale to **1**.

4. Change the Z position to **–0.1**, which is the Z position of the front of the
    shirt.

5. Change Falloff to **LinearZ** and the Z value to **1000%**.

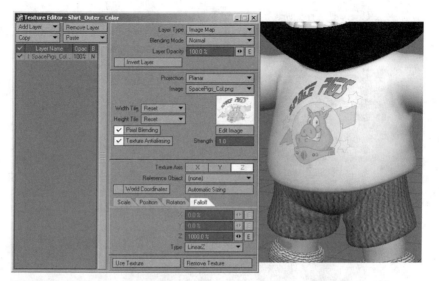

Figure 6.6-72. Scale and position the texture so it's in the right position on the shirt.

6. **Copy** the texture layer and **Paste**, adding to the layers. Change the image to **Images\SpacePigs_A.png** and change Blending Mode to **Alpha**.

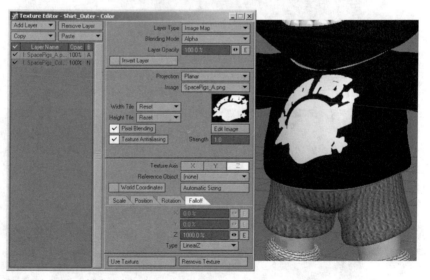

Figure 6.6-73. Add the alpha layer so the texture only appears where we want it.

7. **Copy** the texture layer and **Paste** it into the Specularity channel. Change Blending Mode to **Additive** and set Layer Opacity to **10%**, adding 10% to the specularity for the image area.

8. **Copy** the texture layer and **Paste** it into the Bump channel, leaving it on top of the procedural texture. Change Layer Opacity to **50%**. This halves the amount of procedural bump on the image area.

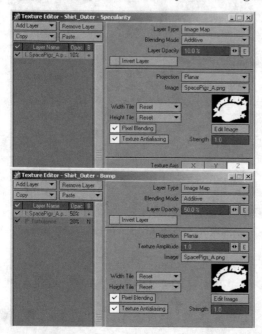

Figure 6.6-74. Giving the texture some added specularity and the bump texture makes it look more like an iron-on transfer.

9. Render the front to check the texture and the back to check that the falloff setting is stopping the texture from projecting on the back of the shirt.

10. Adjust the settings if necessary and save the Hamish object.

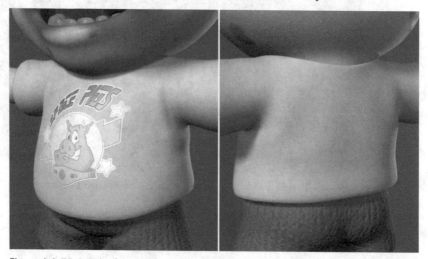

Figure 6.6-75. Result of the shirt texture. The falloff keeps it from reaching the back of the shirt.

6.7 Final Texturing

All the images are created and applied to the object. You'd be forgiven for thinking the job is done, but there are still some final steps.

Converting the Images

Currently all the images are 24 bit, taking up 60 MB of memory. We can drastically reduce this by converting many of the images to 8-bit indexed color or grayscale. If you've created the textures at a higher resolution than the final textures, you also need to adjust the size of the textures at this point. You should always adjust the size before converting to 8 bit.

You can also reduce the resolution of some of the grayscale textures. If a texture only has soft detail, such as many specular maps, they work just as well at half the size. Since the textures for Hamish all include the spots it's safest to leave them at full size, but keep this in mind for other characters.

1. Open all the color textures in the paint package and convert to 8-bit indexed color. Use a selective palette so the best 256 colors are chosen. Before you apply the change you can see a preview. Since each texture for Hamish has only a few colors, the change to indexed color is hardly noticeable. If the image suffers noticeable degradation, cancel and leave it as 24 bit; otherwise change to indexed color and save.

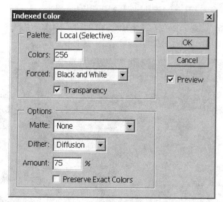

Figure 6.7-1. Indexed color settings.

2. Open all the bump, diffuse, specular, and glossiness textures. If you're using PNGs, convert to indexed color. If you're using TGAs, convert to grayscale. Since even 24-bit images only have 8 bits of gray there is no change in the image quality.

> **Note:**   PNGs and TGAs work a little differently in this aspect. Converting a TGA to grayscale saves it as 8 bit, but converting a PNG to grayscale leaves it as 24 bit.

Final Adjustments

Now with the textures at their final resolution we can finish adjusting the texture settings, especially the bump maps. As I mentioned earlier, bump map strength is related to the image size. The reason we didn't do much with the bump strength earlier is in case you decide to change the final texture size, which would affect the bump strength.

The relationship to texture size also affects the different skin surfaces, as each has a bump map of a different size, so the same strength values on the skin surfaces provide different results. The smaller the bump map the stronger it is, so reduce the Texture Amplitude setting for smaller bump textures and increase it for larger bump textures.

1. Clear the scene in Layout, clearing out all the loaded images, and close Modeler.

2. Load **Hamish_Surfacing.lws** again, loading the new versions of the textures, and open the Image Editor. The textures now take up a quarter of the memory they were using before, only 16 MB, which is far more efficient.

3. Do a close render of the hand. The bump strength on the arm and hand is a little high, so open the Texture Editor for the Bump channel of the **ArmsLegs** surface. Select the image map and change Texture Amplitude to **0.75**. Do the same for the **ArmsLegs_RT** surface.

4. Open the Texture Editor for the Bump channel of the **HandsFeet** surface, select the image map, and change Texture Amplitude to **0.5**.

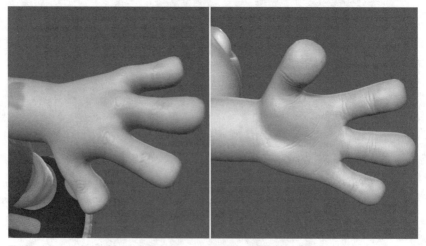

Figure 6.7-2. Adjusted bump strength on the arms and hands.

5. Adjust the Texture Amplitude setting of all the bump textures until you're happy with the results.

> **Note:** Adjusting the Texture Amplitude affects the strength of the entire bump map. If there's a specific area within a texture that needs different bump strength, then you need to adjust the texture itself.

Render closeups of all the areas of the object, adjusting the surface and texture settings where necessary. When you're happy that all the texturing is finished, remember to save the Hamish object and save the scene.

Figure 6.7-3. Final Hamish model.

Lighting Tests

The last stage of texturing is to check the character in different lighting conditions. This is an important step as surfaces can sometimes appear quite different in different lighting conditions. You need to make sure the surfaces of the character work for three lighting conditions: studio (default setup), low light (nighttime), and bright light (sunlight). Once you've done this you can be confident that the character will work well in almost any lighting setup.

Low Light Test

We'll start by checking in low light. The main things to check for here are any luminous areas that shouldn't be there and that the diffuse values of all the surfaces work well together in the low light.

1. In Layout, load \Scenes\Test\Nighttime.lws.
2. Select **File➤Load➤Load Items From Scene…** and load **Hamish_Surfacing.lws**. Choose **No** to loading lights from the scene.
3. Open the Scene Editor and deactivate **Layer2**.
4. Rotate **Light_Master** to get a good view of the character.

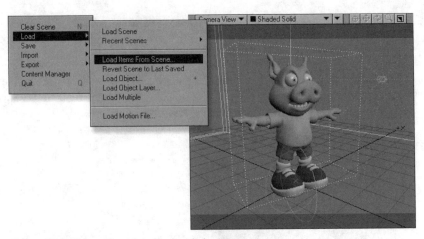

Figure 6.7-4. Set up Hamish in the low-light scene.

5. Press **F9** to create a test render.

Figure 6.7-5. Low-light render of Hamish.

If there are obvious errors in the surfacing, you can tweak them now, but I'm pretty happy with how Hamish is looking in low light.

6. If you've adjusted any surfacing, save the Hamish object.
7. Feel free to save the scene as **Hamish_Nightttime.lws**, then **Clear Scene**.

Bright Light Test

Let's check Hamish in the other extreme — sunlight. The main thing to check for here is diffuse blowout. This is where the diffuse values overtake the specular highlights. A little diffuse blowout is okay, but if it's too much, the diffuse value of the surface might need to be reduced.

1. Load **\Scenes\Test\Sunlight.lws**.

2. Select **File≻Load≻Load Items From Scene...** and load **Hamish_Sur-facing.lws**. Choose **No** to loading lights from the scene.

3. Open the Scene Editor and deactivate **Layer2**.

4. Rotate **Light_Master** to get a good view of the character.

5. Press **F9** to create a test render.

Figure 6.7-6. Bright light render of Hamish.

In the bright light, a little bit of diffuse blowout is okay, but you shouldn't get too much. If a surface is displaying too much blowout, then reduce the diffuse until it's within acceptable levels. If you find any other surface attributes that need adjusting, such as specularity, you can adjust those too.

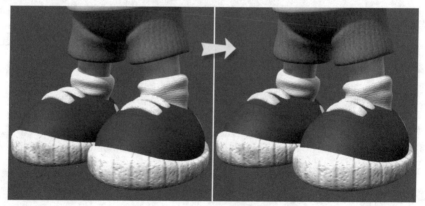

Figure 6.7-7. I've reduced the diffuse of the socks and shoelaces a little.

6. Save the Hamish object to save any surface changes.

7. Save the scene as **Hamish_Sunlight.lws**, then **Clear Scene**.

Finally, load **Hamish_Surfacing.lws** with the default lighting setup to check the results of any changes you made to the surfaces.

Figure 6.7-8.
Hamish with
adjusted surfaces
in the default
lighting setup.

Texturing can be one of the most time-consuming tasks of character creation. The complexity of the texturing largely depends on the type of character, as we've seen with the simple texturing of Morfi and the more detailed texturing of Hamish, but in most cases it takes a decent amount of time and effort to texture a character well.

Keep in mind the delicate balance between memory usage and render time, and create your textures accordingly. Procedural textures use less memory but take longer to render, and image maps use more memory but take less time to render. Making your image maps only as big as they need to be is a big help on the memory requirements too.

We've looked at a variety of texturing methods and how they relate to and complement each other. This has given you a solid base for further experimentation, and there is much more that you can do. The knowledge of how the various surface and texture methods and attributes work allows you to concentrate much more on the art of texturing.

6.8 Render Test

Now that the texturing is complete, the character is ready for a test render. A great way to show off the character to your boss, client, or friends is to create a QuickTimeVR movie. This shows the character from all angles, allowing the viewer to control where they want to look.

QuickTime VR

QuickTime VR plays a movie by dragging the mouse cursor, so you control how fast or slow the movie plays, and you can stop or go backward easily. Character tests usually require only horizontal rotation, although the format also supports vertical rotation, so you can adjust the view to above and below the object as well.

QuickTime VR movies don't have to loop, but they work best when they do. They don't have to rotate around the character either. You could create a looping walk cycle viewed from a single angle, with the benefit of being able to control the playback. You could rotate the camera from a central point to view a location scene. There are all sorts of possibilities for creating previews using QuickTime VR.

QuickTime VR works by first creating a number of horizontal frames. Once you have the horizontal frames you can add vertical frames by replicating the horizontal frames for as many vertical segments as you need, moving the camera to a new position for each repeating set of horizontal frames. If you want to include vertical frames for rotating around a character or object, it's often useful to parent the camera to a null object positioned where you want the pivot of the camera's vertical rotation, and rotate the null instead of moving the camera. The disadvantage of including vertical frames is that it takes a lot longer to render than just horizontal frames.

The default direction of the mouse is reversed from what's expected. Dragging left plays the movie forward; dragging right plays backward. You have the option to flip the controls so dragging right plays forward. It really depends on how you're using QuickTime VR whether you choose to flip the controls or not.

Creating a QuickTime VR

Let's create a simple QuickTime VR character test for Hamish.

1. Load **Hamish_Surfacing.lws** and save as **Hamish_VRTest.lws**.

2. Make sure any keyframes above frame 0 are removed. Select **Plugs**➤**Additional**➤**Motify** and change Delete Mode to **Delete Keys Within Range**, deleting keys from **1** through **60** for **All Items** and all channels, including **All Other Channels**.

> **Note:** Choosing All Other Channels also deletes the keyframes for Morph Mixer, so you don't have to delete those manually. If you have keyframed envelopes for automated motion or effects, don't choose All Other Channels — instead delete the additional keyframes for Morph Mixer manually.

Figure 6.8-1. Mot-ify is a quick way to delete a range of keyframes.

3. Select **Main Null** and set the starting Heading angle at frame **0**. Change the last frame to **120**, and move to frame **120**. In the numeric input, add **+360** to the Heading value for Main Null.

> **Note:** This creates a 120-frame movie. You can make the movie longer or shorter by changing the last frame.

Figure 6.8-2. By rotating the Main Null, the lighting stays consistent as the camera rotates around the character. You could also rotate the Hamish object for similar results.

4. Open the Graph Editor and choose the Heading channel, **Main Null.Rotation.H**. Select the key at frame 120 and change Incoming Curve to **Linear**. Now the camera rotates a full circle around the character between frames 0 and 120.

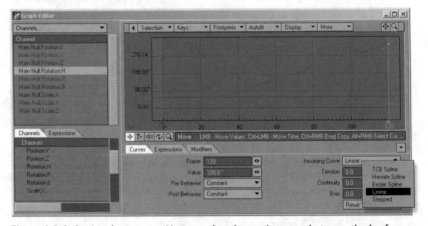

Figure 6.8-3. Setting the curve to Linear makes the motion even between the keyframes.

5. Select the camera and open its properties. Set the resolution to your required resolution, set Antialiasing to **Low**, and turn off **Adaptive Sampling**.

> **Note:** The resolution you choose depends on the delivery format. For a movie you will show over the Internet, use a low resolution, something like 320 x 240. For a movie to show from your computer or on CD, you can set it higher, to 640 x 480 or even better if you want to show more detail.

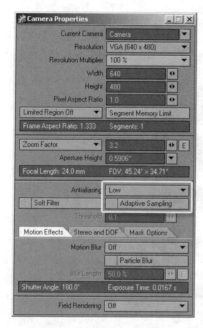

Figure 6.8-4.
Turning off Adaptive
Sampling makes
render times a bit
longer but provides
better results.

6. Select **Render**➤**Render Options**, and set the first frame to **1** and the last frame to **120**. Select the **Output Files** tab, set the animation type to **QuickTime VR Object**, and turn on **Save Animation**. Select where you want to place the movie and call it **Hamish_VR01.mov**. Select **Options** to open the QuickTime VR options.

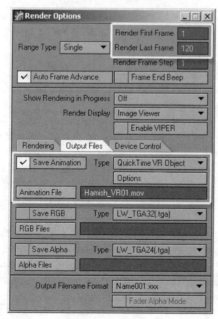

Figure 6.8-5. You
can opt to set the
last render frame
to one frame
before the last
frame to create a
smoothly looping
movie.

7. In the Object Settings tab, change Columns to **120**, turn on **Flip Horizontal Control**, change Rows to **1**, and set Start Tilt and End Tilt to **0**. Select the **Animation Settings** tab and set your preferred compression options.

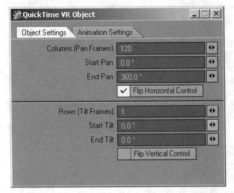

Figure 6.8-6. Set the columns to the number of frames in the movie.

8. Close all the panels and save the scene.
9. Press **F10** to render the movie.

> **Tip:** After the character is rigged, instead of rendering a still turnaround, you can animate the character between frames 0 and 120. Just turning the eyes to follow the camera can make a big difference. If you create some movement, make sure the character is posed exactly the same on frames 0 and 120 so the movie loops properly.

You can find my QuickTime VR scene for Hamish in \Scenes\Chapters\Hamish_VRTest.lws or see the rendered version in \Movies\Hamish_VRTest.mov.

6.9 Conclusion

Congratulations, you've completed the first part of the cartoon character creation series.

You've probably already started creating your own characters using what you've learned, or at least have a few ideas for characters that are begging to be made. I hope this book has not only educated you in the methods of character creation, but given you more insight into how great characters are born and inspired you to create exciting characters of your own. With a solid understanding of the endless possibilities and the tools at your disposal, you now have the ability to create any character that you can imagine.

Please feel free to continue on your own, rigging Hamish or your own characters with the same techniques used to rig Morfi, but I hope you allow me the opportunity to share much more with you. *Volume 2: Rigging & Animation* picks up where we left off in the creation of Hamish, explaining morphs, rigging, and animating your characters in more much detail than I've been able to in this volume.

I wish you the very best of luck in your character creation efforts. I look forward to seeing your characters online or on a screen somewhere so they can inspire us all.

Appendix

A.1 Character Creation Plug-ins

There are hundreds of plug-ins available for LightWave 3D. Some are useful on a regular basis, shaving small amounts of time off common tasks. Others are useful for less common, more demanding tasks, but save much more time or do things that are otherwise impossible. The following is by no means a comprehensive list of useful plug-ins, but includes the plug-ins that I find most useful on a regular basis for character creation.

Free Plug-ins

All of the following free plug-ins are included on the companion CD, but make sure you check the developer web sites for updates and other useful plug-ins.

> **Note:** Make sure you read the manuals provided with each plug-in.

Combine Weightmaps

Kevin Phillips — www.kevman3d.com

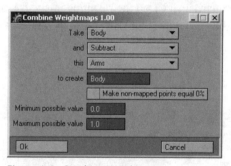

Figure A-1. Combine Weightmaps.

One of the most frustrating parts of weight mapping is working out the correct values for adjoining bone weight maps. Combine Weightmaps makes it easy to create the weight values by letting you subtract one weight map from another. You can also add weight maps together, and multiply or divide them into an existing weight map or a new one.

In addition to setting values for adjoining weight maps as shown in the tutorials, Combine Weightmaps can also be used to create more blending between left and right weight maps. You can do this by creating an additional weight map to determine the blending amount and multiplying the symmetrical weight maps with the additional weight map.

UV Imaginator

Antony Scerri — www.3dcybercorp.com/software

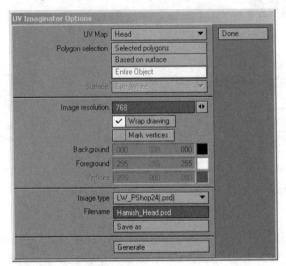

Figure A-2. UV Imaginator.

UV Imaginator is a great alternative to the EPS exporter for creating the initial image files for UV mapped images. Its ability to save an image based on selected polygons, specific surfaces, or entire UV maps makes it very flexible.

Unfortunately, it only creates square images, so the resulting image has to be resized for other aspect ratios, but this is a minor drawback to what is otherwise a very useful tool.

MSort

Scott Martindale

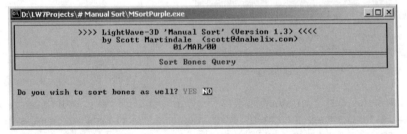

Figure A-3. MSort.

MSort isn't actually a plug-in, but a separate program that works with LightWave scene files. It's most useful for character rigging as it allows you to adjust the order of the bones and control objects so it's easy to change the selected item by pressing the Up and Down Arrow keys. It's also useful for making the bone and object order the same for every character in a production so moving from character to character in a scene is a seamless transition.

It takes a lot of extra time to create items in the proper order when rigging. If you're not careful to create items in order, then extra time is spent during animation. MSort saves that time by giving you the ability to quickly change the order in which bones or objects appear in the selection lists.

A new version of MSort is currently in development as a plug-in instead of a separate program. The new version includes drag and drop editing and much more functionality. When it's finished, the updated version of MSort will be available from my web site.

Commercial Plug-ins

Demo versions or examples from the following commercial plug-ins are included on the companion CD. Check the developer web sites for updates, pricing, and other information.

Relativity

Prem Subrahmanyam — www.premdesign.com

Relativity is an alternative to LightWave expressions. Relativity has many advantages over LightWave expressions, including greater functionality with fewer limitations.

LightWave expressions are very useful and will serve you well in many situations. I recommend learning and using LightWave expressions first, as it'll give you a good basis for understanding how to use Relativity. It'll also give you a better understanding of the advantages of Relativity once you run into problems that LightWave expressions aren't equipped to handle.

FPrime

Worley Labs — www.worley.com

FPrime is an invaluable preview tool for character creation. It creates very quick renders with every change you make to the model, providing real-time feedback instead of having to wait for F9 renders to check your results. FPrime is most useful for texturing and lighting, allowing you to make changes and see the results immediately, which saves considerable time and allows you to work as fast as you can think. Because of the time savings you can spend more time experimenting, ending up with superior results, and still finish well under the time it would take traditionally.

A.2 Auto Rigging Plug-ins

What you've learned in this book and *Volume 2: Rigging & Animation*, together with the improved rigging tools in LightWave 8, give you the ability to create custom character rigs and apply them to multiple characters. Before LightWave 8, it was quite time consuming to transfer rigs from one character to another, so some enterprising plug-in authors wrote some tools to make the job easier.

The main downfall of most auto rigging tools (with the exception of ACS4) is that you're stuck with creating the one rig. While you can add to the rig easily enough once it's been created, this doesn't really help when you have a unique rig of your own that you want to apply to multiple characters. An auto rigging tool gives you a way to quickly rig a character for test poses or to check deformations before sending the character model for final rigging. For character creators comfortable with modeling but less experienced in rigging, this can be very useful. Auto rigging can also be useful for rigging background characters that don't need complex or unique rigs.

Free Plug-ins

All of the following free plug-ins are included on the companion CD, but make sure you check the developer web sites for updates and other useful plug-ins.

> **Note:**   Make sure you read the manuals provided with each plug-in.

Simple Rigger

Christopher Lutz — www.animationsnippets.com/plugins

Simple Rigger creates the animation controls and sets IK for a character object with skelegons, allowing you to choose between FK or IK arms. There are few options available to you, but Simple Rigger creates a decent rig and you can adjust it for your preferred control methods once the rig has been created.

Also look for other useful plug-ins available from Christopher's web site, including a useful replacement for LightWave's Match Goal Orientation.

J Auto Rig

Jacobo Barreiro — www.jacobobarreiro.com

J Auto Rig sets IK for a character object with skelegons. The resulting rig is a little different from the rigs I've covered in this book. Instead of using null objects as the animation controls, the null objects are hidden, allowing you to use the bones themselves as animation controls. This rigging method was made popular by Timothy Albee in his book *LightWave 3D 7 Character Animation*.

Also look for other useful plug-ins available from Jacobo's web site, including a Pose Saver plug-in.

Commercial Plug-ins

Demo versions or examples from the following commercial plug-ins are included on the companion CD. Check the developer web sites for updates, pricing, and other information.

Auto Character Setup 4

Lukasz Pazera and Pawel Olas — acs.polas.net/acs

Auto Character Setup 4 is a very powerful auto rigging tool. There are many different rigs available to choose from, which puts it ahead of most other auto rigging tools, but it's most useful feature is the ability to customize any rig for use with ACS4, allowing you to store IK settings, modifiers, expressions, and more. If you have a lot of characters to rig in a short amount of time, ACS4 will pay for itself very quickly whether you use the provided rigs or put the extra effort into converting a custom rig.

T4D Rigging Tools

Peter Thomas and Samuel Kvaalen — www.thomas4d.com

Thomas 4D Rigging Tools is a suite of tools for rigging and animating characters. Version 2 offers the choice between using bones or null objects as animation controls and IK or FK arms and legs. It also includes a pose saver, a character picker, and joystick controls for facial morphs.

A.3 Internet Resources

The following are some Internet sites useful for character creation, some geared toward LightWave, others geared toward 3D regardless of package. The following resource sites contain tutorials, tips, and plug-ins that will help save your time and sanity when creating characters. The community sites contain inspiring characters and other artwork created by people from all over the world. These communities also offer help; you'll always find someone who can answer a particular question to help solve a problem.

Lightwave Resources

These LightWave resource sites will help you use LightWave 3D to its fullest extent.

Official LightWave 3D Web Site

www.lightwave3d.com

The official LightWave 3D web site includes the latest patches and downloads, tutorials, and interviews with artists using LightWave for production work in many different areas. You can also visit the NewTek forums, which offer a meeting place for everything NewTek.

SpinQuad

www.spinquad.com

SpinQuad is a web site created by William "Proton" Vaughan to be the ultimate LightWave 3D resource.

Flay

www.flay.com

Flay includes the most comprehensive database of LightWave plug-ins available. It also features the latest news, job postings, and tutorials.

LightWave Tutorials on the Web

members.shaw.ca/lightwavetutorials

LightWave Tutorials on the Web contains links to hundreds of LightWave tutorials covering almost every possible use of the package, as well as tutorials for related plug-ins and other packages. If you want to know how to accomplish a task in LightWave 3D, this should be your first stop.

Communities

These community sites are meeting places for 3D artists from around the world. They allow you to find answers to problems and are a great source of inspiration, letting you see the great work that others are doing.

LightWave 3D Mailing List

groups.yahoo.com/group/lw3d

The official LightWave 3D mailing list.

SpinQuad Forums

www.spinquad.com/forums

SpinQuad forums are dedicated to LightWave 3D, where people can meet and discuss pure LightWave issues in a fun and productive way. SpinQuad forums are a great place to visit to find out about recent developments, if you want constructive criticism, or just to show off your latest work.

LightWave Group Forums

www.lwg3d.org

LightWave Group forums include galleries, articles, interviews, and tutorials.

CGTalk

www.cgtalk.com

CGTalk is a huge forum that caters to everything related to computer graphics, both 2D and 3D. There is a forum dedicated to LightWave, but the great benefit is that you can meet people and see work done using all 3D packages.

Friends of NewTek

www.friendsofnewtek.com

Friends of NewTek is a site dedicated to LightWave user groups all over the world. If you're looking for your local user group for face-to-face meetings, this is where you'll find it.

Index

spinQuad

www.spinquad.com
Your LightWave Community

splineGOD

Do You Need Professional Training in LightWave 3D?

Then you need 3D Training Online, http://www.3dtrainingonline.com

When NewTek needed courseware for their educational bundle, who did they turn to? They turned to Larry Shultz of 3D Training Online | FX Academy.

Would you like to learn 3D at a professional level? With Larry's training courses, you can!

What you will get:

Modeling - This part of the course begins with Modeler. Concepts include the LightWave coordinate system, how to navigate through Modeler, and locating tools. Many tools are introduced and explained such as points, polygons, primitives, objects, move, rotate, drag, bevel, smooth shift, extrude, booleans, and so on.

Texturing - Basic surfacing is introduced and discussed, along with how shading works, basic texture mapping techniques, using bitmaps vs. procedurals and gradients, and UV mapping.

Lighting - Basic lighting is covered, using two, three, and multilight setups. The function of key and fill lights, creating and controlling shadows and highlights, and much more are discussed.

Rigging - Getting all the parts set so they can be animated. Various rigging techniques are covered such as inverse kinematics, Cyclist, and Expressions.

Animating - Making it all work together - This part covers keyframing, timing, using the Graph Editor, using the camera, and basic camera work. Students will learn how to use LightWave's powerful renderer.

Visual FX - Creating FX using tools and techniques such as particles, HyperVoxels, geometry, animated procedural textures, and glow.

Online Support - Our courses are self paced. You receive support as long as you need it through our support forum, in which you can post questions to other students and the instructor. You are encouraged to interact with each other, learning from and helping one another.

..and this is just the intro course!

What Others Have Said about 3D Online Training Courses

"Larry is definitely one of the BEST LightWave trainers out there!"

-Philip Nelson, NewTek, Director of Worldwide Sales

"Larry Kicks A$$ at showing you how to work with characters from modeling to rigging to animating....This guy knows his stuff! Be sure to check out more of his training material. Your brain will be overflowing with new skills."

-William "Proton" Vaughan, NewTek, LightWave Evangelist

"Larry's courses are the best on the market. What I learned in a matter of weeks is amazing. Thanks Larry! Looking forward to more of your courses!"

-Wes "kurv" Beckwith - Wordware Publishing

Your LightWave 3D Models...... **Made Real**

LightWave Ninja Model Courtesy of William "Proton" Vaughan

We Create Low Cost Real Parts From Your 3D Files, Perfect For:

- 3D Characters or Creatures
- Toy or Model Prototypes
- Architectural Designs
- Geometric Art
- Concept Models
  and much more

3DArtToPart.com

For additional information or to request a price quote,
Visit us online at : **www.3DArtToPart.com**
1 800 677-4435

LightWave 101

Interactive Training Course and Curriculum Guide™

LightWave 3D is one of the most powerful 3D graphics and animation programs on the market today. If you can dream it, you can build it in LightWave. Many of the awesome 3D graphics you see in movies, on TV, and in print were created with LightWave 3D. Yet with power comes complexity. **Beginners ask, "Where do I start?" The answer is - LightWave 101** - an Interactive Training Course and Curriculum Guide created by the artists and animators at the epic software group.

This CD-Based program contains everything you need to learn LightWave 3D. It takes a completely fresh approach to 3D training, and moves you through the program at a comfortable pace. The number of options available in LightWave can be intimidating to even a seasoned pro. LightWave 101 tames this 3D powerhouse by showing you how to do the right things, the right way, right from lesson one. Before you know it, you'll be creating 3D graphics that will astound both you and your friends.

Although LightWave 101 was originally created for 3D Instructors, we have expanded it to be a perfect learning tool for students, as well. There are six sections to this multimedia training guide:

Section 1 - 3D Interactive
Here you will learn all about the Animation Process.
Multimedia demos are used to illustrate the concepts of 3D.

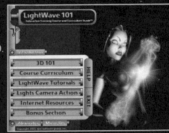

Section 2 - Curriculum Guide
Welcome to our virtual classroom where you'll find a full
semester's curriculum. Easy to follow lessons make this
curriculum guide perfect for both students and teachers.

Section 3 - Intermediate Tutorials
After you have mastered the basics in sections 1 and 2, get ready to put your knowledge to the test. There are over 20 tutorials to help you learn to create everything from animated logos to basic character modeling.

Section 4 - Lights, Camera, Action
Ever watch a blockbuster movie, see a special effect, and wonder - How did they do that? In this section, you'll learn the techniques of the digital cinematographer.

Section 5 - LightWave Resource Guide
This Resource Guide is complete with links to the most popular LightWave 3D web sites, LightWave 3D books, 3D model libraries, listing of popular LightWave plug-in's, texture sources, and so much more. You are always just a click away from anything LightWave, when you are in the Resource section of the program.

Section 6 - Bonus Section
In our Bonus Section, feast your eyes on a gallery of 3D graphics and animations to inspire you. An arcade, complete with 10 games (created with 3D graphics produced in LightWave), will entertain you. We have also included 100 free 3D models from the epic software group 3D model library, for you to use in your scenes.

Special offer for WordWare Customers:

LightWave 101 Interactive Training Course and Curriculum Guide™ is just **$59.95**, plus **$4.95** S&H (North America), $8.95 (International). As a WordWare customer, you can save **20%** by ordering directly from the epic web site (www.epicsoftware.com) and entering discount code **WW-101**, or by calling epic directly at: 281-363-3742.

• LightWave 3D is a registered trademark of NewTek
• All other products or brand names mentioned are trademarks or registered trademarks of their respective holders.

Essential LightWave 3D 7.5
1-55622-226-2 • $44.95
6 x 9 • 424 pp.

LightWave 3D 7.5 Lighting
1-55622-354-4 • $69.95
6 x 9 • 496 pp.

LightWave 3D 8 Lighting
1-55622-094-4 • $54.95
6 x 9 • 536 pp.

LightWave 3D 8 Cartoon Character Creation: Volume II Rigging & Animation
1-55622-254-8 • $49.95
6 x 9 • 440 pp.

LightWave 3D 8 Texturing
1-55622-285-8 • $49.95
6 x 9 • 504 pp.

LightWave 3D 8: 1001 Tips and Tricks
1-55622-090-1 • $39.95
6 x 9 • 648 pp.

CGI Filmmaking: The Creation of Ghost Warrior
1-55622-227-0 • $49.95
9 x 7 • 344 pp.

Just Released

Advanced Lighting and Materials with Shaders
1-55622-292-0 • $44.95
9 x 7 • 360 pp.

Coming Soon

Essential LightWave 3D 8: The Fastest Way to Master LightWave 3D
1-55622-082-0 • $44.95
6 x 9 • 450 pp.

LightWave 3D 8 Character Animation
1-55622-099-5 • $49.95
6 x 9 • 400 pp.

LightWave 3D 8 Modeling: A Definitive Guide
1-55622-289-0 • $49.95
6 x 9 • 500 pp.

Visit us online at **www.wordware.com** for more information.

backlist, and upcoming titles.

Modeling a Character in 3DS Max
1-55622-815-5 • $44.95
7½ x 9¼ • 544 pp.

Coming Soon

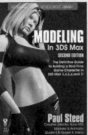

**Modeling a Character in 3DS Max
(2nd Edition)**
1-55622-088-X • $44.95
6 x 9 • 550 pp.

**Game Design: Theory and Practice,
Second Edition**
1-55622-912-7 • $49.95
6 x 9 • 728 pp.

Game Development and Production
1-55622-951-8 • $49.95
6 x 9 • 432 pp.

Game Design Foundations
1-55622-973-9 • $39.95
6 x 9 • 400 pp.

**3D Math Primer for Graphics and
Game Development**
1-55622-911-9 • $49.95
7½ x 9¼ • 448 pp.

Vector Game Math Processors
1-55622-921-6 • $59.95
6 x 9 • 528 pp.

**Memory Management Algorithms
and Implementation in C/C++**
1-55622-347-1 • $59.95
6 x 9 • 392 pp.

Learn FileMaker Pro 7
1-55622-098-7 • $36.95
6 x 9 • 544 pp.

Use the following coupon code for online specials: car1-253X

Check out Wordware's market-leading Game Programming Library featuring the following new releases, backlist, and upcoming titles.

Introduction to 3D Game Programming with DirectX 9.0
1-55622-913-5 • $49.95
6 x 9 • 424 pp.

Advanced 3D Game Programming with DirectX 9.0
1-55622-968-2 • $59.95
6 x 9 • 552 pp.

DirectX 9 User Interfaces: Design and Implementation
1-55622-249-1 • $44.95
6 x 9 • 376 pp.

Strategy Game Programming with DirectX 9.0
1-55622-922-4 • $59.95
6 x 9 • 560 pp.

DirectX 9 Audio Exposed: Interactive Audio Development
1-55622-288-2 • $59.95
6 x 9 • 568 pp.

Learn Vertex and Pixel Shader Programming with DirectX 9
1-55622-287-4 • $34.95
6 x 9 • 304 pp.

ShaderX2: Introductions and Tutorials with DirectX 9
1-55622-902-X • $44.95
6 x 9 • 384 pp.

ShaderX2: Shader Programming Tips & Tricks with DirectX 9
1-55622-988-7 • $59.95
6 x 9 • 728 pp.

New Releases

Programming Multiplayer Games
1-55622-076-6 • $59.95
6 x 9 • 576 pp.

Wireless Game Development in Java with MIDP 2.0
1-55622-998-4 • $39.95
6 x 9 • 360 pp.

Official Butterfly.net Game Developer's Guide
1-55622-044-8 • $49.95
6 x 9 • 424 pp.

Visit us online at **www.wordware.com** for more information.
Use the following coupon code for online specials: **car1-253X**

About the CD

The companion CD is organized into the following directories:

- Book_Illustrations contains all the illustrations from the book.
- LWProjects contains all the files necessary to follow the tutorials, along with plug-in demos and examples.
- LWProjects\LW8_CartoonCreation\Objects\Extra includes extra objects created by William "Proton" Vaughan.
- Movies contains the movies from the book.

Note: For the rigging tutorials to work correctly, it's very important to install the LightWave 8.0.1 update. (See www.newtek.com.) Unfortunately, the 8.0.1 update causes the Textured Filter Scale to work differently than how it's described in Chapter 6. To follow the tutorials correctly, you need to change the scale value to **1/Value**. A value of 0.25 (250 mm) becomes 1/0.25, or 4 (4 m).

The formula for determining the image size as described in Section 6.6 becomes "768 * 0.25 * Textured Filter Scale."

Warning: By opening the CD package, you accept the terms and conditions of the CD/Source Code Usage License Agreement. Additionally, opening the CD package makes this book nonreturnable.

CD/Source Code Usage License Agreement

Please read the following CD/Source Code usage license agreement before opening the CD and using the contents therein:

1. By opening the accompanying software package, you are indicating that you have read and agree to be bound by all terms and conditions of this CD/Source Code usage license agreement.

2. The compilation of code and utilities contained on the CD and in the book are copyrighted and protected by both U.S. copyright law and international copyright treaties, and is owned by Wordware Publishing, Inc. Individual source code, example programs, help files, freeware, shareware, utilities, and evaluation packages, including their copyrights, are owned by the respective authors.

3. No part of the enclosed CD or this book, including all source code, help files, shareware, freeware, utilities, example programs, or evaluation programs, may be made available on a public forum (such as a World Wide Web page, FTP site, bulletin board, or Internet news group) without the express written permission of Wordware Publishing, Inc. or the author of the respective source code, help files, shareware, freeware, utilities, example programs, or evaluation programs.

4. You may not decompile, reverse engineer, disassemble, create a derivative work, or otherwise use the enclosed programs, help files, freeware, shareware, utilities, or evaluation programs except as stated in this agreement.

5. The software, contained on the CD and/or as source code in this book, is sold without warranty of any kind. Wordware Publishing, Inc. and the authors specifically disclaim all other warranties, express or implied, including but not limited to implied warranties of merchantability and fitness for a particular purpose with respect to defects in the disk, the program, source code, sample files, help files, freeware, shareware, utilities, and evaluation programs contained therein, and/or the techniques described in the book and implemented in the example programs. In no event shall Wordware Publishing, Inc., its dealers, its distributors, or the authors be liable or held responsible for any loss of profit or any other alleged or actual private or commercial damage, including but not limited to special, incidental, consequential, or other damages.

6. One (1) copy of the CD or any source code therein may be created for backup purposes. The CD and all accompanying source code, sample files, help files, freeware, shareware, utilities, and evaluation programs may be copied to your hard drive. With the exception of freeware and shareware programs, at no time can any part of the contents of this CD reside on more than one computer at one time. The contents of the CD can be copied to another computer, as long as the contents of the CD contained on the original computer are deleted.

7. You may not include any part of the CD contents, including all source code, example programs, shareware, freeware, help files, utilities, or evaluation programs in any compilation of source code, utilities, help files, example programs, freeware, shareware, or evaluation programs on any media, including but not limited to CD, disk, or Internet distribution, without the express written permission of Wordware Publishing, Inc. or the owner of the individual source code, utilities, help files, example programs, freeware, shareware, or evaluation programs.

8. You may use the source code, techniques, and example programs in your own commercial or private applications unless otherwise noted by additional usage agreements as found on the CD.

Warning: By opening the CD package, you accept the terms and conditions of the CD/Source Code Usage License Agreement.
Additionally, opening the CD package makes this book nonreturnable.